Cocoa Design Patterns

Cocoa Design Patterns

Erik M. Buck
Donald A. Yacktman

♠♦Addison-Wesley

Upper Saddle River, NJ • Boston • Indianapolis • San Francisco
New York • Toronto • Montreal • London • Munich • Paris • Madrid
Cape Town • Sydney • Tokyo • Singapore • Mexico City

Many of the designations used by manufacturers and sellers to distinguish their products are claimed as trademarks. Where those designations appear in this book, and the publisher was aware of a trademark claim, the designations have been printed with initial capital letters or in all capitals.

The authors and publisher have taken care in the preparation of this book but make no expressed or implied warranty of any kind and assume no responsibility for errors or omissions. No liability is assumed for incidental or consequential damages in connection with or arising out of the use of the information or programs contained herein.

The publisher offers excellent discounts on this book when ordered in quantity for bulk purchases or special sales, which may include electronic versions and/or custom covers and content particular to your business, training goals, marketing focus, and branding interests. For more information, please contact

U.S. Corporate and Government Sales
(800) 382-3419
corpsales@pearsontechgroup.com

For sales outside the United States, please contact

International Sales
international@pearson.com

Visit us on the Web: informit.com/aw

Library of Congress Cataloging-in-Publication Data:

Buck, Erik M.

Cocoa design patterns / Erik M. Buck, Donald A. Yacktman.

p. cm.

Includes bibliographical references and index.

ISBN 978-0-321-53502-3 (pbk. : alk. paper) 1. Cocoa (Application development environment) 2. Object-oriented programming (Computer science) 3. Software patterns. 4. Mac OS. I. Yacktman, Donald A. II. Title.

QA76.64.B82 2009

005.26'8—dc22

2009023288

ISBN-13: 978-0-321-53502-3
ISBN-10: 0-321-53502-2
This product is printed digitally on demand.

First printing September 2009

Editor-in-Chief
Karen Gettman

Acquisitions Editor
Chuck Toporek

Development
Editor
Sheri Cain

Managing Editor
Kristy Hart

Project Editor
Jovana San Nicolas-Shirley

Copy Editor
Language
Logistics, LLC

Indexer
Rebecca Salerno

Proofreader
Apostrophe Editing
Services

Publishing
Coordinator
Romny French

Cover Designer
Gary Adair

Compositor
Jake McFarland

*To my beloved wife, Michelle, who makes my life
and every accomplishment possible, and to my children,
Joshua, Emma, and Jacob, for their tireless support
and understanding.*

—Erik M. Buck

❖

*Dedicated to my wife Marcie for her patience and
support and my boys, Joseph and William, for their
never-ending curiosity about how and why things
work the way they do.*

—Donald A. Yacktman

❖

Table of Contents

Foreword

Grumpy old men are represented poorly by our modern culture. They are always depict-ed throwing stuff and bellowing lines like, "Hey, you kids, get off my lawn!" In reality, grumpy old men often say useful things like, "Kid, you should diversify your portfolio—just in case."

As someone who has been developing applications with Cocoa and Objective-C for a long time, one of my important roles is that of a grumpy old man. Programmers who are new to Cocoa come to me and say things like, "Here's my program. It works great. You want to look at the source?"

And I study the source code and growl things like, "Yes, that works, but that isn't how we do it. We grumpy old Cocoa programmers have a system worked out, and you are not following the system."

And the young programmer says, "Well, why is your system so great?"

And I grunt, "Um...well...it just is! Shut up and get off my lawn, kid."

The book you are holding is the answer to two important questions:

- How do the grumpy old Cocoa programmers do things?
- Why is that so great?

Through floundering about with bad solutions, grumpy old Cocoa programmers have figured out some really good solutions to common design problems. The existence of this book means that you are not required to suffer through the same misery that we went through.

Both Erik M. Buck and Donald A. Yacktman have earned their grumpy, old Cocoa programmer status. They each have enough successes and enough failures to recognize what a good Cocoa design looks like. Beyond presenting these idioms and techniques, Erik and Donald have included serious meditations on why it was these patterns emerged from the chaos that was Objective-C programming a decade ago.

Next time some kid shows up at my door asking for a code review, *this* is the book I am going to throw at him. It is a pity there is no hardcover edition.

—*Aaron Hillegass*
Big Nerd Ranch, Inc.
Atlanta, Georgia

Preface

Much of the technology embodied by Apple's Cocoa software has been in commercial use since 1988, and in spite of that maturity, Cocoa is still revolutionary. The technology has been marketed with a variety of names including NEXTSTEP, OPENSTEP, Rhapsody, and Yellow Box. It consists of a collection of reusable software frameworks that contain objects and related resources for building Mac OS X desktop and mobile applications. In recent years, Apple has expanded Cocoa dramatically and added new software developer tools to increase programmer productivity beyond the already famously high levels Cocoa already provided.

Programmers are often overwhelmed by the breadth and sophistication of Cocoa when they first start using the frameworks. Cocoa encompasses a huge set of features, but it's also elegant in its consistency. That consistency results from the application of patterns throughout Cocoa's design. Understanding the patterns enables the most effective use of the frameworks and serves as a guide for writing your own applications.

This book explains the object-oriented design patterns found in Apple's Cocoa frameworks. Design patterns aren't unique to Cocoa; they're recognized in many reusable software libraries and available in any software development environment. Design patterns identify recurring software problems and best practices for solving them. The primary goal of this book is to supply insight into the design and rationale of Cocoa, but with that insight, you'll be able to effectively reuse the tried and true patterns in your own software—even if you aren't using Cocoa.

What Is a Design Pattern?

Design patterns describe high quality practical solutions to recurring programming problems. Design patterns don't require amazing programming tricks. They're a toolbox of reusable solutions and best practices that have been refined over many years into a succinct format. They provide a vocabulary, or shorthand, that programmers can use when explaining complex software to each other. Design patterns don't describe specific algorithms or data structures like linked lists or variable length arrays, which are traditionally implemented in individual classes. The design patterns in this book don't describe specific designs for applications even though examples are provided. What the patterns do provide is a coherent map that leads you through the design of Cocoa itself. Patterns show how and why some of the best and most reusable software ever created was designed the way it was.

At a minimum, design patterns contain four essential elements:

- The pattern name
- A brief description of the motivation for the pattern or the problem solved by the pattern
- A detailed description of the pattern and examples in Cocoa
- The consequences of using the pattern

Parts II, III, and IV of this book contain a catalog of design patterns. Each chapter in the pattern catalog introduces a design pattern and provides the essential information you need to recognize and reuse the pattern.

The pattern's name helps developers communicate efficiently. A shared vocabulary of pattern names is invaluable when explaining a system to colleagues or writing design documentation. Named patterns clarify thought, and the implications of a design—even the rationale behind a design—can be communicated with just a few words.

Programmers familiar with patterns immediately infer the uses and limitations of objects composing a named pattern as well as the overall design employed and the consequences of that design.

Apple's own documentation occasionally uses design pattern names in both class references and programmer's guides, but the documentation doesn't always explain what the patterns are or what they should mean to a developer. In addition, Apple frequently uses its own names for design patterns instead of the terms commonly used throughout the industry. In some cases, the differences in terminology are the result of simultaneous independent discovery. In other cases, the patterns were first recognized in Cocoa or its predecessor NEXTSTEP, and it's the industry that changed the name. The patterns described in this book are identified using both Apple's terminology and the common industry names when applicable so you can see the correlation.

Each design pattern includes a description of the problem(s) and motivation for applying the pattern. Some patterns include a list of problem indicators that suggest the use of the pattern. Because Cocoa contains many patterns that are applicable in diverse situations, the patterns have been carefully organized so that the same problems in different contexts are readily identified. In some cases, related patterns that should be avoided are also identified.

Finally, each pattern identifies the consequences that naturally result from its use. The consequences and trade-offs of design alternatives are crucial when evaluating which patterns to use in a particular situation.

Why Focus on Design Patterns?

When approaching a software technology as vast as Cocoa, it's easy to lose sight of the overall architecture and rationale of the technology. Many programmers comment that they feel lost in the multitude of classes, functions, and data structures that Cocoa provides. They can't see the forest because they're concentrating too much on individual trees. The patterns used in Cocoa provide a structure and organization that helps programmers find their way. The patterns show programmers how to reuse groups of cooperating classes even when the relationships between the classes are not fully explained in the documentation for individual classes.

The goal of object-oriented programming is to maximize programmer productivity by reducing lifetime software development and maintenance costs. The principal technique used to achieve the goal is object reuse. An object that is reused saves the programmer time because the object would otherwise need to be reimplemented for each new project. Another benefit of reusing objects is that when new features are required or bugs are identified, you only need to make changes to a small number of objects, and those changes benefit other projects that rely on the same objects. Most importantly, by reusing objects, fewer total lines of code are written to solve each new problem, and that means there are fewer lines of code to maintain as well.

Design patterns identify successful strategies for achieving reuse on a larger scale than individual objects. The patterns themselves and all of the objects involved in the patterns are proven and have been reused many times. The consistent use of design patterns within Cocoa contributes to the high level of productivity that Cocoa programmers enjoy. Design patterns advance the art of object-oriented programming.

The patterns within Cocoa provide a guide for designing many different types of applications. Cocoa contains some of the most famously well-designed software ever produced, and following the patterns used by Cocoa will make you a better programmer even when you aren't using Cocoa.

This book should satisfy your intellectual curiosity. Design patterns answer "why" as well as "what" and "how." Knowing how patterns are applied and more importantly why patterns contribute so much to productivity makes the daily job of programming more enjoyable.

Guiding Principles of Design

All of the design patterns described in this book have several properties in common. In each case, the goal of the pattern is to solve a problem in a general, reusable way. Several guiding principles of design help ensure that the patterns are flexible and applicable in many contexts. The same strategies that are applied to the design of individual objects are applied to design patterns as well. In fact, patterns that involve many objects benefit even more from good object-oriented design than simpler systems. One reason that patterns exist is to help make sure that productivity gained from reusing the patterns exceeds the productivity gained from using individual objects—the sum is greater than the parts.

Minimize Coupling

As a general design goal, coupling between classes should be minimized. Coupling refers to dependencies between objects. Whenever such dependencies exist, they reduce opportunities for reusing the objects independently. Coupling also applies to subsystems within large systems of objects. It's important to look for designs that avoid coupling whenever possible.

All of the Cocoa design patterns exist in part to limit or avoid coupling. For example, the overarching Model-View-Controller (MVC) pattern described in Part I of this book, "One Pattern to Rule Them All," is used throughout Cocoa to organize subsystems of classes and is applied to the design of entire applications. The primary intent of the MVC pattern is to partition a complex system of objects into three major subsystems and minimize coupling between the subsystems.

Design for Change

It's important to use designs that accommodate changes through the lifecycle of a software system. Designs that are too inflexible ultimately restrict opportunities for reuse. In the worst case, no reuse occurs because it's easier to redesign and reimplement a system than it is to make changes within an existing rigid design.

It's possible to anticipate certain types of changes and accommodate them in a design. For example, the Cocoa Delegates pattern provides a mechanism for one object to modify and control the behavior of another object without introducing coupling between them. Cocoa provides many objects that can be controlled by optional delegates, and the key to the pattern is that the objects acting as delegates might not have even been conceived when Cocoa was designed. All of the Cocoa design patterns exist in part to accommodate change. That's just one of the reasons that Cocoa is so flexible.

Emphasize Interfaces Rather Than Implementations

Interfaces provide a kind of metaphorical contract between an object and the users of the object. An object's interface tells a programmer what the object is able to do but not how it will do it. In the context of reusable frameworks like Cocoa, object interfaces must remain consistent from one version of the framework to the next, or else software written to use one version of the framework may not work correctly with the next. A contract is necessary for programmers to feel confident reusing framework objects, but anyone who has tried to create a truly flexible reusable contract knows that it's a difficult task. When implementation details become part of the contract between an object and its users, it becomes difficult for framework developers to improve objects without breaking backward compatibility.

Find the Optimal Granularity

Many of the design patterns employed by Cocoa operate at different levels of granularity. For example, the MVC pattern is usually applied to large subsystems of cooperating classes and entire applications, but the Singleton pattern is used to make sure that only one instance of a class is ever created and provides access to that instance. The goal of patterns is to enhance software reuse. The granularity of a pattern can have a huge impact on opportunities for reuse.

Certain problems are best solved by small patterns that involve only a few classes, while other problems are solved by reusing grand overarching patterns. The key is to find the optimal balance. In general, the larger patterns provide bigger productivity gains than the smaller ones, but if a pattern is too big or too general to solve a specific, narrow problem, it can't be used. For example, the MVC pattern contributes enormously to most applications, but there are some specific applications that may not benefit from its use, and in those cases the pattern provides no value. In contrast, patterns such as Anonymous Objects and Heterogeneous Containers, Enumerators, Flyweight, and Singleton are small and contribute value in every application. Cocoa provides patterns all along the spectrum. Some of the pattern descriptions address the issues of granularity and the balance that Cocoa strikes.

Use Composition in Preference to Inheritance

It can't be said enough times that coupling is the enemy. It is ironic that inheritance is simultaneously one of the most powerful tools in object-oriented programming and one of the leading causes of coupling. In fact, there is no tighter coupling than the relationship between a class and its inherited superclasses. Many of the patterns described in this book exist in part to reduce the need to create subclasses. The general rule is that when there is an alternative to inheritance, use the alternative.

Audience

This book is intended for Mac OS X programmers who are using or considering the use of Apple's Cocoa frameworks for Mac OS X or the Cocoa Touch frameworks for iPhone and iPod Touch. Much of the information in this book also applies directly to the open source GNUstep project, which is available for Linux and Windows.

Who Should Read This Book

Objective-C, C, C++, and Java programmers should read this book. You should be familiar with the general principals of object-oriented design and object-oriented technology to understand and benefit from the design patterns presented here. Many of Cocoa's design patterns leverage features of the Objective-C language, which are not thoroughly explained in this book; however, Apple includes the document, titled *The Objective-C 2.0 Programming Language*, along with the free Mac OS Xcode Tools (http://developer.apple.com/documentation/Cocoa/Conceptual/ObjectiveC).

Some knowledge of Objective-C is required to understand the implementation of Cocoa, although experienced programmers can pick it up incrementally while reading this book. That said, this book is not a substitute for a language reference such as *The Objective-C 2.0 Programming Language* even though language features that contribute to Cocoa design patterns are explained as needed within the pattern descriptions.

What You Need to Know

This book doesn't require guru-level programming skills. The patterns used in the design of Cocoa are identified and explained in part to demystify the technology. Programmers who are new to Cocoa will benefit from the insights and wisdom embodied by Cocoa just as much as experienced veterans. However, if you are completely new to programming with C or languages derived from C, you'll have difficulty following the in-depth analysis of how and why patterns work. You need to be comfortable with the object-oriented concepts of classes, instances, encapsulation, polymorphism, and inheritance. Without a foundation in the technology of object-oriented software development, the sometimes advanced descriptions of benefits, consequences, and trade-offs in this book could be overwhelming.

This book assumes that you know C, C++, or Java and that you're familiar with object-oriented software development. As mentioned earlier, you need to know Objective-C to get the most value from this book, but Objective-C can be learned along the way.

You need to be running a Mac OS X system with Apple's Xcode Tools installed. If you don't have the Xcode Tools installed on your system, there are a couple things you can do to obtain them:

- If you purchased new Mac hardware or a boxed release of Mac OS X, the Xcode Tools can be found on the Install DVD in the Optional Installs folder.
    - For Mac OS X Leopard (v 10.5), look in the Xcode Tools folder and double-click on the XcodeTools.mpkg file to install Xcode.
    - For Mac OS X Snow Leopard (v 10.6), double-click on the Xcode.mpkg file to install Xcode.
- The latest Xcode Tools are available with a free online membership to the Mac Developer Program which is part of the Apple Developer Connection (ADC) at http://developer.apple.com/. After you've signed up, you can download the Xcode Tools from the ADC website. (Keep in mind, though, that the download is around 1GB, so you'll need a fast connection.)

Note

If you are developing for the iPhone or iPod Touch, you need to register for the iPhone Developer Program (http://developer.apple.com/iphone), and then download and install the iPhone Software Development Kit (SDK) from the iPhone Dev Center after logging in. The iPhone 3.0 SDK requires an Intel-based Mac which means it cannot be used on older, PowerPC-based Macs (for example, Macs with the G3, G4, or G5 processors). The iPhone SDK is available for Mac OS X Leopard (v 10.5) and for Mac OS X Snow Leopard (v 10.6).

This book is written based on Mac OS X (v 10.5), but ultimately you will want to leverage Cocoa's design patterns when creating applications for any version of Mac OS X, iPhone, iPod Touch, or for Windows and Linux with GNUstep.

How This Book Is Organized

This book is organized into five parts. Part I, "One Pattern to Rule Them All," describes the Model-View-Controller pattern that provides the overall structure and organization for Cocoa and most applications that use Cocoa. Part II, "Fundamental Patterns," identifies the patterns in Cocoa with which all other patterns are built. Part III, "Patterns That Primarily Empower by Decoupling," contains patterns that enable you to control and extend objects without introducing unnecessary coupling. Part IV, "Patterns That Primarily Hide Complexity," explains patterns that hide complexity and implementation details so programmers can confidently focus on solving problems. Part V, "Practical Tools for Pattern Application," shows practical applications of the Model-View-Controller design pattern with examples selected from the Cocoa frameworks. Appendix, "Resources," provides additional references for using and understanding Cocoa and design patterns.

Acknowledgments

Acknowledgments from Erik M. Buck

Cocoa Design Patterns would not exist without inspiration and trailblazing provided by *Design Patterns: Elements of Reusable Object-Oriented Software* by Erich Gamma, Richard Helm, Ralph Johnson, and John M. Vlissides.

Cocoa Design Patterns would have no reason to exist if not for the astounding design and engineering accomplishment embodied by the Cocoa frameworks. From NEXTSTEP 0.8 in 1988 to OPENSTEP Enterprise 4.2 for Windows NT, Solaris, and HPUX in 1997 to Mac OS X 10.0 in 2001 and iPhones in 2007, the creators of Cocoa continue to advance the state of the art while setting ever higher standards for elegance and consistency.

Cocoa Design Patterns would have no audience without the vibrant dedication and camaraderie of the Cocoa developer community embodied by the subscribers to Apple's Cocoa-dev mailing list, the countless informative Cocoa-related blogs, and the third-party application developers large and small.

Acknowledgments from Donald A. Yacktman

I'd like to thank my family for their patience and support and those in the community who have helped me learn over the years.

About the Authors

Erik M. Buck founded EMB & Associates, Inc. in 1993 and built the company into a leader in the aerospace and entertainment software industries by leveraging the NeXT/Apple software technology that would later become Apple's Cocoa frameworks. Mr. Buck has also worked in construction, taught science to 8th graders, exhibited oil on canvas portraits, and developed alternative fuel vehicles. Mr. Buck sold his company in 2002 and currently holds the title of Senior Staff at Northrop Grumman Corporation. Mr. Buck received a B.S. degree in computer science from the University of Dayton in 1991 and is a frequent contributor to Cocoa mailing lists and technical forums.

Donald A. Yacktman has been using Cocoa and its predecessor technologies, OpenStep and NextStep, professionally since 1991. He coauthored the book *Cocoa Programming* and has contributed to the Stepwise website as both author and editor. He has worked for Verio/iServer and illumineX in the past. At present he works as an independent consultant assisting in the design and implementation of Cocoa and iPhone applications. Mr. Yacktman received B.S. and M.S. degrees in electrical and computer engineering from Brigham Young University in 1991 and 1994, respectively.

One Pattern to Rule Them All

All of Cocoa is organized according to the Model View Controller (MVC) design pattern. Apple's tools and frameworks encourage and in some cases enforce the use of MVC design. The chapters in Part I explain what MVC is, why it exists, and how it applies to Cocoa programming.

Chapters in this part of the book include

Model View Controller

Model View Controller (MVC) is one of the oldest and most successfully reused software design patterns. It was first introduced with the Smalltalk programming language in the 1970s. MVC defines the overall architecture of the Cocoa frameworks. It's a high-level pattern for organizing large groups of cooperating objects into distinct subsystems: the Model, the View, and the Controller.

To understand the roles that subsystems play in the MVC pattern, it's useful to analyze the capabilities and behavior of common applications. Most applications store information, retrieve information, present information to a user, and enable a user to edit or otherwise manipulate the information. In an object-oriented application, information isn't just bytes; objects encapsulate information along with methods for using the information. Each object within your application should fit into exactly one of the following subsystems:

- **Model.** The Model subsystem is composed of the objects that provide the unique capabilities and information storage for an application. Models contain all of the rules for processing application data. The Model is the key subsystem that makes an application valuable. It's critically important that the Model subsystem is able to stand alone without dependencies on either the View or Controller subsystems.

- **View.** The View subsystem presents information gathered from the Model and provides a way for users to interact with information. The key to understanding Views is to recognize that there are invariably a multitude of Views. For example, there may be a graphical user interface View, a printed report View, a command line View, a Web-based View, and a scripting language View that all interact with the same Model.

- **Controller.** The purpose of the Controller is to decouple the Model from the Views. User interaction with a View results in requests made to the Controller subsystem, which in turn may request changes to information in the Model. The Controller also handles data translation and formatting for presentation to a user. For example, a Model may store data in meters, but based on a user's preference, the Controller may convert the data to feet. A Model may store objects in an unordered collection, but the Controller may sort the objects before providing them to a View for presentation to a user.

The primary purpose of MVC is to decouple the Model subsystem from the Views so that each can change independently. The Controller subsystem enables that decoupling as shown in Figure 1.1. In a typical sequence of operations, the user interacts with a slider or some other interface object. The slider sends a message to tell a Controller object about the change to the slider's value as indicated in step 1 in Figure 1.1. In step 2, the controller identifies which Model objects need to be updated based on the new value. The Controller sends messages to the Model objects to request the updates. In step 3, the Model objects react to the messages about updates. The Model objects might constrain the updated values to fall within application defined limits or perform other validation. Application logic is applied to the updated values, and other Model objects may be updated as a side effect. The Model then notifies the Controller that the Model has changed. Finally, in step 4, the Controller sends messages to View objects so that they reflect the changes that occurred in the Model. There may be many parts of the View that are updated.

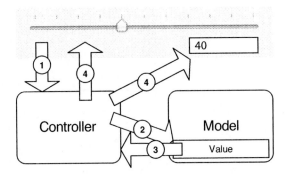

Figure 1.1　The Controller subsystem decouples the Model and the View.

You might be tempted to neglect the Controller subsystem because it's often tricky to design and seems like it adds needless complexity. After all, the flow of information is ultimately between the Model and the Views, so why introduce another layer? The answer is that Views tend to change much more often than Models. Not only are there potentially many Views, but it's the nature of user interfaces that they change based on customer feedback and evolving user interface standards. It's also sometimes important to change the Model without affecting all of the Views. The Controller subsystem provides insulation between the Model and the Views.

The dashed lines in Figure 1.1 emphasize the importance of using messaging approaches that minimize coupling. Ideally, neither the Model nor the View have dependencies on the Controller. For example, View objects often use the Target Action design pattern from Chapter 17, "Outlets, Targets, and Actions," to avoid needing any information about the Controller objects that receive messages when the user interacts with user interface objects. Model objects often use the Notifications pattern in Chapter 14, "Notifications," to broadcast notification of Model changes to anonymous interested objects that may be in the Controller subsystem.

MVC in Cocoa

Cocoa is loosely organized into Model, View, and Controller subsystems, as shown in Figure 1.2. Core Data simplifies the development of Models for many applications. The Application Kit contains objects for use in both the View and Controller subsystems. The Foundation framework provides classes used in all three subsystems. Foundation doesn't directly provide any View or Controller-specific features, but it provides access to operating system services, the NSObject base class, scripting support, and other features used in the implementation of Models, Views, and Controllers.

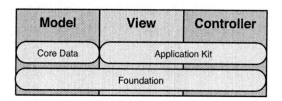

Figure 1.2   The overall MVC organization of Cocoa

Apple supplies a diagram of the classes that comprise the Foundation framework at http://developer.apple.com/documentation/Cocoa/Reference/Foundation/ObjC_classic/Intro/IntroFoundation.html.

Note

Model subsystems are often built in straight C or C++. Some applications use a cross-platform Model that doesn't depend on Cocoa or other platform-specific technology at all. One of the virtues of the MVC design is that the Model has no dependence on other subsystems, so there is little impact to the Controller or View if the Model is written in a completely different programming language or is based on different technology. However, Cocoa's Foundation and Core Data frameworks contain some of the most powerful, flexible, and extensible software available. Building your Model using Cocoa technology is a great choice when cross-platform capabilities are not a primary concern.

In addition to the overall MVC organization of Cocoa, important subsystems within Cocoa repeat the MVC design pattern on a smaller scale, for example, Cocoa's Text Architecture groups collaborating classes into Model, View, and Controller roles within the narrow field of text processing. Cocoa's Document Architecture is similarly divided into separate MVC components. Other Mac OS X technologies that aren't strictly part of Cocoa reuse the MVC design as well. System preference panes, the Quick Time (QT) Kit, and Quartz Composer all separate their subcomponents into distinct MVC roles.

Core Data Support for Model Subsystems

Cocoa's Core Data technology aids Model subsystem development and solves two common implementation challenges: persistent information storage and object relationship management.

Almost every Model needs the ability to store information and later reload it. Many possible implementations of load and store exist. Some applications use binary file formats, others use human readable text files, and some implementations rely on an underlying relational database. Core Data implements load and store with a technique called *object persistence*. The basic approach is to store the Model objects themselves including any encapsulated information and the relationships between the objects. Core Data can load and store the persistent objects from three file formats—human readable XML, binary flat files, or SQLite databases.

Whether Core Data is used, the design of persistent information storage needs to weigh several factors. Is the storage intended for easy information exchange between different applications? If so, a well-defined human readable format like XML is the best choice. How fast does the load and store need to be? Binary formats usually provide the best performance.

Core Data includes reusable infrastructure that abstracts the details of particular storage formats enabling you to concentrate on designing other aspects of your Model. You can change the preferred Core Data storage format for your Model at any time during development and even enable all three supported formats simultaneously.

Almost every Model needs to manage the relationships between objects. Core Data supports one-to-one and also one-to-many relationships between objects. Each relationship can be optional or required. If the members of a family are represented by objects, each member optionally has a relationship to one spouse but always has exactly two biological parents. Each member can have any number of children. Core Data enables you to specify relationships, identify constraints, provide default values, and validate relationships.

Although Core Data relationships can be specified through code, Apple's Xcode tools include a graphical object modeler that lets you define your Model objects called entities and their relationships in a graphical way. The NSManagedObject class provides the built-in support for object relationship management and interacts with an NSManagedObjectContext to provide persistent storage. When designing your Model in Xcode, you can use NSManagedObject instances directly. NSManagedObject uses the Associative Storage pattern, which allows you to add relationships and per-instance information called attributes even without subclassing. Alternatively, you can create your own subclasses of NSManagedObject right in the modeling tool. Core Data natively stores attributes in NSNumber, NSData, NSString, and NSSet instances. Subclassing gives you maximum control over how attributes are stored so that you can use custom objects or C structures as attributes. Subclassing also provides a convenient way to add arbitrary application logic to Model entities.

Core Data is described in more detail in Chapter 30, "Core Data Models." The support for relationship management, attribute changing, and persistent storage naturally integrates with Cocoa's standard undo and redo features. Any change to an attribute or relationship can be undone. Core Data automates Attribute and relationship validation so that you can notify users about inconsistent or invalid changes to Model objects.

Application Kit Support for View Subsystems

Cocoa's Application Kit contains classes used to build both View and Controller subsystems. Figure 1.3 identifies the most important View subsystem classes within the Application Kit. These classes present information and enable user interaction. Apple's diagram of the entire Application Kit is available at http://developer.apple.com/documentation/Cocoa/Reference/ApplicationKit/ObjC_classic/Intro/IntroAppKit.html.

The NSMenu, NSWindow, NSApplication, and NSView classes form the core of Cocoa graphical user interfaces. Almost everything displayed by a Cocoa application is part of a menu or a window. Each Cocoa application uses an instance of the NSApplication class to maintain a connection with the operating system for receiving user input events, displaying an icon in the dock, presenting a main menu, and displaying windows. Subclasses of NSView implement all of the standard user interface elements such as buttons, text, tab views, progress indicators, and image viewers that form the content of windows.

NSApplication, NSView, and NSWindow are all subclasses of NSResponder. The NSResponder class is one of the keys to the design of the Application Kit; it encapsulates handling of user input events and implements the Responder Chain design pattern to ensure events and messages are received by the right objects as described in Chapter 18, "Responder Chain."

Figure 1.3 shows the many standard NSView subclasses that implement user interfaces. You can also create application-specific user interface features by making your own subclasses of NSView. Some of Apple's other frameworks such as Web Kit, QTKit, and Quartz Composer provide specialized NSView subclasses for displaying and editing their respective media types.

NSView implements the Hierarchies pattern (Chapter 16, "Hierarchies") and enables you to compose interfaces that consist of views within views. Any view can contain any number of subviews. Interface Builder lets you easily develop your view hierarchy, and you can build it programmatically with NSView methods such as

-(void)addSubview:(NSView *)aView, -(void)removeFromSuperview, and -(void) replaceSubview:(NSView *)oldView with:(NSView *)newView.

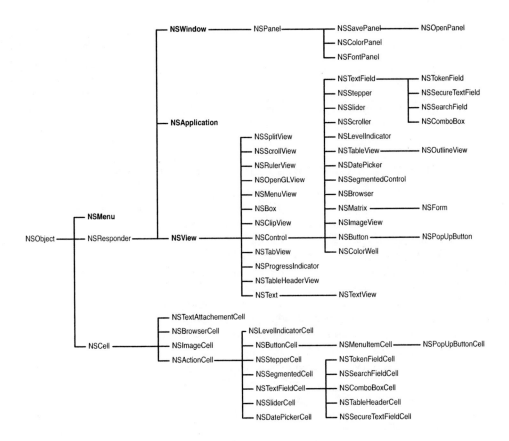

Figure 1.3   Cocoa's principal View subsystem classes

Some of Cocoa's subclasses of NSView visually organize their subviews. For example, the NSBox class can draw a bezel around subviews to visually group them. The NSTabView class provides a visual metaphor for selecting and displaying any of several mutually exclusive subviews. NSSplitView uses a graphical divider bar to separate its subviews either horizontally or vertically. Users drag the divider bar with the mouse to control how much of each subview is visible. NSScrollView repositions its subviews as users drag scroll bars.

Many of Cocoa's standard user interface components are subclasses of the NSControl class. The NSControl class plays key roles in the Targets and Actions and the Responder Chain patterns explained in Chapter 17 and Chapter 18, respectively. For example, when a user selects a date via an NSDatePicker object, an action message is sent to the date picker's target. If no specific target exists, the object that eventually receives the message is determined by the Responder Chain.

The NSCell class implements the Flyweight pattern and is explained in Chapter 22, "Flyweight." Flyweights optimize both execution time and memory consumption. Instances of the NSControl class use NSCell subclasses as an optimization and to add flexibility. NSTableView is a prime example of the way controls use cells. Separate NSCell instances determine the way data is presented in each column. You don't have to subclass NSTableView just to control how information is presented. Instead, configure the standard NSTableView with different embedded cells.

Application Kit Support for Controller Subsystems

Cocoa's NSController class and related classes like NSArrayController fulfill the role of "mediator" between View objects and Model objects. Mediators control the flow of information and in some cases supply default "placeholder" values. For example, if a View object displays data based on the user's current selection, a mediator can supply default data for use when nothing is selected.

The Application Kit supplies the NSController, NSObjectController, NSArrayController, NSUserDefaultsController, and NSTreeController classes that mediate data flow using Cocoa's bindings technology. Bindings establish relationships between objects and are defined either programmatically or in Interface Builder. When a binding exists, changes made at runtime to each bound object result in automatic updates to the other bound object. Bindings can be made directly between Model objects and View objects or even between objects within a single subsystem, for example, between two View objects. However, bindings directly between View and Model objects produce all of the same problems as other dependencies between subsystems. Use NSController and its subclasses to mediate between the Model and the View. Bindings are explained in more detail by Chapter 32, "Bindings and Controllers."

> ### Note
> Cocoa bindings simplify the development of Controller subsystems and potentially replace handwritten code with connections created in Interface Builder. However, even if you choose not to use bindings, you should still use mediating controllers within your applications. Cocoa programmers often create simple subclasses of NSObject to act as mediating controllers and implement handwritten methods to synchronize changes in the Model with the View and vice versa. These custom mediating controllers achieve the MVC goal of decoupling the Model and the View.

In addition to mediating the flow of data between the Model and the View, the Controller subsystem is also responsible for the overall control of application behavior. When multiple View subsystems are available, objects within the Controller subsystem are responsible for determining which Views to present to users. For example, when a script is run to extract data from a Model, there may be no need to display a graphical user interface View. The Controller subsystem is the ideal place to encode logic that determines whether to load and display a graphical user interface View. The Model can't do it because the Model isn't supposed to know what Views exist, and similarly different Views should not depend on each other.

The Application Kit contains several classes that control application behavior. Cocoa's Document Architecture, described later in this chapter, highlights the NSDocumentController, NSViewController, and NSWindowController classes that control application documents, views, and windows, respectively.

Cocoa's Text Architecture

The NSText and NSTextView classes shown in Figure 1.4 provide the user visible portion of Cocoa's MVC text architecture. The NSTextStorage class provides a Model for storing and processing text. In cases in which the layout of text is key to application logic, NSTextContainer is also part of the text architecture's Model. NSTextContainer stores the geometric shape of a block of text. For example, a drawing program that constrains text to a circular area may need to store that shape in the Model so that it's restored if the Model is stored and later reloaded. However, in most applications, default rectangular text layout is sufficient, and no explicit NSTextContainer is needed.

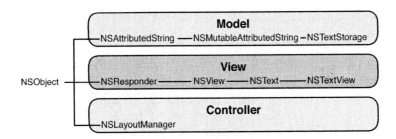

Figure 1.4   The MVC components of Cocoa's text architecture

The NSLayoutManager class acts as a Controller mediating between the View and Model. Each NSTextView instance asks an associated NSLayoutManager instance to provide text to be displayed. The NSLayoutManager in turn accesses instances of NSTextStorage and NSTextContainer to supply the text for display. In the process, NSLayoutManager converts Unicode characters into glyphs (graphical representations of characters) that are appropriate for display based on the current font, underline, and other attributes of the text.

In good MVC style, NSTextStorage is independent of text presentation. A wide range of text processing tasks are possible entirely within the Model subsystem. For example, text attributes can be changed, text itself can be modified, text can be searched, text can be served as web pages over a network, and text can be stored or loaded in a batch processing application that doesn't display any user interface.

Cocoa's text architecture provides a complete solution that meets the needs of most applications. It's common to simply drag instances of NSTextView into your user interface via Apple's Interface Builder application. Apple provides a tutorial to show you exactly how it's done at http://developer.apple.com/documentation/Cocoa/Conceptual/TextArchitecture/Tasks/TextEditor.html. When you do want to customize text processing, the MVC design of the text architecture enables you to focus your effort on the appropriate subsystem. If you want to store nonstandard attributes along with text, use NSTextStorage or its superclass, NSMutableAttributedString, which is implemented in the Foundation framework. NSMutableAttributedString uses the Associative Storage pattern from Chapter 19, "Associative Storage," so that you can most likely do what you want without subclassing. If you need to implement exotic text layout capabilities, start with NSLayoutManager, and if you want fine control over user input or you want to display custom text attributes, use subclass NSTextView.

Cocoa's Document Architecture

Applications for viewing or editing information often adopt the user interface metaphor of "documents" presented in windows on-screen. Examples include spreadsheets, word processors, web browsers, and drawing programs. The Cocoa classes shown in Figure 1.5 implement a reusable MVC document architecture.

The document architecture adds an additional wrinkle to the MVC pattern. The Controller subsystem is divided into the Model Controller and the View Controller. The classes in the Model controller load, store, and access model data. The View Controller classes access already loaded Model data to enable presentation in the View.

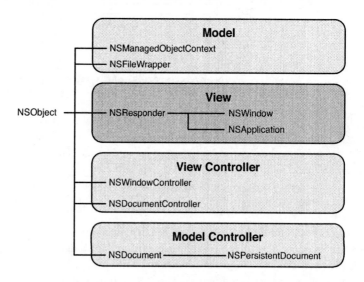

Figure 1.5   The MVC components of Cocoa's document architecture

The division exists in part to simplify the common practice of subclassing the NSDocument class. NSDocument is a prime example of the Template Method pattern described in Chapter 4, "Template Method." NSDocument itself is abstract, so you must subclass it and implement a few critical methods to support loading and saving of Model data unique to your application. Another reason for the separation is that parts of the Controller layer are dynamically created as needed. For example, it's possible to load and interact with a document without necessarily displaying any windows associated with the document. A script might open a document, copy information out of the document, and paste the information somewhere else without any need to display document windows.

The View Controllers, NSDocumentController and NSWindowController, mediate between the View subsystem and the Model to access information to be displayed or edited. There is only one instance of NSDocumentController in a document-based application. At any moment, there are separate instances of NSDocument corresponding to each open document. There may be zero, one, or more NSWindowController instances associated with each open document. The use of different numbers of instances of the various classes is another reason Cocoa distinguishes between document Model Controllers and View Controllers. Without the distinction, a single object would need to control all of the windows representing each document and document loading and saving.

In Mac OS X v10.5, Apple added the NSViewController class that fills a role similar to the NSWindowController class. NSViewController instances mediate between objects loaded from .nib files and objects that are outside the .nib file. Interface Builder makes it easy to establish Cocoa bindings that include NSViewController instances. NSWindowController and NSViewController simplify memory management for objects loaded from .nib files.

Figure 1.6 identifies the collaborations between the classes in Cocoa's document architecture. Within a document-based application, one instance of NSDocumentController receives and processes messages to create new documents, load documents, and remind users to save documents before quitting the application. NSDocumentController also manages the contents of the standard Recent Documents menu. Graphical Cocoa applications contain an instance of the NSApplication class to enable use of menus and windows as described in the section, "Application Kit Support for View Subsystems." The NSDocumentController instance receives delegate messages sent by the NSApplication instance. If you provide a different delegate object, your delegate will receive the messages that enable you to control document management behavior without having to subclass NSDocumentController. The ability to avoid subclassing in some cases is an advantage of the Delegates pattern explained in Chapter 15, "Delegates."

You typically use one instance of the NSWindowController class to control each window associated with a document. A single document may be represented by multiple windows if necessary. For example, one window might present a document's Model information as raw XML and HTML data while simultaneously another window presents the same Model information as a formatted web page. In another example, if a scheduled meeting is stored as a single document, one window might contain a table identifying all of the participants in the meeting, and other windows might display contact information for the people selected in the table.

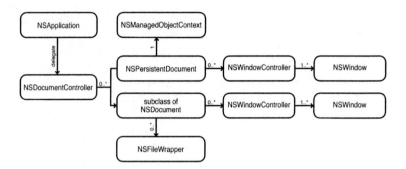

Figure 1.6   Collaboration between the objects in Cocoa's
document architecture

Each NSDocument instance maintains an array of associated window controllers, and
each window controller also knows which document it belongs to. This bidirectional
communication lets the window controllers access the Model via the NSDocument instance. Similarly, when a document is hidden or closed, the NSDocument instance notifies
associated window controllers.

Each instance of NSWindowController has an outlet that is typically connected in Interface Builder to the window to be controlled. You can create your own subclasses of
NSWindowController and add additional Outlets and Actions. The Outlets and Actions
are then connected to View subsystem objects like button and text fields to give the window controller direct access to those objects. An alternative but equally valid design uses
Cocoa's Bindings technology explained in Chapter 32 to configure user interface objects
so that they always reflect the current information obtained from the Model via an
NSDocument instance.

Your application's Model contains the unique information used by the application. If
you use Cocoa's Core Data technology to implement the Model, an instance of
NSManagedObjectContext provides access to the information and relationships within
the Model and persistent storage in XML, binary, or database formats. Apple provides the
NSPersistentDocument class, an already built subclass of NSDocument, to save and load
using an associated NSManagedObjectContext. If you use the Core Data approach, you
can frequently avoid the need to create your own subclass of NSDocument.

If you don't use Core Data, you must create your own custom subclass of NSDocument
and implement methods such as (BOOL)writeToURL:(NSURL *)absoluteURL
ofType:(NSString *)typeName error:(NSError **)outError and
(BOOL)readFromURL:(NSURL *)absoluteURL ofType:(NSString *)typeName
error:(NSError **)outError. Your implementations contain whatever logic and data
conversions are needed to save and load the Model using a specific file type and file system location. The file type information enables document type conversions when saving
and provides the information your code needs to convert from one type to another when

loading. The `error:` parameter provides a way for your code to report any saving or loading errors that should be presented to users.

Whether you use Core Data, there is often a one-to-one correspondence between files on disk and documents. In other words, all of the information for one document is stored in one file. However, if you have more complex storage needs, Cocoa's `NSFileWrapper` class encapsulates the details of using multiple files per document. Each `NSFileWrapper` instance manages a whole folder full of files at the location specified by the URL passed to `-readFromURL:ofType:error:`. `NSFileWrapper` can simplify saving and loading of complex Model information.

Cocoa's MVC document architecture might seem complex at first, but in practice, you usually don't have to spend much time directly interacting with the document architecture. It provides all of the standard behaviors that users expect and requires very little effort on the developer's part. The key benefit of the MVC design is that you can tailor the behavior of multidocument applications without having to touch all of the components that collaborate to implement the full solution.

Apple's Xcode application includes a Cocoa document-based application template that automatically creates an `NSDocument` subclass and other needed components such as the application's `NSDocumentController` instance. The template even provides an Interface Builder file containing a window to use as the starting point for defining your document's View subsystem. There is a similar Core Data document-based application template that automatically uses the `NSPersistentDocument` class.

Cocoa Scriptability

A script interface is much like any other user interface. There are conventions that script writers expect just like there are standard look and feel expectations for graphical user interfaces. In the MVC design, a script interface is just one of the many View subsystems that an application may provide, and like all Views, scripting interfaces should usually interact with the Controller subsystem and not directly with the Model.

When providing a scripting interface, keep in mind that the optimal way in which script writers interact with an application often differs from the way a graphical user interface is used. Although it's possible to write scripts that open windows and simulate button presses or menu selections, that's seldom efficient. Ideally, a scripting interface works even if the application doesn't display anything on screen. Scripts automate complex or tedious tasks and run in a batch mode.

Cocoa automatically provides basic support for scripting interfaces. The `NSApplication` object used in every graphical Cocoa application accepts interprocess messages and commands called "Apple events." Apple events use a Mac OS X standard format for commands, arguments, and return values. The most common and popular scripting language used to send Apple events is Apple's own Applescript. However, the cross-platform Python and Ruby scripting languages included with Mac OS X are also able to send Apple events. You can even generate Apple events from C and Objective-C programs including Cocoa applications. As of Mac OS X 10.5, Apple provides a technology called the Scripting Bridge that simplifies and standardizes the task of integrating scripting interfaces with Cocoa applications.

In addition to NSApplication, other Cocoa Controller layer classes support scripting. The NSDocument and NSDocumentController classes respond to standard AppleEvents related to document selection, loading, and saving. Cocoa's text architecture handles the standard text manipulation Apple events for operations like insertion, deletion, text substitution, and searching.

You expose your application's custom capabilities through new commands provided in a scripting "dictionary" that is stored as an application resource and loaded by the NSApplication class when needed. The scripting dictionary is usually an XML file that specifies how application-specific objects are selected or identified and what commands may be used with the objects. Script writers use the dictionary to determine what commands to send from scripts. Script development tools like Mac OS X's Applescript Studio and Automator applications read the dictionary to validate scripts and detect scripting errors before the scripts are run.

Cocoa's Preference Pane Architecture

Mac OS X's built-in System Preferences application is extensible. It has a plug-in architecture with which new user interfaces called "panes" can be added. When started, the System Preferences application searches a set of standard file system locations to find and load any available plug-in panes. It then displays a window in which users choose among the available loaded preference panes. The System Preferences application as a whole uses the MVC design, and the panes that you add must also use that design.

The System Preferences Model consists of data files where systemwide and per user preferences are stored. Preferences include information like the chosen keyboard repeat speed, the desktop background picture, and the default method of connecting to the Internet. The System Preferences Model is encapsulated by the Core Foundation Preference Services interface, which is used by all applications and the operating system to access the preference values.

Each preference pane contains its own Controller subsystem created by subclassing Cocoa's NSPreferencePane class. NSPreferencePane handles most of the work of interfacing with the System Preferences application. For example, whenever your preference pane is selected by a user, but before it is displayed, the -(void)willSelect message is sent to your Controller. Immediately after your View is displayed, System Preferences sends the -(void)didSelect message to your Controller. Whenever the user unselects your pane by selecting a different pane, closing the preferences window, or quitting System Preferences, the -(NSPreferencePaneUnselectReply)shouldUnselect message is sent to your Controller. Depending on the value returned from your implementation of -shouldUnselect, your pane can postpone the unselect action. As an example, your pane can implement -shouldUnselect to display an error message indicating any problems with the current preference values and warning that the values will not be saved.

Finally, each preference pane provides its own View subsystem so that users can interact with whatever preference values the pane is designed to access. Use Interface Builder to construct the View and connect it to the Controller with the Outlets, Targets, and Actions pattern described in Chapter 17 or bindings described in Chapter 29, "Controllers."

As always in the MVC design, it's critical that the actual preference values are stored in the Model and not just in the pane's user interface. If a value is only stored in the pane's user interface, then the value might as well not exist because the system and other applications will have no way to access it.

Quartz Composer's Architecture

The Quartz Composer application is one of Apple's free developer tools. It builds upon Mac OS X's Quartz Core Imaging technology to create visual compositions using high performance graphical operations called "patches." A group of interconnected patches along with source data such as images, colors, and text comprise the Model. The Model is essentially a recipe for creating visual compositions. The QCView is a subclass of NSView and is able to display final compositions. The QCPatchController class mediates between the Model and the QCView.

When you embed Quartz compositions in your Cocoa applications, you can connect your own user interface controls to an QCPatchController to influence the compositions displayed. For example, a group of patches may use a variable to specify how opaque the resulting composition should be. Your application can use actions or bindings so that the value of a slider sets the opacity variable via the QCPatchController instance.

The QTKit Architecture

Mac OS X's QTKit is an Objective-C framework that manipulates and displays Quick-Time media. The Model used by QTKit is the QTMovie class, which encapsulates movies, audio streams, animations, and other supported QuickTime media formats defined by the international MPEG-4 standard. QTMovieView is a subclass of Cocoa's NSView class and displays QuickTime media to users.

To use the QTMovie and QTMovieView classes in a Cocoa application, you typically implement your own Controller layer. The Controller creates QTMovie instances and loads their content from files or over a network. The Controller then sends messages to tell a QTMovieView instance which QTMovie to play. Play, pause, fast forward, rewind, and other operations are implemented by sending messages to the QTMovieView.

Summary

The MVC pattern reduces coupling within applications, but it also increases complexity in some cases. A clear separation of subsystems pays off in the long term by reducing maintenance costs and enabling incremental enhancements. The MVC design pattern serves you best if you think there might ever be a version 2.0 of the application you're designing, and the larger the application, the more payoff MVC provides.

Another consideration is that it's usually easier to test a Model directly rather than through a user interface. When testing through a user interface, extra effort is required to determine whether a test failure is the result of a bug in the core application logic or a bug in the user interface or both. Furthermore, the Model is often developed by one team and the user interfaces by another. The skills needed to develop the Model may be very different than those needed to produce an excellent user experience.

Even with all of the benefits of the MVC design, it's not the best fit for every software project. At one extreme, a web application that runs on a server and displays information in a web page is the ideal candidate for the MVC design. There is already a clear separation between the View implemented by a web browser and the Model implemented on the server. At the other extreme are operating system device drivers and long-running computation-intensive programs. The application used to configure device drivers might adopt the MVC design, but the drivers themselves must conform to operating system interfaces and don't usually present information directly to users. Long-running calculations are often batch processed and again don't directly provide a user interface. In between the extremes, the combination of MVC and Cocoa proves valuable when applied to a wide range of applications including drawing programs, spreadsheets, games, word processors, and any sort of information viewer or editor.

MVC Analyzed and Applied

This chapter introduces a tiny Pay Calculator application and provides two separate implementations of the application. The first implementation uses a straightforward but naive non-MVC design. The second implementation highlights the improvements realized by using the MVC design pattern.

> **Note**
>
> The two implementations of Pay Calculator serve as a high-level whirlwind tour of Cocoa technologies and developer tools. The example provides a sense of what's possible, but there isn't space in this chapter to describe all of the underlying technology exploited to build Pay Calculator with drag-and-drop in Interface Builder and Xcode. Pay Calculator shows the high altitude view looking down on a trivial application built with Cocoa. Starting in Part II, "Fundamental Patterns," this book introduces the patterns that provide the foundation upon which the technologies employed in this chapter are built.

Non-MVC Design

A Pay Calculator application multiplies an employee's hourly rate of pay times the number of hours worked in the pay period to determine the amount of pay owed to the employee. To make the example slightly more interesting, we'll add the rule that some employees get paid 1.5 times their hourly rate for each hour worked in excess of the standard number of hours. Other employees are exempt from the special "overtime" pay and receive the same pay regardless of the number of hours worked. Figure 2.1 shows the user interface for this simple Pay Calculator.

The Pay Calculator application displays the employee's name. The user can enter the employee's hourly pay rate, the number of hours worked in the current pay period, and the standard number of hours in the pay period. The user can also select whether the employee is exempt from overtime pay. Once all of the information has been entered, pressing the big Calculate button displays the calculated pay amount.

The user interface is constructed using Apple's Interface Builder application that's part of Apple's free developer tools. User interface objects are dragged from palettes of reusable objects and dropped into windows, as shown in Figure 2.2. The objects are then configured and interconnected via Interface Builder without code. A selection of tutorials and documentation for Interface Builder are available at http://developer.apple.com/documentation/DeveloperTools/Conceptual/IBTips/IBTips.html.

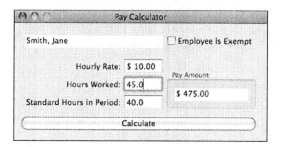

Figure 2.1   The initial user interface for
Pay Calculator

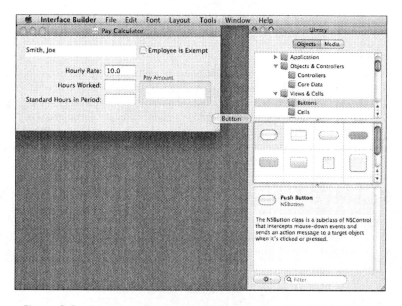

Figure 2.2   A button object is dragged from the Interface Builder Library
to a window under construction.

Note

Interface Builder allows you to work with live objects. Drag-and-drop operations copy fully functioning objects that can be used and tested within Interface Builder. Objects are configured with the desired initial state and then stored in a file. Later, when a Cocoa application reads the file, all of the stored objects are reconstituted to the state they had been in when stored. Interface Builder implements this with the Archiving and Unarchiving design pattern described in Chapter 11, "Archiving and Unarchiving."

The unique application logic for Pay Calculator needs to be implemented with new code, but this example is so small that only one method of one class is needed. The `PayCalculator` class interface declares Outlets to each of the user interface objects and an Action to calculate the pay amount:

```
#import <Cocoa/Cocoa.h>



@interface PayCalculator : NSObject
{
  IBOutlet NSTextField    *employeeNameField;
  IBOutlet NSFormCell     *hourlyRateField;
  IBOutlet NSFormCell     *hoursWorkedField;
  IBOutlet NSFormCell     *standardHoursInPeriodField;
  IBOutlet NSTextField    *payAmountField;
  IBOutlet NSButton       *employeeIsExemptButton;
}


- (IBAction)calculatePayAmount:(id)sender;

@end
```

Outlets are merely pointers to other objects, and Actions are messages that are sent from object to object. Don't worry if the terms are unfamiliar. Chapter 17, "Outlets, Targets, and Actions," explains the technology in detail. The Outlets are connected to other objects such as text input fields in Interface Builder, as shown in Figure 2.3. Similarly, a connection is made from the Calculate button to the `-calculatePayAmount:` Action to specify that the `calculatePayAmount:` message should be sent whenever the button is pressed.

The PayCalculator class implements `-calculatePayAmount:` to set the value of the `payAmountField` based on the information input by the user.

```
#import "PayCalculator.h"



@implementation PayCalculator

- (IBAction)calculatePayAmount:(id)sender
{
  if(NSOnState == [employeeIsExemptButton state])
  { // Pay the hourly rate times the standard number of hours
    // regardless of actual number of hours worked
    [payAmountField setFloatValue:[hourlyRateField floatValue] *
      [standardHoursInPeriodField floatValue]];
  }
  else
```

```
{ // Pay the hourly rate times the actual number of hours worked
  float    payAmount = [hourlyRateField floatValue] *
    [hoursWorkedField floatValue];

  if([hoursWorkedField floatValue] >
    [standardHoursInPeriodField floatValue])
  { // pay 50% extra for overtime hours
    float    overtimePayAmount = 0.5f *
      [hourlyRateField floatValue] *
      ([hoursWorkedField floatValue] -
      [standardHoursInPeriodField floatValue]);

    payAmount = payAmount + overtimePayAmount;
  }

  [payAmountField setFloatValue:payAmount];
  }
}

@end
```

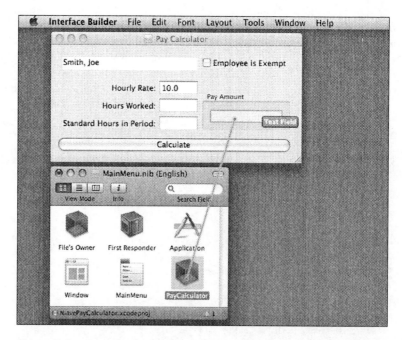

Figure 2.3   A connection from an Outlet to a text field is drawn in Interface
Builder.

Analysis of the Non-MVC Pay Calculator Design

All of the information needed to calculate the pay amount is stored in the objects that compose the user interface. The design is shown in Figure 2.4. When the user presses the Calculate button, the -calculatePayAmount: message is sent to a PayCalculator object as shown in step 1 in Figure 2.4. The implementation of PayCalculator's -calculatePayAmount: method extracts information as floating point values from various user interface objects in step 2. In step 3, the -calculatePayAmount: method sets the value displayed by the payAmount user interface object to the result of the calculation.

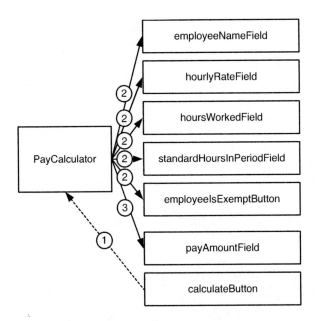

Figure 2.4   Relationships between objects in the non-MVC design

The non-MVC design can certainly be made to work; a sample implementation of the Pay Calculator application is available at www.CocoaDesignPatterns.com. However, even the tiny non-MVC Pay Calculator application example exhibits several serious design problems.

The first problem is that there's no way to save the information entered. Every time the user wants to calculate pay, all of the information has to be entered again. Next, if the user wants to view or enter information for more than one employee at a time, the entire user interface must be duplicated for each employee. The duplication is necessary because the information about each employee is only stored in the user interface objects. The problems just compound from there. Although Cocoa enables users to print the user interface just as it appears on-screen, a more concise presentation is more appropriate for printed output. Already there's a need for two different ways to view the information—a graphical user interface View and a printing View. However, if all of the information is stored in user interface objects, then the user interface objects have to be created even if the result of the calculation is only printed and never displayed on screen.

What happens if user feedback indicates that the `standardHoursInPeriodField` is not needed in the user interface? Perhaps users are confident that the standard will always be 40 hours, so the users request that the `standardHoursInPeriodField` be removed. That simple change to the user interface requires a change to the calculation of pay amounts to make the standard number of hours constant or store the information someplace else. The MVC design pattern exists to prevent situations in which application logic like calculating pay amounts has to be changed just because the user interface has changed.

MVC Design

The Model View Controller pattern is usually applied to large applications, and each of the three subsystems is typically composed of many objects. Nevertheless, MVC can be applied to the simple Pay Calculator application as well. In fact, Cocoa provides objects and technology that enable the implementation of a much more capable Pay Calculator application using the MVC design pattern without requiring much more code than the non-MVC version. Figure 2.5 illustrates an updated user interface for an MVC version of Pay Calculator.

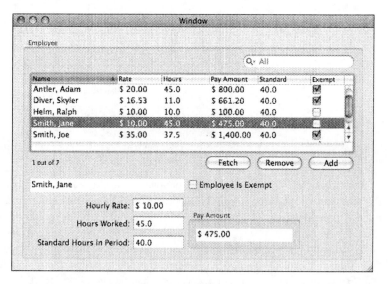

Figure 2.5   The updated user interface for Pay Calculator using MVC

The updated user interface is developed with Interface Builder and doesn't require any code. Interface Builder encourages development of independent View subsystems in two ways: First, it's so easy to develop user interfaces that multiple interfaces can be created and evaluated. Each of the interfaces is a separate View, which naturally leads developers to the habit of making applications work with multiple Views. Second, the objects on Interface Builder's palettes are reusable and therefore can't have any dependence on application-specific information. Just by dragging and dropping reusable objects, you naturally produce a decoupled View subsystem. In fact, the interconnection of objects for the non-MVC version of Pay Calculator actually takes more work to set up than for the MVC version because Interface Builder isn't as well-suited to developing non-MVC applications.

Note

Tools like Interface Builder are handy for developing applications that use the MVC design pattern, but don't confuse the tools and the design itself. The MVC design pattern has existed for a long time and can be used for any kind of software development using any tools. The tools Apple provides and Cocoa itself encourage the use of MVC.

The important change needed to redesign Pay Calculator using MVC is the creation of a proper Model subsystem. In this case, the Model only needs one kind of object, MYEmployee. By creating a MYEmployee class, all of the information for each employee can be stored in separate instances of MYEmployee. Any number of instances can be created to store information about any number of employees. Save and load are implemented by saving and loading the MYEmployee instances in a file. The logic for calculating the pay amount is encapsulated in the MYEmployee class, so the calculation is done one way and in one place no matter how many Views are created.

Before diving into the code for the MYEmployee class, consider the following partial list of features that come for free in the MVC version of Pay Calculator:

- There is automatic support for undo and redo of all changes made to employee information.
- There is automatic support for save and load of employee information.
- There is automatic support for editing of any number of employee objects.
- There is automatic recalculation of the pay amount; no Calculate button is needed.
- Information about different employees can be viewed and edited without the need to duplicate user interface components.

The PayCalculator class from the non-MVC design is no longer needed, and the new MYEmployee class doesn't require much more code than PayCalculator had. The first thing to notice is that the MYEmployee class doesn't need Outlets to access user interface objects. In fact, if MYEmployee had those Outlets, it wouldn't be a very good Model class because it would be coupled to a View:

```
@interface MYEmployee : NSManagedObject
{
}
```

```
- (NSNumber *)payAmount;

@end
```

Another thing to notice is that MYEmployee is a subclass of NSManagedObject. The NSManagedObject class is described in Chapter 30, "Core Data Models." It's essentially a Cocoa class intended to encapsulate persistent data and simplifies the creation of the Model layer for many applications. NSManagedObject uses the Associative Storage pattern in Chapter 19, "Associative Storage," to provide access to data that's stored in memory or in files on the disk or in relational databases. NSManagedObject exists to encapsulate the underlying storage mechanism so that developers don't need to know details about the storage.

The MYEmployee class is designed in the Core Data modeling tool included in Apple's Xcode application. Like Interface Builder, Xcode is a standard component of Apple's free developer tools. Figure 2.6 shows the design of the MYEmployee class.

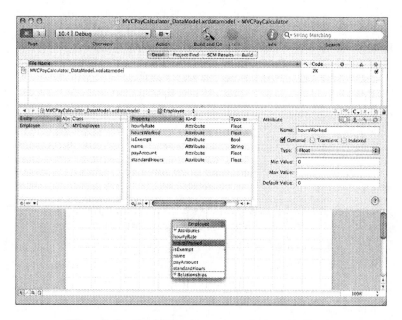

Figure 2.6   The MYEmployee class designed in Xcode

The MYEmployee design identifies all of the attributes needed for the Pay Calculator example: hourlyRate, hoursWorked, isExempt, name, payAmount, and standardHours. It doesn't really matter how the attributes are stored for each instance of the MYEmployee class; NSManagedObject makes the underlying storage irrelevant. All that's needed is to implement the application-specific logic in the MYEmployee class and the Model is complete:

```objc
#import "MYEmployee.h"

@implementation MYEmployee

+ (NSSet *)keyPathsForValuesAffectingPayAmount
{ // return names of attributes that affect payAmount
  return [NSSet setWithObjects:@"isExempt",
      @"hourlyRate", @"hoursWorked", @"standardHours", nil];
}


- (NSNumber *)payAmount
{  // return a calculated pay amount based on other attributes
  float   calculatedPayAmount;
  float   hourlyRate =
    [[self valueForKey:@"hourlyRate"] floatValue];
  float   standardNumberOfHours =
    [[self valueForKey:@"standardHours"] floatValue];

if([[self valueForKey:@"isExempt"] boolValue])
  { // Pay the hourly rate times the standard number of hours
    // regardless of the actual number of hours worked
    calculatedPayAmount = hourlyRate * standardNumberOfHours;
  }
  else
  { // Pay the hourly rate times the actual number of hours worked
    float   numberOfHoursWorked =
      [[self valueForKey:@"hoursWorked"] floatValue];

    calculatedPayAmount = hourlyRate * numberOfHoursWorked;

    if(numberOfHoursWorked > standardNumberOfHours)
    { // pay 50% extra for overtime
      float   overtimePayAmount = 0.5f * hourlyRate *
        (numberOfHoursWorked - standardNumberOfHours);

      calculatedPayAmount = calculatedPayAmount +
        overtimePayAmount;
    }
  }

  return [NSNumber numberWithFloat:calculatedPayAmount];
}

@end
```

The +(NSSet *)keyPathsForValuesAffectingPayAmount method of the
MYEmployee class tells Cocoa that the payAmount attribute depends on the other
MYEmployee attributes, so any time any of the other attributes changes, the payAmount attribute needs to be recalculated. The ability to access attributes and relationships by name
is inherited from the NSManagedObject class, and the attributes that are available are specified in Xcode. The ability to make some attributes depend on others is part of Cocoa's
Key Value Observing technology described in Chapter 32, "Bindings and Controllers."

The -payAmount method is very similar to the -calculatePayAmount: method in the
non-MVC version. The -payAmount method uses expressions like [self value-
ForKey:@"hourlyRate"] to access the values needed to calculate the amount of pay. The
MYEmployee class can calculate the pay amount without accessing any objects outside of
the Model.

The new version of the Pay Calculator application has a View and a Model, so now
the Controller subsystem needs to be addressed. For an application as simple as Pay Calculator, a single instance of Cocoa's NSArrayController class suffices. The
NSArrayController instance is created and configured within Interface Builder to provide access to any and all MYEmployee instances that exist within Pay Calculator when it
runs. No code is needed. The NSArrayController instance even takes care of sorting the
information presented to users into alphabetical order, as shown in Figure 2.5. The table
of employees can be sorted based on any of the columns in the table so that if the user
wants to see them in order of decreasing pay rate, that is also available.

The MVC version of the Pay Calculator application is available at www.CocoaDesign
Patterns.com. The only code in the MVC Pay Calculator that isn't shown here is some
unmodified boilerplate code supplied by the Xcode project template used to create the
project.

Analysis of the MVC Pay Calculator Design

The user interface objects in Figure 2.5 are connected in Interface Builder so that they
communicate exclusively with the NSArrayController instance, as shown in Figure 2.7.
The objects in the View subsystem have no direct knowledge about the Model or its underlying storage and logic. The View objects are configured in Interface Builder to stay
synchronized with either the arrangedObjects or selectedObject properties of the array controller. If the implementation of the View ever changes, only the
NSArrayController instance needs to be reconfigured; the Model is unaffected.

The Model implementation is almost entirely supplied by Cocoa's Core Data components. The example uses Xcode to design a MYEmployee object and store the design in a
configuration file that's automatically loaded by Core Data when Pay Calculator starts.
Core Data and NSArrayController work well together. The array controller can access
any number of MYEmployee instances because it's configured in Interface Builder to ask
Core Data to supply them. The array controller responds to -add:, -remove:, and
-fetch: Action messages by asking Core Data to add, remove, or fetch instances of
MYEmployee.

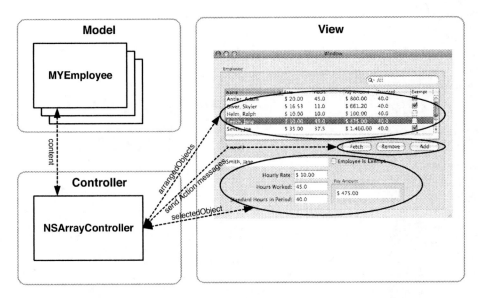

Figure 2.7   Relationships between objects with MVC design

Summary

Cocoa itself is designed using the Model View Controller pattern, and you're encouraged to use MVC in your own applications as well. Apple's developer tools work best when applied to MVC designs. In some cases it's hard to use the tools any other way. Understanding the rationale behind the separation of subsystems in MVC helps you understand how to best use Cocoa. Even the smallest Cocoa applications like the Pay Calculator example acquire sophisticated features by conforming to the design implicit within Cocoa.

II

Fundamental
Patterns

The patterns in this part are fundamental to the architecture
of the Cocoa frameworks. In one sense, you can't use Cocoa
without using these patterns, but in another sense, these patterns are so low-level and ubiquitous that they can quickly
fade from a programmer's consciousness.

Chapters in this part of the book include

$$3$$

Two-Stage Creation

Cocoa relies on conventions established by the NSObject base class to allocate and initialize new instances of Cocoa classes. The reliance on conventions for something as central to an object-oriented language as instance creation may seem problematic at first, but it works well in practice. Several interrelated patterns are used to assure correct allocation and initialization of instances.

Many languages, such as Java, C++, Ruby, and Smalltalk use a method named "new" to allocate and initialize new instances. Even though NSObject implements a +new method, Cocoa developers seldom, if ever, use it. The Two-Stage Creation pattern separates the first stage, object memory allocation, from the second stage, object initialization. The Two-Stage Creation pattern must be followed to effectively use Cocoa.

Motivation

Two-Stage Creation gives programmers control over how objects are allocated in memory and simultaneously provides flexibility when initializing instances. Two-Stage Creation simplifies instance initialization when creating subclasses of Cocoa classes and provides methods for the convenient creation and initialization of temporary objects.

This chapter describes Cocoa's Two-Stage Creation and explains how it achieves the following goals:

- Enable the use of initializers regardless of the way memory is allocated
- Avoid the need to implement too many initializers when subclassing
- Simplify the creation and use of temporary instances

A little history helps to emphasize the reasons why Cocoa uses Two-Stage Creation. Very old versions of the Objective-C class libraries that evolved into Cocoa used class methods to handle both allocation and initialization.

Note

Class methods operate on class objects rather than instances of the class. Objective-C classes are themselves objects that conceptually inherit all of the methods of the base class. Objective-C class methods are superficially similar to static member functions in the

C++ language and static methods in Java. Unlike C++ static member functions, Objective-C class methods have access to the `self` argument that refers to the class object itself. Class methods are fully polymorphic (http://developer.apple.com/documentation/Cocoa/Conceptual/CocoaFundamentals/).

If allocation and initialization are combined in one method, that method has to be a class method because until allocation is complete, there is no instance. The pattern for implementing a single class method to both allocate and initialize an instance looks like the following:

```
+ (id)circleWithCenter:(NSPoint)aPoint radius:(float)radius
{
  // allocation and partial initialization are provided by superclass
  id   newInstance = [[super new] autorelease];

  if(nil != newInstance) // verify new instance was created
  {
  [newInstance setCenter:aPoint];
  [newInstance setRadius:radius];
  [newInstance setLabel:@"default"];
  }

  return newInstance;
}
```

Initializing instances within class methods has many drawbacks. Combined allocation and initialization results in a combinatorial explosion of methods that must be implemented to handle all of the different ways objects might be allocated and initialized. Consider a hypothetical MYImage object that can be initialized with the contents of a file, information downloaded using a network Uniform Resource Locator (URL), arbitrary binary data, the user's current copy/paste buffer, or empty with a specified size. Now consider that storage for images might be allocated from just two different types of memory, regular memory or graphics card memory. The MYImage class could easily end up with all of the following methods:

```
+imageFromRegularMemoryWithContentsOfFile:
+imageFromRegularMemoryWithContentsOfURL:
+imageFromRegularMemoryWithData:
+imageFromRegularMemoryWithPasteboard:
+imageFromRegularMemoryWithSize:
+imageFromGraphicsMemory:(MYCardID)aCard withContentsOfFile:
+imageFromGraphicsMemory:(MYCardID)aCard withContentsOfURL:
+imageFromGraphicsMemory:(MYCardID)aCard withData:
+imageFromGraphicsMemory:(MYCardID)aCard withPasteboard:
+imageFromGraphicsMemory:(MYCardID)aCard withSize:
```

Now imagine that it is also possible to store images in special memory shared between processes or in memory that is mapped into the computer's virtual address space but not actually allocated until needed. There may be additional ways image data is obtained such as by copying an existing image or by screen capture. By the time methods for all of the combinations are created, there are tens if not hundreds of different methods.

The problem of too many methods that create initialized instances really raises its ugly head when you try to create a subclass. It may be necessary for the subclass to reimplement every one of the superclass's instance creation methods and provide new variants for whatever additional parameters are used to create instances of the new class.

Solution

Cocoa's `NSObject` base class provides two methods that allocate memory for new instances, `+(id)alloc` and `+(id)allocWithZone:(NSZone *)aZone`. These methods are inherited by other Cocoa classes and are seldom overridden. The `+alloc` method is implemented to call the `+allocWithZone:` method specifying a default zone argument. Zones are briefly explained in the next section of this chapter. The `+alloc` and `+allocWithZone:` methods each return a pointer to a newly allocated block of memory large enough to store an instance of the class that executed the method. The allocated memory contains zeros except for the one instance variable, `isa`, that all Objective-C objects are required to have. The `isa` variable is automatically initialized to point to the class object that allocated the memory and is the tie-in to the Objective-C language runtime that enables the instance to receive messages such as `-init` that are used to complete initialization.

Zones

Memory zones are a feature of Cocoa intended to improve application performance by keeping the memory for objects that are used together close together in the computer's address space. To explain how the location of objects in memory affects performance, it's necessary to explain what happens when an application needs more memory than the amount of physical memory available.

Each Cocoa application has a very large amount of addressable memory. When an application dynamically allocates memory, the operating system provides memory even if all available physical memory in the computer is already being used. To accommodate the allocation request, the operating system copies the contents of some physical memory to the hard disk in an operation called paging or swapping. The physical memory that formerly contained the data written to disk is then made available to the application that needed more.

When memory that was copied to disk is needed again, the operating system copies a different area of physical memory to the disk and pages the old memory back into memory. The operating system is able to map the address space of each application to the physical memory even when memory is paged to the disk and back. This feature of the operating system is called *virtual memory*.

Using virtual memory affects performance because copying the contents of physical memory to and from the hard disk is time-consuming. Too much paging degrades system performance and is called *thrashing*. The location of memory allocated for object instances is important because if two or more objects that are used together are stored far apart in memory, the likelihood of thrashing increases.

Consider the following scenario: As the memory for one object is needed, it is paged into physical memory from the hard disk. That object then needs to access another object that is still not in physical memory, and even more memory needs be paged in. In the worst case, memory paged in for the second object forces memory for the first object to be paged out again. As the objects that reference each other interact, thrashing results.

Zones are used to make sure the memory allocated for objects that are used together is close together. When one of the objects is needed, the other is almost certainly also needed. Because the objects are in the same zone, the chances are good that all the needed objects are paged into memory at the same time, and when the objects are not needed, they are paged out together as well. Cocoa's NSZone type specifies a C structure that identifies a memory zone. The +allocWithZone: method accepts an NSZone argument and allocates memory from the specified zone. Cocoa provides functions such as NSDefaultMallocZone(), NSCreateZone(), and NSRecycleZone() for managing memory zones. These functions are documented at /Developer/Documentation/Cocoa/ Reference/Foundation/ObjC_classic/Functions/FoundationFunctions.html and online at http://developer.apple.com/.

> **Note**
>
> Zones are a very low level topic, and Apple currently discourages the explicit use of zones in your code. Zones are automatically used within the implementation of Cocoa. As the amount of physical memory in computers continues to increase and the sophistication of the operating system's memory allocation functions improves, the original motivation for using zones is gradually evaporating. With Objective-C 2.0 in Mac OS X 10.5, if your application uses Cocoa's optional automatic memory garbage collection, zones specified with +allocWithZone: are ignored by the frameworks.

Initializing Allocated Memory

Once memory for a new instance is allocated, the memory is initialized by calling an instance method. Such instance methods are called *initializers* and by convention, begin with the word init, and return an id. Some of the advantages of using the id type are described in Chapter 7, "Anonymous Type and Heterogeneous Containers." Allocation and initialization are almost always combined in one line of code with the following pattern: [[SomeClass alloc] init].

Classes can provide any number of initializers, and the different initializers can each accept different arguments. When multiple initializers are provided, one is usually the Designated Initializer. The Designated Initializer for the NSObject class is -(id)init, and the Designated Initializer for the NSView class is -(id)initWithFrame:(NSRect)aFrame. Any of the provided initializers can be the Designated Initializer, but it must be clearly documented. The Designated Initializer is usually the one that accepts the most arguments. All other initializers call the Designated Initializer in their implementations.

> **Note**
>
> When reading Apple's Cocoa documentation for classes, keep an eye out for references to the Designated Initializer for each class. Knowing which method is the Designated Initializer is essential when subclassing Cocoa classes. In a few rare cases such as the `NSCell` class, Cocoa classes have more than one documented Designated Initializer.

In addition to the Designated Initializer, most Cocoa classes provide an `-(id)initWithCoder:(NSCoder *)aCoder` method. The significance of `-initWithCoder:` is explained in Chapter 11, "Archiving and Unarchiving."

Implementing the Designated Initializer

The Designated Initializer for each class must call the Designated Initializer of its superclass. The following simple `MYCircle` class is a subclass of `NSObject`:

```
@interface MYCircle : NSObject
{
NSPoint      center;
float        radius;
}

// Designated Initializer
- (id)initWithCenter:(NSPoint)aPoint radius:(float)aRadius;

@end


@implementation MYCircle

// Designated Initializer
- (id)initWithCenter:(NSPoint)aPoint radius:(float)aRadius
{
self = [super init];

if(nil != self)
 {
 center = aPoint;
 radius = aRadius;
 }

return self;
}

@end
```

The `- (id)initWithCenter:(NSPoint)aPoint radius:(float)aRadius` method first assigns the implicit `self` local variable to the result of calling the superclass's Designated

Initializer. This step is crucial because initializers sometimes return a different object than the one that received the message. This can happen when it is not possible to initialize the receiver correctly for some reason or when a pre-existing instance is returned to avoid the need to initialize a new one.

> **Note**
>
> The `self` variable is present in all Objective-C methods. It is one of two hidden arguments passed to code that implements a method. The initial value of `self` is always the object that received the message that led to the method's execution. The other hidden argument is `_cmd`, which identifies the message received. The `self` and `_cmd` variables are described in Apple's document at /Developer/Documentation/Cocoa/ObjectiveC/ObjC.pdf.

After the `self` variable is set, an `if` statement is used so that instance variables are only initialized if `self` isn't `nil`. This is important because if `self` is `nil`, accessing the memory for the instance variables may be an error. This degree of defensive programming is usually unnecessary because few classes ever return `nil` from their initializers, but `nil` is a valid return value, so getting in the habit of checking for this case will prevent the occasional problem.

Finally, the `-initWithCenter:radius:` method returns `self`. This is the most common pattern for initializers.

Each class that introduces a new Designated Initializer must also override the inherited Designated Initializer to call the new one. Because the `MYCircle` class introduces `-initWithCenter:radius:`, it must also implement `-init` to call `-initWithCenter:radius:` as follows:

```
// Overriden inherited Designated Initializer
- (id)init
{
 static const float MYDefaultRadius = 1.0f;

 // call Designated Initializer with default arguments
 return [self initWithCenter:NSZeroPoint radius:MYDefaultRadius];
}
```

If you adhere to the following guidelines, calling any initializer implemented or inherited by a class will result in a correctly initialized instance:

- Make sure that the Designated Initializer calls its super class' implementation of the super class' Designated Initializer.
- Assign `self` to the object returned by the superclass' Designated Initializer.
- Do not access instance variables if `nil` is returned by the superclass' Designated Initializer.
- Make sure that the superclass' Designated Initializer is overridden to call the new Designated Initializer.

- When subclassing, make sure every new initializer that isn't the Designated Initializer calls the Designated Initializer.

These guidelines greatly simplify the task of creating subclasses. If the guidelines aren't followed and some initializers fail to call the Designated Initializer, the only way a subclass can be implemented to assure correct initialization of instances is to override every inherited initializer.

> **Note**
>
> When subclassing classes that can be archived, it is also necessary to override the inherited -initWithCoder: method to correctly initialize objects that are unarchived as described in Chapter 11.

Using Zones in Initializers

When using memory zones in your own code, it's important to allocate memory used by instance variables from the same zone as the object that owns the instance variables. Storing references to memory outside of an object's zone defeats the whole purpose of zones.

The zone used to allocate an object is determined by sending the -zone message to the object. The MYCircle class can be rewritten so that each instance stores an NSString label allocated from the same zone as the instance itself.

```
@interface MYCircle : NSObject
{
NSPoint     center;
float       radius;
NSString    *label;
}

// Designated Initializer
- (id)initWithCenter:(NSPoint)aPoint radius:(float)aRadius;

@end

@implementation MYCircle

// Designated Initializer
- (id)initWithCenter:(NSPoint)aPoint radius:(float)aRadius
{
 self = [super init];

 if(nil != self)
 {
  center = aPoint;
  radius = aRadius;
  label = [[NSString allocFromZone:[self zone]]
     initWithString:@"default"];
 }
```

```
    return self;
}

// Overriden inherited Designated Initializer
- (id)init
{
 // call Designated Initializer with default arguments
 return [self initWithCenter:NSZeroPoint radius:1.0f];
}

@end
```

Objects aren't the only things that can be allocated from zones. The `NSZoneMalloc()`, `NSZoneCalloc()`, and `NSZoneFree()` functions documented in /Developer/Documentation/ Cocoa/Reference/Foundation/ObjC_classic/Functions/FoundationFunctions.html are used to allocate and free blocks of arbitrary memory from specified zones. In Objective-C 2.0 introduced with Mac OS X 10.5, automatic garbage collection automatically frees memory that is allocated using `void *__strong NSAllocateCollectable(NSUInteger size, NSUInteger options)`. For backward compatibility, calling `NSAllocateCollectable()` with the `NSCollectorDisabledOption` option has the same behavior as calling `NSZoneMalloc()`.

Objects can also be copied and unarchived using specified zones. The `-(id)copyWithZone:(NSZone *)aZone` and `-(id)mutableCopyWithZone::(NSZone *)aZone` methods are explained in Chapter 12, "Copying." The `NSUnarchiver` class provides the `- (void)setObjectZone:(NSZone *)aZone` method used to specify the zone in which unarchived objects are allocated. Archiving and Unarchiving are explained in Chapter 11.

Whenever objects are allocated, they must eventually be deallocated. Cocoa's reference counted memory management system helps to ensure this is the case. It is described in Chapter 10, "Accessors," which explains how to manage the memory used by objects. More information about Cocoa's reference counted memory management is available at /Developer/Documentation/Cocoa/ObjectiveC/4objc_runtime_overview/ Object_Ownership.html.

In Mac OS X 10.5 and later, you can optionally use automatic garbage collection instead of reference counted memory management. However, because automatic garbage collection is optional in Cocoa, it's necessary to correctly implement reference counted memory management in any new classes you create for the foreseeable future unless you require that the users of your class also use automatic garbage collection.

Regardless of whether zones are used, when an object is deallocated, its `-(void)dealloc` method is called. Don't call `-dealloc` yourself. It's called automatically when appropriate. The `-dealloc` method for `MYCircle` is implemented as follows to make sure the `label` instance variable allocated in the Designated Initializer is correctly handled:

```
- (void)dealloc
{
 [label release];

 [super dealloc];
}
```

If automatic garbage collection is used, the - (void)finalize method is automatically called instead of the -dealloc method. The MYCircle example doesn't need to implement -finalize because the automatic garbage collector, if used, automatically collects the memory for the label string. MYCircle doesn't require any special action when its memory is collected. However, it would be necessary to implement the -finalize method if MYCircle had allocated any noncollectible memory via NSAllocateCollectable() with the NSCollectorDisabledOption or needed to perform other end-of-life operations like closing open files.

Creating Temporary Instances

Many Cocoa classes provide methods that combine the two stages of allocating and initializing to return temporary instances. Such methods are called convenience methods. Convenience methods include the name of the class in the method's name. For example, the NSString class provides the +(id)stringWithString:(NSString *)aString convenience method that's similar to the -(id)initWithString:(NSString *)aString initializer method used by the MYCircle class. When not using automatic garbage collection, the primary difference between calling [[NSString alloc] initWithString:@"some string"] and [NSString stringWithString:@"some string"] is that +stringWithString: returns an instance that will be automatically deallocated unless you send it a -retain message to prevent deallocation. When using automatic garbage collection, there is no significant difference between the two techniques for obtaining a new instance.

Methods like +stringWithString: are usually implemented as follows:

```
+ (id)stringWithString:(NSString *)aString
{
 return [[[self alloc] initWithString:aString] autorelease];
}
```

The implications of the -retain message and the -autorelease message are explained in Chapter 10.

The convenience methods for obtaining instances are almost always paired with similarly named initializers. Besides just reducing the amount of code programmers must write to create and initialize instances, the convenience methods also enable certain optimizations and are used with other patterns. In particular, convenience methods are used in the implementation of the Singleton and Class Clusters patterns in Chapter 13, "Singleton," and Chapter 25, "Class Clusters," respectively. Sometimes convenience methods return Flyweight objects, which are described in Chapter 22, "Flyweight." One drawback to using the convenience methods is that you give up flexibility in the way instances are allocated because the allocation technique is hard-coded in the method.

Examples in Cocoa

The Two-Stage Creation pattern is used extensively by Cocoa, and you must adhere to it if you subclass any Cocoa classes. You must be aware of which initializer is the Designated Initializer to create a properly working subclass. Table 3.1 lists several prominent Cocoa classes that are frequently subclassed and identifies the Designated Initializers.

Table 3.1   Prominent Cocoa Classes and Their Designated Initializers

Class	Designated Initializer
NSObject	-init
NSView	-initWithFrame:
NSCell	-initImageCell: and -initTextCell:
NSControl	-initWithFrame:
NSDocument	-init
NSWindowController	-initWithWindow:

The NSCell class actually has two Designated Initializers and both must be overridden in subclasses, but the subclass is free to call either of the superclass' Designated Initializers. As an example of an NSCell subclass, consider a class named MYLabeledBarCell.

MYLabeledBarCell instances each draw a label and a small bar that indicates values between 0.0 and 1.0. These cells can be used to indicate the percentage of battery charge remaining or the speed of mouse acceleration in a preference panel. The bar provides a quick indication of a value, and the label identifies the value. The bar's value is set with the MYLabeledBarCell's - (void)setBarValue:(float)aValue method, and the label is set with the - (void)setLabel:(NSString *)aLabel method or the - (void)setStringValue:(NSString *)aString method inherited from the NSCell class. Figure 3.1 shows several instances of MYLabeledBarCell, a subclass of NSCell.

Figure 3.1   The window shows a matrix of
MYLabelBarCell instances within a scroll view.

The following implementation of MYLabeledBarCell calls the inherited
- (id)initTextCell:(NSString *)aString from the implementations of both
- (id)initImageCell:(NSImage *)anImage and -initTextCell:.

```
#import <Cocoa/Cocoa.h>


@interface MYLabeledBarCell : NSCell
{
 float   barValue;  // values in range 0.0 to 1.0
}

// Overriden Designated Initializers
- (id)initImageCell:(NSImage *)anImage;
- (id)initTextCell:(NSString *)aString;

// Overriden configuration
- (BOOL)isOpaque;

// Accessors
- (void)setLabel:(NSString *)aLabel;
- (NSString *)label;
```

```objc
- (void)setBarValue:(float)aValue;
- (float)barValue;

// New drawing methods
- (void)drawBarInRect:(NSRect)aRect;

@end

#import "MYLabeledBarCell.h"


@implementation MYLabeledBarCell
// Instances of this class store both a text label and a float value,
// barValue. The label is drawn as an attributed string. A green bar is
// drawn along the bottom of the cell based on the value of barValue
// interpreted as a fraction of full length. If barValue is >= 1.0, the
// bar is drawn full length. If barValue is <= 0, no bar is drawn.

- (id)initImageCell:(NSImage *)anImage
// Overriden Designated Initializer calls -initTextCell:
{
  return [self initTextCell:@""];
}



- (id)initTextCell:(NSString *)aString
// Overriden Designated Initializer
{
  self = [super initTextCell:aString];

  if(nil != self)
  {
    [self setBarValue: 1.0f];
    [self setFont:[NSFont labelFontOfSize:[NSFont labelFontSize]]];
  }
  return self;
}



- (BOOL)isOpaque
// Returns NO so that background will show through
{
  return NO;
}


// Constants used to control drawing
static const float BarHeightWithMargins = 4.0f;
static const float BarMarginFraction = 0.25f;
```

```
- (void)drawBarInRect:(NSRect)aRect
// Draw a green bar that fills a portion of aRect specified by barValue
{
  aRect.size.width *= barValue;
  [[NSColor greenColor] set];
  NSRectFill(aRect);
}


- (NSSize)cellSizeForBounds:(NSRect)aRect
// Overridden to return a size large enough for the label and the bar
{
  NSSize   cellSize = [super cellSizeForBounds:aRect];

  // return rectangle large enough for both subcell and text
  return NSMakeSize(cellSize.width, cellSize.height +
    BarHeightWithMargins);
}


- (void)drawInteriorWithFrame:(NSRect)cellFrame
  inView:(NSView *)controlView
// Overridden to draw the label and the bar
{
  NSRect    barRect;
  NSRect    labelRect;

  // calculate the rectangles containing the bar and label
  NSDivideRect(cellFrame, &barRect, &labelRect, BarHeightWithMargins,
    NSMaxYEdge);

  // draw the label with margins around it
  [super drawInteriorWithFrame:labelRect inView:controlView];
  // draw the bar with margins around it
  barRect = NSInsetRect(barRect, 0.0, BarHeightWithMargins *
    BarMarginFraction);
  [self drawBarInRect:barRect];
}


- (void)setLabel:(NSString *)aLabel
{
  // store the label as the receiver's string value
  [self setStringValue:aLabel];
}

- (NSString *)label
{
```

```
  return [self stringValue];
}

- (void)setBarValue:(float)aValue
{
  // store the bar value in instance variable
  barValue = MIN(MAX(aValue, 0.0), 1.0);
}

- (float)barValue
{
  return barValue;
}

@end
```

> **Note**
> Chapter 21, "Prototype," includes an example showing one way to populate a regular grid
> called a matrix with custom cells.

The Two-Stage Creation pattern plays an imports role in Cocoa's Flyweight pattern described in Chapter 22 and the Singleton pattern in Chapter 13, the Archiving and Unarchiving pattern in Chapter 11, and the Class Clusters pattern in Chapter 25. The Accessors pattern simplifies the implementation of initializers as described in Chapter 10.

Consequences

Separating the allocation and initialization stages of instance creation provides many benefits. It's possible to use any variation of the `+alloc` class method to allocate an instance and then use any available initializer with the new instance. This makes it possible to create your own initialization methods without needing to provide alternate implementations of all allocation methods.

New allocation methods are seldom created because the existing methods meet almost every need. However, one or more new initializers are created for almost every class. Due to the separation of allocation and initialization stages, initializer implementations only have to deal with the variables of new instances and can completely ignore the issues surrounding allocation. The separation simplifies the process of writing initializers. Furthermore, Cocoa standard initializers like `-initWithCoder:` work with instances regardless of the way memory for the instance was allocated.

One negative consequence of the separation of allocation and initialization is the need to be aware of conventions such as the designated initializer. You must know which methods are designated initializers and how to create and document new initializers in subclasses. In the long run, using designated initializers simplifies software development, but there is an argument to be made that the Two-Stage Creation pattern adds to the early learning curve for Cocoa developers.

4

Template Method

In many cases, an algorithm or process consists of several steps that are needed by many applications and one or more steps that may be unique to each application. The Template Method pattern implements the common steps within a reusable class while still enabling application-specific customization.

The Template Method pattern is also called the "Hollywood Pattern" because of the Hollywood cliché, "Don't call us; we'll call you." The Template Method pattern identifies one or more methods that will be called automatically as needed by existing code but should not be called directly by application code.

A Template Method is nothing more than a special case of a method that is expected to be overridden in subclasses. The -dealloc method described in Chapter 3, "Two-Stage Creation" is a Template Method. When automatic garbage collection is not used, the -dealloc method must be overridden in each subclass of NSObject that needs to explicitly de-allocate previously allocated resources. The -dealloc method should almost never be called directly from code you write except to invoke the superclass' behavior from within an overridden implementation. Cocoa automatically calls -dealloc when needed. Another prominent Template Method is the -drawRect: method provided by the NSView class. Like -dealloc, -drawRect: should almost never be called directly except to invoke the superclass implementation and is instead called automatically by Cocoa.

Motivation

Use the Template Method pattern to implement common algorithms or processes in a highly reusable way while still enabling customization of some process steps. Application programmers override Template Methods to customize an algorithm or process while benefiting from substantial reuse of code.

Solution

The following small example illustrates the Template Method pattern in action. Consider a drawing application that allows users to draw geometric shapes and then later select the shapes by clicking them with a mouse. In this example, the shapes are represented by the MYShape class as follows:

```
@interface MYShape : NSObject
{
    NSRect          frame; // rectangle that encloses the shape
}


// This is a Template Method to customize selection logic.  The default
// implementation returns YES if aPoint is within frame.  Override this
// method to be more selective.  The default implementation can be
// called from overridden versions.
- (BOOL)doesContainPoint:(NSPoint)aPoint;


@end
```

The `frame` variable stores a rectangle that completely encloses the shape. The intent of the –doesContainPoint: method is to return YES if the receiving shape contains the specified point and NO if it doesn't. The basic algorithm for selection is that whenever the user clicks the mouse to select a shape, the program searches through a collection of MYShape instances to find one that contains the mouse location. The first shape found that contains the mouse location is selected. In other words, the drawing application automatically calls –doesContainPoint: in response to mouse events.

Now consider a subclass of MYShape that draws circles:

```
@interface MYCircleShape : MYShape
{
}


// This method returns YES if aPoint is within a circle inscribed
// within the receiver's bounds and NO otherwise.
- (BOOL)doesContainPoint:(NSPoint)aPoint;


@end
```

Assuming the circle represented by MYCircleShape is inscribed within the frame rectangle inherited from the MYShape class, the circles radius is one-half the width of the frame or one-half the height of the frame, whichever is smaller. The circle's center is the center of the frame. MYCircleShape implements –doesContainPoint: as follows:

```
@implementation MYCircleShape


- (BOOL)doesContainPoint:(NSPoint)aPoint
{
    BOOL      result = [super doesContainPoint:aPoint];

    if(result)
    {
        NSPoint      center = NSMakePoint(NSMidX(frame), NSMidY(frame));
        float        radius = MIN(NSWidth(frame) / 2.0f,
                        NSHeight(frame) / 2.0f);
        float        radiusSquared = radius * radius;
        float        deltaX = aPoint.x - center.x;
        float        deltaY = aPoint.y - center.y;
        float        distanceSquared = (deltaX  * deltaX ) + (deltaY *
                        deltaY);

        result = (distanceSquared <= radiusSquared);
    }

    return result;
}

@end
```

First, the superclass' implementation of -doesContainPoint: is called because if aPoint isn't within the frame, then it also isn't within a circle inscribed in the frame, so there is no reason for further calculation. Next, there's a check to see if the distance squared from aPoint to the center of the circle is less than or equal to the radius squared of the circle. Using the radius squared and the distance squared is just a common trick to avoid having to use a sqrt() function. Algebraically, if one value is less than another, then its square is also less than the other value squared.

If the program contains a mixed collection of shapes, some of which are MYShape instances and some of which are MYCircleShape instances, when the program asks each shape if it contains the selection point, the different shapes will respond differently. MYShape instances will return YES if the selection point is anywhere in the frame. MYCircleShape instances will only return YES if the selection point is within a circle inscribed in the frame. The essential algorithm for selection has remained the same, and yet it has been customized for a particular subclass by overriding the -doesContainPoint: Template Method.

Default Template Methods

Any class that provides Template Methods should provide reasonable default implementations for the methods. Default implementations fall into three general categories that correspond to whether the default implementation can, should, or must be called by overridden versions.

When You *Can* Call the Default Implementation

In many cases, a default implementation does nothing. In such cases, it's safe for the override to call the default implementation, but it certainly doesn't need to call it. The NSView -drawRect: method is such an example: It can be called, but it doesn't do anything.

When You *Should* Call the Default Implementation

NSView provides another Template Method called -hitTest: that functions much like the -doesContainPoint: example. -hitTest: returns the most appropriate object (if any) to receive a mouse event at a specified point. When overriding -hitTest:, the default implementation should almost always be called because the selection of the most appropriate object is based on complex but standard logic that you most likely don't want to reimplement. You might however want to simulate a round NSView subclass or provide other unique application behavior. Override -hitTest: and perform additional tests when it has already been determined that your object is an appropriate receiver for the mouse event.

When You *Must* Call the Default Implementation

The -dealloc Template Method must be called by any overriding method. If the overridden version isn't called from the subclass' version, your program will most likely contain memory leaks, which has serious consequences.

Designing with Template Methods

To use the Template Method pattern in your own reusable classes, follow this design process:

1. Identify the steps of an algorithm and one or more methods to implement each step.

2. Implement the algorithm as a sequence of calls to the identified methods.

3. Factor out the customizable steps of the algorithm into Template Methods and provide a reasonable default implementation for each Template Method.

4. Document whether the base class' implementation of each Template Method can, should, or must be called by subclasses that override them.

Don't neglect any of the steps in the design process, or you will almost certainly experience some or all of the negative consequences described in the Consequences section of this chapter.

Examples in Cocoa

The Template Method pattern is so fundamental to object-oriented programming in general and Cocoa in particular that it isn't practical to identify every occurrence in Cocoa. The `NSView` `-drawRect:` method cited in this chapter is one of the most prominent Cocoa Template Methods, so it's worthwhile to examine in a little more detail the uses of `-drawRect:` and the algorithm that it customizes.

Using the `-drawRect:` Template Method

Any Cocoa application that provides a graphical user interface needs to draw within the application's windows. Cocoa windows contain instances of the `NSView` class for that purpose. Each `NSView` draws in a particular area of the window. The relationship between views and windows is described in more detail in Chapter 16, "Hierarchies," and in Chapter 18, "Responder Chain."

Several distinct steps are needed to draw. First, the framework determines that a portion of a window needs to be redrawn and sends a message to the window. The window sends a `-display` message to each view that is responsible for drawing in the affected portion of the window. `NSView`'s `-display` method configures the graphical coordinate system, implements graphical "clipping" to constrain drawing to the area where view is allowed to draw, calls the `-drawRect:` method to actually draw, and then sends `-display` to any subviews nested within the view. The key to this algorithm is that every step is identical for every view except for the step that actually draws. Within the drawing process, the difference between a view that draws bar charts and a view that draws text is the implementation of the `-drawRect:` method provided by each view.

Cocoa programmers implement application-specific drawing by subclassing `NSView` and overriding the `-drawRect:` Template Method. Cocoa then automatically calls the `-drawRect:` method whenever appropriate. Programmers rarely call `-drawRect:` directly because if they did, they would be skipping all of the other essential drawing-related process steps implemented by Cocoa. Instead of invoking `-drawRect:` directly, Cocoa programmers typically send the `-setNeedsDisplay:` message instead. This will trigger Cocoa to redraw the view at some future time, which will include an invocation of the `-drawRect:` method.

Other Cocoa Template Methods

The one Template Method that almost every Cocoa programmer encounters is `NSObject`'s `-dealloc` method. As of Mac OS X 10.5, the `- (void)finalize` method may also be overridden to support automatic garbage collection. Other Template Methods provided by `NSObject` are identified in Table 4.1. These methods are rarely overridden but essential when they are needed.

Table 4.1   **NSObject Template Methods**

Method	Process Customized
- (id)awakeAfterUsingCoder:(NSCoder *)aDecoder	Chapter 11
- (Class)classForArchiver	Chapter 11
- (Class)classForCoder	Chapter 11
- (Class)classForKeyedArchiver	Chapter 11
- (Class)classForPortCoder	Chapter 11
- (id)replacementObjectForArchiver:(NSArchiver *)anArchiver	Chapter 11
+ (NSArray *)classFallbacksForKeyedArchiver	Chapter 11
- (id)copyWithZone:(NSZone *)zone	Chapter 12
- (id)mutableCopyWithZone:(NSZone *)zone	Chapter 12
- (void)forwardInvocation:(NSInvocation *)anInvocation	Chapter 27
- (NSMethodSignature *)methodSignatureForSelector:(SEL)aSelector	Chapter 27

The optional NSCoding protocol defines the - (void)encodeWithCoder:(NSCoder *)encoder and - (id)initWithCoder:(NSCoder *)decoder Template Methods described in Chapter 11, "Archiving and Unarchiving." If a class you are writing inherits from a class that conforms to the NSCoding protocol, you almost certainly need to override these two methods.

The NSView class provides a large number of Template Methods identified in Table 4.2. Like all Template Methods, these are occasionally overridden but almost never directly called. Cocoa calls these methods as steps in built-in processes like drawing, printing, and event handling.

NSResponder, the superclass of NSView, provides the basic support for handling most user input events in Cocoa applications. It includes Template Methods that you override to control event handling and respond to user input events. Template Methods also customize management of the Responder Chain described in Chapter 18. Table 4.3 lists the most important NSResponder Template Methods.

Table 4.2   NSView Template Methods

Method	Process Customized
+ (NSMenu *)defaultMenu	Event Handling
- (BOOL)acceptsFirstMouse:(NSEvent *)theEvent	Event Handling
- (NSMenu *)menuForEvent:(NSEvent *)theEvent	Event Handling
- (BOOL)needsPanelToBecomeKey	Event Handling
- (NSView *)hitTest:(NSPoint)aPoint	Event Handling
- (BOOL)performKeyEquivalent:(NSEvent *)theEvent	Event Handling
- (void)drawRect:(NSRect)aRect	Drawing
- (BOOL)isOpaque	Drawing
- (BOOL)isFlipped	Drawing
- (BOOL)wantsDefaultClipping	Drawing
- (BOOL)preservesContentDuringLiveResize	Drawing
- (void)adjustPageHeightNew:(CGFloat *)newBottom top:(CGFloat)top bottom:(CGFloat)proposedBottom limit:(CGFloat)bottomLimit	Printing / Pagination
- (void)adjustPageWidthNew:(CGFloat *)newRight left:(CGFloat)left right:(CGFloat)proposedRight limit:(CGFloat)rightLimit	Printing / Pagination
- (BOOL)knowsPageRange:(NSRangePointer)aRange	Printing / Pagination
- (void)beginDocument	Printing / Pagination
- (void)endDocument	Printing / Pagination
- (void)beginPageInRect:(NSRect)aRect atPlacement:(NSPoint)location	Printing / Pagination
- (NSAttributedString *)pageHeader	Printing / Pagination
- (NSAttributedString *)pageFooter	Printing / Pagination

Table 4.2 **NSView Template Methods**

Method	Process Customized
- (void) drawPageBorderWithSize: (NSSize) borderSize	Printing / Pagination
- (void) drawSheetBorderWithSize: (NSSize) borderSize	Printing / Pagination
- (NSRect) adjustScroll: (NSRect) proposedVisibleRect	Scrolling
- (void) didAddSubview: (NSView *) subview	Chapter 16
- (void) resetCursorRects	Mouse Pointer Interaction
- (BOOL) mouseDownCanMoveWindow	Mouse Pointer Interaction

Table 4.3 **NSResponder Template Methods**

Method	Process Customized
- (BOOL) acceptsFirstResponder	Responder Chain Management
- (BOOL) resignFirstResponder	Responder Chain Management
- (void) mouseDown: (NSEvent *) theEvent	Event Handling
- (void) mouseDragged: (NSEvent *) theEvent	Event Handling
- (void) mouseUp: (NSEvent *) theEvent	Event Handling
- (void) mouseMoved: (NSEvent *) theEvent	Event Handling
- (void) mouseEntered: (NSEvent *) theEvent	Event Handling
- (void) mouseExited: (NSEvent *) theEvent	Event Handling
- (void) rightMouseDown: (NSEvent *) theEvent	Event Handling
- (void) rightMouseDragged: (NSEvent *) theEvent	Event Handling
- (void) rightMouseUp: (NSEvent *) theEvent	Event Handling
- (void) otherMouseDown: (NSEvent *) theEvent	Event Handling
- (void) otherMouseDragged: (NSEvent *) theEvent	Event Handling
- (void) otherMouseUp: (NSEvent *) theEvent	Event Handling
- (void) keyDown: (NSEvent *) theEvent	Event Handling
- (void) keyUp: (NSEvent *) theEvent	Event Handling

Table 4.3   **NSResponder Template Methods**

Method	Process Customized
- (void) flagsChanged: (NSEvent *) theEvent	Event Handling
- (void) scrollWheel: (NSEvent *) theEvent	Event Handling
- (id) validRequestorForSendType: (NSString *) sendType returnType: (NSString *) returnType	Services
- (NSUndoManager *) undoManager	Undo / Redo Customization

Many other Cocoa classes provide Template Methods. The `CALayer` class introduced with Mac OS X 10.5 is similar to the `NSView` class and provides almost as many Template Methods. `CALayers` augment `NSView` drawing and in some cases replace `NSView` for hardware accelerated OpenGL-based drawing.

The `NSTableView` class is an interesting example. Although it is an `NSView` subclass, custom subclasses do not typically override -`drawRect:`. Instead, `NSTableView` uses several template methods including -`drawRow:clipRect:`, -`drawBackgroundInClipRect:`, and -`drawGridInClipRect:` to allow specific portions of its rendering to be customized. Layout is also controlled with a Template Method. `NSTableView` and many other complex views such as `NSBrowser` and `NSScrollView` use the -`tile` method to position their subviews. It is interesting to note that the data displayed by an `NSTableView` is not provided by a subclass, nor are Template Methods used. Instead, a Data Source object provides the data. Chapter 15, "Delegates," describes Data Sources in detail.

Whenever you use Apple's Cocoa documentation, keep an eye out for Template Methods. Apple doesn't often use the term Template Method in class reference documentation, but method descriptions for Template Methods usually contain a phrase such as "...overridden in subclasses to..." or "...subclasses can override..." along with information regarding whether your override can, should, or must call the superclass' implementation. Often there is also a warning that you should not directly call the method in question.

Consequences

There are several potentially negative consequences to using the Template Method pattern. First and foremost, the pattern requires the creation of subclasses to override template methods. Subclassing produces the tightest possible coupling between the subclass and its superclass. As always, it's advisable to avoid coupling. If overriding a Template Method is the only reason a subclass is created, there are almost certainly better patterns to apply. In particular, the Delegate pattern described in Chapter 15 is probably more suitable. On the other hand, when there are reasons to create subclasses anyway, Template Methods can be ideal.

Second, it can be difficult to document the intended use of Template Methods. The methods need to be clearly identified so that programmers understand their intended use. Programmers need to know when and why each Template Method can or should be overridden. When overriding a template method, is the new version required to call the inherited version, permitted to call the inherited version, or forbidden to call the inherited version? The special documentation burden of the Template Method pattern must not be overlooked.

Finally, if you need to subclass to customize an algorithm, what happens when several unrelated customizations are required? The Delegate Pattern in Chapter 15 exists in part to avoid the creation of a combinatorial number of subclasses needed to mix and match the different customizations an application might need.

Because there are potentially negative consequences, the Template Method pattern is best reserved for use only in the most mature and stable designs in which the reasons for customization are very well understood. The -drawRect: method of Cocoa's NSView class is an effective Template Method because there is only one reason to override -drawRect:, to perform custom drawing. The -drawRect: method implements one step in a complex drawing algorithm, and overriding it for any other use is almost certainly an error. In a round-about way, Cocoa's implementation of custom drawing via the Template Method pattern communicates the implicit assumption that you must limit what you do in -drawRect: to drawing. Reading between the lines and understanding the consequences of design patterns can reveal seldom-documented aspects of the framework designers' probable intentions.

If you find yourself contemplating the creation of Template Methods in code intended for reuse, first consider Delegates. In many cases, Delegates provide a more flexible alternative to Template Methods.

5

Dynamic Creation

Cocoa utilizes many features of the underlying Objective-C runtime. One powerful feature is the ability to create instances of classes that did not exist at the time an application was compiled and dynamically load and link new classes at runtime. Scripting languages such as AppleScript, Tcl, Ruby, Perl, and Python use this technique to provide interfaces to Cocoa. The core of this pattern is the NSClassFromString() function that returns the class object with a specified name. NSBundle augments this by implementing the method –classNamed:, which can dynamically load code for the class if necessary. Once the named class object is obtained, instances can be created.

Dynamic creation enables scripting language bridges, plug-ins, Interface Builder plug-ins, unarchiving, nib loading, and overriding which classes the Cocoa frameworks will utilize when constructing composite objects or instantiating singletons.

Motivation

Decouple classes from each other and postpone decisions about which class to use until runtime. Provide a simple mechanism for overriding which classes are used for particular tasks within frameworks. Simplify the creation of plug-in architectures.

Solution

The basis of this pattern is a single function, NSClassFromString(). It takes a single argument, an NSString containing the name of a class. An Objective-C class object is returned. Once a class object has been obtained, it can be instantiated or otherwise manipulated. Although this may seem simple, it opens up many powerful options, especially for framework designers. One very important aspect of this power is the fact that this function allows a developer to use an object that was unknown to the compiler and linker when the application was built.

This single function effectively reduces the well-known Factory Method pattern to a single line of code in many cases. The Factory Method pattern typically requires an abstract method to be overridden to return a subclass of the desired type. By instead using NSClassFromString(), the desired subclass type can even be named by a string value in an application's property list, to be resolved into a concrete class object at runtime. Chapter 13, "Singleton," contains sample code that does this, along with a more complete explanation of this technique.

Using Dynamic Creation

As an example of a program that can benefit from Dynamic Creation, consider a basic command line reverse Polish notation (RPN) calculator. Its primary input is a series of numbers punctuated with commands to execute. Each number should be placed onto a stack as it is encountered. Commands manipulate the stack. For example, an "add" command would pop two numbers off the stack, add them together, and then push the result onto the stack. Some commands would not alter the stack in any way. For example, the "print" command displays the value at the top of the stack but makes no modifications.

The Dynamic Creation pattern can be used when it comes time to parse the input and execute the commands. First, a naming convention for the classes that implement the commands must be decided. In this case, the name can be "MYSomethingCommand" in which "Something" is replaced by the command. For example, the command "add" is implemented by the class MYAddCommand. For each input string encountered, an attempt is made to look it up with NSClassFromString(). If an object is found, we have a command, and it is executed. If no object is found, and NSClassFromString() returns nil, then we assume that we have a value to be pushed onto the stack. That's all there is; the details are straightforward from here. Adding new commands to the calculator is as simple as writing a new class, compiling it, and linking it into our application. There is no need to register the new class with the interpreter or list it anywhere. Its mere presence is sufficient to add it to the parsed language.

The first part of the implementation is a simple support class. MYStack is a basic stack that internally uses an NSMutableArray to implement its functionality. The end of the array is considered to be the top of the stack, so appending an object to the array pushes it onto the stack. To pop an object off the stack, it is removed from the end of the array. The method -peekAtIndex: is used to view the stack's contents without actually altering the stack. The interface and implementation are as follows:

```
#import <Cocoa/Cocoa.h>


@interface MYStack : NSObject
{
  NSMutableArray *storage;
}

- (void)push:(id)anObject;
- (id)pop;
- (NSInteger)count;
- (id)peekAtIndex:(NSInteger)index;

@end
```

```objc
#import "MYStack.h"


@implementation MYStack

- (id)init
{
  self = [super init];
  if (self)
  {
    storage = [[NSMutableArray alloc] init];
  }
  return self;
}

- (void)dealloc
{
  [storage release];
  [super dealloc];
}

- (void)push:(id)anObject
{
  if (anObject) [storage addObject:anObject];
}

- (id)pop
{
  id value = nil;
  if ([storage count] > 0)
  {
    value = [storage lastObject];
    [value retain];
    [storage removeObjectAtIndex:([storage count] - 1)];
    [value autorelease];
  }
  return value;
}

- (NSInteger)count
{
  return [storage count];
}

- (id)peekAtIndex:(NSInteger)index
{
```

```
  id value = nil;
  if (index < [self count])
  {
    value = [storage objectAtIndex:([storage count] - 1) - index];
  }
  return value;
}
```

@end

A base class is needed for the various commands. For that, the MYCommand class will be used. To simplify this example, the command objects won't actually be instantiated. Instead, the interpreter will simply call a class method, +executeWithStack:, to perform the command. This method could have been an instance method instead, in which case the command object would have to be instantiated before it could be used. In our example, there is no persistent data or state that needs to be tracked by the MYCommand subclasses, making instantiation an extra, unnecessary step. In a real application, it would be better to use instance methods and instantiate the command objects. There might be some commands that need to store specific state, and that would be best accomplished with an actual instance. The interface for MYCommand defines the +executeWithStack: method and the possible return values for success or failure.

```
#import <Cocoa/Cocoa.h>

@class MYStack;

typedef enum {
     MYSuccess = 0,
     MYError = 1,
     MYHaltExecution = 2
} MYCommandReturn;

@interface MYCommand : NSObject
{
}

+ (MYCommandReturn)executeWithStack:(MYStack *)stack;

@end
```

The implementation of the +executeWithStack: method gives an error message. Because subclasses are supposed to override this method with their own implementations, this code will never be called if the subclasses are written correctly.

```
#import "MYCommand.h"
#import "MYStack.h"
```

```
@implementation MYCommand

+ (MYCommandReturn)executeWithStack:(MYStack *)stack;
{
  NSLog(@"%@: not implemented yet.\n", [self className]);
  return MYError;
}

@end
```

With these two classes in place, it is possible to write an implementation of `main()` for the interpreter. The implementation is not complex. There is some setup code followed by two nested loops. The outer loop reads a line from `stdin` and breaks the input up into an array of strings, separated by whitespace. The inner loop considers each of the strings in the array and either executes it as a command (if the right class exists) or pushes it onto the stack. As a bonus, an `NSDictionary` is used to give alternate names to some of the commands. For example "+" will map to "add," and "*" will map to "multiply." Here is the code:

```
#import <Foundation/Foundation.h>
#import <stdio.h>
#import "MYStack.h"
#import "MYCommand.h"

static NSMutableDictionary *operators = nil;

#define MYMAXSTRING 8192

int main (int argc, const char *argv[])
{
  NSAutoreleasePool *pool = [[NSAutoreleasePool alloc] init];
  MYStack *stack = [[MYStack alloc] init];
  BOOL parsing = YES;
  char cString[MYMAXSTRING];

  // create a substitution dictionary:  every time a key is found,
  // it will be treated as if the user typed the associated
  // object instead
  operators = [[NSMutableDictionary alloc] init];
  [operators setObject:@"add" forKey:@"+"];
  [operators setObject:@"subtract" forKey:@"-"];
  [operators setObject:@"multiply" forKey:@"*"];
  [operators setObject:@"divide" forKey:@"/"];

  // our parsing loop, we parse one line at a time from stdin
  while (parsing)
```

```
{
  NSString *subString;
  // read a line from stdin and break it into
  // substrings separated by whitespace
  fgets(cString, MYMAXSTRING, stdin);
  NSString *inputLine = [NSString stringWithCString:cString];
  NSArray *splitLine = [inputLine
    componentsSeparatedByCharactersInSet:
    [NSCharacterSet whitespaceAndNewlineCharacterSet]];

  // step through the substrings, dealing with them
  // one at a time
  for (subString in splitLine)
  {
    NSString *operator;
    NSString *commandName;
    Class commandClass;

    // if substring is empty, skip it
    if (NSOrderedSame == [subString compare:@""])
    {
      continue;
    }

    // if substring matches an operator, change it
    // into the associated command name
    for (operator in operators)
    {
      if (NSOrderedSame == [operator compare:subString])
      {
        subString = [operators objectForKey:operator];
        break;
      }
    }

    // look for a command to match the string
    commandName = [NSString stringWithFormat:@"MY%@Command",
      [subString capitalizedString]];
    commandClass = NSClassFromString(commandName);

    // if there's a command name
    if (commandClass)
    {
      // that matches, then perform the command
      MYCommandReturn result = [commandClass executeWithStack:stack];
      switch (result)
```

```
   { // handle the return codes appropriately
     case MYHaltExecution:
       parsing = NO;
       break;
     case MYError:
       NSLog(@"Error executing command \"%@\".", subString);
       break;
     case MYSuccess:
     default:
       break;
   }
 }
 else
 { // if there was no command to execute,
   // then push the string onto the stack
   [stack push:subString];
 }
   }
  }

  [stack release];
  [operators release];
  [pool drain];
  return 0;
}
```

As it stands, the interpreter is complete and will run. However, it won't respond to any commands given that none exist. Each command is very simple code. The code needs to define a subclass of MYCommand and implement the -executeWithStack: method. For example, to print out what is at the top of the stack, the "print" command would look like this:

```
#import "MYCommand.h"


@interface MYPrintCommand : MYCommand
{
}

@end

#import "MYPrintCommand.h"
#import "MYStack.h"


@implementation MYPrintCommand

+ (MYCommandReturn)executeWithStack:(MYStack *)stack
```

```
{
  if ([stack count] < 1) return MYError;
  fprintf(stdout,   "%s\n", [[stack peekAtIndex:0]
    cStringUsingEncoding:NSASCIIStringEncoding]);
  return MYSuccess;
}


@end
```

All the commands follow a similar template. Only the class name and code inside the -executeWithStack: method change. For example, here is the code to implement an "add" command that functions as described at the beginning of this example:

```
+ (MYCommandReturn)executeWithStack:(MYStack *)stack
{
  if ([stack count] < 2) return MYError;
  NSString *value1 = [stack pop];
  NSString *value2 = [stack pop];
  double result = [value2 doubleValue] + [value1 doubleValue];
  NSString *resultString = [NSString stringWithFormat:@"%f", result];

  [stack push:resultString];
  return MYSuccess;
}
```

The actual downloadable example code on the book's website also implements commands for quit, subtract, multiply, divide, and dump. "Dump" displays the entire contents of the stack; the other commands are self-explanatory. Because of the use of the Dynamic Creation pattern, it is easy to extend the interpreter with a minimum of code. By simply adding new MYCommand subclasses to the project, the language is extended. As the interpreter parses its input, it will automatically find whatever command classes exist and use them as needed.

Dynamic Creation to Implement Plug-In Architectures

When creating a plug-in architecture, Dynamic Creation greatly simplifies the process. The purpose of plug-ins is to allow new code to be loaded into an application dynamically. The NSBundle class provides a solid foundation for creating plug-ins. A bundle can tie together code, images, Interface Builder interfaces, text and XML files, and so on and localize them, making it a perfect package for housing all the elements a plug-in might require. As such, NSBundle is usually used to implement plug-ins.

The NSBundle class defines a method, -classNamed:, which functions much as NSClassFromString(). Because bundles can contain executable code, the method differs from the function in two key ways. First, it searches only the bundle itself to find the requested class. Second, it will load executable code and link it into the running application if necessary.

NSBundle instances representing plug-ins can be obtained using the
+bundleWithPath: method. Keep in mind that the running application is a special type
of bundle, so sending the message [NSBundle mainBundle] will return an NSBundle instance that represents the application. Because frameworks are also bundles, don't expect
to be able to look up class objects for frameworks in the main bundle.

Once the correct bundle is obtained, there are two methods that can be used to obtain
Objective-C class objects. Most plug-in architectures will use -principalClass to locate
an entry point to the plug-in, given that the names of the classes in the plug-in are probably not known to the application loading them. Each bundle has a property list (Info.plist)
that can be configured to identify an Objective-C class as that bundle's principal class by
putting the class name in the "Principal class" key. The -classNamed: method also can be
used to obtain a class object from a bundle, if you know the name of the class you want.
Both methods will cause the bundle's executable code to be loaded and linked into the
application if necessary.

Underlying all of this NSBundle functionality is the Dynamic Creation pattern. Because this pattern decouples class names from the code using the classes, it helps to avoid
link time issues when an application that uses plug-ins is compiled.

Examples in Cocoa

Cocoa uses this pattern frequently, often in places where it might be convenient to allow
a custom class to be inserted. Chapter 13, which discusses the Singleton pattern, shows
how dynamic creation can be applied in this way. The NSApplication class is an example
of a singleton in Cocoa, which uses dynamic creation as part of its implementation.

Cocoa uses dynamic creation to implement much of its Applescript support. The reference documentation lists several classes such as NSCloneCommand, NSCountCommand,
NSCreateCommand, and so on—class names all ending in "Command." These are used by
Cocoa's Applscript support in a way similar to the RPN example in this chapter. In this
case, Applescript commands are mapped to a Cocoa objects that implement them. Dynamic creation is used to locate and instantiate an object of the correct class for each
command.

In Mac OS X 10.5 (Leopard), Apple added more generic support for scripting languages. These bridge technologies allow Ruby and Python to be used with Cocoa. On
the Objective-C side of the equation, dynamic creation is required to implement the
bridge. Invocations (Chapter 20, "Invocations") and Proxies and Forwarding (Chapter 27,
"Proxies and Forwarding") are also used in the implementation of the bridge.

Core Data relies upon dynamic creation when associating Objective-C classes with
entities. When creating data models in Xcode, it is possible to choose a custom subclass of
NSManagedObject to be used for each entity that is defined. When Core Data instantiates
entities, it uses Dynamic Creation to instantiate an object of the requested class.

When objects are archived, the class name is stored in the archive, and then the class'
data is written. To unarchive an object, the class name is read, and then the dynamic creation is used to instantiate the object. The object is then sent a message to read its data.

These are just a few examples of places in which this pattern is used. Cocoa uses Dynamic Creation pervasively throughout the frameworks to increase their flexibility. As developers gain experience with the frameworks, they begin to spot even more places in which it is being used and often use it more frequently themselves.

Consequences

Dynamic Creation is used to decouple classes from each other, particularly in cases where one class might be substituted for another. This decoupling makes it easy for developers to override sections of the Cocoa frameworks by inserting their own custom subclasses. Because of Dynamic Creation, Cocoa can instantiate and interact with custom classes even though they were unknown to the linker at the time Cocoa was compiled.

Developers can use Dynamic Creation themselves to create code that isn't directly coupled to other code. This is especially useful for creating plug-in architectures. It can also be employed to develop frameworks that are easily extended.

Several of the other Cocoa patterns often use Dynamic Creation in their implementation. Singletons (Chapter 13) often use Dynamic Creation to determine which class to instantiate. Hierarchies (Chapter 16, "Hierarchies") sometimes use Dynamic Creation to determine which classes to use when building up their internal object graphs. Dynamic Creation also makes some features of Bundles (Chapter 24, "Bundles") possible. By using Associative Storage (Chapter 19, "Associative Storage"), it is possible to further enhance the power of this pattern.

6

Category

The Category pattern adds methods to existing classes and provides an alternative to subclassing in many situations. The Category pattern is supported directly by the Objective-C language and is used extensively in the implementation of other Cocoa design patterns. The added methods are inherited by all subclasses of the extended class and are indistinguishable at runtime from methods originally compiled into the class.

The Category pattern can also be used to replace the implementations of methods in existing classes, perhaps to fix bugs in framework classes without needing source code for those classes. However, there is no convenient way to call the original method from the code that replaces it. When replacing a method, you must be certain to duplicate all of the functionality that is replaced, or new bugs will be introduced.

Unlike subclasses, categories can't be used to add instance variables to an existing class, but the Associative Storage pattern described in Chapter 19, "Associative Storage," describes a way to simulate the existence of additional instance variables within a category implementation.

Often Categories are used as a tool to organize class implementations.

Motivation

Use the Category pattern to accomplish the following:

- Extend existing classes without subclassing.
- Create informal protocols.
- Implement different methods of the same class in different frameworks.
- Spread the implementation of individual classes across multiple source files.
- Simplify development when multiple programmers contribute to the definition of individual classes.
- Extend the benefits of incremental compilation.

- Group commonly used methods.
- Fix bugs in existing classes as a last resort when you don't have access to the original source code.

Solution

In Objective-C, a class is declared using the `@interface` compiler directive as follows:

```
@interface ClassName : SuperClass
{
  variable declarations
}

method declarations

@end
```

For example, the following code declares a class called `MYDie` that represents a single six-sided die like the ones used in popular board games and is a subclass of `NSObject`:

```
@interface MYDie : NSObject
{
  int        value;       // stores the last value rolled
}

- (void) roll;            // obtain a new random value
- (int) value;            // returns the last value rolled

@end
```

The class is implemented using the `@implementation` compiler directive, as follows:

```
@implementation ClassName

method definitions

@end
```

Here is one possible implementation for the very simple `MYDie` class:

```
@implementation MYDie

- (void) roll
// rolls the die to obtain a new random value
{
  value = (random() % 6) + 1;  // random number in range (1-6)
}
```

```
- (int)value
// The last value rolled
{
  return value;
}

@end
```

To add methods to an existing class with a category, use the following syntax:

```
@implementation ClassName (CategoryName)

method definitions

@end
```

A category is defined by adding the category name in parentheses after the class name in an implementation. It isn't necessary to provide an interface declaration for a category, but it's a good idea in many situations. Use `@interface ClassName (CategoryName)` followed by method declarations and `@end` to create the interface for a category. The primary reason for creating a category interface is to give the compiler information about the added methods and therefore avoid compiler warnings when code refers to methods defined only in a category. Cocoa sometimes uses category interfaces without corresponding implementations to create something called an informal protocol, described in its own section within this chapter.

> **Note**
>
> The compiler and linker report errors when two categories with the same name are added to the same object. This might happen when multiple developers extend the same framework classes. Avoid the problem by using prefixes in your category names. The Cocoa frameworks use the standard "NS" prefix on the names of all categories they define.

Even in a situation where the source code to the MYDie class isn't available, the following category can still be used. In this case, one method is added to the MYDie class, and the existing - (void)roll method is replaced with a better implementation:

```
@implementation MYDie (_MYCategory)

- (void)roll
// rolls the die to obtain a new random value
{
  // the least significant bits of the value returned by random() are
  // not very random. Shifting those bits out of the way produces
  // better small random numbers
  value = ((random() >> 5) % 6) + 1;  // random number in range (1-6)
}
```

```
- (BOOL)isBoxcar
// Returns YES iff the last rolled value is a six
{
  return (value == 6);
}

@end
```

As another example, the following category adds convenient methods to Cocoa's NSMutableArray class:

```
@interface NSMutableArray (MYAdditions)

- (void)addObjectIfAbsent:(id)anObject;
- (void)addObjectIfNotNil:(id)anObject;

@end

@implementation NSMutableArray (MYAdditions)
// Adds useful methods to mutable arrays

- (void)addObjectIfAbsent:(id)anObject
// Adds anObject to the receiver if and only if anObject is not
// nil and already contained by receiver
{
  if((nil != anObject) && ![self containsObject:anObject])
  {
    [self addObject:anObject];
  }
}


- (void)addObjectIfNotNil:(id)anObject
// Adds anObject to the receiver if and only if anObject is not nil.
{
  if(nil != anObject)
  {
    [self addObject:anObject];
  }
}

@end
```

The - (void)addObjectIfAbsent:(id)anObject method allows you to treat any instance of NSMutableArray like an ordered set. Each object is present in the array at most once, and the order in which the objects were added is preserved.

NSMutableArray raises an exception if an attempt is made to insert a nil object. The - (void) addObjectIfNotNil: (id) anObject method allows you to be a little sloppy in your own code and avoid redundant checks for nil or exception handlers each time your code adds objects to an array.

> **Note**
>
> NSMutableArray is a public interface to a class cluster, which means that subclassing NSMutableArray is troublesome, and many hidden subclasses of NSMutableArray may exist. See Chapter 25, "Class Clusters." By adding methods to NSMutableArray with a category, the need to subclass is avoided, and the added methods are automatically inherited by all of the hidden subclasses of NSMutableArray.

The (MYAdditions) category on NSMutableArray emphasizes one of the reasons categories are sometimes preferred to subclassing. It's difficult but possible to subclass NSMutableArray and add methods in the subclass, but there is no good way to force existing compiled code to return instances of your subclass instead of instances of NSMutableArray. For example, Cocoa's built-in NSArray class responds to the - (id) mutableCopy method by returning an instance of NSMutableArray. That behavior is compiled into the Cocoa frameworks. To force -mutableCopy to return an instance of your hypothetical subclass NSMutableArray, you have to replace the framework's implementation of -mutableCopy. Furthermore, you have to replace every framework method that is compiled to return NSMutableArray if you want them to return your subclass instead. Adding methods via a category sidesteps the problem because methods added by a category are available for all instances of the extended class and its subclasses.

Informal Protocols

In Objective-C, a formal protocol is a language construct that is used to declare methods that an object must implement to be used in certain situations. An object is said to conform to a protocol if it provides all of the methods declared in the protocol. Formal protocol conformance is verified by the Objective-C compiler and can also be checked at runtime. Formal protocols are explained in detail in Apple's documentation at /Developer/Documentation/Cocoa/ObjectiveC/3objc_language_overview/Protocols_1_o_Implement.html if you have Apple's developer tools installed. The document is also available online at http://developer.apple.com/.

Apple's Cocoa documentation uses the term *informal protocol* to mean that the methods described as being part of the protocol are theoretically guaranteed to be available in any object. This guarantee isn't made by the compiler, which has no knowledge of informal protocols. The methods of an informal protocol are usually implemented in a category of the NSObject class. Almost all Cocoa objects inherit directly or indirectly from NSObject, so methods added to NSObject in a category are automatically inherited by almost all Cocoa objects.

However, there's a slight wrinkle when it comes to Cocoa's use of informal protocols. Quite often, the interface for a category that adds methods to NSObject exists, but Cocoa provides no actual implementation of the added methods. In other words, Apple created a category interface but no category implementation to fool the compiler into believing that the added methods are available in almost every class, when in fact they aren't available at all. The reason for doing this is to informally declare methods that will be called in certain circumstances if and only if you actually implement them in one of your classes. Some prime examples are methods that are implemented by a delegate. The Delegate pattern is described in Chapter 15, "Delegates." Many Cocoa classes perform a runtime check to determine if methods are actually available before calling them.

> **Note**
>
> Be careful to avoid conflicts with the method names between multiple categories. Methods implemented in a category always supercede the implementations of methods with the same name in the class itself. However, if multiple categories all implement the same method, there is no guarantee which implementation will be used. To avoid potential name conflicts, some developers add prefixes to the method names in categories. Most find this ugly, however, and avoid it. The Cocoa frameworks typically will use very verbose method names for methods found in informal protocols. This helps reduce the chance for conflict while at the same time improving the readability and self-documenting nature of Cocoa code.

The Anonymous Category

With the introduction of the Objective-C 2.0 in Mac OS X 10.5, Apple added a new language feature called Class Extensions, aka "the anonymous category." The anonymous category works like any other category with a few exceptions. First, the declaration of an anonymous category has no category name in parentheses. The following code declares a `-(void)setValue:(int)aValue` method added to the MYDie class via an anonymous category:

```
@interface MYDie ()

-(void)setValue:(int)aValue;

@end
```

Second, each class can have at most one anonymous category. Finally, the methods declared in an anonymous category must be implemented in the regular `@implementation` block for the class. Unlike named categories, the Objective-C 2.0 compiler verifies that the methods declared in an anonymous category are actually implemented and will emit a warning if any declared anonymous category method is missing.

This language feature is normally used as an informal way of organizing an object's private methods. Objective-C doesn't allow methods to be declared as public or private. By convention, developers put all the private method declarations into a private header that contains the anonymous category's definition. As a result, the private methods do not appear in the public header, yet the compiler will still emit a warning if a declared method in missing from the implementation. If a named category is used, the compiler doesn't offer any warnings for missing method implementations.

> **Note**
>
> Because Objective-C doesn't directly implement private methods in the language, there's no way to prevent messages that use private API from being sent, regardless of how and where private methods are declared. Client code can simply define, but not implement, a new named category that contains the method definitions, and then the compiler will allow messages that invoke the private methods without any error or warning at compile time.

Code Organization

Categories are used to break up the implementation of large classes. Often, the methods of a class can be logically divided into groups of related methods. The larger the code for a class becomes, the more useful it is to break the implementation up into several files, each containing a collection of related methods grouped in a single category. For example, all accessor methods can be one category, while all methods dealing with Applescript support can be in another. As the next section notes, the Cocoa frameworks use this technique to help organize the implementations of many Cocoa classes, including NSObject.

When multiple developers are working on a project, each can be assigned a different category to maintain. This makes revision control much simpler because there are fewer conflicts. Splitting up a class implementation reduces build times because only files with edited method implementations need to be recompiled instead of recompiling the entire class' code. Organizing a large class makes it easier for new team members to digest the code.

When to Use Categories Versus Subclassing

When making the choice between subclassing and categories, there isn't always a clear-cut right or wrong choice. Ultimately it comes down to experience and opinion. Examples of how other Cocoa developers are structuring their code can also be insightful. There are, however, some factors that can be weighed to guide your decision.

If new instance variables need to be added to a class, then subclassing may be the preferred choice. Categories can use Associative Storage (Chapter 19) to simulate the addition of new instance variables, but there is a performance cost in doing so.

Subclassing complex classes, especially those that use the Class Cluster pattern (Chapter 25), is usually discouraged. Categories can be an alternative to subclassing. If the methods being implemented add functionality that can benefit all subclasses of an existing class, then adding a category to the base class is probably the best choice.

Sometimes a hybrid approach can work well, too. A subclass can be created alongside a category. The category implements the methods that are more general extensions to the existing superclass. The subclass then extends the superclass by adding methods that are only applicable to the subclass. In general though, subclassing should be confined to cases where there is a clear need for specialization.

Examples in Cocoa

Cocoa extensively uses Categories, and this chapter has already described several examples. The categories in Cocoa can be organized into three groups:

- Categories that only organize methods
- Categories that define informal protocols
- Categories that spread class implementations across multiple frameworks

The remainder of this chapter describes some of Cocoa's most prominent categories in each group. Several classes have multiple categories that fall into multiple groups.

Using Categories for Organization

Almost every Cocoa class is organized into multiple categories. As of Mac OS X 10.4, the base class, NSObject, has 69 category interfaces defined in Cocoa's public header files. Most of those categories declare methods of informal protocols, but some important features of the base class are organized into the categories shown in Table 6.1.

Table 6.1   **Principle Categories Used to Organize the Methods Implemented by the NSObject Base Class**

Category Name	Description
NSClassDescription	Includes methods required to enable the use of objects with Cocoa's built-in scripting features
NSKeyValueCoding	Provides the methods needed to set and get the values of any object's instance variables
NSKeyValueCodingExtras	Adds even more features for setting and getting the values of instance variables
NSKeyValueCodingException	Declares methods that are called when something goes wrong in the process of setting or getting the values of instance variables
NSDelayedPerforming	Provides methods for sending messages to arbitrary objects after arbitrary delays
NSMainThreadPerformAdditions	Provides methods for sending messages between objects in child threads and objects in the main thread of an application
NSComparisonMethods	Includes methods including -isEqualTo: that are used to compare any two objects
NSScripting	Provides basic scripting support for all Cocoa objects

Table 6.1   **Principle Categories Used to Organize the Methods Implemented by the NSObject Base Class**

Category Name	Description
NSScriptClassDescription	Specifies the -className and -classCode methods that are used to enable scripting. The -className method is also useful in many contexts unrelated to scripting
NSScriptValueCoding	Declares the methods that integrate NSKeyValueCoding with scripting methods
NSScriptObjectSpecifiers	Provides more methods to make arbitrary Cocoa objects interface well with scripting systems
NSScriptingComparisonMethods	Similar to NSComparisonMethods but declares alternate comparison methods for use with scripting systems

Table 6.1 isn't a comprehensive list of all organizational categories for NSObject, but it serves as an indicator of how the code for a class can be broken up. Nine of the 12 categories shown in Table 6.1 are related to scripting. When Apple introduced scripting support in an early version of Cocoa, it chose to implement that one feature in multiple categories.

Using Categories for Informal Protocols

Informal protocols are often defined as a category of NSObject. The methods specified in the category interfaces may or may not be actually implemented by framework classes. Informal protocols are in a kind of design gray area. Formal protocols are checked by the compiler and represent a guarantee about an object's capabilities, but informal protocols make no guarantees—only hints. When reading Apple's documentation, pay special attention when informal protocols are mentioned. Although the documentation is not always explicit, look for information about whether every object already implements the methods in the informal protocol or if the methods will only be called if you implement them in your own classes.

The NSNibAwaking category of NSObject is a prominent example of an informal protocol that you must implement in your own classes. This category interface is in the NSNibLoading.h header, which is part of the Cocoa Application Kit framework. The category declares only one method, -(void)awakeFromNib. That method is not actually implemented. At runtime, an -awakeFromNib message is sent to each object loaded from an Interface Builder nib file after all objects in the nib file have been loaded. Cocoa framework code that loads nib files checks each loaded object to see if it actually implements -awakeFromNib before calling it. In other words, if you implement -awakeFromNib in your custom class, it will be called, but it's not an error if you don't implement it. This level of dynamism can be unsettling at first, but Cocoa programmers soon become accustomed to it.

The NSAccessibility informal protocol is also declared as a category that extends NSObject. Although many of Cocoa's user interface classes implement the NSAccessibility methods, no implementation of the methods is provided for NSObject. If you create a new subclass of NSObject that needs to support the accessibility features of Mac OS X, you need to implement the methods declared in the NSAccessibility category interface.

There are many other examples of informal protocols declared as category interfaces that aren't completely implemented within the Cocoa frameworks. The only way to correctly implement the methods of an informal protocol in your own classes is to carefully read Apple's documentation about the informal protocols and in some cases resort to trial and error. In practice, programmers seldom encounter problems related to the implementation of an informal protocol or for that matter the lack of an implementation.

If a method in an informal protocol is implemented in a class from which your class inherits, your class's implementation of the method almost certainly needs to call the inherited implementation. Look out for places in Apple's class documentation in which the need to call an inherited implementation is specified. The -awakeFromNib method of the NSNibAwaking informal protocol is a prime example and one of the trickiest.

If you know that your superclass implements -awakeFromNib, you should call it directly in your subclass' implementation as follows:

```
- (void)awakeFromNib
{
  [super awakeFromNib];

  // Add code unique to this class
}
```

However, what if you don't have the source code for the superclass, and the available documentation doesn't specify whether the superclass already implements -awakeFromNib? Consider a hypothetical subclass method of Cocoa's NSControl class. The following pattern is a common way to implement -awakeFromNib:

```
- (void)awakeFromNib
{
  if([NSControl instancesRespondToSelector:@selector(awakeFromNib)])
  { // Call superclass implementation
    [super awakeFromNib];
  }

  // Add code unique to this class
}
```

The code meets the direct need: Only call the superclass' implementation of -awakeFromNib if the superclass actually implements it. The preceding code is also future-proof. Suppose NSControl doesn't implement -awakeFromNib. Apple might change NSControl in the next framework version so that it does implement -awakeFromNib. If that happens, the code will do the right thing and call the new superclass implementation. Remember, this is only an issue at all because -awakeFromNib is declared (but not implemented) in an informal protocol.

Another solution to the problem is to provide the base class implementation that Apple "forgot" as follows:

```
@implementation NSObject (MYAdditions)

- (void)awakeFromNib
{
}

@end
```

Once you provide a default implementation in the base class, it's safe for any class' implementation of -awakeFromNib to call [super awakeFromNib].

> Note
>
> Be careful adding your own default implementations for methods like -awakeFromNib. If Apple adds an -awakeFromNib implementation to NSObject in a future framework version, any implementation in your category will replace the new implementation provided by Apple. Your category may prevent you from benefiting from Apple's implementation and may introduce bugs in other framework classes that assume the availability of Apple's version.

When you feel comfortable with Cocoa's use of informal protocols, you may find yourself creating your own informal protocols as categories of NSObject or other classes to support the needs of your applications. As the -awakeFromNib example shows, it's a best practice to provide a default implementation for each method you declare in your informal protocol.

> Note
>
> Objective-C 2.0 (introduced with Mac OS X 10.5) provides two new language keywords that enable you to use formal protocols in situations where you previously had to use informal protocols. The methods in formal protocols can now be declared either @optional or @required. The compiler doesn't need to verify whether methods declared after the @optional keyword are implemented in classes that conform to the protocol. All methods declared after the @required keyword must be implemented. If you don't specify either, all methods in the protocol are @required.

Using Categories for Framework Division

Cocoa uses categories to enable the implementation and maintenance of code in the context where it makes the most sense. For example, the NSAttributedString class is defined in Cocoa's nongraphical Foundation framework and contains many methods related to creating and managing strings. Using only Cocoa's Foundation framework, applications can perform sophisticated text processing with NSAttributedString, but there are no methods to draw attributed strings. Cocoa's Application Kit framework includes a category that extends the NSAttributedString class with methods related to drawing strings and other graphical operations. This provides an ideal organization of the code that implements NSAttributedString. The class can be used in nongraphical applications without including any overhead or dependencies for unneeded drawing logic and resources, but when the class is used in an Application Kit-based graphical application, all of the drawing methods are automatically available.

Other examples include the NSNibAwaking and NSNibLoading categories of NSObject and NSBundle, respectively. NSObject is defined in the Foundation framework and serves as the base class for almost every Cocoa object. NSBundle is also defined in the Foundation framework and provides a simple means to dynamically load objects and resources into a running program. NSNibAwaking and NSNibLoading are implemented in the Application Kit framework and declare the methods needed when objects are loaded from an Interface Builder nib file. By extending Foundation framework classes within the Application Kit framework, it becomes possible to use any foundation object in a nib file even though there is no information about or dependence on nib files within the Foundation framework itself.

The practice of implementing part of a class in one framework and other parts in other frameworks enables the implementation of features where they most make sense and where they are easiest to maintain, but the technique should only be used when the groups of methods are truly independent.

Consequences

The ability to add or replace methods in existing classes makes Cocoa very extensible. Categories are preferred over subclasses in many situations. In particular, categories circumvent the fact that it isn't always possible to force an existing framework to use your subclass instead of whatever class it was compiled to use. The Category pattern is also the preferred way to extend the classes of a class cluster. However, like all powerful tools, categories can be misused.

The Clash of Methods

When multiple categories add or replace the same method, the implementation that ends up replacing all others depends on the order in which code is loaded into a program and can't always be predicted or controlled. This limitation means that it's a bad idea to replace or add the same method more than once. The problem is compounded when you don't necessarily know if other categories already add or replace a method. For example, any plug-in module or framework that is loaded by an application can conceivably contain a category that implements the same methods you implement in your own category. There may be no way to know except to observe that the application has stopped working correctly.

The conflict when multiple categories implement the same method is more of a problem in theory than in practice, but don't discount it. If you think of a useful method to add to a Cocoa class, someone else may have thought of the same thing. The consistency with which methods are named in Cocoa increases the probability of two independent categories that add the same functionality independently using the same method name as well. You can side-step the naming problem in many cases by using a unique prefix in the methods you add. The `-addObjectIfAbsent:` method added to `NSMutableArray` earlier in this chapter can be named `-myAddObjectIfAbsent:` or something similar to reduce the chances of clashing with some other category that extends `NSMutableArray`.

A related problem with categories crops up over time as users upgrade their systems. Suppose Apple adds an `-addObjectIfAbsent:` method to `NSMutableArray` in the next Cocoa framework version. The version provided in this chapter will mask the version in the new framework because an implementation in a category will always supercede the version in the class implementation. If other framework code depends on a side effect of Apple's `-addObjectIfAbsent:` method that isn't present in the category implementation, the framework code can break in very subtle and hard to diagnose ways. The bottom line is that even if a method added in a category doesn't cause problems now, it can start causing problems in the future. Using a unique prefix on methods implemented in a category is the only defense against these problems.

It is strongly recommended that prefixes be used when adding methods to classes defined by the Cocoa frameworks. Of course, when deliberately overriding a method, perhaps to fix a bug in the frameworks, no prefix is desired because you *want* your new implementation to replace the existing one. When this is done, it's wise to retest with every new framework release to see if your override is still necessary and remove it as soon as it becomes obsolete.

Replacing Methods

Categories make it easy to replace existing method implementations, but there is no convenient way to call the replaced methods from the new implementations. You must be very careful to replace all of the behavior of the method including undocumented side effects. As a general rule, it's better to work around a bug in a method implementation than it is to replace the method in a category. Replacing methods is very difficult, requires extensive testing, and should be a last resort.

Software Maintenance

Categories provide an effective way to separate the methods of a class into multiple source files. One reason to do that is to enable different programmers to work on different parts of the same class at the same time. Another reason is to limit the recompilation that is needed when a method implementation is edited. Only the file that contains the edited code needs to be recompiled; other files that implement the same class don't need recompilation. The most compelling reason to divide the implementation of a class into several categories is to implement different methods in different frameworks the way graphics methods are added to Cocoa's Foundation framework NSAttributedString class by a category in the Cocoa's Application Kit framework. However, deciding when it's advisable to divide a class implementation into different frameworks or different subsystems of an application is a tough judgment call. One purpose of the category pattern is to enable the implementation and maintenance of code where it makes the most sense, but misusing categories can actually make software maintenance more difficult.

Keeping all of the method implementations for a class in a single file has the advantage of limiting changes to the class to that one file. If the implementation of a class is dispersed over source files in multiple frameworks and subsystems, the task of isolating code that needs to be modified and verifying that modifications haven't introduced new bugs is complicated. In some cases, the maintainer of a class may not be aware of all of the categories that exist in other frameworks or even in application plug-ins.

This can be mitigated by using a naming convention for source code files that define or implement categories. For example, if the category named MYAdditions is extending the NSArray class, you can name the source files NSArray+MYAdditions.h and NSArray+MYAdditions.m so that it's clear at a glance which class is being affected.

7

Anonymous Type and Heterogeneous Containers

Objective-C defines the type id, which is known as the *Anonymous Type*. The id type tells the compiler that a variable points to an object but doesn't give the compiler any more specific information about the kind of object, hence the object is anonymous. Objective-C programmers quickly become familiar with the pervasive use of the Anonymous Type and forget that this feature is seldom encountered in other languages. Objective-C's Anonymous Type and Cocoa's Heterogeneous Containers deserve special recognition as patterns in their own right and facilitators for other patterns.

Motivation

Use the Anonymous Type pattern to send messages to anonymous objects, including objects that are not available at the time the sending code is compiled. Reduce coupling between classes by limiting the information that each class has about other classes. Use Heterogeneous Containers to provide powerful container classes that can each store any number of objects of any type in any combination.

Solution

Messaging is the key feature of the Objective-C language that makes the language so dynamic and flexible. Every feature that Objective-C adds to the base C language is designed to make it easy to define objects and send messages to them. In fact, the definition of an Objective-C object is "something that can receive messages." Objective-C classes are themselves objects that receive messages. Chapter 3, "Two-Stage Creation," explains how messages are sent to class objects to create instances.

A message is a request for an object to do something. In Objective-C, the syntax for sending a message uses square brackets ([and]) to delimit the start and end of a message sending expression:

```
[receiver selector]
```

The variable *receiver* specifies the object that will receive the message. The variable *selector* identifies the message to send. Messages can include arguments and can return values. The syntax and semantics of messaging are explained in detail in Apple's Objective-C manual at /Developer/Documentation/Cocoa/ObjectiveC/ObjC.pdf *and* http://developer.apple.com.

Messaging is flexible and dynamic because both the receiver and the selector are variables. The determination of exactly which message is sent to which receiver is deferred until a program is running. At the time a program is compiled, it's not always possible to know the type of object that will receive the message. Many other object-oriented languages such as C++ and Java require that the type of every object is known to the compiler. Objective-C has no such requirement.

> ### Note
>
> When Objective-C programmers send messages, what matters most is whether the object can receive the message, not what type of object it is. If an object understands the message, then the type is irrelevant. This language approach is sometimes called *Duck Typing* in reference to an old saying that "if something walks like a duck and quacks like a duck, I would call it a duck." In many other languages, it is important first and foremost to know what type of object you have so you know what messages you can send to it. This is a subtle difference in mindset, but the implications enable and lead to many of the patterns described in this book. Duck typing makes the implementation of many patterns much simpler than they would be in another language.

Arbitrary strings can be converted to selectors while an application is running. The selector to be used can even be provided by user input, though care must be taken to do this safely. It's also possible for the selector to be specified by dynamically loaded code that didn't exist when the code that sends the message was compiled.

Objective-C messaging is so dynamic that the ultimate receiver of a message might not even be in the same process as the expression that sends the message. Chapter 27, "Proxies and Forwarding" explains how Cocoa helps you send messages to objects in different processes on the same or different computers using the same syntax as local messages. In many cases, it is not possible for the compiler to determine the ultimate receiver of a message.

The Anonymous Type

The Objective-C language provides the Anonymous Type, id, which represents a pointer to any object. The id type conveys no more information than the fact that the object referenced by a variable with id type can be the receiver of messages.

The id type is used in the same contexts in which any other C type is used including in the declaration of variables, as a structure or union element, as the type of arguments to functions and methods, and as a return type.

In C any pointer can store the constant NULL, which equals 0. In Objective-C, any pointer to an object can store the constant nil, which also equals 0. Messages sent to nil are not always errors as they would be in Ruby or Java. In Objective-C, such messages immediately return nil.

> **Note**
>
> Don't rely on the value returned from a message to nil unless the message is expected to return a pointer or a type convertible to a pointer. For example, messages that return float or a structure have an undefined return value when sent to nil.

The id type is essential when the maximum flexibility allowed by the Objective-C language is needed, but as a general rule, the compiler should be given as much information about objects as possible. When details about an object are known, use a more specific type than id to convey the details to the compiler. The more information the compiler has, the more assistance it can give you in the form of warnings.

To declare a pointer to an instance of a specific class, use the class name as a type. For example, to declare a reference to an instance of Cocoa's NSArray class, use the following syntax:

```
NSArray    *anArray;
```

When the compiler subsequently encounters anArray as the receiver of a message, the compiler can issue warnings if anArray cannot respond the message being sent. It is considered a best practice to be as specific as possible when defining pointers to objects. For example, if you know you are manipulating an NSTableView, then use that in the variable declaration. If you only know it will be some NSView subclass, but not necessarily which one, then use NSView. Finally, if complete flexibility is required, then it is acceptable to use id.

Objective-C allows the forward declaration of class names using the @class compiler directive. The following declarations tell the compiler that NSArray, NSDictionary, and NSNumber are all the names of classes that have yet to be defined:

```
@class NSArray;
@class NSDictionary, NSNumber;
```

Use forward declaration of class names in the same situations as when standard C structures are forward declared, such as solving circular import dependency problems. In particular, forward declaration of classes is used in class interface declarations so that two or more classes can refer to each other without error as follows:

```
@class MYAcademicStatus

@interface MYStudentRecord : NSObject
{
  MYAcademicStatus  *currentStatus;
}

@end
```

```
@interface MYAcademicStatus : NSObject
{
  BOOL           isEnroled;
  MYStudentRecord *record;
}

@end
```

The initial declaration of MYAcademicStatus is needed to make the declaration of MYStudentRecord possible before the MYAcademicStatus class itself is declared. Once the MYStudentRecord class has been declared, it can be freely used in the declaration of MYAcademicStatus.

The id type can be used instead of specific class names when declaring object instance variables. The MYStudentRecord and MYAcademicStatus classes could have been declared as follows without the need for the forward declaration of any class name, but the compiler would have less information to use when compiling the code:

```
@interface MYStudentRecord : NSObject
{
  id             currentStatus;
}

@end


@interface MYAcademicStatus : NSObject
{
  BOOL           isEnroled;
  id             record;
}

@end
```

Regardless of whether the Anonymous Type or a more specific object type is used, any message can be sent to any object. Providing information to the compiler beyond the information conveyed by id enables the compiler to generate warnings when it can't verify that a receiver responds to a message. Warnings are generated instead of errors because the compiler can never be sure that the receiver doesn't respond to a message. It's possible that the method to respond to a particular message exists but is not known to the compiler. That happens when methods are implemented in a class implementation but not declared in a class interface. It also may happen when methods are added to a class with a Category that is dynamically loaded at runtime. Categories are explained in Chapter 6, "Category."

If a receiver doesn't respond to a message sent at runtime and no special processing is used to forward the message to another receiver, a runtime error occurs. This is often considered a bug of the same severity as an application crash. In practice, errors are easily avoided because it is possible to determine at runtime whether a particular receiver can respond to a particular message before the message is sent. Cocoa's NSObject class provides the -(BOOL)respondsToSelector:(SEL)aSelector method that returns YES if the receiver responds to a specified selector and NO otherwise. The -respondsToSelector: method is inherited by virtually every Cocoa class.

The NSObject class and the -respondsToSelector: method are documented at /Developer/Documentation/Cocoa/Reference/Foundation/ObjC_classic/Classes/NSObject.html. YES and NO are two constants that are stored by Objective-C's BOOL type. BOOL is declared as follows in /usr/include/objc/objc.h:

```
typedef char BOOL;
```

YES and NO are also defined in /usr/include/objc/objc.h:

```
#define YES (BOOL)1
#define NO  (BOOL)0
```

> Note
>
> The header file /usr/include/objc/objc.h also contains the definition of the id type and others of interest when delving into the implementation of the language runtime.

The objc.h header file is not strictly part of Cocoa. It's a component of the Objective-C runtime environment that is provided as part of the underlying open source Darwin operating system used by Mac OS X. Such system files are normally hidden from you by Apple's Finder application, but you can use Finder's Go, Go to Folder...menu item to view any file in the file system including the files in /usr/include. Apple's Terminal application is also available for viewing system files.

> Note
>
> Virtually every Cocoa class is a subclass of NSObject. Many Cocoa classes assume that methods provided by NSObject are available in any object referenced by the id type. In particular, Cocoa's collection classes assume that any object stored in a collection responds to at least the messages declared for NSObject instances. The compiler doesn't assure that any object referenced by an id variable is compatible with NSObject, but when using Cocoa it's usually a safe assumption.

Assignment

Any variable of type id can be assigned to any pointer to an instance of a specific class as follows:

```
id          untypedObject;
NSArray     *anArray;

// Assume untypedObject is initialized here

anArray = untypedObject;    // This assignment is OK
```

Similarly, a pointer to an instance of any class can be assigned to a variable of type `id`:

```
id              untypedObject;
NSArray         *anArray;

// Assume anArray is initialized here

untypedObject = anArray;    // This assignment is OK
```

If you want to verify at runtime that an assignment involving the Anonymous Type makes sense, use the `-isKindOfClass:` method provided by `NSObject`:

```
id              untypedObject;
NSArray         *anArray;

// Assume untypedObject is initialized here

// Verify that an assignment makes sense
if([untypedObject isKindOfClass:[NSArray class])
{
  anArray = untypedObject;    // This assignment is legal
}
```

As an alternative to `-(BOOL)isKindOfClass:(Class)aClass`, the `NSObject` class also provides `-(BOOL)conformsToProtocol:(Protocol *)aProtocol`. An Objective-C protocol is a list of methods that an object promises to implement regardless of the inheritance hierarchy of the class. In addition to the `NSObject` class, Cocoa provides an `NSObject` protocol that declares the methods that almost every Cocoa class is expected to provide. When possible, it is more flexible to test if an anonymous object conforms to a protocol than to check if it inherits from a particular class. Protocols are described in Apple's Objective-C reference at /Developer/Documentation/Cocoa/ObjectiveC/ObjC.pdf and http://developer.apple.com.

It is possible to use protocols to get a compromise between anonymous and static typing. For example, suppose we don't care about an object's class, but we do care that it conforms to `MYProtocol`. We can define a variable in this way:

```
id <MYProtocol, NSObject> myProtocolObject;
```

By using `id`, `myProtocolObject` is still an anonymous type. The object to which it points could be of any class. But at the same time, the compiler knows what messages are safe to send to the object, and it can emit a warning if an attempt is made to send a message that is not in one of the listed protocols.

Note

Because protocols can inherit from other protocols, and even multiple inheritance is supported, `MYProtocol` could be defined to inherit from the `NSObject` protocol. Then only `MYProtocol` would have been listed in the variable declaration.

Heterogeneous Containers

Cocoa provides a small number of collection classes designed to meet most application needs. Each collection is designed to store variables of type id. As a result, the collections are called *heterogeneous*, meaning that references to objects of any type can be stored in any combination. The collection classes automatically reserve extra storage as needed to hold as many objects as required.

> **Note**
>
> Cocoa's collection classes use the id type to store references to any type of object. However, unless the optional automatic memory garbage collection introduced in Mac OS X 10.5 is used, the collection classes require that any object referenced within a collection implements Cocoa's reference counted memory management conventions described in Chapter 10, "Accessors."

Cocoa uses the Enumerator pattern described in Chapter 8, "Enumerators," to provide flexible access to the objects stored in collections. Using Enumerators frees you to change the specific collection classes used as an application evolves while minimizing disruption to program logic.

Cocoa's collection classes are implemented using the Class Cluster pattern explained in Chapter 25, "Class Clusters." The Class Cluster pattern provides simple interfaces to the collection classes and wide range of behind the scenes optimizations, but the cost of using the Class Cluster pattern is increased difficulty when subclassing existing collection classes. Fortunately, Cocoa's collection classes are time-tested with more that ten years of use. They meet most application needs and are seldom subclassed.

The collection classes are implemented in both mutable and immutable forms. The contents stored by mutable collections can be changed throughout the execution of a program. Immutable collections are created with particular contents, and the contents do not change.

The NSArray and NSMutableArray classes store ordered collections of object references. The NSDictionary and NSMutableDictionary classes store associations of keys and values for rapid retrieval. The NSSet and NSMutableSet classes store unordered collections of unique object references; each object can be referenced at most once in any particular set. Finally, NSCountedSet, a subclass of NSMutableSet, provides an unordered collection, but it allows multiple references to the same object within one collection.

The collection classes are all provided in Cocoa's Foundation framework. The classes are used extensively throughout Cocoa and can be adapted to almost any need. They are documented within the /Developer/Documentation/Cocoa//Reference/Foundation/ObjC_classic/Classes/ folder installed with Apple's developer tools and at http://developer.apple.com/.

Examples in Cocoa

Many of Cocoa's design patterns leverage the Anonymous Type. In particular, powerful features of Cocoa's Application Kit framework rely on the Anonymous type. Outlets and Targets, described in Chapter 17, "Outlets, Targets, and Actions," use the Anonymous Type to avoid coupling between user interface objects and custom objects so that both can be reused with maximum flexibility. The same is true of the Notification pattern described in Chapter 14, "Notifications," and Delegates described in Chapter 15, "Delegates."

Consequences

Errors that might be detected at compile time by some languages cannot be detected until runtime with Objective-C. The Objective-C compiler can never determine for sure whether the receiver of a message will be able to respond to it. The level of flexibility and dynamism provided by the Anonymous Type might seem dangerous, but in practice, messages to objects that cannot respond to them are rare, and runtime checks can be used to detect and prevent errors.

One of the benefits of Objective-C's Anonymous Type is the simplicity that it enables. Objective-C provides a rich object-oriented infrastructure with minimal additions to the base C language in part because of the Anonymous Type. The Anonymous Type eliminates the need for complex language features like C++ templates and Ada generic packages. When used with other patterns, the Anonymous Type can dramatically reduce the amount of code needed to solve common problems. The Anonymous Type also promotes loose coupling of code.

Finally, the ability to send any message to any receiver and do so without compiler warnings eliminates the need for complex and error prone ad-hoc extensions to the Objective-C language. To implement remote messaging and support dynamic loading of code, many languages require helper languages like Corba's Interface Definition Language (IDL) described at http://www.corba.org/. Technologies such as Sun's Enterprise JavaBeans (EJB) and Microsoft's COM and DCOM exist to enable objects in separately compiled code bases to communicate without being statically linked together. Objective-C's Anonymous Type and messaging make it possible for Proxies and Forwarding (Chapter 27) to provide an elegant solution for remote messaging without unwieldy language extensions.

8

Enumerators

Enumerators provide a mechanism for accessing all of the objects in a collection sequentially without exposing the collection's underlying data structures. Enumerators are used to write flexible and efficient code for using collection classes without tying applications to specific implementations. Furthermore, enumerators provide a uniform interface to collection classes that can be extended to meet a wide range of needs including alternative traversal orders and algorithms.

Enumerators rely on the Anonymous Type pattern and make Heterogeneous Containers more powerful. Objective-C 2.0, available with Mac OS 10.5, Leopard, adds language features to further enhance Enumerators by reducing the amount of repetitive code needed to use the pattern. In non-Cocoa settings, this pattern is often called an Iterator or a Cursor.

Motivation

Enumerators provide a uniform means of traversing a collection's underlying data structures. The interface presented by Enumerators is independent of the traversal order and algorithms used for traversal. Enumerators decouple a collection class from code that traverses it. It is also possible to have multiple traversals active simultaneously, but Cocoa generally disallows the modification of mutable collections while they are being traversed.

Solution

To traverse a collection, it is necessary to obtain an enumerator object and then construct a loop that will extract objects from the enumerator one at a time until all objects are exhausted. A developer implementing a custom collection class will want to also create their own NSEnumerator subclass. Fast enumeration in Objective-C 2.0 simplifies the looping code at the expense of requiring extra code to be added to a collection class. The following sections show in detail how to use Enumerator objects and fast enumeration, how to create new Enumerators, and how to implement fast enumeration.

Using Enumerator Objects

In Cocoa, the Enumerator pattern is defined by the abstract NSEnumerator class. Nearly every collection in Cocoa offers one or more methods that return an instance of a concrete NSEnumerator subclass. Many other Cocoa objects also have methods to return an NSEnumerator to iterate over relevant sets of objects. Most commonly the -objectEnumerator method is used to obtain a relevant Enumerator.

For example, NSArray offers the two methods -objectEnumerator and -reverseObjectEnumerator to obtain enumerators. Using the -objectEnumerator method traverses the array's contents in order from first element to last, starting with the object at index 0, which is what is normally desired. To traverse the other direction, from the end to the beginning of the array, use -reverseObjectEnumerator instead. The NSDictionary class also offers the -objectEnumerator method for traversing a list of all the contained objects. Alternatively, the -keyEnumerator method can be used to iterate over the dictionary's keys instead of the objects it contains. To find out what traversals are possible for a particular collection, simply look for methods that return NSEnumerator objects.

No matter how you obtain an Enumerator or what objects it will be traversing, it is always used the same way. The Enumerator's encapsulation hides the specific traversal algorithms from you to present a simple, uniform interface.

The NSEnumerator class defines only two methods: -nextObject and -allObjects. Usually only the -nextObject method is used. The first time it's called, the first object in the traversal is returned. Subsequent calls return objects one at a time until the list is exhausted. Once all objects have been traversed, -nextObject returns nil. You typically write code like the following to traverse an enumeration:

```
id instance;
NSEnumerator *enumerator = [myCollection objectEnumerator];
while (instance = [enumerator nextObject])
{
  // do something with instance
}
```

Use the -allObjects method to obtain an NSArray filled with all the objects remaining to be enumerated. The -nextObject method always returns nil after the -allObjects method has been used.

> **Note**
>
> The -allObjects method name can be somewhat confusing, given that the returned NSArray contains only the objects *remaining* to be enumerated. The only way for the returned array to actually contain all the objects in the collection is if -allObjects is called before any calls to -nextObject.

For safety, each NSEnumerator subclass retains the collection it is traversing until the traversal is complete so that the underlying data will not be deallocated while traversal is underway. Also if a collection is mutable, it's considered unsafe to modify the collection during traversal. Doing so may lead to undesireable behaviors including skipped objects or repeated objects during traversal, raised exceptions, and even application crashes.

Using Fast Enumeration

Fast enumeration was introduced in Objective-C 2.0 as a way to both simplify and potentially speed up enumeration loops. With fast enumeration, the code from the previous section is reduced to either of these loops:

```
id instance;
for (instance in myCollection)
{
  // do something with instance
}
// or, alternatively:
for (id instance2 in myCollection)
{
  // do something with instance2
}
```

This decreases the amount of code written, making the programmer's intent more clear. In turn, the possibility of bugs is reduced. If the collection class implements fast enumeration correctly, then using fast enumeration can be more efficient and safer. Because modifying mutable collections while they are being traversed isn't allowed in Cocoa, fast enumeration offers some automatic safeguards to detect such activity and throw exceptions when it occurs. Not all NSEnumerator subclasses properly detect mutation of the data they are traversing, which can lead to unpredictable application behavior or crashing if a collection is modified while it is being enumerated.

Typically the order of enumeration performed by fast enumeration is the same as the order of enumeration performed by the NSEnumerator instance returned by a call to the -objectEnumerator method. However, the NSEnumerator class itself supports fast enumeration and can be used in the for () statement. For example, here is the code to enumerate an NSArray in reverse with fast enumeration:

```
id instance;
for (instance in [myArrayInstance reverseObjectEnumerator])
{
  // do something with instance
}
```

Creating Custom Enumerators

If you create a custom collection class or have some other object whose contents might need to be enumerated, then it is necessary to create your own subclass of NSEnumerator to handle your custom class and add a method to your class that creates and initializes an instance of this new Enumerator type. For example, suppose you have a very simple linked list class, built off this interface:

```
@interface MYLinkedList : NSObject
{
  unsigned long     listLength;
  MYLinkedListNode *firstNode;
  MYLinkedListNode *lastNode;
  MYLinkedListNode *markerNode;
}

- (void)appendObject:(id)newObject;

@property (readwrite, retain) MYLinkedListNode *firstNode;
@property (readwrite, retain) MYLinkedListNode *lastNode;
@property (readonly) MYLinkedListNode *markerNode;
@property (readonly) unsigned long listLength;

@end
```

The private helper class `MYLinkedListNode` is a simple helper that defines two properties, `object` for the contained object and `nextNode` as a pointer to the next `MYLinkedListNode` in the list. The code isn't shown here, but is part of the downloadable example on the book's website at www.CocoaDesignPatterns.com. The only modification this linked list class supports is appending new nodes to the end of the list.

The one slightly unusual trait of this class is `markerNode`, which denotes the end of the list. Usually a `nil` marks the end of the list, but because of the implementation details of fast enumeration as shown later in this chapter, a non-`nil` marker must always be kept at the end of the list.

Here's a simple starting implementation of the class as defined:

```
@implementation MYLinkedList

@synthesize firstNode;
@synthesize lastNode;
@synthesize markerNode;
@synthesize listLength;

- init
{
  self = [super init];
  markerNode = [[MYLinkedListNode alloc] init];
  markerNode.object = [NSNull null];
  markerNode.nextNode = nil;
  self.firstNode = self.markerNode;
  self.lastNode = self.markerNode;
  listLength = 0;
  return self;
}
```

```
- (void)appendObject:(id)newObject
{
  MYLinkedListNode *newNode = [[MYLinkedListNode alloc] init];
  newNode.object = newObject;
  newNode.nextNode = markerNode;
  if (self.markerNode == self.firstNode)
  { // first object added
    self.firstNode = newNode;
    self.lastNode = newNode;
  }
  else
  {
    self.lastNode.nextNode = newNode;
    self.lastNode = newNode;
  }
  listLength++;
}

- (void)dealloc
{
  MYLinkedListNode *node = firstNode;
  MYLinkedListNode *next = firstNode.nextNode;
  while (node != markerNode)
  {
    [node release];
    node = next;
    next = next.nextNode;
  }
  firstNode = nil; lastNode = nil;
  [markerNode release]; markerNode = nil;
  [super dealloc];
}
```

`@end`

Now it is time to add a custom `NSEnumerator` subclass that can enumerate this collection. We need to create an initialization method that can be used by `MYLinkedList` to set up a new enumeration. The only method we need to override in `NSEnumerator` is `-nextObject`. The Enumerator needs to keep track of the collection it is enumerating and retain it. It also needs to be aware of its current position in the traversal of the collection's objects. Finally, to be safe, it should somehow track modifications to the original list, just in case something is modified while the enumeration is still active. Considering our list supports only the single action append that increases the length of the list, we can track the length of the list to detect modification. Here's an interface for the new Enumerator meeting these requirements:

```
@interface MYLinkedListEnumerator : NSEnumerator
{
  MYLinkedList      *list;
  MYLinkedListNode *currentNode;
  unsigned long     originalListLength;
}


- (id)initForList:(MYLinkedList *)theList;

@property (readwrite, retain, nonatomic) MYLinkedList *list;
@property (readwrite, retain, nonatomic) MYLinkedListNode *currentNode;
@property (readonly) unsigned long originalListLength;

@end
```

The following code provides a basic implementation that meets the specification:

```
@implementation MYLinkedListEnumerator

@synthesize list;
@synthesize currentNode;
@synthesize originalListLength;

- (id)initForList:(MYLinkedList *)theList
{
  self = [super init];
  self.list = theList;
  self.currentNode = theList.firstNode;
  originalListLength = theList.listLength;
  return self;
}

- (id)nextObject
{
  id object = nil; // we return nil if at the end of the list
  MYLinkedListNode *nextNode = self.currentNode.nextNode;

  // detect mutation and throw an exception if found
  if (list.listLength != self.originalListLength)
  {
    NSException *exception = [NSException exceptionWithName:
      @"MYLinkedListMutationException" reason:
      @"MYLinkedList was mutated during an enumeration"
      userInfo:nil];
    @throw exception;
  }
```

```
  // if not at the end, get the next object and return it
  if (self.currentNode != self.list.markerNode)
  {
    object = self.currentNode.object;
    self.currentNode = nextNode;
  }
  return object;
}


@end
```

The initialization method -initForList: simply sets up the internal state of the Enumerator. The overridden -nextObject does all the work. First it checks to make sure that the list hasn't mutated. In a more robust implementation that allows more list manipulation options, it might make sense to have the list have a property named numberOfMutations that gets incremented every time the list is altered. Then use numberOfMutations to detect mutations such as two objects swapping places in the list. Regardless of how mutations are tracked, if one mutation is discovered during enumeration, it's a good idea to throw an exception. Finally, as long as we are not at the end of the list, the next object is returned to the message sender, and our currentNode is updated to point to the next node in the list.

Note that we did not override the -allObjects method. NSEnumerator actually implements a very basic version of this method so that we don't have to. A naïve implementation, if we wanted one, might look something like this:

```
- (NSArray *)allObjects
{
  NSMutableArray *array = [NSMutableArray
    arrayWithCapacity:originalListLength];
  id object;

  // fill the array with all remaining objects to be enumerated
  while ((object = [self nextObject]))
  {
    [array addObject:object];
  }
  return array;
}
```

That implementation will work fine but is rather inefficient. If there is a better way to implement -allObjects based on the data structure of your custom collection, then it usually makes sense to optimize the -allObjects implementation. The last thing to do is add the -objectEnumerator method to the MYLinkedList class. All it needs to do is return an auto-released instance of the Enumerator that is set up and ready to go, like this:

```
- (NSEnumerator *)objectEnumerator
{
```

```
MYLinkedListEnumerator *enumerator =
  [[MYLinkedListEnumerator alloc] initForList:self];
[enumerator autorelease];
return enumerator;
}
```

With that method complete, it's possible to use the normal enumeration `while()`
statement to enumerate `MYLinkedList` in the same way any Foundation collection class is
enumerated. It's possible to create multiple NSEnumerator subclasses for any given collection. Different subclasses might implement other traversal orders or different algorithms.

For example, suppose your data structure has two well-known traversal algorithms.
Further suppose that one algorithm is much faster for large data sets, while the other is
best for small data sets. In that case, consider implementing the `-objectEnumerator`
method to return an appropriate subclass of `NSEnumerator` based on analysis of the data
to be traversed. When used this way, `NSEnumerator` subclasses can take on some aspects of
the well-known Strategy pattern described at http://en.wikipedia.org/wiki/
Strategy_pattern.

Just as arrays allow for reverse enumeration, other possibilities exist, limited only by
developer creativity. For example, a tree data structure might have an associated Enumerator
class that provides a depth first traversal and another to provide a breadth first traversal.
If you have a class which is an Aggregate, made up of several collection instances, use a
custom Enumerator to provide a way of traversing all the collections in turn while hiding
the underlying implementation complexity.

Implementing Fast Enumeration

To use fast enumeration on `MYLinkedList`, it is necessary to adopt the
`NSFastEnumeration` protocol. This protocol requires the implementation of a single
method, `-countByEnumeratingWithState:objects:count:`. As might be imagined from
the name, implementing this method is often nontrivial. Here is the method prototype:

```
-(NSUInteger)countByEnumeratingWithState:
    (NSFastEnumerationState *)state
  objects:(id *)stackbuf
  count:(NSUInteger)len
```

The method is set up to allow iterations to be performed in batches. Each time it is
called, one or more objects are indirectly returned; the return value of the method is the
number of objects being returned in each batch. The method will be called multiple
times until the collection has been traversed completely. When the enumeration is complete, zero is returned to signal the end. As a consequence, even if all the collection's objects are sent in a single batch, this method will still be called at least twice per
enumeration.

The first parameter to this method, `state`, is the most important. It is a pointer to a
structure of the type `NSFastEnumerationState`. This structure serves two purposes. First,
it gives you a place to store state information so that you can pick up where you left off

when it comes time to prepare the next batch. Second, the actual objects being enumerated are returned via this structure. It is defined like this:

```
typedef struct {
  unsigned long state;
  id            *itemsPtr;
  unsigned long *mutationsPtr;
  unsigned long extra[5];
} NSFastEnumerationState;
```

The structure member `state` is yours, to store whatever information you need to keep to continue your traversal from where you left off. For traversing a linked list such as the one in our previous example, it makes sense to simply store a pointer to the current node here. If you need to preserve more state than just a pointer to a single object, you should create a new object to hold all the state information and put a pointer to that object here instead.

The `itemsPtr` member should be a pointer to a C array of object pointers. The objects in the C array are the actual objects being returned in the current batch. The return value of this method tells fast enumeration how many objects are in the array pointed to by `itemsPtr`. If you provide your own storage array, then it can be of any length you wish, allowing you to control the batch size.

To guard against mutation while enumerating, the `mutationsPtr` should be set to point to some property of the actual collection object that will accurately flag whether the object has changed. In the previous example, the `NSEnumerator` class used the length of the list to guard against mutation; that works here, too. If it's possible to mutate your collection class without change to the length of the collection, then a different means of detecting mutations is required. If you don't detect mutations, fast enumeration will still function, but undesirable side effects like skipped elements during enumeration may result.

Finally, the `extra` member of the structure can be safely ignored. It's possible to safely store extra state information in the `extra` member. However, wrapping all state information into an object stored in `state` is preferred, because it's a more objected-oriented approach.

The other two parameters of the `-countByEnumeratingWithState:objects:count:` method are `stackbuf` and `len`. If you are providing your own C array to hold your batches of objects, then both can safely be ignored. The parameter `stackbuf` is a C array of object pointers that you can use to store your objects, and `len` tells you the maximum number of objects you can store. If you want to use this storage instead of managing your own, then `state->itemsPtr` should be set to be the same as `stackbuf`.

Now that we know what the method is supposed to do, it's possible to come up with a few possible implementations. For example, if a custom class that is implementing fast enumeration just wants to allow traversal over a group of objects already contained in a Foundation collection class, then the easiest way to implement fast enumeration is to defer to the collection class itself, like this:

```
- (NSUInteger) countByEnumeratingWithState:
    (NSFastEnumerationState *) state
  objects:(id *) stackbuf count:(NSUInteger)len
{
  return [myCollection countByEnumeratingWithState:state
    objects:stackbuf count:len];
}
```

If a custom class has an actual C array of objects already, and is immutable, the implementation is straightforward. Assume that the C array is called myCArrayOfObjects and that there is an unsigned long integer property named myObjectsCount that holds the number of objects in the C array. This yields one of the simplest implementations possible and sends everything in a single batch:

```
- (NSUInteger) countByEnumeratingWithState:
    (NSFastEnumerationState *) state
  objects:(id *) stackbuf count:(NSUInteger)len
{
  if (state->state == 0)
  { // first call
    state->state = 1; // to flag we've been called
    state->itemsPtr = myCArrayOfObjects;
  }
  else
  { // later calls, only one batch so zero returned now
    return 0;
  }
  return myObjectsCount;
}
```

In the previous example of MYLinkedList, there is no such convenient C array available, so an implementation for that class is best served by using the passed-in storage array. Here is a sample implementation:

```
- (NSUInteger) countByEnumeratingWithState:
    (NSFastEnumerationState *) state
  objects:(id *) stackbuf count:(NSUInteger)len
{
  MYLinkedListNode *currentNode;
  if (nil == (MYLinkedListNode *)state->state)
  { // first call, begin at the start of our list
    currentNode = self.firstNode;
  }
  else
  { // pick up where we left off
    currentNode = (MYLinkedListNode *)state->state;
  }
```

```
  // fill stackbuf with objects from our list
  // until storage is full or we run out of objects
  NSUInteger nodeCount = 0;
  while ((currentNode != self.markerNode) && (nodeCount < len))
  {
    stackbuf[nodeCount] = currentNode.object;
    currentNode = currentNode.nextNode;
    nodeCount++;
  }
  state->state = (unsigned long)currentNode;
  state->itemsPtr = stackbuf;

  // this will change if we are mutated so it's a good guard
  state->mutationsPtr = &listLength;
  return nodeCount;
}
```

Now it is possible to use fast enumeration on `MYLinkedList` instances just as if they were instances of any Foundation collection class. Because `NSEnumerator` already has it's own support for fast enumeration, it is not necessary to make any changes to `MYLinkedListEnumerator` at all. It already supports fast enumeration as it is. Of course, the default implementation is generic and therefore not as efficient as a custom implementation. It is possible to add batching code similar to what we added to `MYLinkedList` to improve the performance of fast enumeration when used with `MYLinkedListEnumerator`, but such improvements are left as an exercise. The main concern is to keep the state information between the Enumerator itself and the fast enumeration code in sync.

For further exploration, download the example code from the book website www.CocoaDesignPatterns.com. The enumeration example creates a `MYLinkedList` with 20 nodes and then iterates through it using a variety of enumeration approaches. It also demonstrates how mutating the list in the middle of enumeration will raise an exception. Finally, by adding a logging statement at the end of the fast enumeration code, it is possible to observe the behavior of the batching process:

```
2008-10-03 17:57:04.436 Enumeration[13663:10b] Fast enumeration called with buffer
size 16; 16 objects loaded.
2008-10-03 17:57:04.437 Enumeration[13663:10b] 1:   String #1
2008-10-03 17:57:04.437 Enumeration[13663:10b] 2:   String #2
2008-10-03 17:57:04.438 Enumeration[13663:10b] 3:   String #3
2008-10-03 17:57:04.438 Enumeration[13663:10b] 4:   String #4
2008-10-03 17:57:04.438 Enumeration[13663:10b] 5:   String #5
2008-10-03 17:57:04.439 Enumeration[13663:10b] 6:   String #6
2008-10-03 17:57:04.439 Enumeration[13663:10b] 7:   String #7
2008-10-03 17:57:04.439 Enumeration[13663:10b] 8:   String #8
2008-10-03 17:57:04.440 Enumeration[13663:10b] 9:   String #9
2008-10-03 17:57:04.446 Enumeration[13663:10b] 10:  String #10
```

```
2008-10-03 17:57:04.449 Enumeration[13663:10b] 11:   String #11
2008-10-03 17:57:04.449 Enumeration[13663:10b] 12:   String #12
2008-10-03 17:57:04.450 Enumeration[13663:10b] 13:   String #13
2008-10-03 17:57:04.451 Enumeration[13663:10b] 14:   String #14
2008-10-03 17:57:04.451 Enumeration[13663:10b] 15:   String #15
2008-10-03 17:57:04.451 Enumeration[13663:10b] 16:   String #16
2008-10-03 17:57:04.452 Enumeration[13663:10b] Fast enumeration called with buffer
size 16; 4 objects loaded.
2008-10-03 17:57:04.452 Enumeration[13663:10b] 17:   String #17
2008-10-03 17:57:04.452 Enumeration[13663:10b] 18:   String #18
2008-10-03 17:57:04.453 Enumeration[13663:10b] 19:   String #19
2008-10-03 17:57:04.453 Enumeration[13663:10b] 20:   String #20
2008-10-03 17:57:04.453 Enumeration[13663:10b] Fast enumeration called with buffer
size 16; 0 objects loaded.
```

Obviously, three method calls will be a bit faster than 20, making fast enumeration more efficient than a standard NSEnumerator loop.

Internal Enumeration

All of the enumeration that has been discussed here is what is known as external or active iteration, meaning that the iteration loop is completely under control of the programmer and external to the collection classes themselves. Cocoa does support another type of iteration, known as internal or passive iteration. Internal or passive iteration is an implied iteration; there is no explicit control over the loop itself, even though the existence of a loop is implied.

For example, consider these two NSArray methods:

```
- (void)makeObjectsPerformSelector:(SEL)aSelector
- (void)makeObjectsPerformSelector:(SEL)aSelector
  withObject:(id)anObject
```

Both of these methods send the same message to every object in an array. They are a shortcut that eliminates the need for an explicit enumeration loop. There is still an unseen loop, of course; the latter of these methods is very likely implemented using fast enumeration as follows:

```
- (void)makeObjectsPerformSelector:(SEL)aSelector
  withObject:(id)anObject
{
  id object;
  for (object in self)
  {
    [object performSelector:aSelector withObject:anObject];
  }
}
```

Examples in Cocoa

It is nearly impossible to do much in Cocoa without encountering enumeration in some form. Most collection classes such as NSArray, NSDictionary, NSSet, NSCountedSet, NSHashTable, NSMapTable, and so on all implement the -objectEnumerator method to return an Enumerator instance. Many collections have other methods that return other Enumerators. NSArray has -reverseObjectEnumerator to perform a different traversal order. NSDictionary and NSMapTable use -keyEnumerator for traversing their keys instead of the contained objects.

Typically the same classes that can create and return Enumerators also support fast enumeration. In general, when fast enumeration is used the traversal will be the same as if the Enumerator returned by the -objectEnumerator method were used normally. Notable exceptions to this are NSDictionary and NSMapTable, which iterate over their keys when fast enumeration is used. When in doubt, always consult Apple's class documentation.

One interesting special case is the NSPointerArray, a new class introduced in 10.5, which can store NULL values. NSEnumerator doesn't work with NSPointerArray because the first NULL returned during contents traversal ends the traversal. The NSPointerArray class does, however, support fast enumeration. This works because fast enumeration implementations return how many references are being batched together. This means that they can return NULL values for some of the objects in the traversal without causing the loop to be exited because loop termination conditions do not depend on the return of a NULL or nil value.

Consequences

Enumerators provide a consistent means of traversing a collection of objects independent of collection type and traversal algorithm. This decoupling allows a developer to change from one type of collection to another or choose different traversal algorithms without incurring the need to change all their collection traversal code.

In Cocoa, enumeration is implemented by subclassing NSEnumerator and by adopting the NSFastEnumeration protocol. In other frameworks, the role of an NSEnumerator is commonly called the Iterator pattern, though Enumerators can also act as a special case of the Strategy pattern by allowing a flexible choice of traversal algorithm.

Because Enumerators retain their own state information, it is possible to have multiple traversals of a given collection pending simultaneously. Typically NSEnumerator subclasses are tightly coupled to specific collection classes and have privileged access to the internal details of the collection's data structures so that they can implement as efficient a traversal algorithm as possible.

Cocoa forbids the modification of mutable collections while they are being enumerated. Some environments attempt to create robust iterators that allow modification of underlying collections. Because of the overhead and complexity of this approach, and the fact that this ability is seldom required in practice, Cocoa chooses to disallow modifications in favor of enhanced thread safety and faster, more efficient code.

Enumerators in Cocoa are unidirectional and cannot be reset. Once the end of an iteration loop is reached, the Enumerator is no longer useful. To traverse again, a new Enumerator must be requested. It's possible to create custom subclasses that have more cursor-like behavior, with the ability to move both forward and backward through a list and even jump to the start, end, or an arbitrary position, but the standard interface defined by Cocoa doesn't support any such behaviors.

9

Perform Selector and Delayed Perform

Selectors identify the messages that are sent to Objective-C objects. They're used by the receivers of messages to select which methods will be performed. Selectors provide much of the power, flexibility, and dynamism of the Objective-C language, and they're used to implement other Cocoa design patterns. In particular, selectors are key to Cocoa's implementation of the Notifications, Delegates, Targets and Actions, Invocations, and Forwarding patterns. Using selectors, Cocoa objects can be asked to perform methods immediately or after arbitrary time delays. Delaying the performance of methods can be very handy and is sometimes used to keep a user interface responsive while long-running tasks complete, implement animation, or provide other time-based application features.

Selectors are an object-oriented substitute for C function pointers. A function pointer is a variable that stores the address of a compiled function. In the C programming language and languages derived from it like Objective-C and C++, compilers and linkers convert explicit function calls in program source code into machine language jumps to code at predetermined fixed addresses in memory. The conversion of code to fixed addresses in sometimes called *binding*. Using a function pointer variable enables programmers to postpone binding of a function call until the program is running. For example, the value of a function pointer might be partly determined by user input at runtime. The technique is sometimes called *late-binding*. Just like using function pointers can postpone specification of precisely what function will be called, using selectors can postpone specification of precisely what message will be sent to an object.

What makes selectors more object-oriented than function pointers, and why are they used instead of function pointers? That's a bit of a trick question because ultimately, Objective-C uses function pointers. The answer involves the implementation of Objective-C message sending as described in the "Solution" section of this chapter, but simply stated, selectors are used by objects to select which method is performed, and then the implementation of the selected method is accessed via a function pointer. The role of the object in the selection of a method is key to object orientation.

Motivation

Use Perform Selector to postpone specifying the message that will be sent to an object until runtime. Reduce coupling between objects by limiting the information that message senders need about the message sent.

Use Perform Selector in combination with the Anonymous Type and Heterogeneous Containers patterns described in Chapter 7, "Anonymous Type and Heterogeneous Containers," to completely decouple the sender of a message from the receiver. At compile time, the sender of a message doesn't need to know what message is sent or what object will receive the message. This capability underlies the Targets and Actions pattern.

Use Delayed Perform to schedule messages to be sent at a specified time in the future.

Use Cocoa's related ability to send messages that will execute in the main thread even if sent from a different thread.

Solution

To describe the detailed role of selectors in Objective-C messaging, it's necessary to introduce the following interdependent concepts:

- Objects have *methods* of performing operations. A *method* is composed of program code that's part of the implementation of an object. The emphasis on the *method* of performing an operation as opposed to the operation itself is important to object-oriented programming because different objects might have different methods of performing the same operation.

- A *message* is a request for an object to *perform* an operation. The object determines which method will be used to perform the operation. The same message can be sent to different objects and produce different results.

- A *selector* identifies the *message* sent to an object, and the object that receives the message uses the selector to select which method to invoke. In some cases, the object might apply complex logic to select a method, or it might forward the message to another object.

With those concepts in mind, using selectors is very straight-forward. Objective-C provides the SEL data type used to declare variables that store selectors.

```
SEL   aSelector;  // declare a variable that stores a selector
```

A selector variable can be initialized using Objective-C's @selector() syntax as follows:

```
SEL   aSelector = @selector(update);
```

Cocoa's NSObject base class provides the -(id)performSelector:(SEL)aSelector method, which is used to send a variable message at runtime. The -performSelector: method can be used in any situation where the message to be sent has no arguments and returns an object.

```
SEL     aSelector = @selector(update);

// These three lines are interchangeable
id      result1 = [someObject update];
id      result2 = [someObject performSelector:@selector(update)];
id      result3 = [someObject performSelector:aSelector];
```

The selector used with -performSelector: doesn't have to be specified at compile time. For example, Cocoa provides the SEL NSSelectorFromString(NSString *) C function that converts a string into a selector. The string could come from any source; it might even be based on user input. A selector can be converted back into a string using Cocoa's NSStringFromSelector() C function.

> Note
>
> Objective-C allows any message to be sent to any object. If the receiver of a message has no specific method of responding to the message, the receiver has many options including forwarding the message to another object, ignoring the message, generating an exception, or reporting an error.

NSObject provides the -(BOOL)respondsToSelector:(SEL)aSelector method that can be used to verify that an object responds to a selector before sending a message. The following code converts a string into a selector but doesn't use the selector unless the object asked to perform can actually respond to the selector:

```
id MYSendMessageToObject(NSString *userEnteredString, someObject)
{
    SEL     aSelector = NSSelectorFromString(userEnteredString)];
    id      result = nil;

    if([someObject respondsToSelector:aSelector])
    {
        result = [someObject performSelector:aSelector];
    }

    return result;
}
```

To send a variable message that requires a single object argument, use NSObject's -(id)performSelector:(SEL)aSelector withObject:(id)anObject method. You can send messages that require two object arguments using NSObject's -(id)performSelector:(SEL)aSelector withObject:(id)anObject withObject:(id)anotherObject method. However, if you need to send a variable message that requires more than two arguments or requires nonobject arguments or returns a nonobject value, you need to use Cocoa's NSInvocation class and the Invocations pattern described in Chapter 20, "Invocations."

Delayed Perform

To send a message after a delay, use NSObject's - (void)performSelector:(SEL)aSelector withObject:(id)anArgument afterDelay:(NSTimeInterval)delay method. The message with the specified selector and argument is scheduled and sent sometime after the specified delay measured in seconds.

Delayed Perform is actually implemented by Cocoa's NSRunLoop class. NSRunLoop is responsible for accepting user input and monitoring a Cocoa application's communication with the underlying operating system. Requests to send delayed messages are queued with the run loop associated with the thread making the request. Each time the run loop checks for user input, it also checks for queued requests. If enough time has elapsed since a queued request was made, the run loop sends the requested message with the specified argument. The run loop may not get a chance to run because the application is busy doing something else. Therefore, the run loop can't guarantee that the requested message will be sent at a precise time. It can only guarantee that it won't be sent too soon. If a zero delay is specified when requesting the delayed message, the message is sent as soon as possible the next time the run loop runs. In all cases, - performSelector:withObject:afterDelay: returns before the requested message is sent.

The NSObject class method, + (void)cancelPreviousPerformRequestsWithTarget: (id)aTarget selector:(SEL)aSelector object:(id)anArgument, can be used to cancel a previously requested delayed message. This will cancel all delayed messages matching the target, selector, and argument specified and queued by the run loop for the thread canceling the request.

The NSRunLoop class can operate in several different modes. The modes determine which sources of input are read by the run loop. The - performSelector:withObject: afterDelay: method schedules requests in the NSDefaultRunLoopMode, so if the run loop isn't in that mode, the requested message won't be sent. To specify which run loop modes are used to queue the delayed message request, use NSObject's - (void)performSelector: (SEL)aSelector withObject:(id)anArgument afterDelay:(NSTimeInterval)delay inModes:(NSArray *)modes method.

The Implementation of Objective-C Message Sending

Message sending using selectors is so fundamental to the design of Cocoa that it's worthwhile to dig into the underlying Objective-C implementation of message sending. You don't necessarily need this information to use the Perform Selector and Delayed Perform patterns in your own code. The implementation of Objective-C messaging is relatively simple, extremely elegant, and makes Cocoa possible.

> Note
>
> Apple's Objective-C runtime is open source and available as part of the Darwin project at http://www.opensource.apple.com/projects/darwin. The GNU Compiler Collection also provides a version of the Objective-C runtime at http://gcc.gnu.org/. Both Apple and the GNU

Compiler Collection's maintainers endeavor to keep the two runtimes compatible and share source code, but historically, features that appear in one version have sometimes taken a while to appear in the other.

The Objective-C language uses a small, fast library of functions and data structures called a *runtime*. Many programming languages use a runtime; Java's Virtual Machine is one of the best known runtimes, but C++ and even C also have runtimes. Objective-C's runtime is primarily written in standard C and can be used from C or C++ programs even if those programs aren't compiled with an Objective-C or Objective-C++ compiler. The Objective-C runtime provides supporting technology used to implement all of Cocoa's design patterns, but some of the patterns in this book are little more than specific applications of language runtime features:

- The runtime enables dynamic loading of Objective-C objects making the Bundles pattern possible.
- The runtime creates all object instances and underlies the Dynamic Creation pattern.
- The runtime directly implements the Category pattern to add methods to existing classes.
- The runtime implements the messaging that is key to the Perform Selector and Delayed Perform patterns and the Proxies and Forwarding patterns.

Messaging is implemented with the following two C functions or variations based on return types and platform-specific function calling conventions:

```
id objc_msgSend(id self, SEL op, ...);
id objc_msgSendSuper(struct objc_super *super, SEL op, ...);
```

The messaging functions are the core of Objective-C. When the Objective-C compiler encounters a messaging expression such as [receiver someMessageSelector], it replaces that expression with code to call objc_msgSend(receiver, @selector(someMessageSelector)) in the compiled result. The objc_msgSend() function searches for a method implemented by the receiver that corresponds to the specified selector. More details about the search for a method that corresponds to a selector are provided in the "How Messaging Works" section of Apple's documentation at http://developer.apple.com/documentation/Cocoa/Conceptual/ObjectiveC/Articles/chapter_4_6.html. If the search doesn't find a suitable method, the message may be forwarded to another object as described by the Proxies and Forwarding patterns.

If a suitable method is found, a corresponding C function pointer is used to call a function that implements the method. Function pointers that correspond to method implementations are stored in variables with the IMP type declared as follows: typedef id (*IMP)(id self, SEL _cmd, ...);.

The first two arguments to the function referenced by an IMP are the same receiver and selector arguments passed to objc_msgSend(id self, SEL op, ...). Within the method implementation, the receiver is the self variable used by the method. Additional arguments to a method are also passed to the method implementation. Apple's Objective-C runtime uses platform-specific assembly language to make additional arguments available to the method implementation. The GNU Objective-C runtime uses portable C code to achieve the same result but suffers a small performance penalty when used with some CPU platforms.

The `objc_msgSendSuper(struct objc_super *super, SEL op, ...)` function works exactly the same way as `objc_msgSend(id self, SEL op, ...)` except that `objc_msgSendSuper(struct objc_super *super, SEL op, ...)` begins the search for a method with the receiver's superclass and doesn't consider any methods implemented by the receiver itself. The Objective-C compiler generates a call to `objc_msgSendSuper()` when it encounters a messaging expression containing the `super` keyword such as `[super someMessageSelector]`.

> **Note**
>
> Searching for a method to invoke can be time-consuming. Apple's Objective-C runtime avoids the search in most cases by caching the IMP for each selector within the class itself. When the messaging functions are called, they check the cache for an IMP that corresponds to the specified selector. Most of the time, the IMP is found in the cache, and no search takes place.

You can convert any code that sends messages into a function call via an IMP. Cocoa's NSObject base class provides methods to obtain an IMP directly:

```
- (IMP)methodForSelector:(SEL)aSelector;
+ (IMP)instanceMethodForSelector:(SEL)aSelector;
```

Now all of the pieces are in place, and the `- (id)performSelector:(SEL)aSelector` method itself can be implemented with the following code:

```
- (id) performSelector:(SEL)aSelector
{
    IMP      methodImplementation = [self methodForSelector:aSelector];

    return (*IMP)(self, aSelector);
}
```

Examples in Cocoa

Selectors are used extensively in Cocoa. The `-performSelector:` method and related support provided by the NSObject base class are extended in a variety ways. Two of Cocoa's collection classes, NSArray and NSSet, implement the following methods to send a variable message to every object in the collection:

```
- (void)makeObjectsPerformSelector:(SEL)aSel
- (void)makeObjectsPerformSelector:(SEL)aSel withObject:(id)anObject
```

Cocoa's other prominent collection class, `NSDictionary`, provides arrays of all contained values and all contained keys via the `- (NSArray *)allValues` and `- (NSArray *)allKeys` methods, respectively. You can use the arrays to indirectly send a variable message to all objects contained in a dictionary.

Sending messages to the objects in a collection can often be used instead of the Enumerators pattern described in Chapter 8, "Enumerators." You shouldn't rely on the order in which messages are sent to a collection's contents when using the `-makeObjectsPerformSelector:` and `-makeObjectsPerformSelector:withObject:` methods. Nor should the messages sent change the collections themselves. Enumerators are a better choice if the order is important or you need the return values from the individual messages that are sent.

The Notifications pattern in Chapter 14, "Notifications," enables objects to register for messages to be sent in response to future events. The message to be sent is variable and specified using a selector. Inside the implementation of the `NSNotificationCenter` class, the `-perfromSelector:withObject:` method is used to actually send the messages.

The messages sent to a Delegate object are usually predefined, but the object that sends the delegate messages must first determine whether the delegate can respond. The Delegates pattern in Chapter 15, "Delegates," shows an example using `NSObject`'s `-respondsToSelector:` method.

Cocoa's Invocation pattern is used in several situations including automatic undo/redo support and distributed messaging via the Proxies pattern. Invocation is described in Chapter 20, and Proxies are described in Chapter 27, "Proxies and Forwarding." The Invocation pattern and the `NSInvocation` class provide a more complete implementation of late binding of messages than the simple `-performSelector:` method. `NSInvocation` can store messages that have nonobject return types or require complex arguments. `NSInvocation` stores the selector of the message to send along with the receiver of the message and all arguments.

Cocoa's Targets and Actions Pattern in Chapter 17, "Outlets, Targets, and Actions," shows how powerful and flexible late binding with selector can be. An Action is really just a variable selector, and the target is just an anonymous object as described in Chapter 7. It's late binding, the ability to postpone the specification of the Action, and the Target until runtime that makes the Targets and Actions pattern so useful.

Last but not least, one of Cocoa's most interesting variations of the Perform Selector pattern is the ability to safely send messages that will execute in the main thread even if the messages originate from a different thread. This isn't a general solution for interthread messaging, but it can be supremely handy. The main thread is the one in which the `main()` C function executes. For example, most AppKit drawing has to be performed on the main thread. Nonmain threads send messages to the main thread to request AppKit-based drawing.

Just like Cocoa's implementation of Delayed Perform, messages sent from other threads can be queued with the main thread's run loop for future execution. Also like Delayed Perform, the mode of the run loop must sometimes be considered. The following methods make it possible:

```
- (void)performSelectorOnMainThread:(SEL)aSelector withObject:(id)arg
waitUntilDone:(BOOL)wait
```

```
- (void)performSelectorOnMainThread:(SEL)aSelector withObject:(id)arg
waitUntilDone:(BOOL)wait modes:(NSArray *)array
```

When sending a message to be performed on the main thread, it's not possible to retrieve the return value, if any, from the message. The `waitUntilDone:` argument enables you to specify whether the sending thread should continue to execute asynchronously or block until the message has been executed on the main thread. Unlike with Delayed Perform, once a message has been queued to execute in the main thread, it can't be canceled.

Consequences

The Perform Selector and Delayed Perform patterns make it possible to send variable messages and send messages at variable times in the future. These patterns provide a partial substitute for the famous Command design pattern described at http://en.wikipedia.org/wiki/Command_pattern. The Invocations pattern explained in Chapter 20 is a more complete implementation of the Command pattern.

From a software engineering perspective, Perform Selector and Delayed Perform are an application of late-binding to object-oriented systems. Objective-C and programming languages such as Smalltalk, Ruby, and Python have language level runtime support for various forms of late binding. Microsoft's Common Language Runtime and the C# programming language also support late-binding. To understand the consequences of language level support for late binding as used by Cocoa and implemented by Objective-C, it's helpful to compare it to the alternative approaches.

Framework developers have attempted to bolt-on object-oriented implementations of late binding for many programming languages. Some prominent examples include Microsoft's Component Object Model (COM) and later the Distributed Component Object Model (DCOM), which became known as Active-X. COM provides late binding, and DCOM uses the late binding to enable communication between objects over a network. The Object Management Group's Common Object Request Broker Architecture (CORBA) adds late binding and a variation of messaging over a network to a wide variety of programming languages. All of the bolt-on approaches either require that programmers learn and use an additional language like CORBA's Interface Definition Language (IDL) or write extensive and tedious code to use late binding.

In contrast, Cocoa uses late binding ubiquitously and therefore doesn't require extensive use of the Command pattern or an Interface Definition Language. All Objective-C messages use late binding, so there is no extra code to write when late binding is needed. The .NET framework and frameworks for Smalltalk, Ruby, and Python similarly enable late binding with little or no special code. Frameworks built on top of languages that intrinsically support late binding are able to implement distributed communication between objects without requiring a lot of special effort from programmers. For example, Cocoa's Proxies and Forwarding patterns enable programmers to send messages to anonymous objects over a network in exactly the same way the messages are sent to local objects. The .NET framework uses a similar technique.

10

Accessors

The Accessors pattern (also known as "setters and getters") describes a technique for funneling all access to an object's properties through well-defined and easy to recognize methods called *accessors*. Properties are often stored as instance variables but in some cases may be stored a different way or calculated as needed. The Accessors pattern maximizes implementation flexibility while minimizing opportunities for errors. The Accessors pattern provides the following benefits:

- **Implementation flexibility.** Properties can be stored as instance variables or using other techniques such as the Associative Storage pattern, and the implementation can be changed without breaking other code.

- **Minimum maintenance burden.** All uses of an object's properties are funneled through a few methods limiting the number of places where code needs to change if properties change.

- **Simple usage of Cocoa's reference counted memory management conventions.** Restricting memory management to Accessor methods provides the simplest way to adhere to Cocoa's conventions and isolates memory management code to just a few methods.

- **Support Cocoa Key Value Coding and Key Value Observing technologies.** The Key Value Coding and Key Value Observing technologies won't work with your classes unless you provide correctly named Accessor methods. Cocoa Bindings (Chapter 32, "Binding and Controllers") require Key Value Coding and Key Value Observing.

- Enable special processing when Outlets connected in Interface Builder are reestablished during .nib loading.

The crucial role that accessors play in the Associative Storage pattern is described in Chapter 19, "Associative Storage." The Accessor pattern helps to encapsulate data and operations on that data in the best tradition of object-oriented programming. Consistent use of the Accessor pattern is particularly important when using Cocoa without the optional automatic memory garbage collection introduced with Mac OS X 10.5. Without garbage collection, Cocoa's reference counted memory management conventions must be followed to avoid serious errors. Many of the bugs in computer programs are byproducts of dynamic memory allocation problems, and the Accessor pattern helps to reduce the number of places in code where memory allocation problems can occur.

This chapter describes several common implementations of accessors and focuses on the interaction between accessors and Cocoa's reference counted memory management conventions. Reference counted memory management is explained in detail because Cocoa objects need to support it for the foreseeable future—at least until automatic memory garbage collection becomes ubiquitous. Using accessors reduces the programming burden of reference counted memory management.

> ### Note
>
> The Objective C 2.0 language introduced the @property and @synthesize compiler directives to formalize property declaration and generate correctly named accessor methods for you. This chapter explains how to write your own accessor methods and the code that is generated by @synthesize. Objective C 2.0 @property syntax is briefly explained in the "Copying Objective-C 2.0 Properties" section of Chapter 12, "Copying."

Motivation

Funnel access to an object's properties through methods to hide implementation details and confine code related to memory management to those methods. Cocoa's reference counted memory management provides a relatively simple pragmatic solution to the difficult problem of memory management, but patterns must be applied to use reference counting correctly, and accessors play a pivotal role in keeping memory management simple.

Enable use of higher level Cocoa technologies like Bindings, Key Value Coding, and key Value Observing with your custom classes.

Solution

Accessors are methods used to set and get the properties of an object. The simplest accessor is a method that returns the value of a nonobject instance variable. For example, given an object that stores an interest rate as a floating point instance variable named interestRate, the following method implementation returns that value:

```
- (float)interestRate
{
  return interestRate;
}
```

Even though the method is extremely simple, it's still a good idea to provide the accessor method rather than directly accessing to the variable throughout your code. If all code that uses the interest rate calls the accessor to obtain the value, the implementation of the class can safely be changed in the future. For example, it may not be necessary to store the interest rate in an instance variable if the value can be computed as needed. When using accessors, the implementation of the - (float)interestRate method can be changed to return a calculated value or a value obtained from a server without concern that the change will break code elsewhere in an application.

Accessors that return values directly are named after the value returned. The `interestRate` value is returned by the `-interestRate` method. Cocoa uses the word `get` in the name of an accessor to indicate that a value will be returned indirectly by reference. The following implementation returns the interest rate by reference:

```
- (void)getInterestRate:(float *)aFloatPtr
{
  if(NULL != aFloatPtr)
  {
    *aFloatPtr = interestRate;
  }
}
```

There is seldom a reason to return values by reference, and accessors with the word `get` in their names are rare within Cocoa. Cocoa normally returns even complex C structures by value. As long as the size of the value to be returned is constant, the value should be returned directly. Methods like NSData's `- (void)getBytes:(void *)aBuffer` return values by reference because the number of bytes that will be returned can't be determined at compile time. Other examples of `get` methods include NSArray's `- (void)getObjects:(id *)aBuffer`, NSString's `- (void)getCharacters:(unichar *)aBuffer`, and NSValue's `- (void)getValue:(void *)aBuffer`. In each case, the size of the value copied into the referenced memory is variable. Another reason for returning values by reference is to enable the return of more than one value from a single method. A good example of that is NSColor's `- (void)getRed:(CGFloat *)red green:(CGFloat *)green blue:(CGFloat *)blue alpha:(CGFloat *)alpha` method, which returns four floating point values by reference.

Accessors for setting nonobject properties are also straightforward. The interest rate stored by an object can be set by calling a `- (void)setInterestRate:(float)aRate` method with the following implementation:

```
- (void)setInterestRate:(float)aRate
{
    interestRate = aRate;
}
```

It's important to provide `set` accessors for the same reasons accessors that return values are important. As long as there is only one method used to set a property of an object, the technique used to store that property can be changed without affecting other code. Confining property changes to the implementation of accessors simplifies debugging. During debugging, if a property has an incorrect or suspicious value, a debugger break-point set within the implementation of an accessor halts execution whenever the property is changed and helps track down how and why the value is being changed incorrectly.

The accessors that set values are often more complex than the implementation shown so far. `Set` accessors are a natural place to implement application logic that constrains values, notifies other objects of changes to a property, or prompts recalculation of values based on the property changed. For objects that display values, schedule redisplay after a property is changed within an accessor. For example, the NSTextField class in the Application Kit Framework implements its - (void) setIntValue: (int) aValue method as similar to the following:

```
- (void)setIntValue:(int)aValue
{
  [[self cell] setIntValue:aValue];   // Set the value stored by the associated
                                      // NSCell instance
  [self setNeedsDisplay:YES];         // Schedule redisplay
}
```

Cocoa consistently provides accessors for nonobject properties, and doing so in your own classes is usually a good idea. Accessors for object properties are even more important because they provide an ideal place to centralize memory management in code. Cocoa's reference counted memory management system is simple, powerful, and flexible, but a clear understanding of the system is essential for correct use of Cocoa classes and for the implementation of accessors in your own classes.

Reference Counted Memory Management

The memory used by Cocoa objects is allocated dynamically as needed. Whenever memory is allocated, the application has to keep track of the memory and remember to deallocate (free) it when it is no longer needed. Failure to deallocate memory that is no longer needed constitutes a memory leak and can cause serious performance problems as a program runs. A severe memory leak will eventually cause an application to crash.

As of Mac OS X 10.5, Cocoa provides a built-in memory management feature called *automatic garbage collection*. With automatic garbage collection, the programming language runtime environment detects when allocated memory is no longer used and automatically deallocates it. Automatic garbage collection can prevent many memory allocation errors, but it doesn't come for free. Historically, automatic garbage collection has had a negative performance impact on software and in some cases restricts the type of software that can be written. For example, it's difficult to use automatic garbage collection in conjunction with the type of distributed messaging technology provided by Cocoa. Cocoa provides a high performance multithreaded garbage collector, but it's optional. The garbage collector is not available for the iPhone as of version 3.0. If you use any code that doesn't work with automatic garbage collection (perhaps because the code predates the introduction of automatic garbage collection), you need to support the older reference counted memory management.

The NSObject base class provides a set of methods for incrementing and decrementing a counter that is automatically stored for each object as needed. The counters keep track of how many other objects reference (use) each object. Chapter 19 includes an example that shows a partial implementation of the reference counting system.

When a Cocoa object is first allocated, it has an implicit reference count of one. If the reference count ever reaches zero, the object is immediately deallocated. If an object needs to store a reference to another object, the reference count of the referenced object is increased by calling the `-retain` method declared in `NSObject`. When an object no longer needs a reference to another object, the reference count of the referenced objects is decreased by calling the `-release` method. Each object starts out with a reference count of one; therefore, it will not be deallocated until it is released as many times as it has been retained plus one additional release corresponding to the original allocation. As long as objects follow the convention of calling `-retain` and `-release` when appropriate, no object is deallocated while it is still being used, and all objects are deallocated as soon they are no longer being used.

Reference counted memory management is less convenient than automatic garbage collection because programmers must remember to call `-retain` and `-release` instead of relying on the language runtime to take care of things. Furthermore, reference counted memory management is a bit more complicated than has been revealed so far, but it's flexible, fast, convenient, and works well with distributed objects. Information about Cocoa's reference counted memory management is available from many sources including Apple's own Objective-C documentation provided with the developer tools at /Developer/Documentation/Cocoa/ObjectiveC/4objc_runtime_overview/Object_Ownership.html. General guidelines and more detailed explanations are available at http://www.stepwise.com/Articles/Technical/MemoryManagement.html, http://www.stepwise.com/Articles/Technical/2001-03-11.01.html, and http://www.stepwise.com/Articles/Technical/HoldMe.html.

Accessors That Manage Retain Counts

The following examples of accessor methods take into account Cocoa memory management conventions when setting and returning object properties. The simplest way to return an object value from an accessor is to return it directly. Given an object that stores a "title" property as an `NSString` instance variable named `_myTitle`, the title is returned by the `-(NSString *)title` method as follows:

```
- (NSString *)title
{
  return _myTitle;
}
```

Note

In the example, a property named "title" is stored in an instance variable named `_myTitle`. The Accessor method name must match the property name to be presented to users of a class, but the implementation of the method is free to supply the property value using any appropriate logic. Property names and instance variable names do not have to correspond.

The `-title` implementation is adequate in most cases, but a more sophisticated technique may be necessary if the application using the title is multithreaded. In a multithreaded application, there is a chance that another thread of execution may alter _myTitle or release it after it has been returned from the -title method but before the code that called -title has had an opportunity to retain the returned object. In that case, _myTitle's retain count may reach zero, and the object may be deallocated, leaving the code that called -title with a pointer to a deallocated (invalid) object.

One solution that supports the multithreaded case is to retain and autorelease the object being returned as follows:

```
- (NSString *)title
{
  id        result;

  // Lock
  result = [[_myTitle retain] autorelease];
  // Unlock

  return result];
}
```

Each call to -autorelease schedules a call to -release that will happen after a delay. The -autorelease method can be called in any situation that -release is called, but it's less efficient than -release because of extra logic and data structures needed to implement the delay. Retaining and autoreleasing the object to be returned assures that the object's reference count will not reach zero before the calling code has an opportunity to retain it.

The comments that specify Lock and Unlock show where *locks* are needed to assure thread safety. You must use locks and be aware of possible *deadlock* scenarios in some cases. Locks and deadlocks are described in an online document that is frequently updated at http://developer.apple.com/techpubs/macosx/Cocoa/TasksAndConcepts/ProgrammingTopics/Multithreading/Multithreading.html. Links on that page describe a variety of safe interthread and interprocess communication strategies. A version of the document is also installed with Apple's developer tools at /Developer/Documentation/Cocoa/TasksAndConcepts/ProgrammingTopics/Multithreading/index.html.

> **Note**
>
> In most cases, a lock used in a get accessor must also be used in the corresponding set accessor. In addition, the lock object must be created before any calls to either accessor. Multithreaded programming is a difficult topic outside the scope of this book.

The most common implementation of a set accessor for an object property uses the pattern shown in the following implementation of the -(void)setTitle:(NSString *)aTitle method:

```
- (void)setTitle:(NSString *)aTitle
{
  [aTitle retain];
```

```
[_myTitle release];

_myTitle = aTitle;
}
```

The `aTitle` argument will be stored as the new value of the `_myTitle` instance variable. The new object to be stored must be retained so that it isn't deallocated while it is still being used. The old object stored in the instance variable is released because it is no longer being used. If no other object has retained the old value, it is immediately deallocated when it is released. Finally, the `_myTitle` instance variable is assigned the new value.

Note

Objective-C objects are always stored and passed by reference. The `_myTitle` instance variable is actually a pointer to an object. The `aTitle` argument is a pointer to another object. When the statement `_myTitle = aTitle;` is executed, only a pointer is copied. The `_myTtle` instance variable is set to point to the same object as `aTitle`.

The order in which a new object value is retained and the old value released is important. The `set` Accessor can be called with a `nil` argument, an object argument that references a different object than one already stored, or an argument that references the same object already stored. In any of these cases, the existing stored object property may be `nil`. The following describes the `set` Accessor's behavior in each case:

- The argument to the `set` Accessor is `nil`—The retain message is harmlessly sent to `nil`. It's safe to send any message to `nil` as long as you don't count on any return value. The currently stored object is released. Finally, `nil` is stored as the new value of the object property.
- The argument references an object that isn't already stored—The new object is retained so that it will not be deallocated. The old object is released and will be deallocated if it's not retained by any other objects. Finally, a pointer to the new object is stored as the value of the property being set.
- The argument references the same object that is already stored—The referenced object already has a retain count of at least one because it is being used. The first thing the `set` Accessor does is retain the object causing its retain count to be no less than two. The object reference already stored is released, but because it is the same object that was just retained, its retain count drops to no less than one. Finally a harmless pointer assignment that sets the property to the same value already stored takes place.

The case in which the object passed as an argument to a `set` Accessor is the same as the object already stored is critical. If the order of the retain and release is changed, it is possible that the object value will be released and immediately deallocated before the assignment takes place. Then the object property is left storing a pointer to a deallocated object.

The set Accessor pattern shown for the -setTitle: method must be implemented differently to address multithreading issues. The multithread safe version uses the following pattern:

```
- (void)setTitle:(NSString *)aTitle
{
  id     oldValue;

  [aTitle retain];

  // Lock
  oldValue = _myTitle;
  _myTitle = aTitle;
  // Unlock

  [oldValue release];
}
```

There are many subtle issues related to multithreading, and using the accessor implementations shown or related variations is necessary but not sufficient to ensure correct behavior in all cases. In most cases, it isn't worthwhile to try and implement thread safe accessors. When the same object must be used within multiple threads, it's often better to require explicit locks in the code that calls the accessors or use one of the interthread communications techniques described at /Developer/Documentation/Cocoa/TasksAndConcepts/ProgrammingTopics/Multithreading/index.html.

Confining Memory Management to Accessors

If the Accessors pattern is consistently applied, almost all memory management for objects can be confined to accessors. When initializing object instances, use a set accessor to set the value of each object property. For example, the following implementation of -(id)initWithStringValue:(NSString *)aValue method uses an accessor to store the string value rather than making a direct assignment to an instance variable:

```
- (id)initWithStringValue:(NSString *)aValue
{
  self = [super init];

  [self setStringValue:aValue]; // set the initial value of the property

  return self;
}
```

The process of initializing instances is described in Chapter 3, "Two-Stage Creation."

The -dealloc method can indirectly release referenced objects using the set accessors and avoid memory management code in its implementation as follows:

```
- (void)dealloc
{
  [self setStringValue:nil];      // any previous string value is released

  [super dealloc];
}
```

Note

Some programmers have historically avoided using accessors within initializer methods and -dealloc because a subclass may override inherited accessors to cause side effects. Using the overridden accessors within the superclass's initializer might invoke side effects before the subclass instance is fully initialized. Similarly, accessors called from within the superclass's -dealloc may cause side effects in partially deallocated instances. However, there is no practical alternative to using accessors when you use synthesized instance variables with the modern Objective-C 2.0 runtime or use properties that are not implemented as instance variables. In such cases, accessors provide the only way to initialize the properties or set the properties to nil.

Mutability

The accessors described so far have been implemented to set and return the values of instance variables directly. When setting or returning the values of object instance variables, the mutability of objects must be considered. Mutability refers to the ability of objects to change state during their lifetimes. If an object is immutable, it is created with a certain state or set of properties that don't change until the object is deallocated. The state or properties of mutable objects can be changed any number of times. Many classes in Cocoa's Foundation framework are available in both immutable and mutable forms. For example, both the NSString and NSMutableString classes exist along with the NSArray and NSMutableArray classes and others.

If a pointer to a mutable instance variable is returned from an Accessor method, the encapsulation of the class that owns the instance variable might be violated. The state or properties of the returned object could be changed without the knowledge of other objects that store references to the modified object. This isn't a danger when immutable objects are returned.

So far, the examples of accessors for the _myTitle instance variable have assumed that the object stored by _myTitle is immutable. If _myTitle is stored as a mutable string, it can still be safely returned from a get Accessor that claims to return an immutable object. The following complete class definition shows variations on Accessor methods when mutable objects are involved:

```
@interface MYTitleStorage
{
  NSMutableString    *_myTitle;
}
```

```
@end
```

```objc
@implementation MYTitleStorage

- (id)init
{
  self = [super init];

  [self setTitle:@"Default Title"];

  return self;
}


- (NSString *)title
{
  return _myTitle;  // This is safe because the type we claim to return
                    // is immutable, and other programmers should
                    // respect that
}

- (NSMutableString *)mutableTitle
{
  // Return a copy of the instance variable so that changes made to
  // the copy do not affect the instance variable
  return [[_myTitle mutableCopy] autorelease];
}


- (void)setTitle:(NSString *)aTitle
{
  NSMutableString    *newValue = [aTitle mutableCopy];

  [_myTitle release];
  _myTitle = newValue;
}


- (void)dealloc
{
  [self setTitle:nil];

  [super dealloc];
}

@end
```

Accessors that handle mutable object properties often use the `- (id)mutableCopy` method declared by the NSMutableCopying protocol to copy the object passed in or returned so that no reference to the mutable instance variable is available outside the class where it's stored. When the -mutableCopy message is received by an object, a new copy of the receiver is returned. The returned object has a retain count of one and must eventually be released or autoreleased. The Copying pattern is explained in Chapter 12 and the -mutableCopy method is documented in the Foundation framework and at /Developer/Documentation/Cocoa/Reference/Foundation/ObjC_classic/Protocols/NSMutableCopying.html.

NSKeyValueCoding

Cocoa's NSKeyValueCoding informal protocol is defined as part of the Foundation framework and documented at /Developer/Documentation/Cocoa/Reference/Foundation/ObjC_classic/Protocols/NSKeyValueCoding.html. Informal protocols are explained in Chapter 6, "Category." In the simplest terms, informal protocols are groups of methods that you can assume are available for use even when you are dealing with an anonymous object.

NSKeyValueCoding defines a mechanism for accessing an object's properties by name. The primary methods that enable this access are -setValue:(id)aValue forKey:(NSString *)aKey and -(id)valueForKey:(NSString *)aKey, which set and get named properties, respectively. In all cases, the Key: argument is a reference to an NSString instance that stores the name of the property being accessed. The Value: argument of the -setValue:forKey: method requires a reference to an object as its argument, and -valueForKey: returns an object reference. Nonobject properties are set and returned by wrapping them in instances of Cocoa's NSValue class.

In some respects, the NSKeyValueCoding protocol provides an alternative to using accessor methods. However, accessor methods are such a good idea that even NSKeyValueCoding protocol methods operate with the help of accessor methods whenever possible. To set or return an object's properties, the NSKeyValueCoding methods use the following techniques in order:

1. Check for the existence of accessor methods named -<key> or -get<Key> and use the methods if possible to return a value. Check for the existence of a method named -set<Key>: and use it to set values. For both the -get<Key> and -set<Key>: methods, the first letter of the Key string is made uppercase to be consistent with Cocoa's method naming conventions.

2. If an accessor method based directly on the key name is not available, check methods named -_<key>, -_get<Key>, and -_set<Key>:.

3. If no accessor method is found, attempt to directly access an instance variable. The instance variable can be named either <key> or _<key>.

4. Finally, if the property cannot be accessed through accessor methods or directly through an instance variable, invoke one of the NSKeyValueCoding methods -handleQueryWithUnboundKey: or -handleTakeValue:forUnboundKey: as appropriate. The default implementations of these methods raise an exception, but you can override the methods to do something else.

The NSKeyValueCoding protocol declares other methods that are not described here. The important thing about NSKeyValueCoding in the context of accessors is the fact that even NSKeyValueCoding methods use accessors. If you implement appropriate accessors, you can be confident that they will be called whenever your object's properties are accessed.

> **Note**
>
> Cocoa's nib file loading code doesn't use NSKeyValueCoding methods as of Mac OS X version 10.2, but nib loading employs similar strategies for setting object properties. If you provide Accessor methods, the nib loading code will use them. If you don't, your object's properties will be set directly when possible. The Cocoa frameworks don't raise exceptions if properties are not available or can't be set when loading a nib file.

Interface Builder Outlets

Outlets are instance variables that can be connected to point to other objects within Apple's Interface Builder application as explained in Chapter 17, "Outlets, Targets, and Actions." Interface Builder saves all of the interconnected objects into files with the .xib extension by using the Archiving and Unarchiving pattern explained in Chapter 11, "Archiving and Unarchiving." As the objects are loaded (unarchived) into a running Cocoa application, the outlets are reconnected. If you provide properly named accessor methods for your object's outlets, your methods will be called to set the values of the outlets. Your accessor methods are free to perform additional processing as needed. It's very important that if you implement set accessor methods, they actually set the value of the affected outlets, or else the connections established in Interface Builder will not be reestablised when the .nib file is loaded. If you don't provide a properly named set accessor method for each outlet, Cocoa's .nib loading code will set the outlet variable directly using Objective-C runtime functions.

Objective-C 2.0 Properties

The Objective-C 2.0 language introduced with Mac OS X 10.5 provides new syntax for declaring object properties and reduces the amount of typing needed to use the Accessors pattern in your own classes. If you use the @synthesize directive, the Objective-C 2.0 compiler automatically generates Accessor methods for you based on the way you have declared Properties. The new Properties syntax is self-documenting. It clarifies how the Accessor methods behave right in the class declaration.

The new Property declaration syntax is explained at http://developer.apple.com/documentation/Cocoa/Conceptual/ObjectiveC/Introduction/chapter_1_1.html. The key to understanding the new syntax is to realize that it's optional and doesn't provide any significant new capability. Using Properties syntax primarily just reduces the amount of typing needed to implement new classes. However, the code generated by the compiler in response to @synthesize does not suffer from human error and automatically works correctly with memory management, Key Value Coding, Key Value Observing, and Interface Builder whether you are using automatic garbage collection.

Examples in Cocoa

Cocoa classes provide accessors for all properties that can be examined or set outside the class where they are used. Generally, there is no reason to ever directly access the instance variables of a Cocoa class except when writing a subclass, and even then the practice is uncommon. For example, when writing a subclass of Cocoa's NSView class, it is possible to directly access NSView's _subviews instance variable. However, it's almost always better to access the property through NSView's -(NSArray *)subviews method. Using the accessor makes the subclass's code more flexible and leaves open the possibility that the implementation of the superclass can change without automatically breaking all subclasses. The same principle applies in almost every case when subclassing a Cocoa object.

As a further example of the ability to preserve flexibility in the implementation of classes by using accessors instead of direct references, consider another property of NSView. Each NSView instance stores a reference to its superview and a reference to the window that contains the view respectively in the _superview and _window instance variables. Because each NSView instance is always in the same window as its superview, the implementation of NSView could be changed so that a single instance variable stores either a reference to a superview or a reference to a window. Views that have a superview store that reference. Views that don't have a superview store a reference to the window that contains the view. NSView's -(id)window method is then implemented to return the window if there is no superview or the result of [[self superview] window] if there is a superview. This example is a bit contrived because there is no compelling reason to optimize the storage of NSView instances by reducing the number of instance variables, but it shows the degree of flexibility enabled by consistent use of accessors. The flexibility provided by accessors is even more important in classes that you choose to redesign or reimplement many times in the life of a software product.

Cocoa accessors that return nonobject properties by value are so common that there is no point in listing them here. Just keep in mind that nonobject properties are almost always returned by value even if the properties have complex types. For example, methods like NSView's -(NSRect)frame and -(NSRect)bounds return NSRect structures by value. The -(void)setFrame:(NSRect)aRect and -setBounds:(NSRect)aRect Accessors require NSRect structure arguments passed by value. As another example, NSValue's -(NSRange)rangeValue Accessor returns an NSRange structure by value.

Cocoa classes rarely provide accessors that return nonobject properties by reference, and such Accessor methods always include the word "get" in their names. This type of Accessor is only used when the size of the property returned is variable or multiple values are returned by one method. Table 10.1 lists all of the common Cocoa Accessor methods that return nonobject values by reference and the classes that provide the methods.

Table 10.1   **The Accessor Methods That Return Nonobject Values by Reference**

Class	Accessor
NSArray	- (void)getObjects:(id *)objects - (void)getObjects:(id *)objects range:(NSRange)range
NSData	- (void)getBytes:(void *)buffer - (void)getBytes:(void *)buffer length:(unsigned)length - (void)getBytes:(void *)buffer range:(NSRange)range
NSFormatter	- (BOOL)getObjectValue:(id *)obj forString:(NSString *)string errorDescription:(NSString **)error
NSInvocation	- (void)getReturnValue:(void *)retLoc - (void)getArgument:(void *)argumentLocation atIndex:(int)index
NSMethodSignature	- (const char *)getArgumentTypeAtIndex:(unsigned)index
NSPathUtilities	- (BOOL)getFileSystemRepresentation:(char *)cname maxLength:(unsigned)max
NSRunLoop	- (CFRunLoopRef)getCFRunLoop
NSString	- (void)getCharacters:(unichar *)buffer - (void)getCharacters:(unichar *)buffer range:(NSRange)aRange - (void)getLineStart:(unsigned *)startPtr end:(unsigned *)lineEndPtr contentsEnd:(unsigned *)contentsEndPtr forRange:(NSRange)range - (void)getCString:(char *)bytes - (void)getCString:(char *)bytes maxLength:(unsigned)maxLength - (void)getCString:(char *)bytes maxLength:(unsigned)maxLength range:(NSRange)aRange remainingRange:(NSRangePointer)leftoverRange
NSBezierPath	- (void)getLineDash:(float *)pattern count:(int *)count phase:(float *)phase
NSValue	- (void)getValue:(void *)value
NSBitmapImageRep	- (void)getBitmapDataPlanes:(unsigned char **)data - (void)getCompression:(NSTIFFCompression *)compression factor:(float *)factor + (void)getTIFFCompressionTypes:(const NSTIFFCompression **)list count:(int *)numTypes
NSButtonCell	- (void)getPeriodicDelay:(float *)delay interval:(float *)interval

Table 10.1   **The Accessor Methods That Return Nonobject Values by Reference**

Class	Accessor
NSButton	- (void)getPeriodicDelay:(float *)delay interval:(float *)interval
NSCell	- (void)getPeriodicDelay:(float *)delay interval:(float *)interval
NSColor	- (void)getRed:(float *)red green:(float *)green blue:(float *)blue alpha:(float *)alpha
	- (void)getHue:(float *)hue saturation:(float *)saturation brightness:(float *)brightness alpha:(float *)alpha
	- (void)getWhite:(float *)white alpha:(float *)alpha
	- (void)getCyan:(float *)cyan magenta:(float *)magenta yellow:(float *)yellow black:(float *)black alpha:(float *)alpha
NSLayoutManager	- (unsigned)getGlyphs:(NSGlyph *)glyphArray range:(NSRange)glyphRange
	- (void)getFirstUnlaidCharacterIndex:(unsigned *)charIndex glyphIndex:(unsigned *)glyphIndex
	- (unsigned)getGlyphsInRange:(NSRange)glyphsRange glyphs:(NSGlyph *)glyphBuffer characterIndexes:(unsigned *)charIndexBuffer glyphInscriptions:(NSGlyphInscription *)inscribeBuffer elasticBits:(BOOL *)elasticBuffer bidiLevels:(unsigned char *)bidiLevelBuffer
	- (unsigned)getGlyphsInRange:(NSRange)glyphsRange glyphs:(NSGlyph *)glyphBuffer characterIndexes:(unsigned *)charIndexBuffer glyphInscriptions:(NSGlyphInscription *)inscribeBuffer elasticBits:(BOOL *)elasticBuffer
NSMatrix	- (void)getNumberOfRows:(int *)rowCount columns:(int *)colCount
	- (BOOL)getRow:(int *)row column:(int *)col ofCell:(NSCell *)aCell
	- (BOOL)getRow:(int *)row column:(int *)col forPoint:(NSPoint)aPoint
NSOpenGL	- (void)getValues:(long*)vals forAttribute:(NSOpenGLPixelFormatAttribute)attrib forVirtualScreen:(int)screen
	- (void)getValues:(long *)vals forParameter:(NSOpenGLContextParameter)param
NSWorkspace	- (BOOL)getInfoForFile:(NSString *)fullPath application:(NSString **)appName type:(NSString **)type
	- (BOOL)getFileSystemInfoForPath:(NSString *)fullPath isRemovable:(BOOL *)removableFlag isWritable:(BOOL *)writableFlag isUnmountable:(BOOL *)unmountableFlag description:(NSString **)description type:(NSString **)fileSystemType

Consequences

Using accessors is almost always the best solution for getting and setting an object's properties by code that is not within of the object's own implementation. In many cases, the accessors are used exclusively to access instance variables even within the implementation of a class. Using accessors limits the number of places in code where explicit memory management is needed and provides many other benefits.

However, accessors require the overhead of at least one method call and usually several. It's always more efficient to access instance variables directly. Use accessors until it has been proven through profiling and other techniques that more performance is required. Then replace the use of accessors with direct use of variables only when necessary.

Archiving and Unarchiving

Archiving preserves objects including any interrelationships or dependencies among the archived objects. Unarchiving re-creates the objects and relationships that were previously archived. Some common object-oriented programming languages such as Ruby, Python, Java, and C# use the term "Serialization" to describe the Archiving and Unarchiving pattern.

Cocoa includes built-in support for interprocess communication that relies on Archiving and Unarchiving to copy objects from one process to another. Objects archived by one process are unarchived in another via the `NSPortCoder` and `NSDistributedNotificationCenter` classes.

Apple's Interface Builder application archives the objects that are configured and connected within the tool. Cocoa applications later unarchive the objects stored in Interface Builder files to restore the configured objects and connections. A similar process takes place when Interface Builder enters "Simulation" mode. The objects to be tested are archived into a memory buffer and then unarchived to produce a fully functioning copy of the objects ready for you to test.

Archived objects are most commonly stored as binary data. Binary data tends to be fast to read and write from memory or disk and fast to transmit over a network. However, in cases where it's helpful to store the objects in a human readable text format, Cocoa supports archiving and unarchiving from XML files with a few limitations described in this chapter.

Motivation

Use the Archiving and Unarchiving pattern any time you need to copy or store a group of interrelated objects. Some Cocoa applications adopt this approach to store application data in files. Because most Cocoa objects automatically work with the Archiving and Unarchiving pattern, it's straightforward to save application data by just archiving your application's objects. To reload the application data, unarchive the objects. The previous application state is restored.

The Archiving and Unarchiving pattern is sometimes used to implement the "deep" Copying pattern as explained in Chapter 12 "Copying."

Solution

The Archiving and Unarchiving pattern relies on objects to encode their own internal state into an archive and later decode themselves from an archive. By implementing their own encoding and decoding, the objects safeguard encapsulation and data hiding. Objects that reference other objects typically give the referenced objects an opportunity to en-code themselves as well. Therefore, the act of encoding one object may add many objects to an archive. For example, if an object being encoded has instance variables that are ob-jects, the instance variables are usually also encoded. If an object doesn't encode its in-stance variables, it might be incomplete when later unarchived. On the other hand, if an instance variable has a default value or can be calculated from other instance variables, it often makes sense not to encode it. Each object must make its own determination regard-ing which instance variables to encode.

The key to implementing the Archiving and Unarchiving pattern is the treatment of interrelated objects. No matter how complex the relationships between objects, each object in an archive is only encoded once in that archive. This minimizes the storage re-quired for an archive, but more importantly, it simplifies the restoration of relationships when unarchiving. If many archived objects reference the same object, the unarchived copies will also all reference a single copy of that same object. Similarly, within any group of objects that are being archived, two or more objects might reference each other. Such circular references are resolved automatically in part because of the rule that each object is only represented once in an archive.

Cocoa's implementation of the Archiving and Unarchiving pattern handles data type size and byte order issues inherent with cross-platform data exchange. That way, archives created on a 32-bit computer can be unarchived on a 64-bit computer and vice versa. Even if objects are archived with a PowerPC processor that uses one byte order for multibyte values, it's possible to unarchive the objects with an Intel processor using the opposite byte order. Automatic byte order conversions are also essential for interprocess communication between dissimilar computers on a network.

Built-in object versioning provides the ability to unarchive objects that were archived with different application versions or different operating system releases. Cocoa supports object substitution during unarchiving. For example, Interface Builder sometimes archives placeholder objects that have stored connections to other objects within the archive. When the objects are unarchived into a running application, an application-specific object is substituted for the placeholder, and connections set in Interface Builder end up being restored to the application-specific object. Object substitution is combined with versioning to automatically update objects as they are unarchived. Consider what happens when a class is deprecated or replaced between version 1.0 and version 2.0 of an application. When the version 2.0 application unarchives an instance of the old class, the application can optionally substitute an instance of the new class and perform any necessary data conversions during the substitution.

Conditional Encoding

Conditional encoding constrains which objects are archived in situations where many objects are inter-related but not all relationships need to be preserved. Objects can be either unconditionally encoded or conditionally encoded. When an object is unconditionally encoded, it's always added to the archive if it isn't already there. When unarchived, all objects that referenced the unconditionally encoded object have their references restored. Conditional encoding of an object means that references to the object should only be restored if the object ends up in the archive. To be in an archive, an object has to be unconditionally encoded at least once. If a conditionally encoded object does end up in an archive, then references to the object are restored as normal when unarchived. However, if the object doesn't make it into the archive, all objects that formerly referenced that conditionally encoded object have their references set to `nil` when unarchived. Figure 11.1 illustrates what happens when a particular object is exclusively conditionally encoded. The object, C, that was conditionally encoded no longer exists when the objects are decoded.

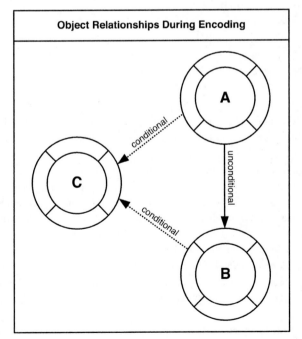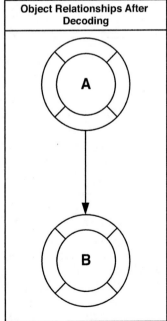

Figure 11.1   Exclusively conditionally encoded objects no longer exist when decoded.

However, if an object is unconditionally encoded by at least one referencing object, then when decoded, all references are restored regardless of whether each reference was conditional or unconditional. Figure 11.2 shows what happens to conditionally encoded object references when the referenced object is also unconditionally encoded by another object.

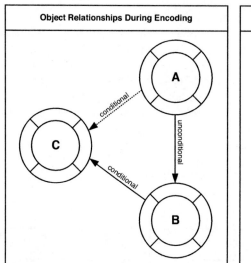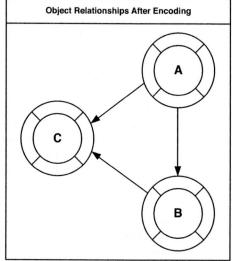

Figure 11.2   Conditional references are preserved if even one object unconditionally encodes the referenced object.

Use conditional encoding when only a subset of the objects in a group needs to be archived. For example, each Cocoa NSView object has a single reference to its "parent" ("superview") and references to all of its "child" views ("subviews"). The relationships between Cocoa NSView instances are explained in Chapter 16, "Hierarchies." Each view conceptually "owns" its subviews and treats them as an intrinsic part itself. Therefore, when an NSView instance encodes itself, all of the view's subviews are unconditionally encoded. In contrast, views have little knowledge about their superview and work correctly regardless of the specific view that owns them. NSView conditionally encodes its superview. The concepts of object ownership are elaborated in Apple's documentation provided with the developer tools at /Developer/Documentation/Cocoa/ObjectiveC/ 4objc_runtime_overview/Object_Ownership.html and in http://developer.apple.com/ documentation/Cocoa/Conceptual/MemoryMgmt/Concepts/ObjectOwnership.html online.

The fact that NSView conditionally encodes its superview enables you to archive a portion of a view hierarchy without having to archive the entire hierarchy. If you choose to archive a view in the middle of a hierarchy, the view that you archive will encode all of its subviews but not necessarily its superview.

Examples in Cocoa

The best way to create an archive of interrelated objects is to use the `NSKeyedArchiver` class as shown in the following example:

```
[NSKeyedArchiver archivedDataWithRootObject:someObject];
```

The `+(NSData *)archivedDataWithRootObject:(id)rootObject` method sends a message asking the specified root object to unconditionally encode itself. The root object in turn asks any referenced objects to either conditionally or unconditionally encode themselves. The one line of code that archives a root object is sufficient to archive an entire hierarchy of objects. The root object can be any object that conforms to the `NSCoding` protocol including an instance of `NSArray` or `NSDictionary`. The `NSData` instance returned from `+archivedDataWithRootObject:` may be stored in a file, as a Core Data attribute, or as a default value in user defaults.

Unarchive an object with `NSKeyedUnarchiver`'s `+(id)unarchiveObjectWithData:(NSData *)data` method as follows:

```
[NSKeyedUnarchiver unarchiveObjectWithData:someData];
```

`NSKeyedUnarchiver` asks the previously encoded root object to decode itself. In the process of decoding itself, the root object asks referenced objects to decode themselves. As a result, the entire hierarchy of encoded objects is decoded, and the relationships between objects are restored.

To see how the Archiving and Unarchiving pattern is used in practice, consider how a Cocoa application stores a color in user defaults. User defaults provide a standard way to store system, user, and application preferences or default values. You access user defaults via the `NSUserDefaults` class, which uses the Associative Storage pattern from Chapter 19, "Associative Storage," to store key value pairs. Code like the following can store a string value in user defaults:

```
[[NSUserDefaults standardUserDefaults]
    setObject:@"http://www.stepwise.com"
    forKey:@"homePage"];
```

However, `NSUserDefaults` is only able store to objects that are instances of the following classes: `NSData`, `NSString`, `NSNumber`, `NSDate`, `NSArray`, or `NSDictionary`. Cocoa encapsulates colors with the `NSColor` class, which is not in the list of classes directly supported by `NSUserDefaults`. If you want to store a color in user defaults, combine the Category pattern from Chapter 6, "Category," with Archiving and Unarchiving to extend `NSUserDefaults`. The following category methods take advantage of the fact that `NSColor` objects already conform to the `NSCoding` protocol to store and retrieve any `NSColor` in user defaults:

```
@implementation NSUserDefaults (ColorHandling)


- (void)setColor:(NSColor *)theColor forKey:(NSString *)key
{
  NSData *data = [NSKeyedArchiver archivedDataWithRootObject:
      theColor];
  [self setObject:data forKey:key];
}

- (NSColor *)colorForKey:(NSString *)key
{
  NSData *data = [self dataForKey:key];
  return [NSKeyedUnarchiver unarchiveObjectWithData:data];
}


@end
```

Using a similar technique, any object that conforms to the NSCoding protocol can be archived and stored in user defaults as NSData.

Implementing the NSCoding Protocol

The NSCoding protocol defines only two methods, -encodeWithCoder: and -initWithCoder:. Objects encode themselves into archives by implementing the - (void)encodeWithCoder:(NSCoder *)coder method. They decode themselves by implementing the - (id)initWithCoder:(NSCoder *)coder method. Cocoa's NSObject base class doesn't conform to the NSCoding protocol, but most other Cocoa classes do. If your class inherits from a Cocoa class that already conforms to the NSCoding protocol, you must override the NSCoding methods to call the inherited implementations and then encode or decode the unique information for your class.

> **Note**
>
> The - encodeWithCoder: and - initWithCoder: methods are prime examples of the Template Method pattern in Chapter 4, "Template Method." These methods are overridden in each subclass you create, and the methods are called automatically by Cocoa when appropriate. You shouldn't call these methods directly except to invoke the superclass' implementation from within an override.

To add encoding and decoding support to a class that does not inherit NSCoding conformance, the class must adopt the NSCoding protocol and implement the -encodeWithCoder: and -initWithCoder: methods. The following code is excerpted from the WordInformation class in the WordPuzzle example program available at www.CocoaDesignPatterns.com.

```
@interface WordInformation : NSObject <NSCoding>
{
  NSString             *word;
  NSString             *clue;
  NSMutableDictionary  *puzzleSpecificAttributes;
}

@end

// Coding keys
static NSString    *CodingKeyWord = @"word";
static NSString    *CodingKeyClue = @"clue";
static NSString    *CodingKeyPuzzleSpecificAttributes =
    @"puzzleSpecificAttributes";


- (id)initWithCoder:(NSCoder *)coder
{
  if (nil != (self = [super init]))
  {
    [self setWord:[coder decodeObjectForKey:CodingKeyWord]];
    [self setClue:[coder decodeObjectForKey:CodingKeyClue]];
    [self setPuzzleSpecificAttributes:[coder decodeObjectForKey:
        CodingKeyPuzzleSpecificAttributes]];
  }
  return self;
}


- (void)encodeWithCoder:(NSCoder *)coder
{
  [coder encodeObject:[self word] forKey:CodingKeyWord];
  [coder encodeObject:[self clue] forKey:CodingKeyClue];
  [coder encodeObject:[self puzzleSpecificAttributes] forKey:
      CodingKeyPuzzleSpecificAttributes];
}
```

WordInformation is a direct subclass of NSObject. Most of the methods of the WordInformation class are omitted from the example to keep it short, but the implementation of the NSCoding protocol is shown. The -encodeWithCoder: method unconditionally encodes each of the receiver's instance variables using the Accessors pattern from Chapter 10, "Accessors," to access the variables. The -initWithCoder: method decodes the encoded objects and sets the instance variables using the Accessor methods. Using the Accessor methods help ensure correct memory management for decoded objects whether automatic garbage collection is used.

Like other initializers explained in Chapter 3, "Two-Stage Creation," the -initWithCoder: method assigns self to the value returned from the superclass' designated initializer.

The assignment of self is necessary because the inherited initializer is free to return a different object from the one that received the message.

As a direct subclass of NSObject, WordInformation doesn't call any inherited NSCoding methods because NSObject doesn't conform to NSCoding. If your class inherits NSCoding protocol conformance, you not only need to implement the NSCoding methods, but you must call the inherited versions as shown in the next code example. The assignment of self is still required, but instead of calling the class' designated initializer, you must call the inherited version of -initWithCoder:. The following code excerpt is from the WordMatchPuzzleView class in the WordPuzzle example program:

```
// Coding keys
static NSString *CodingKeyDataSource = @"dataSource";
static NSString *CodingKeyPrototypeWordView = @"prototypeWordView";
static NSString *CodingKeyPrototypeClueView = @"prototypeClueView";
static NSString *CodingKeyWordConnectionPoints =
    @"wordConnectionPoints";
static NSString *CodingKeyClueConnectionPoints =
    @"clueConnectionPoints";
static NSString *CodingKeyConnectionLines = @"connectionLines";

// Coding methods
- (id)initWithCoder:(NSCoder *)coder
{
  if (nil != (self = [super initWithCoder:coder]))
  {
    [self setDataSource:[coder decodeObjectForKey:
        CodingKeyDataSource]];
    [self setPrototypeWordView:[coder decodeObjectForKey:
        CodingKeyPrototypeWordView]];
    [self setPrototypeClueView:[coder decodeObjectForKey:
        CodingKeyPrototypeClueView]];
    [self setWordConnectionPoints:[coder decodeObjectForKey:
        CodingKeyWordConnectionPoints]];
    [self setClueConnectionPoints:[coder decodeObjectForKey:
        CodingKeyClueConnectionPoints]];
    [self setConnectionLines:[coder decodeObjectForKey:
        CodingKeyConnectionLines]];
  }
  return self;
}


- (void)encodeWithCoder:(NSCoder *)coder
{
  [super encodeWithCoder:coder];
  [coder encodeConditionalObject:[self dataSource] forKey:
      CodingKeyDataSource];
```

```
[coder encodeObject:[self prototypeWordView] forKey:
    CodingKeyPrototypeWordView];
[coder encodeObject:[self prototypeClueView] forKey:
    CodingKeyPrototypeClueView];
[coder encodeObject:[self wordConnectionPoints] forKey:
    CodingKeyWordConnectionPoints];
[coder encodeObject:[self clueConnectionPoints] forKey:
    CodingKeyClueConnectionPoints];
[coder encodeObject:[self connectionLines] forKey:
    CodingKeyConnectionLines];
}
```

WordMatchPuzzleView conditionally encodes its dataSource instance variable. As a result, if a WordMatchPuzzleView is encoded by itself, the dataSource will not end up in the archive. In the WordPuzzle application, the dataSource is used to automatically initialize a blank puzzle with words and clues. If you archive an already initialized WordMatchPuzzleView instance by itself, there is no need to preserve the dataSource used to initialize the instance. On the other hand, if you are archiving a larger group of objects including the dataSource and one or more WordMatchPuzzleView instances, the dataSource will end up in the archive and therefore will be available to generate new puzzles after the group of objects is unarchived.

Encoding and Decoding Nonobject Types

NSKeyedArchiver and NSKeyedUnarchiver provide methods for encoding and decoding nonobject values including floating point types and 32-bit or 64-bit integers. The Cocoa BOOL data type and some commonly used C structures such as NSPoint, NSSize, and NSRect are also directly supported.

The next example of NSCoding is an excerpt from the WordConnectionPoint class in the same WordPuzzle program. In this example, some nonobject values are encoded and decoded:

```
// Coding keys
static NSString    *CodingKeyFrame = @"frame";
static NSString    *CodingKeyColor = @"color";
static NSString    *CodingKeyIsFilled = @"isFilled";
static NSString    *CodingKeyLineWidth = @"lineWidth";
static NSString    *CodingKeyAssociatedWordInformation =
    @"associatedWordInformation";


// Coding methods
- (id)initWithCoder:(NSCoder *)coder
{
  if(nil != (self = [super init]))
  {
    [self setFrame:[coder decodeRectForKey:CodingKeyFrame]];
    [self setColor:[coder decodeObjectForKey:CodingKeyColor]];
    [self setIsFilled:[coder decodeBoolForKey:CodingKeyIsFilled]];
```

```
    [self setLineWidth:[coder decodeFloatForKey:
        CodingKeyLineWidth]];
    [self setAssociatedWordInformation:[coder decodeObjectForKey:
        CodingKeyAssociatedWordInformation]];
  }
  return self;
}


- (void)encodeWithCoder:(NSCoder *)coder
{
  [coder encodeRect:[self frame] forKey:CodingKeyFrame];
  [coder encodeObject:[self color] forKey:CodingKeyColor];
  [coder encodeBool:[self isFilled] forKey:CodingKeyIsFilled];
  [coder encodeFloat:[self lineWidth] forKey:CodingKeyLineWidth];
  [coder encodeConditionalObject:[self associatedWordInformation]
      forKey:CodingKeyAssociatedWordInformation];
}
```

Cocoa does not provide built-in support for other data types such as arbitrary C structures, unions, bit fields, nonobject pointers, or arrays of values other than bytes. Apple supplies extensive advice regarding how to encode unsupported data types in archives at http://developer.apple.com/documentation/Cocoa/Conceptual/Archiving/Tasks/codingctypes.html. However, the advice boils down to the following two approaches: Either wrap the unsupported data types in objects that conform to the NSCoding protocol and then encode those objects, or break the data types down to supported components like int and float and encode the individual components.

If you wrap multibyte values in NSData objects, you must handle any byte order (endian) issues in the event that the data is decoded on a different platform. Furthermore, in all but the simplest cases, wrapping C structures in NSData objects is unworkable. The memory representation of C structures is not defined by any standard, and as a result different compilers store structures differently. In particular, compilers are free to insert padding bytes between structure members or bit fields so that the same structure definition may have different memory sizes when compiled with different compilers. Similarly, any encoded structure members that are pointers will become useless gibberish when decoded into an application running in a different memory space.

> ### Note
> By default, objects that are decoded are allocated in the default memory zone. If you need to decode objects using a different memory zone, specify the zone via NSKeyedUnarchiver's - (void)setObjectZone:(NSZone *)zone method before any objects are decoded. You can find out what zone NSKeyedArchiver is using via the - (NSZone *)objectZone method. In almost every case, the objects being decoded should be allocated in the same zone as the object that is decoding them. You can find out the zone of the object requesting the decoding via NSObject's - (NSZone *)zone method.

Object Substitution

During encoding, the object being encoded can substitute a replacement class or instance for itself. As each object is encoded, `NSKeyedArchiver` calls the object's `- (Class) classForKeyedArchiver` method. You can override `-classForKeyedArchiver` to return a class different from the class of the object being encoded. Next, `NSKeyedArchiver` calls the `- (id)replacementObjectForKeyedArchiver:(NSKeyedArchiver *)archiver` method of the object being encoded. Override `-replacementObjectForKeyedArchiver:` to substitute a different instance for the instance being encoded. Finally, `NSKeyedArchiver` calls `+ (NSArray *)classFallbacksForKeyedArchiver:` and encodes the array returned, if any, along with the encoded object. If the actual class of an object doesn't exist at the time the object is decoded, `NSKeyedUnarchiver` substitutes the first class in the array that does exist to decode the object. Override `+classFallbacksForKeyedArchiver:` to provide some compatibility hints so that objects can be decoded in different application versions that use different classes.

NSKeyedUnarchiver allows an optional delegate object to control substitution during decoding. Delegates are explained in Chapter 15, "Delegates." When `NSKeyedUnarchiver` is unable to decode an object, it tries to send the `- (Class)unarchiver:(NSKeyedUnarchiver *)unarchiver cannotDecodeObjectOfClassName:(NSString *)name originalClasses:(NSArray *)classNames` message to its delegate. The delegate can optionally implement the `-unarchiver:cannotDecodeObjectOfClassName:originalClasses:` method to return the class that should be used to continue decoding.

Finally, after an object has been decoded, the `-awakeAfterUsingCoder:` message is sent to the decoded object. You can override `-awakeAfterUsingCoder:` to calculate values for instance variables that were not successfully decoded or to return a different object than the one just decoded.

Nib Awaking

A problem can arise when objects that have been encoded into an Interface Builder `.nib` file are decoded. As an object is decoded, it might need to send messages to a referenced object that has not yet been decoded. How does an object know when during decoding it is safe to access the objects to which it has relationships? The answer is the `-awakeFromNib` method.

When objects are decoded from a `.nib` file, the Application Kit automatically sends the `-awakeFromNib` message to every decoded object that can respond to it. The `-awakeFromNib` message is only called after all the objects in the archive have been decoded and initialized. Therefore, when an object receives an `-awakeFromNib` message, it's guaranteed to have all its outlet instance variables set. The `-awakeFromNib` message is also sent to objects when Interface Builder enters "Simulation" mode because Interface Builder encodes objects into a `.nib` archive in memory and then immediately decodes them.

When `.nib` files are unarchived by a Cocoa application, the application specifies an object outside the `.nib` that will "own" the objects decoded from the `.nib`. This outside object is represented by an icon labeled "File's Owner" within Interface Builder. Any connections or references to the File's Owner made within the .nib file are reconstituted to reference the application supplied owner via object substitution. The object specified as the owner also receives an -awakeFromNib message each time a .nib is unarchived with that object as the owner. Use the owner's implementation of -awakeFromNib to complete any initialization that happens each time a .nib file is loaded. Keep in mind that the owner's -awakeFromNib method will be called multiple times if the same owner is used multiple times to load .nibs.

Consequences

Archiving and Unarchiving provide a convenient standard way to preserve or copy interconnected objects. The pattern supports Cocoa's implementation of distributed messaging. Objects that are passed between applications via distributed messaging are sometimes archived and unarchived to create copies in the receiving application. As an alternative to copying the objects, proxies may be used as, described in Chapter 27, "Proxies and Forwarding."

Most Cocoa classes conform to the NSCoding protocol and can therefore be used with Archiving and Unarchiving. Some extra work is needed when creating custom classes to implement the necessary NSCoding methods. Programmer effort is also required to achieve backward and forward compatibility between applications and archives so that older applications can use newer archives and vice versa. Some other languages and frameworks provide more automatic support for this pattern than Objective-C and Cocoa. However, Cocoa's approach maximizes program control of archiving and unarchiving. Cocoa's implementation is extensible and flexible. It provides many hooks like -awakeAfterUsingCoder: for object substitution, and if necessary, you can create your own NSCoder subclasses to implement Archiving and Unarchiving using your own archive formats.

There are a couple of common alternative techniques for Cocoa object persistence. Consider using Cocoa property lists if all of the objects you want to store can be converted to property list types. Property lists are documented at http://developer.apple.com/documentation/Cocoa/Conceptual/PropertyLists/PropertyLists.html. The user defaults cited in this chapter are actually stored as property lists.

Cocoa's Core Data framework stores objects and their relationships using technology adapted from relational databases. Core Data and its patterns are explained in Chapter 30, "Core Data Models." Core Data can be used as an alternative to storing application data in archives, but like property lists, Core Data supports only a limited number of data types directly. Fortunately, Core Data includes support for storing NSData objects, so it's possible to mix approaches and store archived objects via Core Data.

12

Copying

The Copying pattern is used to create new object instances by copying existing instances. The act of copying objects is not always as clear cut as you might expect. For example, if you copy an object that contains other objects, should the copy contain the exact same objects as the original, or should the copy contain copies of the objects in the original?

Copying serves as an alternative to the Two-Stage Creation pattern introduced in Chapter 3, "Two-Stage Creation," and enables the Prototype pattern in Chapter 21, "Prototype." Copying also plays a role in the Accessor pattern from Chapter 10, "Accessors." At a higher level, user interface actions, like copy and paste or drag and drop, are often implemented by copying application objects.

Motivation

Use the Copying pattern any time you want to create a new object that is a copy of another object. Copying captures the state of an object at a moment in time.

The C programming language uses a technique called *pass-by-value* to supply arguments to functions. Pass-by-value means that arguments are implicitly copied so that changes made to the arguments within a function affect only the copies and not the original values. If you're an experienced C or Objective-C programmer, skip to the next section of this chapter. The remainder of this section briefly explains pass-by-value semantics and why Objective-C objects may need to be explicitly copied when used as arguments to functions or methods. The following command line program is available at www.CocoaDesignPatterns.com and demonstrates pass-by-value semantics with C types:

```
#import <Foundation/Foundation.h>


static void SimplePassByValue(float floatArgument)
{
  floatArgument = floatArgument * 3.0f;
  NSLog(@"Inside SimplePassByValue, floatArgument = %f",
      floatArgument);
}
```

```
int main (int argc, const char * argv[])
{
  NSAutoreleasePool *pool = [[NSAutoreleasePool alloc] init];

  float         floatArgument = 1.0f;
  NSLog(@"Before SimplePassByValue, floatArgument = %f",
      floatArgument);
  SimplePassByValue(floatArgument);
  NSLog(@"After SimplePassByValue, floatArgument = %f",
      floatArgument);

  [pool release];
  return 0;
}
```

The program generates the following output, which shows that although floatArgument is changed inside the SimplePassByValue() function, the changes affect only the implicit copy of floatArgument within SimplePassByValue() and not the variable declared in main().

```
Before SimplePassByValue, floatArgument = 1.000000
Inside SimplePassByValue, floatArgument = 3.000000
After SimplePassByValue, floatArgument = 1.000000
```

C and therefore Objective-C always passes arguments by value. Even C structures like Cocoa's NSRect are passed by value and implicitly copied. However, it's possible to pass a pointer to a value and then modify a value indirectly via the pointer. The pointer itself is implicitly copied, but the value the pointer addresses is not copied. The next example and its output show what happens when pointers to values are used as arguments. The value of floatArgument within main() is changed by the call to PassPointer().

```
#import <Foundation/Foundation.h>

static void PassPointer(float *floatPointer)
{
  *floatPointer = *floatPointer * 3.0f;
  NSLog(@"Inside PassPointer, *floatPointer = %f", *floatPointer);
}

int main (int argc, const char *argv[])
{
  NSAutoreleasePool *pool = [[NSAutoreleasePool alloc] init];

  float         floatArgument = 1.0f;
```

```
NSLog(@"Before PassPointer, floatArgument = %f", floatArgument);
PassPointer(&floatArgument);
NSLog(@"After PassPointer, floatArgument = %f", floatArgument);

[pool release];
return 0;
}
```

```
Before PassPointer, floatArgument = 1.000000
Inside PassPointer, *floatPointer = 3.000000
After PassPointer, floatArgument = 3.000000
```

Objective-C objects are always passed as pointers. You'll get a compiler error if you attempt to pass an object itself rather than a pointer to the object. So in the following example, the NSMutableString, aString, in the main() function is changed by the PassObjectPointer() function:

```
#import <Foundation/Foundation.h>

static void PassObjectPointer(NSMutableString *aString)
{
  [aString setString:@"Changed"];
  NSLog(@"Inside PassObjectPointer, aString = %@", aString);
}


int main (int argc, const char *argv[])
{
  NSAutoreleasePool *pool = [[NSAutoreleasePool alloc] init];

  NSMutableString    *aString = [NSMutableString stringWithString:
      @"Original"];
  NSLog(@"Before PassObjectPointer, aString = %@", aString);
  PassObjectPointer(aString);
  NSLog(@"After PassObjectPointer, aString = %@", aString);

  [pool release];
  return 0;
}
```

```
Before PassObjectPointer, aString = Original
Inside PassObjectPointer, aString = Changed
After PassObjectPointer, aString = Changed
```

Objective-C programmers quickly become familiar with the effects of passing objects by pointer and expect that any C function or Objective-C method that accepts an object pointer as an argument can modify the object via the pointer. It's the standard and most often desired behavior. If you need to pass a pointer to one of your objects, but you want to make sure the object isn't changed, one approach is to copy the object and pass a pointer to the copy instead of a pointer to the original. No matter what changes are made to the copy, the original is preserved.

If you are writing a function or method that will store a pointer to an object, you may actually want to create a copy and store a pointer to the copy. That way, changes that are later made to the original object won't affect the stored copy.

Solution

Not all objects can be meaningfully copied. If an object encapsulates a unique or scarce resource, it doesn't make sense to copy the object. For example, Cocoa's NSHost class encapsulates information about the unique network names and Internet addresses of a computer. It doesn't make sense to copy an NSHost instance because doing so would duplicate the network names and Internet addresses that are supposed to be unique. The NSApplication class encapsulates a connection to Mac OS X's Quartz window server so that Cocoa applications can draw windows on the screen. Each Cocoa application is permitted exactly one connection to the window server. For that reason, NSApplication uses the Singleton pattern introduced in Chapter 13, "Singleton." It makes no sense to copy an instance of NSApplication because only one instance is permitted in each program.

When copying is supported, consider whether the copy operation is shallow or deep. A shallow copy is a copy of the object itself, but not any objects contained by the object being copied. In other words, when an object is shallow copied, the result is a new object that contains pointers to the exact same objects contained by the first. A deep copy copies the contained objects as well. The result of a deep copy is a new object that contains pointers to copies of the objects contained by the original. Usually, deep copies are as deep as possible. Objects within objects within objects are also copied to as deep a level as necessary to copy every object in the containment hierarchy.

Cocoa classes that support copying all implement the Copying pattern to return a shallow copy. The result of copying an NSArray instance is a new instance that contains pointers to the same objects as the original. You are free to implement the pattern in your own classes to produce shallow or deep copies depending on the needs of your applications.

One convenient way to obtain deep copies of Cocoa objects uses the Archiving and Unarchiving pattern explained in Chapter 11, "Archiving and Unarchiving." If the object to be copied and all the objects contained within that object conform to Cocoa's NSCoding protocol, the following code will produce a deep copy. NSCoding is the Objective-C protocol needed to support Archiving and Unarchiving.

```
id MYDeepCopyObject(id <NSCoding> anObject)
// This function accepts any object conforming the NSCoding protocol
// and returns a deep copy of that object.  The object returned must
// be explicitly released unless automatic garbage collection is used.
{
  return [[NSKeyedUnarchiver unarchiveObjectWithData:[NSKeyedArchiver
```

```
    archivedDataWithRootObject:anObject]] retain];
}
```

Another issue to consider is the mutability of objects produced by copying. Mutability refers to the ability to "mutate" or change an instance after the instance is created. An object that can't be changed after creation is called *immutable*. For example, once an instance of Cocoa's NSString class is created, the string data encapsulated by the NSString instance can't be changed. NSString doesn't provide any methods that modify the contained string directly. However, Cocoa provides a subclass of NSString, NSMutableString, that does have methods for changing the contents of the string. There are also mutable and immutable variants of other classes. For example, Cocoa provides NSArray and its subclass NSMutableArray, NSDictionary and its subclass NSMutableDictionary, and NSSet and its subclass NSMutableSet. Some common Cocoa classes exist only in immutable forms. A partial list of immutable objects includes NSColor, NSNumber, NSDate, and NSNotification.

Many, but not all, Cocoa classes use the concept of mutability, and programmers new to Cocoa often ask why immutable objects exist. The best answer is to refer back to the issue of pass-by-value semantics described in the Motivation section of this chapter. Copying an object prevents changes made to the original from affecting the copy and vice versa. However, if an object is immutable and therefore can't be changed, there is no need to make a copy. It's safe to store the pointer to the immutable object without making a copy. Immutable objects can be used as if they were ordinary pass-by-value C language data types.

If a Cocoa object has both mutable and immutable variants, and the object is copied, the resulting new object is always immutable. For example, if you send the -copy message to an NSMutableSet instance, the object returned is an instance of the immutable NSSet class.

In some cases, a -(id)mutableCopy method is available that will return a mutable copy. For example, sending the -mutableCopy message to either an NSMutableSet or an NSSet will return an instance of NSMutableSet. Mutable copying and the NSMutableCopying protocol are explained in the next section.

Examples in Cocoa

Cocoa also defines the NSCopying Objective-C protocol to which objects that can be copied conform. NSCopying declares exactly one method, -(id)copyWithZone:(NSZone *)zone. The NSZone type and memory zones are introduced in Chapter 3. Cocoa's NSObject base class defines the -(id)copy method and implements the -copy method to check whether the receiver of the -copy message conforms to the NSCopying protocol. If the receiver does conform to NSCopying, the -copy method calls [self copyWithZone:[self zone]]. However, NSObject's implementation of the -copy method generates an Objective-C exception if the receiver doesn't conform to the NSCopying protocol. Therefore, if you create a subclass of NSObject and your subclass instances can be copied, your subclass must either conform to the NSCopying protocol or override the inherited -copy method.

Implementing NSCopying

The following WordInformation class is a direct subclass of NSObject. WordInformation is immutable and implements NSCopying to produce a shallow copy and is part of the WordPuzzle example program available at www.CocoaDesignPatterns. com. WordInformation is used in Chapter 11 and is extended here to implement NSCopying:

```
@interface WordInformation : NSObject <NSCoding, NSCopying>
{
  NSString            *word;
  NSString            *clue;
  NSMutableDictionary *puzzleSpecificAttributes;
}

@end


@implementation WordInformation


// Several methods are omitted to simplify this example

// NSCopying
- (id)copyWithZone:(NSZone *)aZone
{
  return [self retain];
}

@end
```

The implementation of -copyWithZone: for an immutable class doesn't need to make a copy at all. It's sufficient to return a retained pointer to the object because there is no danger of the object being changed after it's returned. Many Cocoa Accessor methods are implemented using the -copy method, and the ability of immutable objects to skip actually copying when used in those Accessors is a substantial optimization.

The WordMutableInformation class is a mutable subclass of WordInformation. WordMutableInformation implements shallow copying for a mutable object as follows:

```
@interface WordMutableInformation : WordInformation
{
}

@end

@implementation WordMutableInformation
```

```
// Several methods are omitted to simplify this example

// NSCopying
- (id)copyWithZone:(NSZone *)aZone
{
  // initializer is called for the new instance of the
  // immutable class
  id     result = [[[self class] allocWithZone:aZone]
      initWithWord:[self word] clue:[self clue]];

  [[result puzzleSpecificAttributes] addEntriesFromDictionary:
      [self puzzleSpecificAttributes]];

  return self;
}

@end
```

There is no need for the @interface declaration of WordMutableInformation to include the <NSCopying> protocol conformance identification because protocol conformance is inherited from the WordInformation class. The WordMutableInformation implementation of -copyWithZone: allocates a new instance of the immutable WordInformation class from the specified memory zone. The new instance is then initialized, and its properties are set to match the original's.

Implementing Deep Copying

The following code extends the WordInformation class using the Category pattern and the Archiving and Unarchiving pattern to provide deep copying. There is no formal NSDeepCopying protocol, so the name of the - (id)deepCopy method that follows is arbitrary:

```
@interface WordInformation (WordDeepCopyingSupport)

- (id)deepCopy;

@end

@implementation WordInformation (WordDeepCopyingSupport)

- (id)deepCopy
{
  return [[NSKeyedUnarchiver unarchiveObjectWithData:[NSKeyedArchiver
      archivedDataWithRootObject:self]] retain];
}

@end
```

The example -deepCopy method doesn't specify a memory zone because zones are seldom used in modern Cocoa applications. The requirement to specify a zone for the -copyWithZone: method is really just a hold-over that provided backward compatibility for ancient code.

The -(id)deepCopy method added to WordInformation is automatically inherited by WordMutableInformation. The implementation of deep copying is the same regardless of whether an object is mutable. There is a subtlety however; a shallow copy of a mutable object returns an immutable object, but the implementation of -deepCopy for mutable objects returns a mutable object.

To following Category adds support for deep copying to every object that conforms to the NSCoding protocol:

```
@interface NSObject (DeepCopyingSupport)

- (id)deepCopy;

@end


@implementation NSObject (DeepCopyingSupport)

- (id)deepCopy
{
  return [[NSKeyedUnarchiver unarchiveObjectWithData:[NSKeyedArchiver
      archivedDataWithRootObject:self]] retain];
}

@end
```

NSKeyedArchiver's -archivedDataWithRootObject: method will raise an Objective-C exception if the object to be archived, self, doesn't conform to NSCoding.

Implementing NSMutableCopying

Cocoa's NSMutableCopying protocol declares exactly one method, -(id)mutableCopyWithZone:(NSZone *)aZone. Just like NSObject provides an implementation of -copy that calls -copyWithZone:, NSObject also provides a default -(id)mutableCopy method that calls -mutableCopyWithZone:. If you send the -mutableCopy message to an object that doesn't either conform NSMutableCopying or override the -mutableCopy method, NSObjects's -mutableCopy implementation raises an exception.

The following example extends the WordInformation class with an implementation of shallow NSMutableCopying:

```
@interface WordInformation : NSObject <NSCoding, NSCopying,
  NSMutableCopying>
```

```
{
  NSString           *word;
  NSString           *clue;
  NSMutableDictionary *puzzleSpecificAttributes;
}

@end

@implementation WordInformation

// Several methods are omitted to simplify this example

// NSCopying
- (id)copyWithZone:(NSZone *)aZone
{
  return [self retain];
}

// NSMutableCopying
- (id)mutableCopyWithZone:(NSZone *)aZone
{
  // initializer is called for the new instance of the
  // mutable class
  id     result = [[[self class] allocWithZone:aZone]
      initWithWord:[self word] clue:[self clue]];

  [[result puzzleSpecificAttributes] addEntriesFromDictionary:
      [self puzzleSpecificAttributes]];

  return self;
}

@end
```

There is no need to override WordInformation's implementation of -mutableCopyWithZone: in the WordMutableInformation class. WordInformation's implementation does everything needed regardless of whether the receiver of -mutableCopyWithZone: is mutable.

Required Copying

When using your own classes with Cocoa, there are a few cases in which your classes must implement NSCopying. For example, Cocoa's NSDictionary class copies objects that are used as keys. Therefore, every object used as a key in an NSDictionary must conform to the NSCopying protocol. The Prototype pattern in Chapter 21 uses the Copying pattern. Prototype objects are copied as needed. For example, instances of the

NSCell class are copied to fill the rows and columns of an NSMatrix instance. NSCell and
NSMatrix are described in Chapter 21 and in Apple's Cocoa documentation at
http://developer.apple.com/documentation/Cocoa/.

Copying Objective-C 2.0 Properties

The Objective-C 2.0 Properties syntax introduced with Mac OS X 10.5 interacts with
the Copying pattern. The Properties syntax is used to automatically generate accessors for
an object's properties. Properties are usually instance variables, but they can be implemented using the Associative Storage pattern in Chapter 19, "Associative Storage," or with
other techniques. Using the Objective-C 2.0 syntax, the publicly immutable
WordInformation class is declared as follows:

```
@interface WordInformation : NSObject <NSCoding, NSCopying,
  NSMutableCopying>
{
  NSString            *word;
  NSString            *clue;
  NSMutableDictionary *puzzleSpecificAttributes;
}

@property (readonly, retain) NSString *word;
@property (readonly, retain) NSString *clue;
@property (readonly, copy) NSMutableDictionary
   *puzzleSpecificAttributes;

@end
```

The @property (readonly, retain) NSString *word; declaration tells users of the
class and the Objective-C 2.0 compiler how accessor methods that correspond to the
word property are implemented. The word and clue properties are declared readonly in
the class interface so that users of the class know a -(NSString *)word accessor method
will exist but can't assume that a -(void)setWord:(NSString *)aString method will
exist. The fact that the word property is declared retain has no relevance to users of the
class, but it is very important within the implementation of WordInformation. Properties
that are initially declared readonly are frequently redeclared readwrite in a class extension as follows: (Class extensions are explained in Chapter 6, "Category.")

```
@interface WordInformation ()

@property (readwrite, retain) NSString *word;
@property (readwrite, retain) NSString *clue;
@property (readwrite, copy) NSMutableDictionary
   *puzzleSpecificAttributes;

@end
```

The redeclarations tell the compiler that `-setWord:`, `-setClue:`, and
`-setPuzzleSpecificAttributes:` Accessor methods exist for use solely within the class
implementation. In other words, the `WordInformation` class interface tells users of the
class that it is externally immutable even though the internal implementation of the class
may mutate properties. The compiler allows redeclarations to replace `readonly` with
`readwrite`, but no other attributes of the property can be changed in a redeclaration. The
`retain` attribute of the `word` and `clue` properties means that the corresponding
`-setWord:` and `-setClue:` methods retain their arguments as opposed to copying them.

The `WordInformation` class extension redeclares the `puzzleSpecificAttributes`
property as `@property (readwrite, copy) NSMutableDictionary`
`*puzzleSpecificAttributes;`. The copy attribute specifies that the argument to the
`-setPuzzleSpecificAttributes:` method will be copied within the implementation
as opposed to being merely retained. Therefore, the object passed to
`-setPuzzleSpecificAttributes:` must conform to the `NSCopying` protocol.

The Objective-C 2.0 compiler uses the `assign` attribute of properties when neither
`retain` nor `copy` is specified. Using either `@property (readonly, assign)` or
`@property (readonly)` produces identical results. However, the Objective-C 2.0 compiler generates a warning when a property declaration defaults to using the `assign` attribute for an object property that conforms to the `NSCopying` protocol. To avoid the
warning, you must explicitly specify one of the `assign`, `retain`, or `copy` attributes.

Use the following Objective-C 2.0 syntax to declare the `WordMutableInformation`
class:

```
@interface WordMutableInformation : WordInformation
{
}

@property (readwrite, retain) NSString *word;
@property (readwrite, retain) NSString *clue;
@property (readwrite, copy) NSMutableDictionary
   *puzzleSpecificAttributes;

@end
```

Because the properties are declared `readwrite` in the class interface, users of the
`WordMutableInformation` class know its instances are mutable. The compiler will ensure
that accessor methods exist to both set and return the properties. The `-(void)set-`
`Word:(NSString *)aString` and `-(void)setClue::(NSString *)aString` methods retain the respective properties. The `-(void)setPuzzleSpecificAttributes:`
`(NSMutableDictionary *)aDictionary` method copies the specified dictionary with
code similar to the following:

```
-(void)setPuzzleSpecificAttributes:(NSMutableDictionary *)aDictionary
{
   if(puzzleSpecificAttributes != aDictionary)
```

```
    {
        [puzzleSpecificAttributes release];
        puzzleSpecificAttributes = [aDictionary copy];
    }
}
```

Avoid `NSCopyObject()`

Cocoa provides a C function called `NSCopyObject()`. Don't use it. The `NSCopyObject()` function makes an exact byte for byte copy of an object. If the object being copied has instance variables that point to other objects, the pointers are copied, but the retain counts of the objects are not incremented as required for Cocoa's reference counted memory management. Even if you use Objective-C 2.0 and automatic memory garbage collection, `NSCopyObject()` doesn't respect `@property` declarations and circumvents the optional __strong and __weak declaration modifiers used with garbage collection. The __strong and __weak declaration modifiers are documented at http://developer.apple.com/documentation/Cocoa/Conceptual/GarbageCollection/Articles/gcAPI.html.

Consequences

The ability to copy objects is almost as fundamental as the ability to allocate and initialize new instances. Cocoa relies on framework level conventions to allocate and initialize new instances as explained in Chapter 3. The Copying pattern also relies on mere conventions established by the Cocoa frameworks. The Copying pattern enables the use of value semantics with objects and is used in the implementation of Accessors and the Prototype pattern. However, correct implementation of copying conventions requires some forethought by class designers. Support for Cocoa's reference counted memory management must be considered in the implementation of the Copying pattern.

The interdependence of Objective-C 2.0 properties and the `NSCopying` protocol blurs the lines between framework features and compiler level language support. Prior to Objective-C 2.0, it was possible to use every feature of the Objective-C language without using Cocoa frameworks at all. Apple's implementation of Objective-C 2.0 depends on the `NSCopying` protocol and the Copying pattern as implemented by Cocoa. The source code for the Objective-C 2.0 compiler is available from the Gnu Compiler Collection at http://gcc.gnu.org/. Future versions may implement Objective-C 2.0 properties syntax without dependence on Cocoa-specific protocols.

III

Patterns That Primarily Empower by Decoupling

The patterns in Part III provide powerful built-in framework features and enable you to control and extend those features without introducing unnecessary coupling between objects. Minimal coupling is a key guiding principle of Cocoa's design and the quality that most contributes to programmer productivity. These patterns are some of the most prominent and reused patterns in Cocoa.

Chapters in this part of the book include

13

Singleton

The Singleton pattern is used when there must be exactly one instance of a class, and it must be easily accessible to other objects in an application. Usually, the Cocoa documentation uses the term *shared instance* when the Singleton pattern is in use.

In Cocoa, one example of a Singleton is the NSApplication class. It maintains the application's connection to the window server for drawing and receiving events. Cocoa optionally takes advantage of Dynamic Creation and Bundles to substitute an instance of your own class for the default NSApplication instance.

Motivation

Define conventions for the creation of and access to an instance in cases where only one instance of a class should be created. Often singletons represent physical devices. At other times they represent virtual resources or other system properties that are singular and cannot or should not be duplicated. It is useful to have a one-to-one relationship between instances and the devices or concepts they represent.

Solution

Any class that uses the Singleton pattern must achieve three goals:

- Encapsulate a shared resource.
- Provide a standard way to create one shared instance.
- Provide a standard way to access the one shared instance.

Each goal has its own challenges and can be implemented many different ways using Objective-C. The following sections describe the techniques used to implement the Singleton pattern in Cocoa and the trade-offs made.

Encapsulating a Shared Resource

A common question arises whenever the Singleton pattern is used with Objective-C: Why create an instance instead of just using a class object? After all, Objective-C provides true class objects that can receive messages and can be used in any context where other objects are used, and Objective-C's runtime assures that each class object is only stored in memory once per application. The answer is subtle and has to do with flexibility and the maintainability. A class can certainly be used to encapsulate a shared resource. Consider a game written in Cocoa that includes a hypothetical class for managing storage of player high scores on a particular computer. It might have an interface such as this:

```
@interface MYGameHighScoreManager : NSObject
{
}

+ (void)registerScore:(NSNumber *)score playerName:(NSString *)name;
+ (NSEnumerator *)scoreEnumerator;
```

The MYGameHighScoreManager class could provide a much more complicated interface if necessary, but as long as all of the methods are class methods as denoted with the + symbol, the class can be used without ever creating an instance. For example, when a game is over, the player's score may be registered by sending the +registerScore:playerName: message directly to the MYGameHighScoreManager in code similar to the following:

```
[MYGameHighScoreManager
    registerScore:[NSNumber numberWithInt:[self score]]
    playerName:[self playerName]];
```

The problem with using the class directly arises when it becomes necessary to subclass MYGameHighScoreManager. If a subclass of MYGameHighScoreManager called MYGameNetworkHighScoreManager is created, it becomes necessary to modify existing code everywhere the MYGameHighScoreManager class is specified and use the MYGameNetworkHighScoreManager class instead. In other words, hard coding the class name everywhere the class is used reduces the flexibility to use a different class in the future.

Many techniques could be used to avoid hard coding a class name. The simplest approach is to use a global variable that stores a pointer to the class that should be used. For example, the code to register a high score could be altered like this:

```
extern Class GameHighScoreClass;

[GameHighScoreClass
    registerScore:[NSNumber numberWithInt:[self score]]
    playerName:[self playerName]];
```

The global variable GameHighScoreClass would have to be initialized first, of course. One of the following lines of code would have to appear during the application's

initialization, perhaps in the -applicationWillFinishLaunching: method of the
NSApplication's delegate:

```
// Set up the default high score controller
GameHighScoreClass = [MYGameHighScoreManager class];

// Or alternatively, set up a specialized subclass to be used instead
GameHighScoreClass = [MYGameNetworkHighScoreManager class];
```

With the added flexibility of a global variable, it is no longer necessary to edit multiple lines of code just to change the class used to manage high scores. However, using a global variable brings with it all of the maintenance problems of unencapsulated variables.

One of the important features of object-oriented programming is a reduction of the need for such global variables. Using a class to encapsulate a global variable is an ideal solution. Classes exist to encapsulate information about instances and provide a single interface for creating instances. Using an instance of MYGameHighScoreManager to manage scores and using the MYGameHighScoreManager class itself to encapsulate access to the instance is the cleanest way to achieve the goals of flexibility and maintainability.

The remainder of this chapter describes techniques for encapsulating the creation of a single shared instance and providing access to the shared instance. Although a basic high scores list as encapsulated by the MYGameHighScoreManager class is a simple shared resource, the pattern is applicable to any situation where a shared resource is used.

Creating and Accessing a Shared Instance

To have a shared instance, it is necessary to change the interface of MYGameHighScoreManager so that the management is done with instance methods. A class method also needs to be added to allow for access to the shared instance. A commonly chosen name is +sharedInstance. Here is the new interface:

```
@interface MYGameHighScoreManager : NSObject
{
}

+ (id)sharedInstance;
- (void)registerScore:(NSNumber *)score playerName:(NSString *)name;
- (NSEnumerator *)scoreEnumerator;
```

A basic implementation of the +sharedInstance method might be like this:

```
+ (MYGameHighScoreManager *)sharedInstance
{
  static MYGameHighScoreManager *myInstance = nil;
  if (!myInstance)
  {
    myInstance = [[[self class] alloc] init];
    // any other special initialization as required here
  }
```

```
    return myInstance;
}
```

In this implementation, a local static variable is used to hold a pointer to the shared instance. This forces all access to this value to pass through the +sharedInstance method. It is initialized to nil by the compiler. The first time the method is called, the code to create and initialize the shared object will be executed. Finally, the shared object is returned to the caller.

Of special note is the call to +alloc. Instead of sending it to MYGameHighScoreManager directly, we instead send it to [self class]. Normally they would give the same result. We use this implementation because we want to take full advantage of Objective-C's polymorphism. By dynamically looking up the class object at runtime, this allows for the shared instance to be an instance of a particular subclass. So to have the shared instance be a MYGameNetworkHighScoreManager object, code like this would be placed in the application's initialization code, probably in the -applicationDidFinishLaunching: method of the NSApplication's delegate:

```
extern Class MYGameNetworkHighScoreManager;
[MYGameNetworkHighScoreManager sharedInstance];
```

In this example, the return value is thrown away because the actual object isn't needed. The message is being sent only to trigger the creation of the shared instance and to ensure it is of the desired class. A similar technique can be used for most other Cocoa singletons if you want to make certain that your custom subclass is used for the shared instance.

One obvious exception would the NSApplication shared instance, however. It is created automatically by Cocoa before any of your code is executed! To solve this problem, the Dynamic Creation pattern is used. To choose a particular subclass of NSApplication, select the application target in Xcode, open the Info panel, and select Properties. In the middle of the panel is a field titled Principal Class, where the name of your NSApplication subclass can be specified, as shown in Figure 13.1 where MyApplicationSubclass has been entered.

Making that change in Xcode actually sets the key NSPrincipalClass in the application's Info.plist file to the value you set. When Cocoa starts the application, it looks at this value and uses Dynamic Creation to instantiate the requested class to be used as the shared application object. If we wanted, we could use a similar scheme to avoid having to call +sharedInstance early on in the application initialization. Here is the code for +sharedInstance updated to look up the class name in the application's Info.plist, using the key MYGameHighScoreManagerClass.

```
+ (MYGameHighScoreManager *)sharedInstance
{
    static MYGameHighScoreManager *myInstance = nil;
    if (!myInstance)
    {
        NSBundle *mainBundle = [NSBundle mainBundle];
```

```
    NSDictionary *info = [mainBundle infoDictionary];
    NSString *className = [info objectForKey:
        @"MYGameHighScoreManagerClass"];
    Class *myClass = NSClassFromString(className);
    if (!myClass)
    {
      myClass = self;  // self is a class within a class method
    }
    myInstance = [[myClass alloc] init];
    // any other special initialization as required here
  }
  return myInstance;
}
```

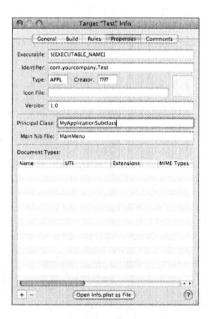

Figure 13.1   Setting the NSApplication class in
Xcode

Now, to select the subclass to use, a value would be placed in the Application's
Info.plist for the key MYGameHighScoreManagerClass. Notice that if the key is missing or
the lookup otherwise fails, this implementation falls back to the value returned by a call
to [self class].

Controlling Instantiation

To fully implement the Singleton pattern, it is necessary to prevent the creation of multiple instances of a class. While the +sharedInstance method implementation controls the creation and access of a single instance, it does not prevent other code from calling +alloc to manufacture more instances. It is therefore necessary to make a few more changes. Every method that causes the allocation of a new instance needs to be overridden to prevent instantiation. Methods of concern would be +new, +alloc, +allocWithZone:, -copyWithZone:, and -mutableCopyWithZone:. Our +sharedInstance method needs to be adjusted as well so that it can allocate an instance without calling the now overridden +alloc method. Here's one way to accomplish this:

```
+ (id) hiddenAlloc
{
  return [super alloc];
}


+ (id) alloc
{
  NSLog(@"%@: use +sharedInstance instead of +alloc",
      [[self class] name]);
  return nil;
}


+ (id) new
{
  return [self alloc];
}


+ (id) allocWithZone: (NSZone *) zone
{
  return [self alloc];
}


- (id) copyWithZone: (NSZone *) zone
{ // -copy inherited from NSObject calls -copyWithZone:
  NSLog(@"MYGameHighScoreManager: attempt to -copy may be a bug.");
  [self retain];
  return self;
}


- (id) mutableCopyWithZone: (NSZone *) zone
{
  // -mutableCopy inherited from NSObject calls -mutableCopyWithZone:

  return [self copyWithZone:zone];
}
```

```
+ (MYGameHighScoreManager *)sharedInstance
{
  static MYGameHighScoreManager *myInstance = nil;
  if (!myInstance)
  {
    NSBundle *mainBundle = [NSBundle mainBundle];
    NSDictionary *info = [mainBundle infoDictionary];
    NSString *className = [info objectForKey:
        @"MYGameHighScoreManagerClass"];
    Class *myClass = NSClassFromString(className);
    if (!myClass)
    {
      myClass = self;
    }
    myInstance  = [[myClass hiddenAlloc] init];
    // any other special initialization as required here
  }
  return myInstance;
}
```

The method +hiddenAlloc is considered private and is not declared in the class header. This method could be omitted all together if the singleton will never be subclassed because a call to [super alloc] would work. However, because we want to allow myClass to be determined dynamically at runtime, it is likely that the overridden +alloc will be called when the +alloc message is sent. Calling +hiddenAlloc prevents this problem. Furthermore, if there is the possibility of subclassing, then it may be necessary for subclass code to call or override the original super implementation of +alloc. By creating +hiddenAlloc, there is now a hook that subclassers may use if needed.

The new implementations of the object creation methods now log an error and return nil. Alternatively, they could return the results of a call to +sharedInstance if a subsequent call to -init would be harmless. Often, it's best to return nil. Some developers will prefer to throw an exception instead of just returning nil, though that would be considered extreme by others.

The new copying methods simply increase the retain count of the object so that the semantics of the reference counting system remain unchanged. They do not return a new instance, however. This preserves the Singleton nature of the class. Because technically copying a singleton is an error that may signal a deeper bug in the calling code, it makes sense to at least log a message when copying is attempted, though this isn't strictly required. Depending on the context and programmer preferences, throwing an exception or simply leaving out the log message might be preferred over this behavior.

Deallocation

Another issue with Singletons is the destruction of the shared instance. Because the instance is created in +sharedInstance and never released, there should always be a retain count of at least one as long as no buggy code calls -release more times than it should have. So in theory the instance will never be deallocated. If a shared instance represents a physical device, however, it may need to be given the opportunity to shut down cleanly if the application is terminating. The best way to do this is to have the shared object register for the NSApplicationWillTerminateNotification notification and shut down when it is received.

Usually, a shared instance should be instantiated only once during the lifetime of an application and only be shut down when the application terminates. In some applications of this pattern, however, it may make sense to allow the shared instance to be deallocated and then create a new instance later if it is needed again. If this is the case, things get a bit messy. First, the myInstance static variable needs to be moved out of the implementation of the +sharedInstance method so that other class methods can access it. Then a method like +attemptDealloc needs to be created and called whenever your code wants to try to deallocate the shared instance:

```
+ (void)attemptDealloc
{
    if ([myInstance retainCount] != 1) return;
    [myInstance release];
    myInstance = nil;
}
```

If some other object is still retaining the shared object, then we don't want to actually attempt to deallocate it. If the class object is the only place left that is still retaining the shared instance, then it's safe to send the release message. And of course, this only works if -dealloc hasn't been overridden to prevent deallocation.

Considering it's quite common to assume a shared instance will live until application death, it's also quite common for other objects to not retain it even if they keep references to it. This is a dangerous practice, though. It is safer to never keep a pointer to the shared instance and instead call +sharedInstance every time a reference is required.

Determining if the Singleton Has Been Created

In some cases it is useful to know if the shared instance has been created yet. Some Cocoa classes allow this to be determined; others do not. For example, NSSpellChecker implements the method +sharedSpellCheckerExists that will return YES or NO. On the other hand, NSApplication has no such method, given that it's pretty safe to assume the answer is always YES.

To add such a method to our singleton implementation, the static variable myInstance needs to be moved out of the implementation of the +sharedInstance method so that other class methods can access it. Then an implementation of +sharedInstanceExists might look like this:

```
+ (BOOL)sharedInstanceExists
{
  return (nil != myInstance);
}
```

Thread Safety

When a singleton is intended for use by multiple threads in a multithreaded application, it is crucial to implement it in a thread-safe manner. The previous example code omits any attempt at being thread-safe to keep it simple and clear. This can still work well, given that it is reasonable to assume that a game's high score table will only be accessed from the main thread. If a singleton will be used by multiple threads, however, care should be taken to make properties atomic as deemed necessary and to use @synchronized() blocks or NSLock instances as appropriate.

Working with Interface Builder

If a singleton will be used in Interface Builder, then it is necessary to make some alterations to the previous example code. To make connections or bindings to the singleton, it must be instantiated in Interface Builder, but this instantiation will operate through the +alloc and -init methods and expect the normal semantic. Having +alloc return nil will break things. The easiest way to fix this is to no longer treat a call to +alloc as an error and just have it call +sharedInstance like this:

```
+ (id)alloc
{
  return [self sharedInstance];
}
```

There is one additional concern, however. The -init method may now potentially be called multiple times and therefore needs to be made re-entrant. For most singletons, the best solution is to just have -init return immediately if it has already been called once. For example:

```
- (id)init
{
  if (![[self class] sharedInstanceExists])
  {
    // Normal initialization code goes here
  }
  return self;
}
```

Examples in Cocoa

There are several classes in Cocoa that are singletons. As mentioned at the start of this chapter, NSApplication is one such example. It encapsulates the connection between a Cocoa application and the window server. It receives events and distributes them to the correct objects via the First Responder pattern. It also sends drawing commands. Finally, it represents the application itself, handling all application-level events such as hiding and quitting. The global variable NSApp is a pointer to the shared NSApplication instance.

Another example is NSWorkspace, which encapsulates the application's communication with the Mac OS X Finder and underlying file systems. Because there is only one Finder and it doesn't make sense to have multiple connections to it, a singleton is used for this class.

The NSFontManager class is also a singleton. It represents the collection of all the fonts installed on the system and manages access to them so that all font objects can be shared. This helps keep an application efficient given that NSFontManager will ensure that only one instance of NSFont will ever be created for a given font installed on the system. Because the system only has a single collection of fonts, the manager needs to be a singleton itself.

Other examples are NSDocumentController, NSHelpManager, NSNull, NSProcessInfo, NSScriptExecutionContext, and NSUserDefaults. Some of the standard panels such as NSColorPanel and NSFontPanel are also shared. As you learn about new Cocoa objects, a quick glance at the class documentation will usually tell you if a class is a singleton. Simply look for a class method with the word "shared" in the name.

In Cocoa, usually the method used to obtain a shared instance includes the word "shared" and the name of the class minus the "NS" prefix. For example, use the method +sharedWorkspace to obtain the shared NSWorkspace instance or +sharedApplication to obtain the shared NSApplication instance. You might also see the more generic +sharedInstance method used for some objects.

Shared instances can sometimes be obtained by calling the +new class method. This use of the +new method is left over from prior versions of the frameworks and is deprecated. The +new method played a crucial role in the earliest frameworks that were developed for Objective-C but should not be used with Cocoa.

As Cocoa has matured, the shared nature of some Cocoa classes has changed. For example, before the advent of sheets, there were single print and page layout panels for the entire application. Bringing up either one would halt work in all windows until the panel was dismissed. As such, the NSPrintPanel and NSPageLayout classes were singletons. Now that they can appear multiple times simultaneously, as sheets on an application's windows, they are no longer shared objects.

Although these types of occurrences are rare, they can affect code that makes too many assumptions about the shared nature of these objects. For example, some developers would set up the print panel with some defaults early on and then assume that this setup would appear automatically every time the panel was displayed. After sheets created the possibility of more than one print panel, this no longer held true, and code had to be modified.

Consequences

One of the simplest patterns seen in Cocoa is called the "shared object" in Cocoa's documentation. This is commonly known as a "Singleton." A shared object is used in cases where a particular class should be instantiated once and only once.

Perhaps the most obvious example of a shared object is the central application object. Every Cocoa application has a single NSApplication instance. This makes sense; an object that represents a running application should only appear once per application.

Several other Cocoa classes are also shared objects. These include objects representing certain user interface panels such as the color and font panel and lower level objects such as the font manager, some scripting objects, and objects representing system resources such as the Finder. Any Cocoa objects that have a class method with the word "shared" in the name are using some variant of this pattern.

It is not difficult to write code for new classes to make them behave as singletons. As shown in this chapter, it is important to be aware of all class methods that have to do with object creation, copying, and destruction. Documentation should direct users of the class to use a specific method to obtain the shared instance.

To implement this pattern, the class object provides a method that is globally accessible and can be used to obtain the shared-object instance. At the same time, the +alloc method is disabled to prevent you from creating extra instances. The single, shared instance is created the first time you ask for it, and then the same instance is returned every time thereafter.

It is important to not over-apply this pattern when designing objects. Only make a class be a singleton when it represents something that truly should exist only once. Sometimes things that initially seem to fit this criteria will no longer fit as an application evolves. For example, if the hypothetical game used as an example in this chapter expands to have multiple game play variants, then each will need its own high score table. The Singleton approach for the high score table is no longer applicable in this case. Often, the Manager pattern described in Chapter 28, "Managers," becomes a better alternative. To demonstrate this, the high score table example presented in this chapter is extended to support multiple high score tables in Chapter 28.

14

Notifications

The Notification pattern enables communication between objects without tight coupling. An object is able to broadcast information to any number of other objects without any specific information about the other objects. An instance of Cocoa's NSNotification class encapsulates the information to be broadcast. Objects that are interested in receiving the information register themselves with an instance of Cocoa's NSNotificationCenter class. Registered objects are called observers, and the Notification pattern is sometimes called the "Observer" pattern in other frameworks. Registered observers specify the types of communication desired.

When a notification is sent to a notification center, the notification center distributes the notification to appropriate observers. A single notification may be broadcast to any number of observers. The object that sends a message to a notification center doesn't need to know what observers exist or how many observers ultimately receive the notification. Similarly, the observers don't necessarily need to know where notifications originate. Figure 14.1 illustrates the relationships between a notification sender, a notification center, and the observers.

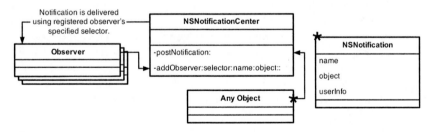

Figure 14.1   Relationships between notification
centers and observers

The NSNotificationCenter class stores registered observers as Anonymous Objects using the Heterogeneous Container pattern described in Chapter 7, "Anonymous Type and Heterogeneous Containers." Notification and Delegation are related patterns, and

Delegation is explained in Chapter 15, "Delegates." Notification is also similar to the Key Value Observing pattern described in Chapter 32, "Bindings and Controllers."

Motivation

Use the Notification pattern to establish anonymous communication between objects at runtime. Within the Model View Controller design pattern, notifications safely cross subsystem boundaries without tying the subsystems together. Model objects often generate notifications that are ultimately received by controller objects, which react by updating view objects. In the other direction, model and controller objects observe notifications that may originate in the view or controller subsystems. For example, when a Cocoa application is about to terminate, the NSApplication controller object posts the NSApplicationWillTerminateNotification to the application's default notification center. Model objects that need to perform clean-up processing before the application terminates register as observers to receive the NSApplicationWillTerminateNotification.

Use the Notification pattern to broadcast messages. Notifications may be posted by any number of objects and received by any number of objects. The Notification pattern enables one-to-many and many-to-many relationships between objects.

Use the Notification pattern with Cocoa's NSDistributedNotificationCenter class to achieve simple asynchronous interprocess communication.

Use the Notification pattern when anonymous objects need to passively observe and react to important events. In contrast, use the Delegates pattern when anonymous objects need to actively influence events as they happen.

Solution

The Notification pattern is not unique to Cocoa, and a simple version can be readily implemented using Foundation classes along with the Anonymous Object, Heterogeneous Containers, and Perform Selector patterns. The code in this section illustrates how design patterns are combined to implement the Notification pattern, but the example doesn't necessarily reflect the internal implementations of Cocoa classes. A real application should reuse Cocoa's NSNotification and NSNotificationCenter classes. If you're just interested in observing and sending notifications but not necessarily in how the pattern can be implemented with other Cocoa patterns, skip ahead to the "Examples in Cocoa" section of this chapter.

MYNotification

First, create a MYNotification class that will fill a role similar to Cocoa's NSNotification class. Instances of the MYNotification class encapsulate information about notifications, as shown in the following code:

```
@class MYNotification : NSObject
{
  NSString      *name;          // Identifies the notification
  id            object;         // an anonymous object
```

```
  NSDictionary     *infoDictionary;  // arbitrary associated info
}

- (id)initWithName:(NSString *)aName object:(id)anObject
    userInfo:(NSDictionary *)someUserInfo;

@property (readonly, copy) NSString *name;
@property (readonly, assign) id object;
@property (readonly, copy) NSDictionary *infoDictionary;

@end
```

The MYNotification class has the following straightforward implementation:

```
@interface MYNotification ()

// Re-declare the properties so that their values can be set by methods
// within the implementation of this class.
@property (readwrite, copy) NSString *name;
@property (readwrite, assign) id object;
@property (readwrite, copy) NSDictionary *infoDictionary;

@end


@implementation MYNotification

@synthesize name;
@synthesize object;
@synthesize infoDictionary;

- (id)initWithName:(NSString *)aName object:(id)anObject
    userInfo:(NSDictionary *)someUserInfo
{
  [self setName:aName];
  [self setObject:anObject];
  [self setInfoDictionary:someUserInfo];

  return self;
}


- (void)dealloc
{
  [self setName:nil];
  [self setObject:nil];
  [self setInfoDictionary:nil];
  [super dealloc];
}

@end
```

MYNotificationCenter

Instances of the MYNotificationCenter class store information about observers in a Heterogeneous Container called observersDictionary. MYNotificationCenter is similar to Cocoa's NSNotificationCenter class.

```
@class MYNotificationCenter : NSObject
{
  NSMutableDictionary    *observersDictionary;
}

+ (id)defaultCenter;

- (void)addObserver:(id)notificationObserver
    selector:(SEL)notificationSelector
    name:(NSString *)notificationName
    object:(id)objectOfInterest;

- (void)removeObserver:(id)notificationObserver;

- (void)postNotification:(MYNotification *)aNotification;

- (void)postNotificationName:(NSString *)aName
    object:(id)objectOfInterest userInfo:(NSDictionary *)someUserInfo;
@end
```

Call MYNotificationCenter's -addObserver:selector:name:object: method to register an observer. The first argument is the observer being registered. The second argument is a selector that identifies the Objective-C message to be sent to the observer when an appropriate notification is posted. The selector must specify a method that takes one argument, and that argument must be a pointer to a notification instance. Selectors are explained in Chapter 9, "Perform Selector and Delayed Perform." The third and fourth arguments, name: and object:, identify which notifications the observer is interested in receiving. Only notifications with names that match the specified name are delivered to the registered observer. If an observer wants to receive multiple kinds of notification, the observer can register with the notification center multiple times, specifying a different notification name each time. Similarly, the object: argument identifies an object of interest to the observer. Only notifications with objects that match the specified object are delivered to the registered observer. The MYNotificationCenter class provides a little bit more flexibility with object argument: If nil is specified, all notifications that match the specified name are delivered regardless of the notification's object.

In many respects, MYNotificationCenter duplicates the capability of NSNotificationCenter. However, when using Cocoa's NSNotificationCenter class, if the name: argument to -addObserver:selector:name:object is nil, the observer is registered to receive all notifications associated with the specified `object:` argument. The `MYNotificationCenter` class doesn't allow registration with a `nil` notification name.

Objects that are registered to observe notifications eventually need to be unregistered. The convention adopted by Cocoa is that registered observers unregister themselves by calling the notification center's `-removeObserver:` method. One call to a notification center's `-removeObserver:` unregisters all of the observer's previous registrations with that center. The most common place to call `-removeObserver:` is within the observer's `-dealloc` implementation. It's an error to leave a deallocated object registered as an observer.

> ### Note
> When using Cocoa's automated memory garbage collection introduced in Objective-C 2.0 with Mac OS X 10.5, `NSNotificationCenter` automatically unregisters observers that are no longer in use somewhere else in the application.

Neither `MYNotificationCenter` nor Cocoa's `NSNotificationCenter` retain observers or the objects observers are interested in. If they did retain registered observers, it would likely cause retain cycles that prevent observer deallocation. The observers' `-dealloc` would never be called because each observer would still retained by the notification center.

The following simple private class stores the information about registered observers but doesn't retain the observer or the object of interest to the observer:

```
@interface _MYNotificationObserverRecord : NSObject
{
  id    object;     // anonymous object of interest
  id    observer;   // anonymous observer
  SEL   selector;   // selector to call
}

@property (readwrite, assign) id object;
@property (readwrite, assign) id observer;
@property (readwrite, assign) SEL selector;

@end
```

The implementation of `_MYNotificationObserverRecord` includes only the synthesis of methods for accessing the class' properties.

```
@implementation _MYNotificationObserverRecord

@synthesize object;
@synthesize observer;
```

```
@synthesize selector;

@end
```

MYNotificationCenter stores _MYNotificationObserverRecords indirectly: MYNotificationCenter's observersDictionary is a mutable dictionary of mutable arrays keyed to notification names, and each array stores MYNotificationObserverRecord instances.

```
@interface MYNotificationCenter ()

@property (readwrite, retain) NSMutableDictionary *observersDictionary;

@end


@implementation MYNotificationCenter

@synthesize observersDictionary;


+ (id)defaultCenter
{
  // The shared "default" instance created as needed
  static id           sharedNotificationCenter = nil;

  if(nil == sharedNotificationCenter)
  {
    sharedNotificationCenter = [[MYNotificationCenter alloc] init];
  }

  return sharedNotificationCenter;
}


// Designated initializer
- (id)init
{
  if(nil != (self = [super init]))
  {
    [self setObserversDictionary:[NSMutableDictionary dictionary]];
  }

  return self;
}
```

```
- (void)dealloc
{
  [self setObserversDictionary:nil];
  [super dealloc];
}


- (void)addObserver:(id)notificationObserver
    selector:(SEL)notificationSelector
    name:(NSString *)notificationName
    object:(id)objectOfInterest
{ // This class requires a non-nil notificationName, NSNotification
  // has no corresponding restriction.
  NSParameterAssert(notificationName);

  _MYNotificationObserverRecord  *newRecord =
      [[[_MYNotificationObserverRecord alloc] init] autorelease];

  [newRecord setObject:objectOfInterest];
  [newRecord setObserver:notificationObserver];
  [newRecord setSelector:notificationSelector];

  // There is an array of observer records for each notification name
  NSArray  *observers = [observersDictionary
      objectForKey:notificationName];

  if(nil != observers)
  {
    [observers addObject:newRecord];
  }
  else
  { // This is the first observer record for notificationName so
    // create the array to store this observer record and all
    // future observer records for the same notificationName.
    [observersDictionary setObject:[NSMutableArray
        arrayWithObject:newRecord]
        forKey:notificationName];
  }
}


- (void)removeObserver:(id)notificationObserver
{
  if(nil != notificationObserver)
  {
    for(NSMutableArray *observers in [self observersDictionary])
```

```
   {
     NSInteger       i;

     for(i = [observers count] - 1; i >= 0; i—)
     {
       currentObserverRecord = [observers objectAtIndex:i];
       if(notificationObserver == [currentObserverRecord
           observer])
       {
         [observers removeObjectAtIndex:i];
       }
     }
   }
 }
}


- (void)postNotification:(MYNotification *)aNotification
{
  NSParameterAssert(aNotification);
  NSAssert(nil != [aNotification name], @"nil notification name");

  NSArray  *observers = [observersDictionary objectForKey:
      [aNotification name]];

  for(id currentObserverRecord in observers)
  {
    id      object = [currentObserverRecord object];

    if(nil == object || object == [aNotification object])
    { // observer is either interested in notifications for all
      // objects or at least this object.
      [[currentObserverRecord observer] performSelector:
          [currentObserverRecord selector] withObject:
          aNotification];
    }
  }
}


- (void)postNotificationName:(NSString *)aName
    object:(id)objectOfInterest
    userInfo:(NSDictionary *)someUserInfo;
{ // This method creates a suitable MYNotification instances and
  // then posts it.
  MYNotification   *newNotification = [[[MYNotification alloc]
```

```
    initWithName:aName object:objectOfInterest
    userInfo:someUserInfo] autorelease];

  [self postNotification:newNotification];
}


@end
```

The sample application provided at www.CocoaDesignPatterns.com includes some test cases for the MYNotification and MYNotificationCenter classes.

Associative Storage

The MYNotificationCenter implementation uses the Associative Storage pattern explained in Chapter 19, "Associative Storage." Associative Storage, embodied by Cocoa's NSDictionary class, allows you to store arbitrary objects associated with other objects called *keys*. The idea is that you can later quickly look up the object based on its key. In the MYNotificationCenter example, notification names are used as keys to look up arrays that contain _MYNotificationObserverRecord instances.

There is another subtler use of Associative Storage: Both the MYNotification class and Cocoa's NSNotification class allow you to pass along a "userInfo" dictionary with each notification. The "userInfo" dictionary can contain any combination of key value pairs that makes sense for your application. Some of the notifications posted by Cocoa classes make use of the extra information passing capability. For example, Cocoa's NSTextView class posts the NSTextViewDidChangeSelectionNotification whenever the user's selection changes. The NSTextViewDidChangeSelectionNotification provides the range of the previous selection using the key, NSOldSelectedCharacterRange, in the notification's "userInfo" dictionary. The following code shows how an object registers itself to receive the NSTextViewDidChangeSelectionNotification notification.

```
[[NSNotificationCenter defaultCenter]
    addObserver:self
    selector:@selector(textViewSelectionDidChange:)
    name:NSTextViewDidChangeSelectionNotification
    object:nil];
```

An implementation of -(void)textViewSelectionDidChange:(NSNotification *)aNotification uses the notification's "userInfo" as follows:

```
-(void)textViewSelectionDidChange:(NSNotification *)aNotification
{
  NSValue    *oldSelectionRangeValue = [[aNotification userInfo]
    objectForKey:@"NSOldSelectedCharacterRange"];

  NSRange    oldSelectionRange = [oldSelectionRangeValue rangeValue];

  // Do something with oldSelectionRange
}
```

Examples in Cocoa

The Notification pattern is commonly used within Cocoa, and Apple provides a "Notifications" section in the documentation for each class that posts notifications. Cocoa classes post their notifications to the default notification center obtained via NSNotificationCenter's +defaultCenter method. You are also free to use the default notification center. Programmers rarely create application-specific notification centers.

Global Notification Names

Notification names are NSString instances. Cocoa class documentation lists the notifications posted by each class by identifying global notification names with symbols like NSApplicationDidFinishLaunchingNotification, NSApplicationDidUpdateNotification, and NSTableViewColumnDidResizeNotification. Apple recommends that you copy and paste the notification name symbols into your code exactly as shown in the documentation.

If you look in the Cocoa header files, you will find declarations like the following:

```
extern NSString *NSTableViewColumnDidResizeNotification;
```

If you could see Apple's source code, you would find the NSTableViewColumnDidResizeNotification global variable initialized similar to the following:

```
NSString *NSTableViewColumnDidResizeNotification =
    @"NSTableViewColumnDidResizeNotification";
```

What this means is that for practical purposes, the following two code samples produce the same result:

```
// Register for notifications using the global symbol
[[NSNotificationCenter defaultCenter]
    addObserver:self
    selector:@selector(tableViewColumnDidResize:)
    name:NSTableViewColumnDidResizeNotification
    object:nil];

//Register for notifications using a local NSString constant
[[NSNotificationCenter defaultCenter]
    addObserver:self
    selector:@selector(tableViewColumnDidResize:)
    name:@"NSTableViewColumnDidResizeNotification"
    object:nil];
```

The global strings declared in the Cocoa header files can be used interchangeably with the same string values defined as local variables in your code. Use the framework supplied global variable to avoid hard coding constant strings in your code.

"Will" and "Did" Notifications

Cocoa's notification names consistently use a naming pattern that helps you determine which notifications you want to observe. Names that include the word "Will" are used for notification that tell observers about something that is about to happen. Names that include the word "Did" are for notifications that tell observers about something that already happened. In some cases, both types of notification are provided for the same event. For example, NSApplication posts both NSApplicationWillHideNotification and NSApplicationDidHideNotification.

Synchronous Versus Asynchronous Notifications

Posting a notification to an NSNotificationCenter is synchronous. What that means is that when you post a notification with -postNotification: or any of the related NSNotificationCenter methods, the notification is delivered to all appropriate registered observers before -postNotification: returns control to your code. The synchronous behavior also means that you should be mindful of the consequences when you implement methods to react to notifications. If you perform lengthy operations in your notification handling code, you delay the receipt of the notification by other objects and delay return to the code that posted the notification.

One common trick used to initiate complex processing in response to a notification is to use delayed perform. In your notification handling code, schedule a future message and return immediately as follows:

```
- (void)tableViewSelectionDidChange:(NSNotification *)aNotification
{   // schedule a future message and return from the method
    [self performSelector:@selector(doComplexProcessing:)
        withObject:[aNotification object] afterDelay:0.0f];
}

- (void)doComplexProcessing:(id)anObject
{   // Do some complex processing based on anObject
}
```

When you need more complex asynchronous behavior than just delaying a message, use Cocoa's NSNotificationQueue class. NSNotificationQueue instances implement an asynchronous First In First Out (FIFO) queue. When you call NSNotificationQueue's - (void)enqueueNotification:(NSNotification *)notification postingStyle:(NSPostingStyle)postingStyle coalesceMask:(NSUInteger)coalesceMask forModes:(NSArray *)modes method, the specified notification is placed in the back of a queue, and control is returned to the caller. Based on the values of postingStyle, coalesceMask, and modes, at some later time the NSNotificationQueue posts the notification to an NSNotificationCenter. From that point on, the notification is processed synchronously by the NSNotificationCenter. Figure 14.2 identifies the relationships between the object that enqueues a notification, the notification queue, the notification center, and the registered observers.

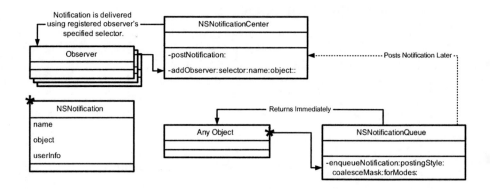

Figure 14.2   Relationships between notification queues and notification centers

Every thread in a Cocoa application has a default notification queue instance that's accessed via the NSNotificationQueue class method, + (NSNotificationQueue *)defaultQueue. The default notification queue posts notifications to its thread's default notification center. Just like you can create your own application-specific notification centers, you can also create application-specific notification queues. For example, the following code allocates two new notification queues that will both post notifications to the same hypothetical pre-existing myApplicationSpecificNotificationCenter object.

```
NSNotificationQueue *applicationSpecificNotificationQueue1 =
   [[NSNotificationQueue alloc]
   initWithNotificationCenter:myApplicationSpecificNotificationCenter];


NSNotificationQueue *applicationSpecificNotificationQueue2 =
   [[NSNotificationQueue alloc]
   initWithNotificationCenter:myApplicationSpecificNotificationCenter];
```

The postingStyle: argument to NSNotificationQueue's -enqueueNotification: postingStyle:coalesceMask:forModes: supports three styles: NSPostASAP, NSPostWhenIdle, and NSPostNow. The NSPostASAP style directs the queue to post the notification at the beginning of the next run loop iteration and is effectively identical to the -performSelector:withObject:afterDelay: example provided earlier in this section. Cocoa's run loop is documented at http://developer.apple.com/documentation/Cocoa/ Reference/Foundation/Classes/NSRunLoop_Class/Reference/Reference.html. The NSPostWhenIdle style directs the queue to post the notification the next time the Cocoa run loop is idle, meaning that there are no user events or other input sources with data ready for processing. Finally, the NSPostNow style directs the queue to post the notification immediately and synchronously. The only difference between enqueuing a notification with NSPostNow style and just calling a Notificationcenter's -postNotification:

method is that NSNotificationQueue will still coalesce duplicate notifications that might have been waiting in the queue. Coalescing just means that multiple similar enqueued notifications can be combined into one and only posted once.

The coalesceMask: argument allows you to specify how you want the queue to handle multiple similar notifications. The available options are NSNotificationNoCoalescing, NSNotificationCoalescingOnName, and NSNotificationCoalescingOnSender. You can specify both NSNotification CoalescingOnName and NSNotificationCoalescingOnSender by using the C language bit-wise "or" operator. If they are both specified, only enqueued notifications that share both the same name and the same object are coalesced.

The forModes: argument allows you to specify an array of run loop modes in which the queue is allowed to post notifications. If you specify nil for the forModes: argument, the queue will only post notifications when the run loop is in NSDefaultRunLoopMode. The NSRunLoop class documentation provides a description of the available modes.

Distributed Notifications

Cocoa provides a mechanism for posting notifications that are transmitted to all applications running on the same computer. These distributed notifications have some limitations and are relatively inefficient compared to other interapplication communication techniques, but they are very simple to use. Each Cocoa application has a default instance of the NSDistributedNotificationCenter class that is accessed via NSDistributed NotificationCenter's +defaultCenter method.

NSDistributedNotificationCenter is a subclass of NSNotificationCenter, so notifications are posted to the default NSDistributedNotificationCenter in the same way they are posted to a regular NSNotificationCenter, via the -postNotification: method. Notifications posted to distributed notification centers are asynchronous and are therefore not received immediately when they are posted. NSDistributedNotification Center provides the -(void)postNotificationName: (NSString *)notificationName object: (NSString *)notificationSender userInfo: (NSDictionary *)userInfo deliverImmediately: (BOOL)deliverImmediately method so that you are able to specify how to handle the situation when some of the observers are suspended by the operating system and therefore not running.

The object: argument of notifications that are posted to a NSNotificationCenter is required to be an instance of NSString. With distributed notifications, the object: arguments originate in different applications from the observers. Therefore, distributed notifications are filtered based on the string value of the object: argument instead of its address. The userInfo: argument to distributed notifications is encoded via the Archiving and Unarchiving pattern explained in Chapter 11, "Archiving and Unarchiving." Therefore, all objects in the userInfo: dictionary are required to implement Archiving and Unarchiving.

Objects are registered to observe distributed notifications by using one of two NSDistributedNotificationCenter methods: -(void)addObserver: (id)anObserver

```
selector:(SEL)aSelector name:(NSString *)notificationName object:
(NSString *)anObject or -(void)addObserver:(id)anObserver selector:(SEL)
aSelector name:(NSString *)notificationName object:(NSString *)anObject
suspensionBehavior:(NSNotificationSuspensionBehavior)suspensionBehavior.
```

NSDistributedNotificationCenter's -setSuspended: method is used to suspend distribution of distributed notifications to observers. If -setSuspended: is called with YES as the argument, the distributed notification center for that application temporarily stops receiving notifications. The NSApplication object in Application Kit-based applications automatically calls -setSuspended:YES when the application is inactive and calls -setSuspended:NO when the application becomes active. Cocoa applications that don't use the Application Kit framework need to explicitly manage suspension of distributed notifications by calling -setSuspended: when appropriate.

The notifications that are posted but not received by a suspended application are handled in one of four ways depending on the suspensionBehavior: argument to -addObserver:selector:name:object:suspensionBehavior:. The available behaviors are enumerated by Cocoa's NSNotificationSuspensionBehavior type, which defines the following constants: NSNotificationSuspensionBehaviorDrop, NSNotification SuspensionBehaviorCoalesce, NSNotificationSuspensionBehaviorHold, and NSNotificationSuspensionBehaviorDeliverImmediately.

If NSNotificationSuspensionBehaviorDrop is used, distributed notifications that would otherwise be received are not received and are not queued for later delivery. If NSNotificationSuspensionBehaviorCoalesce is used, at most one notification with each matching name and object arguments queued for delivery when the observer is no longer suspended. If NSNotificationSuspensionBehaviorHold is used, notifications are queued, and they are all delivered when the observer is no longer suspended. The number of notifications that can be queued is undefined but is likely subject to operating system resource constraints. For that reason, caution must be used when specifying NSNotificationSuspensionBehaviorHold to avoid misuse of system resources. Finally, if NSNotificationSuspensionBehaviorDeliverImmediately is used, notifications are sent to observers immediately regardless of whether the distributed notifications are suspended. The "deliver immediately" behavior should only be used for critical notifications that cannot be delayed or ignored.

Observers are removed for the distributed notification center with the -remove Observer:name:object: method that NSDistributedNotificationCenter inherits from its superclass, NSNotificationCenter. When an object registered to observe distributed notifications is deallocated, the observer must remove itself from all notification centers, or there is a risk that notifications will be sent to deallocated objects.

Consequences

The biggest weakness of the Notification pattern is that class designers must anticipate the need for notifications. The developers at Apple were able to anticipate that programmers would want to do something special when a window is about to be closed and provided the NSWindowWillCloseNotification. There is a trade-off. Posting a notification takes some processor time even when there are no registered observers for the notification. It's not practical to post a notification for every single application state change. Therefore, designers must find a balance between too many and too few notifications.

The Delegates pattern in Chapter 15 is closely related to the Notification pattern. In fact, Cocoa classes use the Delegate pattern in many of the same cases that notifications are used. As a general rule, use Notifications when there are potentially many objects that may observe the notification. Use the Delegates pattern when exactly one object is given an opportunity to influence or react to changes as they are happening.

15

Delegates

A delegate is an object that's given an opportunity to react to changes in another object or influence the behavior of another object. The basic idea is that two objects coordinate to solve a problem. One object is very general and intended for reuse in a wide variety of situations. It stores a reference to another object, its delegate, and sends messages to the delegate at critical times. The messages may just inform the delegate that something has happened, giving the delegate an opportunity to do extra processing, or the messages may ask the delegate for critical information that will control what happens. The delegate is typically a unique custom object within the Controller subsystem of your application.

Delegates are one of the simplest and most flexible patterns in Cocoa and are made possible by the use of the Anonymous Type pattern described in Chapter 7, "Anonymous Type and Heterogenous Containers." Delegates highlight key advantages of using anonymous objects when designing reusable classes.

Motivation

Delegates simplify the customization of object behavior while minimizing coupling between objects. Cocoa's NSWindow class uses a delegate to control window behavior. NSWindow is a very general class that encapsulates all aspects of windows in a graphical user interface. Windows can be resized and moved. They have embedded controls for closing, minimizing, or maximizing the window. Almost all graphical Cocoa applications use windows, yet window handling must be customized in many cases. For example, an application may need to constrain the size of a window or give users a chance to save changes to the content of a window before the window closes.

One way to customize the behavior of the standard NSWindow class is to subclass it and implement new behaviors in the subclass. However, subclassing requires very tight coupling between the subclass and its superclass. Overuse of subclassing results in the creation of many classes that are application-specific and not very reusable. Subclassing statically establishes the relationship between the subclass and its superclass at compile time. In many cases, runtime flexibility is desired. For example, constraints on the resizing behavior of a window might change based on user actions at runtime. More importantly, the logic used to customize window behavior may depend on details of the application's implementation. In the Model View Controller pattern emphasized throughout Cocoa, windows are clearly part of the view subsystem, but application details are better encapsulated within the model or controller subsystems. Subclassing NSWindow to add application logic causes a contamination between the separate subsystems.

Thanks to the use of delegates, there is usually no need to subclass the NSWindow. The NSWindow class has a delegate and sends messages to the delegate just before the window is resized, closed, or otherwise modified. When the window's delegate receives messages sent by the window, the delegate can perform necessary application-specific processing such as checking to see if the window contains any unsaved changes before it is closed and if so, giving the user a chance to save the changes or cancel the operation. The delegate can be part of the controller subsystem and have little coupling to other subsystems. All the delegate has to do is implement the appropriate methods corresponding to messages that the window will send to it.

Using delegates simplifies application development. In many cases, this pattern is simultaneously simpler to implement and more flexible than the alternative. The delegate is free to implement some, all, or none of the methods corresponding to delegate messages. A single object can be the delegate of multiple objects. For example, a single object might be the delegate for all of the windows in an application. Conversely, every window might have a different delegate, or the delegate might be changed at runtime.

To further explore the motivation behind the Delegates pattern, consider the client side of a hypothetical client-server application. The client application establishes a single network connection to a server and displays any number of data windows containing information obtained from the server. The client application may provide many other types of windows as well such as font panels, spelling checkers, user preferences, and so on. If at any time, the user closes the last data window, he or she should be presented with the option to close the network connection to the server or leave it open for future use. Now consider the information needed to implement this functionality. Determining whether the window being closed is the last open data window requires information about (coupling with) all other open data windows. The ability to close a network connection requires detailed information about (coupling with) networking classes. Implementing this behavior within a subclass of NSWindow couples that subclass, which is part of the View subsystem, to networking classes that are clearly not part of the View subsystem. Furthermore, giving every open data window information about every other open data window can easily result in difficult to maintain spaghetti code as suggested by Figure 15.1 in which arrows indicate coupling between objects.

In contrast, when the Delegates pattern is used, each window only has information about its delegate. Figure 15.2 identifies the coupling between the windows and one object that serves as the delegate for all data windows. The lines are drawn dashed to indicate that the coupling is very weak. Each window has little information about its delegate except that the delegate may be able to receive some of the messages the window might send. The delegate merely keeps a count of the number of open data windows without any specific information about the windows themselves.

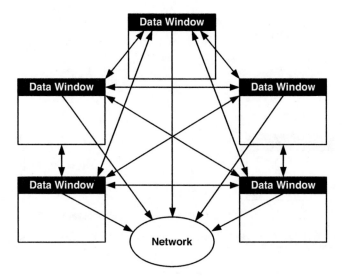

Figure 15.1   Coupling between objects when NSWindow is
subclassed to implement application behavior

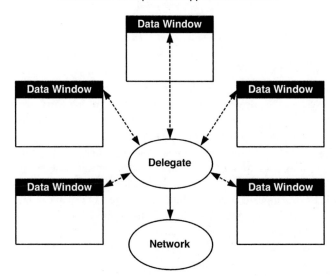

Figure 15.2   Coupling between objects when the Delegates
pattern is used

Because the coupling between the data windows and the delegate is so loose, it's very likely that modification to either the windows or the delegate can be made without affecting the other objects, and that's a worthwhile goal. For example, consider what happens when the client application is enhanced so that different data windows can show data from different servers. Figure 15.3 shows one possible implementation that takes advantage of the Delegates pattern.

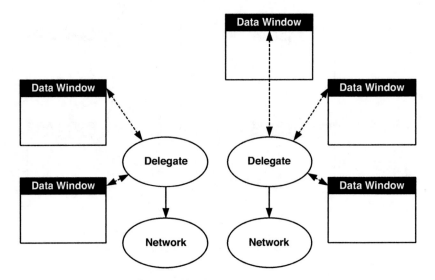

Figure 15.3   Coupling between objects when multiple delegates are used

Because the Delegates pattern is used, there is no need to change any code to enable multiple network connections. The delegate referenced by each window is assigned at runtime. When the last window that shows data from one particular server is closed, the delegate can give the user the option to close the connection to that server without impact to connections maintained by other delegates to other servers.

Delegates eliminate one of the most common situations in which multiple-inheritance may be desired. If the design goal is to close a network connection when the last window that displays content from the connection is closed, it might be tempting to try and create a new class that inherits both the ability to manage a network connection and the ability to manage window closing. However, multiple-inheritance is not supported by the Objective-C language, and the Delegates pattern provides a more flexible and simpler solution than trying to merge two separate inheritance hierarchies.

The Delegates pattern is very general and can be used in many situations. The emphasis so far on NSWindow's delegate just shows one of the most obvious examples. Many Cocoa classes support the use of delegates as an alternative to subclassing. For example, Cocoa's NSApplication class uses a delegate to provide specialized processing in common situations such as when a Cocoa application has just finished launching or when it's about to be quit.

Having an alternative to subclassing becomes more and more important as classes get more complex. Cocoa classes such as NSBrowser are sufficiently complex that subclassing them without introducing errors is challenging. In contrast, a class created to act as the delegate for an NSBrowser instance may be a direct subclass of NSObject, and it can be implemented very simply with a focus on only the capabilities unique to the application being built.

> Note
>
> Apple's class documentation for each Cocoa class that uses a delegate includes a section titled "Methods Implemented by the Delegate." The section describes each message that instances of the class send to a delegate and the circumstances under which the message will be sent. Objects acting as delegates are free to implement any subset of the documented delegate messages.

Solution

A delegate is an object referenced using Objective-C's anonymous type, id. The reference to the delegate is typically an instance variable named delegate, and methods that use the Accessors pattern described in Chapter 10, "Accessors," are provided to set or return the current delegate object. The following simple MYBarView class provides a typical implementation of delegate support:

```
@interface MYBarView : NSView
{
  IBOutlet id delegate;      //! The delegate if any
  NSColor     *barColor;     //! The color of the bar
  float       barValue;      //! The value (0.0 to 1.0) to indicate
}

//! Accessors
- (id)delegate;
- (void)setDelegate:(id)anObject;
- (float)barValue;
- (void)setBarValue:(float)aValue;
- (NSColor *)barColor;
- (void)setBarColor:(NSColor *)aColor;

//! Actions
- (IBAction)takeBarValueFrom:(id)sender;

@end
```

In Cocoa, the NSView class encapsulates a rectangular area within a window and enables drawing within that area. MYBarView is a subclass of NSView that fills a portion of its area with a colored bar. Figure 15.4 shows a screen shot of a simple Cocoa application that displays several instance of the MYBarView class.

The MYBarView class implemented in the remainder of this section allows a delegate to control instance operation: The delegate object can provide easy application-specific control over the range of values that can be shown by each instance of MYBarView. The delegate object can also implement application-specific side effects to value changes such as changing the color of the bar based on its value. Using a delegate allows customization of behavior without the need to subclass MYBarView. Using different delegate objects for different MYBarView instances or basing the delegate object's logic on the specific MYBarView instance that called each delegate method enables per-instance customization.

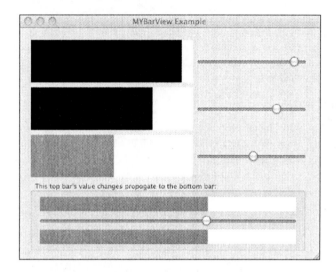

Figure 15.4   A simple application that uses several instances of MYBarView with delegates

Implementing Delegate Support

The first key to providing support for a delegate is the delegate instance variable defined as an IBOutlet of type id. The IBOutlet symbol used in the declaration of an instance variable is just a hint to Apple's graphical Interface Builder application that instance variable accepts connections to other objects. Such instance variables are described in Chapter 17, "Outlets, Targets, and Actions." Declaring the delegate variable with type id tells the Objective-C compiler that any object can be used as the delegate. This use of the id type is explained in Chapter 7. The -delegate and -setDelegate:(id)anObject methods are accessors (Chapter 10) that provide a programmatic way to set and get the delegate objects at runtime.

> **Note**
>
> When an Interface Builder .nib file is loaded, the -setDelegate: accessor method will be called automatically to re-create any connection to the delegate outlet that was made in Interface Builder. The automatic use of appropriately named accessor methods is explained in Chapter 10.

The next step to supporting delegates is to define the messages that may be sent to a delegate. The following Objective-C 2.0 formal protocol defines the messages with the @optional key word so that delegates that conform to the protocol don't have to implement all of the methods:

```
//! Formal protocol defines messages sent from MYBarView to its
// delegate
@protocol MYBarViewDelegate

@optional
- (float)barView:(id)barView shouldChangeValue:(float)newValue;
- (void)barViewWillChangeValue:(NSNotification *)aNotification;
- (void)barViewDidChangeValue:(NSNotification *)aNotification;


@end
```

All versions of Objective-C that are used with Cocoa support informal protocols. The following category of NSObject is an informal protocol that declares MYBarView's delegate messages:

```
//! Informal protocol defines messages sent from MYBarView to its
// delegate
@interface NSObject (MYBarViewDelegateSupport)

- (float)barView:(id)barView shouldChangeValue:(float)newValue;
- (void)barViewWillChangeValue:(NSNotification *)aNotification;
- (void)barViewDidChangeValue:(NSNotification *)aNotification;


@end
```

Categories and informal protocols are an Objective-C feature used frequently in the implementation of Cocoa. Some of the common Cocoa delegate messages have an NSNotification argument. Notifications are described by the Notifications pattern in Chapter 14, "Notifications." The Notifications pattern is closely related to the Delegates pattern. In fact, some of the delegate messages provided by the MYBarView class have corresponding notifications. The practice of providing both delegate messages and notifications is common in Cocoa and is reflected in the MYBarView class. Whenever notifications are used, it's important to provide unique names for the notifications. The notifications sent by MYBarView correspond to the related delegate messages and are named with the following definitions:

```
//! Notification names
extern NSString  *MYBarViewDidChangeValueNotification;
extern NSString  *MYBarViewWillChangeValueNotification;
```

> **Tip**
>
> **Naming Delegate Messages**
>
> There is a convention to the way messages sent to delegates are named. Each such message starts with an identification of the type of object that sends the message. The delegate messages sent by the `MYBarView` class all start with `barView`. Delegate messages usually include one of three verbs: `should`, `will`, or `did`.
>
> Messages that use `should` are expected to return a value and usually take an argument that directly identifies the object sending the message. These messages are sent to the delegate before a change to the object sending the message. The delegate is given an opportunity to influence the change. For example, Cocoa's `NSText` object sends the `-textShouldBeginEditing:` message to its delegate and expects a Boolean return value. If the delegate returns `NO`, editing does not begin. In this way, the delegate influences the behavior of the object that sends the messages.
>
> Messages that use `will` are not expected to return values. These messages are sent before a change happens and are strictly informative. The delegate can implement a method to synchronize the application's state or perform additional processing when such a message is received.
>
> Finally, the `did` messages are sent after a change happens. These messages are also strictly informative and give the delegate an opportunity to perform processing after the change.

`MYBarView`'s `@interface` declaration contains all of the information needed to configure a `MYBarView` instance in Interface Builder and connect it to a delegate. Before examining how the delegate itself is written, consider how the `MYBarView` class is implemented to use its delegate. The full source code for the `MYBarView` class is provided at www.CocoaDesignPatterns.com as part of an example application. The online example shows how all of the features of the class including drawing and initialization are implemented. The following code focuses on the implementation of delegate support independent of the other features of the `MYBarView` class.

`MYBarView`'s accessor methods are typical and are shown here to emphasize what they don't contain. Accessors generally should not send any messages to the delegate because the delegate may call the accessors, and calling back to the delegate might then result in infinite recursion.

```
//! Accessors
- (float)barValue
//! Returns the receiver's value
{
  return barValue;
}

- (void)setBarValue:(float)aValue
//! Sets the receiver's value
{
  barValue = aValue;
  [self setNeedsDisplay:YES];
```

```
}

- (NSColor *)barColor
//! Returns the receiver's color
{
    return barColor;
}

- (void)setBarColor:(NSColor *)aColor
//! Sets the receiver's color
{
    [aColor retain];
    [barColor release];
    barColor = aColor;
    [self setNeedsDisplay:YES];
}
```

The `- (void) setBarValue:(float)aValue` and `- (void) setBarColor:(NSColor *)aColor` methods use the most common implementations of accessor methods for a nonobject and an object property, respectively. In Cocoa, the NSColor class encapsulates colors, and `-setBarColor:` is essentially boilerplate code. A critical distinction exists between a standard accessor like `-setBarColor:` and the accessor used to set the delegate object as follows:

```
- (id)delegate
//! Returns the receiver's delegate
{
    return delegate;
}

- (void)setDelegate:(id)anObject
//! Sets the receiver's delegate
{
    delegate = anObject;  // Note: not retained!
}
```

The color object set by `-setBarColor:` is retained, but the delegate object set by `- (void) setDelegate:(id)anObject` is not retained. This is a subtle but important nuance that exists to avoid retain cycles. A retain cycle occurs when two or more objects each retain a reference to the other(s), resulting in a situation where none of the objects ever can be deallocated because each is still being used by another. Cocoa conventions for memory management are briefly explained as part of the Accessor pattern in Chapter 10, and the specific issue with retain cycles is described in the "Memory Management" section of /Developer/Documentation/Cocoa/ObjectiveC/ObjC.pdf.

The general philosophy is that because objects that support a delegate can and do work perfectly well without any delegate at all, the delegate is not a critical property that should be retained. Objects are not considered to "own" their delegates and thus shouldn't retain them. Objects implemented within the Cocoa frameworks do not retain their delegates. If an object still has a pointer to its delegate after the delegate has been deallocated, errors including application crash may result when messages are sent to the deallocated delegate. Therefore, objects that serve as delegates should implement -dealloc to send -setDelegate:nil messages as necessary to make sure no other objects have pointers to the soon to be deallocated object.

MYBarView's accessor method implementations are shown in this example to accentuate the differences between the implementations for delegates and other properties. With Objective-C 2.0, you could have used the following @property declarations in the MYBarView interface:

```
@property (assign, nonatomic, readwrite) IBOutlet id delegate;
@property (retain, nonatomic, readwrite) NSColor *barColor;
@property (nonatomic, readwrite) float barValue;
```

The implementation of MYBarView's - (IBAction) takeBarValueFrom: (id) sender method calls private methods of the MYBarView class to send delegate messages to a delegate object:

```
//! Actions
- (IBAction)takeBarValueFrom:(id)sender
/*! Sets receiver's value to sender's floatValue.  The receiver's
 delegate is given an opportunity to change the new value before it is
 set and the delegate is notified of the change before and after the
 value is set. */
{
  float newValue = [sender floatValue];

  newValue = [self _myBarShouldChangeValue:newValue];
  [self _myBarWillChangeValue];
  [self setBarValue:newValue];
  [self _myBarDidChangeValue];
}
```

The -takeBarValueFrom: method is typical of Action methods described in Chapter 17. It can be called by any Cocoa objects that use the Outlets, Targets, and Actions pattern, and it can be conveniently connected in Interface Builder. Within the implementation of the method, three private methods are called to indirectly send messages to the delegate. The first private method is

- (float)_myBarShouldChangeValue:(float)newValue.

Note

In Objective-C, any message can be sent to any receiver. Methods are only private to the extent that their existence is not advertised in a class interface within a public header file. The convention of naming so-called private methods with an underscore and a prefix reduces the chance that someone might inadvertently override or call the method.

```
- (float)_myBarShouldChangeValue:(float)newValue
/*! Give the delegate a chance to change the new value */
{
  if([[self delegate] respondsToSelector:
      @selector(barView:shouldChangeValue:)])
  {
    newValue = [[self delegate] barView:self
        shouldChangeValue:newValue];
  }

  return newValue;
}
```

If the delegate can respond to a -barView:shouldChangeValue: message, the message is sent to the delegate, and the value returned by the delegate is used as the new value of the MYBarView. If the delegate can't respond to -barView:shouldChangeValue:, the new value is used unchanged. A delegate that implements -barView:shouldChangeValue: can veto the change by returning the calling object's existing value. Similarly, the delegate can limit or scale the value returned.

The next delegate message is sent by the -(void)_myBarWillChangeValue method:

```
- (void)_myBarWillChangeValue
/*! Notify the delegate and default notification center that the value
    is about to change.*/
{
  NSNotification      *notification;

  notification = [NSNotification notificationWithName:
      MYBarViewWillChangeValueNotification object:self];

  if([[self delegate] respondsToSelector:
    @selector(barViewWillChangeValue:)])
  {
    [[self delegate] barViewWillChangeValue:notification];
  }
  [[NSNotificationCenter defaultCenter]
      postNotification:notification];
}
```

A temporary NSNotification instance is created and initialized with a name and the MYBarView instance that is sending the notification. Just before posting the notification to the default notification center, the delegate is checked to determine if it responds to the -barViewWillChangeValue: delegate message. If the delegate does respond, the message is sent with the notification object as an argument. The delegate that receives the message can use the object property of the notification to determine which bar view sent the message. The NSNotification class and its object property are described in Apple's developer documentation.

The -(void)_myBarDidChangeValue private method is similar to
-_myBarWillChangeValue: and is called after the bar view's value is changed.

```
- (void)_myBarDidChangeValue
/*! Notify the delegate and default notification center that the value
    just changed. */
{
  NSNotification    *notification;

  notification = [NSNotification notificationWithName:
     MYBarViewDidChangeValueNotification object:self];

  if([[self delegate] respondsToSelector:
     @selector(barViewDidChangeValue)])
  {
    [[self delegate] barViewDidChangeValue:notification];
  }
  [[NSNotificationCenter defaultCenter]
     postNotification:notification];
}
```

Implementing a Delegate

To implement an object that will act as a delegate, simply implement methods corresponding to whichever delegate messages you want to receive. In the following example, the
MYValueLimitColorChanger class implements methods for only two of the three delegate messages a MYBarView object might send. The methods are implemented to constrain
a bar view so that it cannot indicate values less that 0.25 and to change the color of the
bar based on the value being indicated. These are arbitrary behaviors, but they are representative of the type of role a delegate can play to provide application-specific behavior.

```
@implementation MYValueLimitColorChanger

//! Delegate messages
- (float)barView:(id)barView shouldChangeValue:(float)newValue
{
  float     result = newValue;

  if(0.25f > result)
  {
    result = 0.25f;
  }

  return result;
}
```

```
- (void)barViewDidChangeValue:(NSNotification *)aNotification
{
  if(0.75f < [[aNotification object] barValue])
  {
    [[aNotification object] setBarColor:[NSColor blackColor]];
  }
  else
  {
    [[aNotification object] setBarColor:[NSColor grayColor]];
  }
}

@end
```

An instance of MYValueLimitColorChanger can be created in Interface Builder and connected as the delegate of any number of MYBarView instances. Alternatively, an instance of MYValueLimitColorChanger can be created programmatically and set as the delegate of one or more bar views via MYBarView's -setDelegate: method.

The MYValueLimitColorChanger class is as simple as can be. The only methods it adds to its superclass are methods to handle delegate messages. The real power of delegation is best shown in more complex situations. The delegate might interact with the bar view based on complex application logic that depends on many other objects. The following MYValuePropagator class implements only one of MYBarView's delegate methods. MYValuePropagator sets the value of another bar view to mach the value adopted by the bar view that sent the message.

```
@class MYBarView;

@interface MYValuePropagator : NSObject
{
  IBOutlet MYBarView *barViewToControl;     //! The object to control
}

//! Declare accessor as Objective C 2.0 @property
@property (readwrite, retain, nonatomic)
    IBOutlet MYBarView *barViewToControl;

@end


@implementation MYValuePropagator

//! Let the Objective C 2.0 compiler generate the accessor code
@synthesize barViewToControl;
```

```
- (void)barViewDidChangeValue:(NSNotification *)aNotification
{
  if([aNotification object] != [self barViewToControl])
  {
    [[self barViewToControl] setBarValue:
        [[aNotification object] barValue]];
  }
}

@end
```

Data Sources

Data sources are similar to delegates, but they play a different role. Delegates react to changes or control other objects. A data source provides data to another object whenever needed. Delegates are always optional; the object that uses a delegate falls back to default behavior if there is no delegate assigned. An object that uses a data source may not be functional without a valid data source to supply data.

For example, Cocoa's NSTableView class retrieves data as needed from a data source. Using a data source provides several advantages. First and most importantly, using a data source preserves the separation of subsystems in the Model-View-Controller pattern. The graphical table drawing and editing features of NSTableView clearly belong in the View subsystem. Calculation, retrieval, and storage of the data values to be displayed are clearly part of the Model subsystem. The calculations and storage of data remains the same even if the mechanism used to display the data changes. The same Model data could be displayed in a pie chart or output to a file or sent to a printer. The object acting as a data source for an instance of NSTableView is typically part of the Controller subsystem. The data source responds to the NSTableView's requests for data by retrieving the data from the Model. NSTableView is decoupled from details regarding the retrieval of data from the Model. Similarly, classes in the Model subsystem have no coupling to the View objects that display data.

Using a data source has the added advantage of enabling efficient data processing and memory usage. For example, even if a table has a million rows, at most a few dozen rows can be seen on the screen at once. NSTableView only asks its data source for the data needed to display the currently visible rows. If the Model subsystem needs to calculate the data or the data must be fetched over a network from a database, there is no need to calculate or fetch a million rows of data at once.

Like a delegate, the data source object is not retained by the object that uses it. A single object acting as a data source may provide data to any number of objects. Apple identifies the messages that will be sent to a data source in the class documentation for the classes that require a data source. Just like delegate methods, there is typically an informal protocol that declares the methods a data source must implement.

Examples in Cocoa

The following Cocoa classes use a delegate: NSApplication, NSBrowser, NSControl, NSDrawer, NSFontManager, NSFontPanel, NSMatrix, NSOutlineView, NSSplitView, NSTableView, NSTabView, NSText, NSTextField, NSTextView, and NSWindow. The NSOutlineView and NSTableView classes also use a data source. Apple's WebKit framework also contains several Objective-C classes that use data sources and delegates.

Almost every nontrivial graphical Cocoa application includes an object that acts as the delegate for the application's shared NSApplication instance. NSApplication provides a little over two dozen delegate methods. They range from -(void)application:(NSApplication *)sender openFiles:(NSArray *)filenames, which you can implement to control how your application opens files, to -(NSApplicationTerminateReply)applicationShouldTerminate:(NSApplication *)sender, which allows you to control whether the application terminates.

Before you consider subclassing a Cocoa object, make sure you can't achieve what you want via a delegate method.

Consequences

The Delegates pattern dramatically reduces the need to subclass Cocoa objects to implement application-specific behavior. Many of the more complex Cocoa classes such as NSApplication, NSBrowser, NSTableView, NSText, and NSWindow are rarely if ever subclassed because the Delegates pattern provides a better alternative.

The Delegates pattern reduces the coupling between objects. Subclassing creates the tightest possible coupling between the subclass and its superclass. The Delegates pattern substitutes a much looser relationship based on anonymous objects. The coupling between an object and its delegate is so loose that the object can function without any delegate at all, and a delegate is free to implement any subset of the potential delegate methods.

The Delegates pattern provides runtime flexibility. Each instance of a class that supports delegates can have a different delegate. Each object's delegate can be set in Interface Builder or at runtime and can then be changed as needed at runtime.

Using a data source simplifies the separation between the View subsystem and the Model subsystem in a Model-View-Controller–based application. Just like with delegates, using Objective-C's id type reduces coupling between the data source and the object that needs data. That reduced coupling enhances the opportunities to separately reuse objects in the View subsystem and the Model subsystem while simultaneously enabling application-specific behavior.

However, the need for a delegate or a data source must be foreseen by a class designer. If no delegate support is provided or delegate messages are not sent in the right situations, there may be no alternative to subclassing to implement application-specific behavior.

Providing support for a delegate or a data source in your own classes requires several lines of code, and specific idioms for using Objective-C and Cocoa's conventions must be followed. For example, it's critical that the object using a delegate or a data source doesn't retain the delegate/data source even though that seems contrary to the standard Cocoa conventions. The practice of not retaining delegates and data sources avoids retain cycles, but it also means that you must be careful about the order in which objects are deallocated. If a data source is deallocated before the object(s) that asks it for data, runtime errors may result.

16

Hierarchies

In Cocoa, hierarchical nesting is often used to organize objects. A hierarchy of view objects is used to organize and control drawing and coordinate systems in Cocoa. The Responder Chain pattern, described in depth in Chapter 18, "Responder Chain," leverages the view hierarchy. Hierarchies are also seen in many data models and parse trees given that most are hierarchical in nature.

Hierarchies define relationships between objects to avoid ambiguity about which objects are responsible for storage of other objects. In addition, hierarchies provide an alternative to subclassing. In Cocoa, hierarchies are used when objects have a "has-a" relationship, while subclassing is used only for a true "is-a" relationship. Hierarchies in Cocoa are closely related to the well-known Composite pattern.

Motivation

Express a has-a relationship between objects. Allow groups of cooperating objects to be treated as a single object. Enable customization without a need for subclassing by allowing objects within a group to be reconfigured or swapped out for alternate objects. Reduce the complexity of a parent class by sharing responsibility for data and behaviors between child objects. Allow groups of objects to be treated the same as a single object.

Solution

It is common for developers to encounter data that can be stored, manipulated, and searched most efficiently if it is stored in a tree structure. Likewise, the objects in an application often derive similar benefits when they are organized into tree-like structures.

For example, it is common for vector drawing, layout, and diagramming applications to allow the grouping of objects so that the user can move a complex figure as if it were a single graphical object. Many such applications even offer a library or palette of prebuilt, commonly used objects. Internally there is usually a base class, such as MYGraphic, that is used as a parent for all the graphical elements that the user can manipulate. Typical subclasses might be MYSquare, MYCircle, and so on.

To implement groups of objects, a class called MYGroup would be created. The MYGroup class would also be a subclass of MYGraphic. By designing the data model this way, a group of objects may now be treated just as if it were any normal graphic object. A group can be resized, and all the child graphics would be resized simultaneously, keeping their relative sizes constant. The code sending the resize message to the graphic doesn't need to know whether it is dealing with one graphic or many. When asked for an object's bounding box, the group object would accumulate the bounds of all its children and return a single bound encompassing all its children. Code requesting the bounding box would get the right answer whether it is dealing with a single graphic or a group, and it wouldn't need to know the difference between them.

Graphical applications are not the only ones that can benefit from this kind of a structure. For example, consider a scripting subsystem that can parse and execute program scripts. Besides individual statements, there are also blocks of statements. In Objective-C, a block is all the code found between two brackets. Typically loops and if/then statements control the execution of blocks. Because a block is actually just a collection of statements grouped together, a hierarchical structure emerges when a script is parsed.

The elements of a parsed script might be represented as MYStatement objects. Blocks would then be represented by MYBlock objects, which are a subclass of MYStatement. By making a block be just another kind of statement, code that manipulates a script becomes much simpler. Rather than checking to see whether it is a statement or a block of statements to execute, the code running the script can simply call an -execute method, defined by the MYStatement object. This allows single statements and blocks to be treated the same.

In the end, there still has to be a decision about which code to run because the code to execute a single statement is obviously different than the code to execute a block. The block code would require a loop to execute each of the child statements, some of which may in turn be other blocks. However, instead of forcing the calling code to be aware of the differences between statements and blocks and pick the right code, the Objective-C runtime is being leveraged. Based on the object's class, the right code will be called automatically as a result of the structure of the parsed object hierarchy.

Implementing a Hierarchy

Returning to the example of an application that manipulates graphics and groups of graphics, the actual code required to support a hierarchical structure is simple. Even without a specific application design in mind, it is still possible to show the parts of the MYGraphic and MYGroup classes that would support a hierarchy. Suppose that the MyGraphic class has the following (simplified) interface:

```
@interface MYGraphic : NSObject
{
  NSRect bounds;
}
```

```
- (NSRect)bounds;
- (void)draw;

@end
```

In a real application there would also be methods for setting the bounds and accessors for other attributes of the graphic such as color, line width, rotation, and so on. Because this is an abstract base class, the implementation of this class for the methods just shown would be very simple:

```
@implementation MYGraphic

- (id)init
{
  self = [super init];
  if (!self) return nil;
  bounds = NSMakeRect(0.0, 0.0, 0.0, 0.0);
  return self;
}

- (NSRect)bounds
{
  return bounds;
}

- (void)draw
{
  // overridden by subclasses to do actual drawing
}

@end
```

To implement a MYGroup object, some methods are needed to manipulate the child objects. An array can be added and used to store the children. A basic interface might be as follows:

```
@interface MYGroup : MYGraphic
{
  NSMutableArray *children;
}

- (void)addChild:(MYGraphic *)aChild;
- (NSArray *)children;

@end
```

In addition to the new methods for handling child objects, the -bounds and -draw methods need to be overridden to loop through all the children. In the case of -bounds, the resultant bounding box is stored in the inherited `bounds` instance variable. An alternative approach would be to update the `bounds` variable whenever a child is added or removed, in which case the `-bounds` method would not need to be overridden at all. Here is one possible implementation:

```
@implementation MYGroup


- (id)init
{
  self = [super init];
  if (!self) return nil;
  children = [[NSMutableArray alloc] init];
  return self;
}

- (void)dealloc
{
  [children release];
  [super dealloc];
}

- (void)addChild:(MYGraphic *)aChild
{
  [children addObject: aChild];
}

- (NSArray *)children
{
  return [[children copy] autorelease];
}

- (NSRect)bounds
{
  if ([children count] == 0)
  {
    bounds = NSZeroRect;
    return bounds;
  }
  else
  {
    bounds = [[children objectAtIndex:0] bounds];
    for (MYGraphic *child in children)
    {
      bounds = NSUnionRect(bounds, [child bounds]);
    }
  }
```

```
  return bounds;
}

- (void)draw
{
  for (MYGraphic *child in children)
  {
    [child draw];
  }
}

@end
```

When dealing with a `MYGraphic` subclass, the calling code can obtain a bounding box with the `-bounds` method without needing to know if there are child graphics. Likewise, when drawing, there is no need to distinguish between a single graphic and a group. The `MYGroup` object simply passes the `-draw` message on to each of the children.

Sometimes it is useful for child objects to have a pointer that points at their parent objects. Adding such pointers sometimes makes it easier to implement context-dependent behaviors. Pointers to parent objects need to be updated whenever an object is added or removed as a child to another. As an example of the utility of pointers to the parent objects, consider how `NSView` objects, described later in this chapter, are also part of a responder chain as described in Chapter 18. The responder chain wouldn't be possible at all if views didn't have pointers to their parent object, also known as their *superview*.

When implementing a hierarchy, there are two other ways that the code can be organized besides what was shown in the previous example. One is to put prototype child handling messages such as `-addChild:` into the `MYGraphic` class interface. The default implementation would then raise an exception. This approach allows all objects in the hierarchy to be treated uniformly, but at the risk of raising runtime exceptions. It doesn't make sense to add circles to a square, though it would make sense to add them to a group of objects.

The other way this could have been organized and implemented would have been to move the child handling messages into the `MYGraphic` class and *also* move the `children` instance variable and the child handling code to the `MYGraphic` class. Then there would be no runtime exception if a child were added to another graphic. The downside of this is that, at least for this particular data model, it doesn't make sense to allow every kind of graphic to contain child graphics. Cocoa does take this latter approach with its `NSView` hierarchy, however. Every Cocoa view is capable of containing subviews.

The Cocoa View Hierarchy

Every graphical Cocoa application has windows, and every window contains a hierarchy of `NSView` objects. Although `NSView` is an abstract class, it does contain all the code and storage to add and manipulate child objects, known as *subviews*. In fact, despite being basically abstract in nature, actual NSView instances are found at the top of the view hierarchy in most Cocoa windows.

In Figure 16.1 a typical view hierarchy is shown. The actual user interface is on the left, and the views in the window are listed on the right. The NSView at the top is the window's content view. The four views below it are its subviews, and so on.

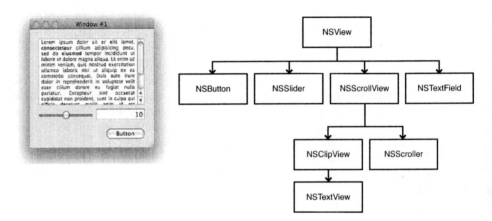

Figure 16.1   Example of a View hierarchy

As is easy to see in Figure 16.1, many of the more complex Cocoa user interface elements, such a text editors, are actually composed of several NSView subclasses working together. NSTableView is another such composite object. The actual NSTableView or NSTextView objects are really at the bottom of a hierarchy that includes NSScrollView, NSClipView, and NSScroller instances.

The real power of this design comes into play when customizations of standard view classes are desired. For example, suppose a developer wants to add a pop-up button to select the scale of the view that is being controlled by an NSScrollView instance. The button can be added as a subview to an NSScrollView, and the -tile method can be overridden in a subclass. All -tile does is set the frames of each of the subviews so that they are laid out properly next to each other. For an example implementation of this, look at the example code in /Developer/Examples/AppKit/Sketch.

More often than not, no subclassing is required. It is common to lay out complex user interfaces in Interface Builder using a combination of standard Cocoa classes. In general, Cocoa's design favors constructing user interfaces by composition rather than by subclassing. The advantage to developers is that this reduces the number of classes to maintain and often simplifies any code that needs to be written.

Coordinate Systems in the View Hierarchy

Every NSView object has its own coordinate system. Drawing done by the view object treats the lower-left corner of the view as the origin. Because of this, each view actually keeps track of two rectangles. The bounds rectangle is a rectangle around the view's drawing area, as is the frame rectangle. The difference is that bounds is represented in the view's coordinate system, while frame is in the superview's coordinate system. This makes it possible to translate points between different views' coordinate systems.

Because the bounds and frame rectangles can have different values for their sizes and different origins, the coordinate systems are not necessarily simple translations. It is also possible for there to be scaling involved. Because of the inherent complexity of translating points from one coordinate space to another, Cocoa implements several NSView methods to help.

To convert points from one coordinate system to another, the NSView class defines the methods -convertPoint:fromView: and -convertPoint:toView:. There are also -convertSize:... and -convertRect:... methods. In the "fromView" versions of these methods, the point, size, or rectangle is being converted from another view's coordinate system to that of the receiver. The "toView" methods go the opposite direction, from the receiver's coordinate system to that of the argument. Whenever the view argument is nil, the conversion is to or from the window's coordinate system. The only limitation is that both views, the receiver and the argument, must be in the same window. In other words, they both must be part of the same view hierarchy.

Having multiple coordinate systems like this can become very confusing, so it is reasonable to ask why Cocoa goes to so much trouble to offer this feature. One of the key reasons is so that groups of views can be repositioned and resized relative to each other. Entire hierarchies of views can be moved around in a window or moved from one window to another, and only the frame of the topmost view in the hierarchy needs to be altered. This greatly simplifies the manipulation of multiple view objects. Having separate coordinate systems for each view also makes the drawing code for a particular view much easier to write, given that translation and scaling do not need to be taken into account when writing the drawing code.

Browsing the View Hierarchy

One of the best ways to understand how something is put together is to look at each individual piece in context. Walking through a view hierarchy to see how different Cocoa interface objects are assembled is often more helpful than simply reading about them. The ViewFinder application is designed to let a developer browse a view hierarchy. This example can be downloaded from the book's website.

The main interface is an NSBrowser object that lists all the views found in the application's current "main" window. Clicking a window to make it the main window and then selecting any view listed in the browser draws a highlight around the actual view. Figure 16.2 shows the application running.

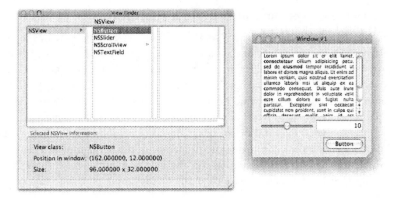

Figure 16.2   ViewFinder example interface

To highlight the selected views, an overlay window is used. The ViewFinder application uses a custom NSView subclass that draws a rectangle around its bounds. This view is then placed in a transparent window that is set above the actual window on the screen. Because this view needs no instance variables, the header only declares it to be a subclass of NSView:

```
#import <Cocoa/Cocoa.h>


@interface MYHighlightingView : NSView
{
}


@end
```

The code simply draws a semi-transparent, red rectangle around the view's bounds. By making the view nonopaque, any mouse clicks will pass through to the window below so that the highlight doesn't interrupt the functionality of the window or view beneath it.

```
#import "MYHighlightingView.h"


@implementation MYHighlightingView


- (void)drawRect:(NSRect)rect
{
  NSRect myBounds = [self bounds];
  [[[NSColor redColor] colorWithAlphaComponent:0.5] set];
  NSFrameRectWithWidthUsingOperation(myBounds, 2.0,
      NSCompositeSourceOver);
}


- (BOOL)isOpaque
```

```
{
  return NO;
}
```

@end

The controller class for the application and the delegate for the NSBrowser in the graphical user interface is the MYViewFinderController class. The header defines a few outlets that should be connected to the user interface items in the browser panel. It also defines the -broswerSelectionChanged: method, which should be the action sent by the NSBrowser object. The array browserPath is used to keep track of the user's selection in the NSBrowser.

```
#import <Cocoa/Cocoa.h>


@interface MYViewFinderController : NSObject
{
  IBOutlet NSBrowser    *browser;
  IBOutlet NSTextField *viewClassField;
  IBOutlet NSTextField *windowPositionField;
  IBOutlet NSTextField *sizeField;
  NSWindow             *viewedWindow;
  NSMutableArray       *browserPath;
  NSWindow             *highlightWindow;
}

- (void)mainWindowChanged:(id)sender;
- (IBAction)browserSelectionChanged:(id)sender;

@end
```

The implementation begins with the -init method. It allocates the browserPath array and creates the window that will be used to highlight selected NSView objects. By making the window nonopaque with a clear background, it will effectively ignore all events. This is so that the view being highlighted can still be used. The -dealloc method contains the usual clean-up code.

```
#import "MYViewFinderController.h"
#import "MYHighlightingView.h"


@implementation MYViewFinderController

- (id)init
{
  if (nil != (self = [super init]))
  {
    browserPath = [[NSMutableArray alloc] init];
```

```
      highlightWindow = [[NSWindow alloc]
          initWithContentRect:NSMakeRect(-10.0, 10.0, 5.0, 5.0)
          styleMask:NSBorderlessWindowMask
          backing:NSBackingStoreBuffered defer:NO];
      [highlightWindow setBackgroundColor: [NSColor clearColor]];
      [highlightWindow setAlphaValue:1.0];
      [highlightWindow setOpaque:NO];
      [highlightWindow setLevel:(NSNormalWindowLevel + 1)];

      MYHighlightingView *highlightView = [[[MYHighlightingView alloc]
          initWithFrame:NSMakeRect(0.0, 0.0, 5.0, 5.0)] autorelease];
      [highlightView setAutoresizingMask:
          (NSViewWidthSizable | NSViewHeightSizable)];
      [highlightWindow setContentView:highlightView];
    }
    return self;
}


- (void)dealloc
{
    [highlightWindow orderOut:self];
    [highlightWindow release];
    [browserPath release];
    [super dealloc];
}
```

The browser needs to be reset whenever the application's main window changes and initially upon launch of the application. This is done by having this controller object be the application's delegate and having some of the NSApplication notifications send a -mainWindowChanged: message to the controller. When the main window changes, the browser is reset, and the user interface is cleared.

```
- (void)applicationDidUpdate:(NSNotification *)aNotification
{
    [self mainWindowChanged:self];
}


- (void)applicationDidUnhide:(NSNotification *)aNotification
{
    [self mainWindowChanged:self];
}


- (void)applicationDidFinishLaunching:(NSNotification *)aNotification
{
    [self performSelector:@selector(mainWindowChanged:)
        withObject:self afterDelay:0.0];
}
```

```
- (void)mainWindowChanged:(id)sender
{
  NSWindow *mainWindow = [NSApp mainWindow];
  if (mainWindow && (viewedWindow != mainWindow))
  {
    viewedWindow = mainWindow;
    [browserPath removeAllObjects];
    [browserPath addObject:[viewedWindow contentView]];
    [browser loadColumnZero];
    [viewClassField setStringValue:@""];
    [windowPositionField setStringValue:@""];
    [sizeField setStringValue:@""];
    [highlightWindow orderOut:self];
    [browser selectRow:0 inColumn:0];
  }
}
```

To implement the required NSBrowser delegate methods, it will be helpful to have a method that can locate an NSView in the hierarchy when given a browser column and row as identifiers. As objects are selected in the browser, they will be added to the controller's browserPath array. Therefore, the requested column can be used as an index to this array to find the superview. Then the requested row can be used as the index to the subview array to find the right object. Add some bounds checking, and here's the code:

```
-(NSView *)representedViewAtRow:(NSInteger)row
    column:(NSInteger)column
{
  NSView *representedView = nil;
  if (column == 0)
  {
    if (row != 0) return nil; // should never happen
    representedView = [browserPath objectAtIndex:0];
  }
  else
  {
    NSView *parent = [browserPath objectAtIndex:(column - 1)];
    NSArray *children = [parent subviews];
    int numChildren = [children count];
    if ((row >= 0) && (row < numChildren))
    {
      representedView = [children objectAtIndex:row];
    }
  }
  return representedView;
}
```

The first browser delegate method we need, -brower:numberOfRowsInColumn:, is used by the browser to determine the number of rows in a given column. The method starts with a little housekeeping to ensure that the browserPath array is up to date. Next, if it is the item count for column zero that is being requested, then there is always one object, the window's content view. Otherwise, the number of subviews of the object selected in the previous column is needed. The selected object is provided by the browserPath array.

```
- (NSInteger)browser:(NSBrowser *)sender
    numberOfRowsInColumn:(NSInteger)column
{
  int ret = 0;
  int columnCount = [browserPath count];

  if (column >= columnCount)
  {
    [self browser:sender selectRow:
        [sender selectedRowInColumn:(column - 1)]
        inColumn:(column - 1)];
    columnCount = [browserPath count];
    if (column > columnCount)
    {
      return 0;
    }
  }

  if (column == 0)
  {
    if (columnCount > 0)
    {
      ret = 1;
    }
    else
    {
      ret = 0;
    }
  }
  else
  {
    ret = [[[browserPath objectAtIndex:(column - 1)]
        subviews] count];
  }
  return ret;
}
```

When the browser is about to display one of its cells, the delegate is asked to populate it. The previously shown method -representedViewAtRow:column: is used to obtain the view that this cell represents. The title of the cell is set to the object's class name. If the object has no subviews, then it is a leaf node.

```
- (void)browser:(NSBrowser *)sender willDisplayCell:(id)cell
    atRow:(NSInteger)row column:(NSInteger)column
{
  NSView *representedView =
      [self representedViewAtRow:row column:column];

  if (representedView)
  {
    [cell setTitle:[representedView className]];
    [cell setLeaf:(([[representedView subviews] count] > 0) ?
        NO : YES)];
  }
  [cell setLoaded:YES];
}
```

The next method is used to keep the browserPath array up to date as the selection in the browser changes. If a selection is made in a browser column to the left of the previous selection, then objects are removed from browserPath. The object most recently selected is then added to the end of the array.

```
- (BOOL)browser:(NSBrowser *)sender selectRow:(NSInteger)row
    inColumn:(NSInteger)column
{
  if ((row < 0) || (column < 0)) return NO;

  if (column == 0)
  {
    while ([browserPath count] > 1)
    {
      [browserPath removeLastObject];
    }
  }
  else
  {
    NSView *representedView =
        [self representedViewAtRow:row column:column];

    while ([browserPath count] > column)
    {
      [browserPath removeLastObject];
    }
```

```
  if (!representedView)
  { // should never happen
    return NO;
  }
  [browserPath addObject:representedView];
}
return YES;
}
```

The last method required to complete the application's functionality is the action method -browerSelectionChanged:. It is called whenever the user clicks a cell in the browser. This method first makes sure that the browserPath array is updated. Then it takes the currently selected view, the last item in the array, and displays information about its class, position in the window, and size. Finally, the highlighting window is resized so that its frame is the same as the view's frame rectangle. This causes the red rectangle around the selected view to be drawn.

```
- (IBAction)browserSelectionChanged:(id)sender
{
  NSView *selectedView = nil;
  NSRect selectedFrame;
  NSRect windowFrame;
  NSRect showFrame;
  int lastColumn = [sender selectedColumn];
  int row = [sender selectedRowInColumn:lastColumn];

  if (row < 0)
  {
    lastColumn-;
    row = [sender selectedRowInColumn:lastColumn];
  }
  [self browser:sender selectRow:row inColumn:lastColumn];
  selectedView = [browserPath lastObject];
  [viewClassField setStringValue:[selectedView className]];
  selectedFrame = [selectedView convertRect:
      [selectedView bounds] toView:nil];
  [windowPositionField setStringValue:
      [NSString stringWithFormat:@"(%f, %f)",
       selectedFrame.origin.x,
       selectedFrame.origin.y]];
  [sizeField setStringValue:
      [NSString stringWithFormat:@"%f x %f",
       selectedFrame.size.width,
       selectedFrame.size.height]];
  windowFrame = [viewedWindow frame];
  showFrame = NSMakeRect(
      windowFrame.origin.x + selectedFrame.origin.x,
```

```
        windowFrame.origin.y + selectedFrame.origin.y,
        selectedFrame.size.width,
        selectedFrame.size.height);
    [highlightWindow setFrame:showFrame display:YES];
    [highlightWindow orderFront:self];
}
```

Examples in Cocoa

As already discussed in this chapter, the most commonly encountered hierarchy in Cocoa is the NSView hierarchy used to build complex user interfaces. All drawing and user interaction with a graphical user interface-based Cocoa application funnels through view objects.

Another hierarchy, which is nongraphical in nature, is encountered when working with XML documents. After parsing XML documents, the NSXML class provides an NSXMLDocument object as output. This object contains the complete parse tree for the XML document as a hierarchy of objects. The NSXMLNode class is the base class for the objects found in the parse tree such as NSXMLDocument and NSXMLElement. NSXMLNode has methods to add and remove child objects inherited by all the parsed elements of the document.

Developers will often use hierarchies to create their data models. The collection classes in Cocoa's Foundation make this easy. Usually NSMutableArray is used to store child objects, but NSMutableSet can be used whenever the ordering of the child classes is unimportant.

Consequences

Because Cocoa uses a hierarchy of views to represent user interfaces, it is possible to reduce the need for subclassing. Developers are encouraged to add views to each other as subviews, building up complex user interfaces from simpler building blocks. Because each view has its own coordinate system, complex groupings of view objects can be assembled and then easily moved from one window to another, or swapped in and out of a space in a single window.

Similar benefits can be realized in custom object models by organizing model objects into hierarchies when appropriate. Hierarchies should be chosen instead of subclassing when the relationship between two objects is has-a instead of is-a. The flexibility of Objective-C and the Cocoa Foundation's collection classes make this easy to accomplish.

17

Outlets, Targets, and Actions

When you build a graphical user interface, you need a way to configure user interface objects, such as buttons, sliders, text fields, and menu items, and connect them to application-specific operations. For example, an application might provide a menu item to center selected text and another menu item to send a seating request to an airline reservation system. Finding a good way to connect user interface objects to application-specific operations is a common recurring problem.

One potential solution is to create application-specific subclasses of the user interface objects like menu items. For example, you could create a CenterTextMenuItem class and a SendSeatingRequestMenuItem class. However, there are a number of shortcomings to creating application-specific subclasses of user interface objects.

The first shortcoming is the number of classes and amount of code you write. You'll have to create separate new subclasses for every operation supported by your application, and you'll have to do it all again for the next application. The second shortcoming is that operations like sending a seating request are clearly part of the Model or Controller subsystems when using the Model View Controller design pattern. Menu items are clearly part of the View subsystem. Extending a menu item specifically to send a seating request couples the menu item to objects that have nothing to do with presentation to a user. Having numerous subclasses promotes code duplication. What happens when you also provide a scripting interface to send seating requests or you provide a button and a menu item? You'll end up using the similar code related to seat requests in each of the objects that send requests.

Some object-oriented frameworks provide an alternative to using numerous subclasses by assigning unique identifiers to each object in the user interface. You search through the user interface objects to find the one with a desired unique identifier whenever you want to configure specific objects. When a button or menu item is pressed by the user, the application uses a table or C language switch statement to determine what action to take based on the identifier of the object that was pressed. However, the need to coordinate the meaning of identifiers between user interface objects and application logic still introduces coupling. There can be issues maintaining the unique identifiers. For example, when designing a user interface, you might copy and paste user interface objects from one interface design to another. If the identifiers assigned to each object are copied with the objects, how to you make sure the copied identifiers are unique in each application? There may also be concerns regarding the way unique identifiers are correlated with operations to be taken within the application. Ideally, you shouldn't have to hand code a giant switch statement or manually populate a look-up table.

What's needed is a way for applications to configure user interface objects and for user interface objects to invoke application-specific operations without creating otherwise unneeded subclasses, without writing any new code in the View subsystem, without coupling between the View subsystem and other application subsystems, and without manual correlation of unique identifiers with operations. Furthermore, the solution needs to enable context-sensitive behavior. For example, when the user presses the menu item to center selected text, it matters what specific text is selected at that moment. The result of pressing the menu item needs to change based on user interaction. If there is no text selected, the menu item should probably be disabled to show that it would have no effect if pressed.

Cocoa provides the needed solution by applying the Outlets, Targets, and Actions design pattern, which simplify user interface implementation and contribute to the flexibility and productivity enabled by tools like Interface Builder.

Motivation

Use Cocoa's Outlets, Targets, and Actions design pattern to achieve the following objectives:

- Support direct programmatic configuration of user interface objects.
- Specify what application actions should take place as the result of user interactions with user interface objects.
- Avoid coupling between generic reusable user interface objects and application-specific behavior.
- Avoid code duplication when multiple user interfaces invoke the same application-specific actions.
- Enable context-sensitive behavior as the result of user interaction with user interface objects.

Solution

An outlet is an instance variable that stores a reference (pointer) to another object such as a user interface object. Outlets can be set with the Interface Builder tool or programmatically. In Interface Builder, connection lines are drawn from objects that have outlets to the objects that are referenced. Outlets are set programmatically with the help of Accessor methods (Chapter 10, "Accessors") or by using Cocoa's Key Value Coding technology described in Chapter 19, "Associative Storage."

Targets are special outlets. You draw connection lines in Interface Builder as shown in Figure 17.1 to set the object referenced by an outlet. It works the same way for all outlets, but Figure 17.1 shows connection of a target outlet.

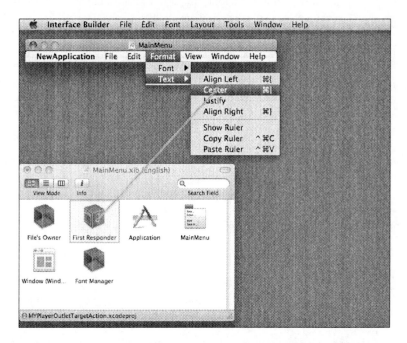

Figure 17.1   Draw connection lines to set outlets in Interface Builder.

When you connect a target, Interface Builder allows you to select an action message to be sent to the target, as shown in Figure 17.2. Action messages can also be specified programmatically via an Accessor method.

Interface Builder identifies outlets based on criteria shown in the following MYController class declaration. Any instance variable with type id and a name that doesn't start with an underscore character is automatically considered an outlet. In addition, any instance variable that is a pointer to an object and includes the IBOutlet macro in its declaration is treated as an outlet.

```
@interface MYController : NSObject
{
    id                  sampleOutlet;   // IB Considers this an outlet
    IBOutlet NSMatrix *sampleMatrix;    // IB Considers this an outlet
    id                  _myPrivateIVar; // IB ignores this because of the
                                        // leading underscore '_'
    NSView             *sampleView;     // IB ignores this because the
                                        // type is not id and the
```

```
                                  //   IBOutlet macro is not used
    IBOutlet NSView   *_myOtherView;  //   IB Considers this an outlet
                                  //   in spite of the leading '_'
                                  //   because IBOutlet is used
}

@end
```

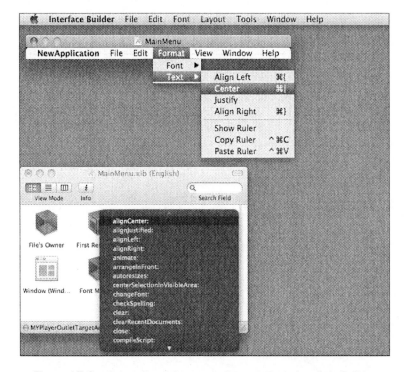

Figure 17.2   Select the action to send to a target in Interface Builder.

The IBOutlet macro is defined in NSNibDeclarations.h, which is part of Cocoa's Application Kit framework, and the C preprocessor replaces it with a single space character whenever it's encountered in source code. IBOutlet doesn't change the meaning of compiled code at all. It is just a hint to Interface Builder that identifies outlets with types more specific than id. When a specific type is declared, Interface Builder will respect it and use that information to limit what types of objects may be connected to that outlet.

Interface Builder stores information about connections from outlets to other objects using a class called NSNibOutletConnector. When objects are loaded from a .nib file into a running application, any loaded NSNibOutletConnector instances automatically receive an -establishConnection message, which directs them to assigning the values of associated outlet instance variables. NSNibOutletConnector implements

-establishConnection to use the Accessors pattern if a suitable Accessor method is available. At runtime, NSNibOutletConnector looks for an implemented method with the name -set<Outlet>: where <Outlet> is the name of an instance variable with its first letter capitalized. For example, given the following MYController class, NSNibOutletConnector instances representing Interface Builder connections to sampleOutlet, sampleMatrix, and _myOtherView will automatically call -setSampleOutlet:, -setSampleMatrix:, and -set_myOtherView: to re-establish connections when objects are loaded from a .nib file.

```
@interface MYController : NSObject
{
  id                    sampleOutlet;    // IB Considers this an outlet
  IBOutlet NSMatrix *sampleMatrix;   // IB Considers this an outlet
  id                    _myPrivateIVar; // IB ignores this because of the
                                         // leading underscore '_'
  NSView              *sampleView;    // IB ignores this because the
                                         // type is not id and the
                                         // IBOutlet macro is not used
  IBOutlet NSView    *_myOtherView;  // IB Considers this an outlet
                                         // in spite of the leading '_'
                                         // because IBOutlet is used
}

@end


@implementation MYController

- (void)setSampleOutlet:(id)anObject;
- (void)setSampleMatrix:(NSMatrix *)aMatrix;
- (void)set_myOtherView:(NSView *)aView;

@end
```

The -set_myOtherView: method doesn't fit the pattern for accessor names. Ordinarily, the first letter in the second word is capitalized like -set_MyOtherView:, but in all versions of Mac OS X up to and including version 10.5, NSNibOutletConnector doesn't follow that convention. Future versions may use Cocoa's Key Value Coding system to implement NSNibOutletConnector, and this behavior could change to become more standard.

If no appropriate Accessor method is available, NSNibOutletConnector uses information stored in the Objective-C runtime to find the address of each outlet in the memory and then directly assigns each outlet's value.

Outlets

Outlets are like any other instance variable and can be used programmatically in application code. After all objects have been loaded and initialized from a `.nib` file, an `-awakeFromNib` message is sent to each object that was loaded. By the time an object receives the `-awakeFromNib` message, all of its outlets have been set to the values they were given in Interface Builder.

The `-awakeFromNib` message is also sent to the object that is specified as the "owner" of the nib when the `.nib` file is loaded. Nib files are usually loaded with the `NSBundle` class `+loadNibNamed:owner:` method documented at /Developer/Documentation/ Cocoa/TasksAndConcepts/ProgrammingTopics/LoadingResources/index.html. If the same object is used as the owner in multiple invocations of `+loadNibNamed:owner:`, `-awakeFromNib` will be sent to the owner again each time a `.nib` file is loaded.

Caution is needed when implementing Accessor methods for objects that may be loaded from a `.nib` file. Accessor methods are called whenever possible as `.nib` files are loaded, but the order in which objects are loaded from the `.nib` file is undefined. Accessors can be called in any order, so dependencies on the state of instance variables other than the one being set need to be avoided. By the time `-awakeFromNib` is called, all objects have been restored to the state they were given in Interface Builder. Implement `-awakeFromNib` to perform any final initialization logic that depends on multiple outlets or the state of other objects loaded from the `.nib`.

The Archiving and Unarchiving design pattern in Chapter 11, "Archiving and Unarchiving," provides a more complete description of the process applied to create and load `.nib` files.

Targets

Cocoa's `NSControl`, `NSActionCell`, and `NSMenuItem` classes each provide an outlet named `target` and a corresponding instance variable named `action`. Interface Builder handles connections to the `target` outlet as a special case and allows you to specify an associated action message to be sent to the object referenced by `target`. Actions are explained in the "Actions" section of this chapter. Together, the target and action provide much of the flexibility and power associated with Cocoa.

Any class that provides both target and action instance variables can be used with this pattern. Interface Builder stores Target/Action connections as instances of the `NSNibControlConnector` class. When `.nib` files are loaded, the Target/Action connections are reestablished in much same way as outlet connections. The `-establishConnection` message is sent automatically and `NSNibControlConnector` instances respond by restoring the `target` and `action` instance variables to the states given in Interface Builder.

The ability of the target to point to any object and the fact that the action is variable provides tremendous flexibility. A single user interface object like `NSButton`, a subclass of `NSControl`, can be used to send any action to any target without the need to subclass or write custom code; it can be configured entirely in Interface Builder.

NSControl, NSActionCell, and NSMenuItem each implement the -target and -setTarget: Accessor methods for programmatically getting and setting the target.

Actions

Any method that returns void and accepts one object argument can be used as an action. NSControl and NSActionCell each provide the -action and -setAction: methods for programmatically accessing the action. Actions are stored as Objective-C selectors. A selector is a unique identifier for an Objective-C message as described in Chapter 9, "Perform Selector and Delayed Perform."

There are several ways to obtain selectors. The easiest way is to use Objective-C's @selector() compiler directive. The following example sends a -setAction: message with the selector for the -copy: message as an argument:

```
[someControl setAction:@selector(copy:)];
```

Any message name can be converted into a selector with Cocoa's NSSelectorFromString() function, and any selector can be converted into a string with NSStringFromSelector(). The following example sets the action of an object and then obtains that action and converts it to a string:

```
[someControl setAction:NSSelectorFromString(@"copy")];

NSLog(NSStringFromSelector([someControl action]);
```

The @selector() compiler directive is documented in Apple's Objective-C manual at /Developer/Documentation/Cocoa/ObjectiveC/ObjC.pdf. The NSSelectorFromString() and NSStringFromSelector() functions are documented at /Developer/Documentation/Cocoa/Reference/Foundation/ObjC_classic/Functions/FoundationFunctions.htm.

Each subclass of NSControl or NSActionCell sends its action message to its target in different circumstances. The NSButton subclass of NSControl normally sends its action message after the mouse button has been pressed and released while the mouse pointer is over the button, but it can be configured for other behaviors. The NSSlider subclass of NSControl can be configured to send its action message each time the slider is moved or only when the user releases the slider. Sliders can also be configured to only send values that correspond to tick marks drawn along the slider's range of motion. NSButton and NSSlider are two of the simplest controls. More complex controls like NSMatrix and NSTableView provide more sophisticated behavior.

Regardless of why an action message is sent, it's always sent using the NSApplication class's -sendAction:to:from: method. NSApplication is an example of the Singleton pattern, meaning that exactly one instance of the class is used in each application. The NSApplication instance is obtained by sending the +sharedApplication message to the NSApplication class as follows:

```
[NSApplication sharedApplication];
```

There is also a global variable, NSApp, that points to the single NSApplication instance.

The NSControl and NSActionCell classes send action messages to targets with code similar to the following:

```
[[NSApplication sharedApplication] sendAction:[self action]
                                   to:[self target]
                                   from:self];
```

The first argument to -sendAction:to:from: is the selector stored in the action instance variable and identifies the message to send. The second argument is the target object referenced by the target instance variable. The final argument is the object argument passed to the method identified by the action selector. The from: argument is usually the sender of the message. The receiver of the message can use the argument to get more information such as the value of the control that sent the message. For example, when a slider is moved, it sends its action message to its target with itself as the argument. When the target object receives the message, it uses the sender argument to get the value represented by the slider. The following code implements a hypothetical -volumeSliderDidChange: method called as the action of an NSSlider instance:

```
- (void)volumeSliderDidChange:(id)sender
{
  // make sure the anonymous sender responds to -floatValue
  if([sender respondsToSelector:@selector(floatValue)])
  {
    // set our own volume to the float value of the sender
    [self setVolume:[sender floatValue]];
  }
}
```

Actions and Responder Chains

The role of the shared NSApplication object in the Target/Action implementation is crucial. If the to: argument to NSApplication's -sendAction:to:from: method is a valid object, the action message is sent directly to the target, but if the to: argument is nil, the eventual receiver of the action message is determined by the application's current state and the user interface object that has the user's attention.

When the target of an action message is nil, the -sendAction:to:from: method uses an expanded version of the Responder Chain to find an object that can respond to the action and sends the action to that object. As a result, setting the target of a Cocoa object to nil makes the object's action context-sensitive. As the user interacts with an application, the Responder Chain continuously reflects the current context. Each time the Responder Chain changes, the set of potential receivers for action messages changes.

For example, a menu item can be configured to send the -copy: message when the menu item is selected. If the menu item has a nil target, the object that receives the -copy: message depends on the **first responder** in the **Key** window. The first responder is the object with the user's focus. The Key window is the currently front-most window that will receive keyboard input from the user. If the First Responder is a text field, then that text field receives the -copy: action message sent from the menu item. If another object has the user's focus, or then that object receives the -copy: action message instead.

When Target/Action connections are made to the first responder object in Interface Builder, as shown in Figure 17.1, the target is actually set to nil. The first responder object in Interface Builder is just a placeholder that represents whatever object has the user's focus at any given moment while an application is running. Figure 17.3 shows Interface Builder Inspector panel "Identity" tab, which enables you to define new action messages that can be sent up the Responder Chain.

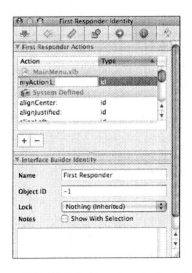

Figure 17.3   Interface Builder's Inspector lets you define new action messages that can be sent to First Responder.

Chapter 18, "Responder Chain," explains Cocoa's Responder Chain pattern, including the sequence in which the Responder Chain is searched to find a receiver for each action message sent to nil. The first object that can respond to an action message in the search order receives the message. If no object in the Responder Chain can respond to the action message, Cocoa's default behavior is to play a beep sound. However, action messages that can't be handled by any object in the Responder Chain are rare because Cocoa's automatic menu and control validation feature uses the same chain of objects to determine if each object that sends the action is enabled. Normally, if there is no responder for an object's action message, the object is automatically disabled and can't send the action message. Automatic validation is described at /Developer/Documentation/Cocoa/TasksAndConcepts/

ProgrammingTopics/MenuList/Tasls/EnablingMenuItems.html and /Developer/
Documentation/Cocoa/TasksAndConcepts/ProgrammingTopics/Toolbars/Tasls/
ValidatingTBItems.html.

Interface Builder and Xcode communicate to automatically discover the actions provided by each class. Any method declared with the following pattern is an action method
that Interface Builder can use:

```
- (IBAction)someAction:(id)sender;
```

The IBAction type is actually a preprocessor macro that evaluates to the void type.
Action methods are required to return void and accept a single object argument. Use the
IBAction macro in the declaration of methods to help Interface Builder find them.

The object argument to an Action method does not need to have the id type. Any
pointer to an object type can be used. For example, the following declaration is a suitable
Action method:

```
- (IBAction)volumeSliderDidChange:(NSSlider *)sender
```

Examples in Cocoa

Almost every introductory tutorial for Cocoa uses Outlets, Targets, and Actions. Apple
provides an online tutorial to get you started with them at http://developer.apple.com/
documentation/Cocoa/Conceptual/ObjCTutorial.

One key to using Outlets, Targets, and Actions when creating your applications is an
understanding of the Responder Chain. NSApplication's -sendAction:to:from:
method does all of the work needed to correctly dispatch action messages sent to any target and handles the case when no specific target is specified and the context is used to
find a receiver.

The Outlets, Targets, and Actions design pattern is used in all Cocoa applications that
provide user interfaces via the Model View Controller pattern. Targets usually point to
objects in the View or Controller subsystems. Objects in the Model subsystem should not
have outlets because outlets are intended to point to View or Controller objects, and
Models should not have any dependence on View or Controller objects. Model objects
should not have action methods either because actions are sent by View subsystem objects, and Model objects should not have direct interaction with the View subsystem.
Figure 17.4 provides an example of the typical connections and sequence of operations
involving Outlets, Targets, and Actions in a Model View Controller application.

Figure 17.4 represents part of the design of a simple song playing application. The ability to store songs, play songs, keep track of the current song that's playing, and change the
volume of the current song are all parts of the Model subsystem. The Model should work
regardless of how the user interacts with it. Figure 17.4 shows an application that provides
a "play" button, a "pause" button, and a slider to control volume, but the Model should
work regardless of the user interface. For example, the user might have a script that selects
songs from a play list and asks the player to play them one after another. There might be a
menu item that pauses play or a "mute" button that sets the volume to zero.

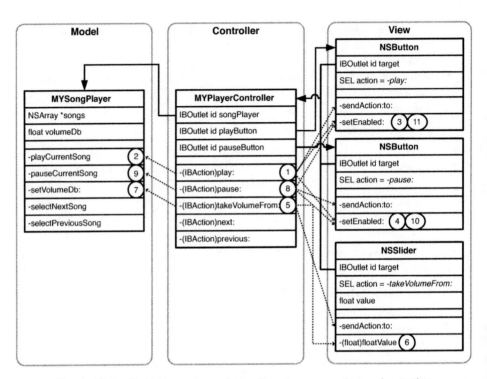

Figure 17.4   Typical sequences of operations in response to user interaction

The two buttons and the slider in the View subsystem each have their respective targets set to point to the same MYPlayerController instance in the Controller subsystem. When a button is pressed or a slider is moved, the button or slider's own -sendAction:to: method is invoked, which in turn invokes NSApplication's -sendAction:to:from: method, passing the affected button or slider as the from: argument, which is usually called sender. The targets are explicitly set for each of the buttons and the slider, so NSApplication will send each action message directly to the MYPlayerController instance. MYPlayerController has outlets that are connected to each of the two buttons and to the MYSongPlayer instance in the Model. With regard to coupling, the MYPlayerController class knows about the MYSongPlayer object in the Model and is therefore coupled to the Model, but the Model knows nothing about the Controller subsystem. The MYPlayerController instance also has outlets that are connected to View objects. The Controller is slightly coupled to the View but knows very little about the View objects with which it communicates. The View has no dependence on the Controller. The buttons and slider have targets defined with type id, which means they could be connected to any objects that respond to the assigned action messages.

The following sequence of operations is depicted in Figure 17.4: In step 1, the user presses the "Play" button, and MYPlayerController's -play: method is called with the pressed button as the `sender` argument. In step 2, `MYPlayerController` reacts by calling `[[self songPlayer] playCurrentSong];`, which causes `MYSongPlayer` to start playing the current song. `MYPlayerController` just ignores the `sender` argument within the implementation of `-play:`. In step 3, `MYPlayerController` calls `[[self playButton] setEnabled:NO];` because the song is now already playing and it does no good to press "Play" again. In step 4, `MYPlayerController` calls `[[self pauseButton] setEnabled:YES];` because now that a song is playing, it makes sense to be able to pause it.

> **Note**
>
> There is no assumption in the design of `MYPlayerController` that the `playButton` and `pauseButton` outlets will be connected to buttons. In reality, the outlets could be connected to any objects that respond to the `-setEnabled:` message, and all descendants of Cocoa's `NSControl` and `NSActionCell` classes respond to `-setEnabled:` and `-floatValue`. `MYPlayerController` is only slightly coupled to the View objects because you could replace the buttons with menu items or other user interface objects without any change or effect on the operation of the `MYPlayerController` class.

In step 5, the user adjusts the "Volume" slider, and the `-takeVolumeFrom:` action message is sent to the `MYPlayerController` instance. The slider itself is passed as the `sender` of the action message. `MYPlayerController` implements `-takeVolumeFrom:` as follows:

```
- (IBAction)takeVolumeFrom:(id)sender
{
  if([sender respondsToSelector:@selector(floatValue)])
  {
    float     newVolume = [sender floatValue];  // step 6
    [[self songPlayer] setVolumeDb:newVolume];  // step 7
  }
}
```

In step 6, `MYPlayerController` asks the sender to provide its floating point value. In this design, the `sender` is a slider, but the `sender` could have been a text field or any other object that can respond to the `-floatValue` message. In step 7, `MYSongPlayer`'s `-setVolumeDb:` method is called, and `MYSongPlayer` reacts by validating the argument passed and changing the song volume.

In step 8, the user presses the "Pause" button, which results in the `-pause:` action message being sent with the pressed button as the `sender` argument. In step 9, the `MYPlayerController` instance calls `MYSongPlayer`'s `-pauseCurrentSong` method. In step 10, `MYPlayerController` calls `[[self playButton] setEnabled:YES];` because now that the song is paused, it makes sense to press "Play" again. In step 11, `MYPlayerController` calls `[[self pauseButton] setEnabled:NO];` because the user can't pause an already paused song.

The user interface design expressed in Figure 17.4 does not require any code in the View subsystem at all. Once the class interface for `MYPlayerController` is created in Xcode, the entire user interface can be built and connected in Interface Builder with no custom subclasses of View objects and no generated code. Even if a different interface is created for scripting or with menu items and text fields instead of buttons and a slider, you shouldn't have to change the Controller or Model subsystems at all.

If the `MYSongPlayer` class is ever changed, there's a good chance that you can still use the `MYPlayerController` class unmodified. In the worst case, you will have to update `MYPlayerController` to communicate with a new Model, but under no circumstances should a change to the Model require any changes to the View.

Consequences

Objective-C's language level support for selectors and the ability to send any message to any object provide a flexible solution to the problem of integrating user interface objects with application code. For example, using Objective-C's dynamic message sending facilities eliminates the need for manual event handling systems common in other frameworks. Many user interface frameworks are implemented to post events identified by unique integer tags when user interface objects change state. The objects that receive events are then responsible for decoding them and interpreting any information sent with the events. The need to decode events results in the duplication of code such as switch statements or table lookup in multiple places and quickly becomes a maintenance burden. Objective-C's built-in messaging system makes manual event processing unnecessary.

The popular Signals and Slots pattern developed by Trolltec for its Qt C++ cross-platform framework replicates some of the Outlets, Targets, and Actions pattern. Programmers must subclass framework user interface classes to add application-specific Signals and Slots. Trolltec provides a tool called the Meta Object Compiler that pre-processes application C++ code to generate code that implements the Signals and Slots. Once the specialized code is generated and compiled into an application, the Signals approximate Cocoa's actions, and the Slots approximate Cocoa's targets. Cocoa and Apple's development tools avoid the need for pre-processing and code generation by using Objective-C's dynamism including the Perform Selector, Anonymous Object, and Responder Chain design patterns.

The ability of tools like Interface Builder to set outlets and actions graphically reduces the amount of code needed to implement user interfaces and integrate them with application code. In many cases, Cocoa applications do not require any custom code to implement a user interface. Even when tools are used to produce user interfaces with other frameworks, the tools usually generate code to handle interactions between user interface objects and other objects. The generated code needs to be maintained over the life of a project and can easily become a source of bugs. Interface Builder does not generate code. It creates instances of existing classes, sets the state of the instances, and archives them in .nib files for later unarchiving by running applications as explained in Chapter 11. No user interface source code is generated. In many cases, no recompiling is needed when the user interface is changed.

Cocoa user interface classes are seldom subclassed. Outlets, Targets, and Actions provide all of the flexibility needed for most applications. Reduced subclassing results in reduced coupling and less code to maintain. The Notifications and Delegates patterns in Chapter 14, "Notifications," and Chapter 15, "Delegates," provide additional flexibility that diminish the need to create subclasses of most View subsystem classes.

Cocoa Bindings provide an automated mechanism for keeping variables synchronized between objects. When two or more variables are bound together, if one changes value, the values of all bound variables are automatically changed to correspond. Cocoa Bindings are described in Chapter 29, "Controllers," and can sometimes be used as an alternative to Outlets, Targets, and Actions.

18

Responder Chain

Cocoa's Responder Chain is a central and essential element of every graphical Cocoa application. It routes user events to the correct objects and simplifies the implementation of context-sensitive application features. The Responder Chain is also known as the Chain of Responsibility pattern.

This chapter describes the behavioral and logic problems that the Responder Chain solves. Application features as diverse as user input, automated menu item validation, undo and redo, copy and paste, font selection, error presentation, and all forms of context-sensitive input are simplified by the Responder Chain. It is closely related to the Hierarchies pattern explained in Chapter 16, "Hierarchies." Hierarchies are primarily structural in nature; the Responder Chain leverages that structure to implement context-dependent behaviors.

Motivation

Control the routing of user input to the correct user interface element. Allow the dynamic retargeting of action messages to currently active or selected user interface elements. Provide a way for user interface elements to automatically update their status in response to user input or application state changes. Simplify the creation of context-sensitive application features.

Solution

Most graphical user interface applications have the notion of a user being focused on a particular user interface element in a specific window. A common problem is that of routing messages and events to the currently focused object. As the user's focus changes, the target needs to change dynamically to follow the focus. Cocoa solves this by using the Chain of Responsibility pattern to implement what is commonly called the *Responder Chain*.

The Chain of Responsibility pattern is designed to decouple a message's sender from the receiver. A message or event is passed down a linked list of objects until one of them handles the message, giving multiple objects the opportunity to handle or ignore the message. Because of the dynamism of Objective-C, the Cocoa implementation of this pattern is amazingly powerful and in most cases is also simpler than its counterpart in other application frameworks.

Terminology

In Cocoa, all objects that respond to user input are subclasses of the abstract class NSResponder. A responder's primary task is to respond to user input, which usually comes from the keyboard or mouse. Because the NSApplication, NSWindow, and NSView classes are all subclasses of NSResponder, the majority of AppKit classes encountered and used by Cocoa developers are responders. The NSWindowController, NSViewController, and NSDrawer classes are also subclasses of NSResponder.

As a user works with an application, Cocoa automatically tracks where the user's focus is. The window currently receiving keyboard input is known as the "key" window. The currently focused document is known as the "main" window. Usually a user is working directly in the document, so the key and main windows are the same. Sometimes the user's focus is actually on two windows, however. For example, in a multidocument application with utility panels, the user might be focused on a particular document while entering something into a utility panel. The input to the utility panel is expected to modify the focused document in some way. In this case, the utility panel would be the key window, while the document it affects is the main window.

The application object tracks both the key and main windows. References to the current key and main NSWindow objects can be obtained from an NSApplication instance with the -keyWindow and -mainWindow messages, respectively.

Within a given window, the user will usually be focused on a specific view object. For example, a user click on a text field will change focus to that field so that the user is able to type in it. The currently focused view is known as the *first responder*. This is the start of the Responder Chain. To obtain a reference to the object that is currently a window's first responder, send the -firstResponder message to the window object.

The Responder Chain

Responders are chained together to allow multiple responders to handle an event. If the first responder cannot handle the user's input or chooses not to handle it, then it passes the input to the next responder in the chain. Any responder can be sent the -nextResponder message to find out which object is next in the chain. The -setNextResponder: message can be used to modify a Responder Chain.

Chapter 16 described the hierarchy of view objects used by Cocoa. This hierarchy defines most of the Responder Chain. Usually a view's next responder is its superview. Sometimes other objects might be inserted into the chain between a view and its superview, but this is less common. A window's content view will point to the window itself as its next responder. Most windows usually have nil as their next responder, ending the chain. A window that is being managed by an NSWindowController will point to the window controller, and the controller will in most cases point to nil. All Responder Chains eventually end in nil to prevent infinite looping.

Figure 18.1 shows an example Responder Chain. The window containing the chain is shown on the left. If the user has clicked the NSTextView to enter some text, then it will be the first responder. The resulting Responder Chain for this circumstance is shown on the right. The NSTextView is first, and then its enclosing NSClipView and NSScrollView. The window's content view, an NSView, is next. The NSWindow is last.

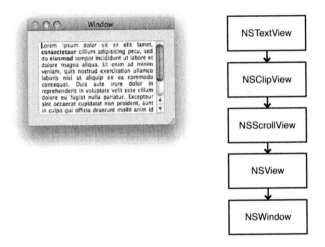

Figure 18.1   An example of a Responder Chain

In this fashion, each window has its own Responder Chain. As the user changes focus from one view to another within a window, the Responder Chain for that window is updated. To change focus, an object is first asked if it is willing to become the next responder via the -acceptsFirstResponder message. Typically only views that can handle keyboard input will say YES. If so, the current first responder is asked to relinquish its first responder status by being sent the -resignFirstResponder message. Sometimes, in the case of text fields that validate input, the answer might be NO until valid data is entered. Finally, the object to become the new first responder is sent the -becomeFirstResponder message.

Incoming keyboard and mouse events are converted to NSEvent objects by the NSApplication object and then dispatched to the correct responder object by passing them down a Responder Chain. For a keyboard events and mouse moved events, the first responder of the key window is the head of the chain. For mouse clicks, the most deeply nested view directly under the mouse is the head. If a responder doesn't want to handle the event, then it will pass the event on to the next responder in the chain until either an object handles the event or the event reaches the end of the chain.

Cocoa handles events in this way to make event dispatching become directed by the hierarchical structure of the objects in the user interface. Input sources are never directly coupled to the objects that receive the input. Instead, an ordered list of objects based on the user's current focus is given the opportunity to respond. User input is automatically routed by the application's current context.

The Extended Responder Chain

A difficult problem to solve when designing an application framework is the question of how to route messages sent by menu items. Consider some of the more common action messages that might be sent by a menu item. A message like -copy: will probably be handled by the first responder of the key window. The -miniaturize: method would apply to the key window. The main window's delegate, often an NSDocument instance, can probably handle the -save: message. The message to quit an application, -terminate:, should be handled by the shared NSApplication instance. Finally, the message to create a new document, -new:, should be handled by the shared NSDocumentController. Routing all these messages to the correct object is a tricky problem.

Some frameworks send menu events to the currently active window, leaving it up to the window to determine how to further dispatch the event. This often requires subclasses of the window object to be created just to handle events generated by menu items.

Cocoa's solution removes the need for any special subclassing while actually being more precise than simply sending an event to a window. Cocoa sends target/action messages down a Responder Chain, starting with the key window's first responder. The target/action message is sent to the first object that responds to it.

The Responder Chain in the key window is not sufficient to cover all the possibilities, however. In the earlier example of a document window and utility panel, some menu items such as "Save" need to operate on the document itself, not the utility panel. Therefore, messages need to be passed down the Responder Chains in both the key and the main window if these are two different windows. Furthermore, some messages should go to the application object, and it is also convenient if the window and application delegates get an opportunity to respond. In a document-based application, the NSDocumentController also implements some actions, such as "New Document" and "Save All."

Putting this all together, the extended Responder Chain used by Cocoa's Target/ Action mechanism is as follows:

1. Start with the first responder of the key window.

2. Follow the Responder Chain up the view hierarchy.

3. Try the window object.

4. Try the window's delegate, which is often an NSDocument instance.

5. Next is an NSWindowController instance, if there is one.

6. Repeat 1–5 starting with the first responder of the main window.

7. Try the NSApplication object and its delegate.

8. Try the NSDocumentController, if there is one.

Unfortunately, even though some NSView objects support delegates, those delegates do not participate in this extended Responder Chain. Only the window and application objects' delegates are included.

Figure 18.2 shows an extended Responder Chain for a window and utility panel. The window at the top is the main window and is part of an NSDocument. The panel at the bottom is the key window. In both windows, the NSTextView is the first responder. The resulting extended Responder Chain is shown at the right. Additional labels are shown to the right of some objects to highlight their roles, such as delegates. If the main and key windows are the same, this chain is shorter because only one window's view hierarchy needs to be traversed. In an application that doesn't use the Cocoa document architecture, the document and document controller objects are left out as well.

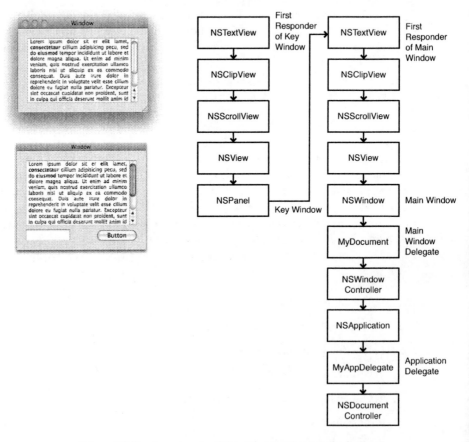

Figure 18.2   An example of the extended Responder Chain

When a menu item is connected to the first responder object in an Interface Builder document, it really means that the action message will be passed down this extended Responder Chain until an object is found that can respond to the message. Just like with mouse and keyboard events, this decouples the targets from the senders and automatically makes menu actions become context-sensitive.

When a developer connects a control in Interface Builder to the "first responder" placeholder, what happens under the hood is that the action's target is set to nil. To manually configure a control to send an action down the extended Responder Chain, set the action normally and use nil as the target. For example, to set an NSControl to send the -terminate: message (which is what the "Quit" menu item sends), you would use this code:

```
[myControl setAction:@selector(terminate)];
[myControl setTarget:nil];
```

To send a message down the extended Responder Chain, NSApplication implements the -sendAction:to:from: method. To find out which object would respond if a message were sent down the chain, without actually sending the message, the NSApplication method -targetForAction:to:from: would be used instead. For example:

```
[NSApp sendAction:@selector(terminate) to:nil from:self];
id myTarget = [NSApp targetForAction:@selector(terminate)
    to:nil from:self];
```

Walking Through the Extended Responder Chain

While learning about the Responder Chain, sometimes it is helpful to see what objects are actually in the chain at a given moment and to see how application context changes what objects are present. By including a simple object in any application, you can easily dump a trace of the Responder Chain to the console. The interface is simple; the -trace: action method is the most important feature:

```
#import <Cocoa/Cocoa.h>

@interface MyResponderChainTracer : NSObject
{
  int count;
}

- (void)traceChain:(id)currentResponder;
- (IBAction)trace:(id)sender;

@end
```

The implementation simply follows the Responder Chain linked lists for the key and main windows, printing a line to the log for every object it finds:

```objc
#import "MyResponderChainTracer.h"


@implementation MyResponderChainTracer

- (void)traceChain:(id)currentResponder
{
  while (currentResponder)
  {
    NSLog(@"Responder %d:  %@", count, currentResponder);
    count++;
    if ([currentResponder isKindOfClass:[NSWindow class]] ||
        [currentResponder isKindOfClass:[NSApplication class]])
    {
      id delegate = [currentResponder delegate];
      if (delegate)
      {
        NSLog(@"Responder %d (delegate):  %@", count,
            [currentResponder delegate]);
        count++;
      }
    }

    if ([currentResponder respondsToSelector:
        @selector(nextResponder)])
    {
      currentResponder = [currentResponder nextResponder];
    }
    else
    {
      currentResponder = nil;
    }
  }
}

- (IBAction)trace:(id)sender
{
  NSWindow *keyWindow = [NSApp keyWindow];
  NSWindow *mainWindow = [NSApp mainWindow];
  count = 1;
  NSLog(@"***** Begin Trace *****");
  [self traceChain:[keyWindow firstResponder]];
  if (keyWindow != mainWindow)
```

```
{
  [self traceChain:[mainWindow firstResponder]];
}
[self traceChain:NSApp];
// omit this line if not in an NSDocument-based app:
[self traceChain:
    [NSDocumentController sharedDocumentController]];
NSLog(@"***** End Trace *****");
}
```

`@end`

To use this object, instantiate it in your application's Main.nib and create a menu item that sends the `-trace:` action to the `MyResponderChainTracer` instance. When the application is run, simply select the menu item at any time to see the Responder Chain at that given moment.

Inserting Objects into the Responder Chain

It is possible to manually manipulate the Responder Chain to insert other objects. The only requirement is that inserted objects be subclasses of `NSResponder`. For example, the `NSViewController` class is a subclass of `NSResponder`. Sometimes it makes sense to insert a view controller into the Responder Chain between the view it is controlling and that view's superview. This is especially true if the view controller is a custom subclass that implements an event handling method or Target/Action method. When a view is added to another as a subview, the next responder is set automatically. Therefore, the time to alter the chain is after the view hierarchy has been created. For example, to insert a view controller, code like this might be used:

```
// myView has been added to it's superview already
NSResponder *theNextResponder = [myView nextResponder];
[myView setNextResponder:myViewController];
[myViewController setNextResponder:theNextResponder];
```

One reason for something like this might be if the view controller overrides `-keyDown:` to allow some keyboard shortcuts to be used, such as the use of the Delete key. When the view controller is inserted into the chain after the view, it will only respond when the view itself is active. This makes sense if a given window has more than one view/controller pair. If the view is the only one like it in the window, or the controller's actions must be active always, then it might make sense to insert it after the window controller instead. By inserting it into different parts of the chain, it is possible to alter behaviors and select when the controller will or won't respond to user input.

Leveraging the Responder Chain

Any time a developer wants to implement context-sensitive features, it is easiest to do so by taking advantage of the existing Responder Chains. For example, in the early days of NeXTStep, Cocoa's predecessor, menu items had to be enabled or disabled manually. Eventually automatic menu item validation was added. To make this new feature easy for developers to adopt, the Responder Chain was used at the core of the implementation.

Cocoa's menu validation is a straightforward use of the Responder Chain. If no object in the Responder Chain responds to the action sent by the menu item, it should obviously be disabled. In the simplest form of validation, if the user changes focus to a user interface element that responds to the menu item's action message, then the menu item can be enabled. However, consider a text object. The cut-and-copy actions do not make sense if no text is selected. Therefore, it is reasonable to add an optional validation method, -validateMenuItem: that returns YES or NO to enable the menu item. In effect, the menu item is asking the target user interface object if the action makes sense given the object's current state.

By implementing menu validation in this way, a lot of old code supporting enabling and disabling menu items could be thrown away, greatly simplifying Cocoa applications. A similar approach can be taken when trying to implement similar context-dependent behaviors. As an example, consider creating a button subclass that can automatically validate itself in the same way NSMenuItem objects do now. The object would not need to declare any new instance variables or methods, so the header would be simple:

```
#import <Cocoa/Cocoa.h>


@interface MyValidatingButton : NSButton
{
}


@end
```

The implementation does two things. First, the button is set up to observe the NSApplicationDidUpdateNotification notification so that it can periodically validate itself. This will cause validation checks that are much more frequent than necessary, but it is easier than a more efficient alternative and allows us to focus on the validation itself.

To actually validate the button, it is necessary to determine the button's target and then call a validation method on the target. If the validation result requires the button to change its enabled state, then the change can be made. The complete implementation for the validating button is as follows:

```
#import "MyValidatingButton.h"
```

```
@implementation MyValidatingButton

- (void)awakeFromNib
{
  [[NSNotificationCenter defaultCenter] addObserver:self
      selector:@selector(applicationDidUpdate)
      name:NSApplicationDidUpdateNotification object:nil];
}


- (void)applicationDidUpdate:(id)userInfo
{
  BOOL validated = NO;
  id myTarget = [NSApp targetForAction:[self action]
      to:[self target] from:self];

  if (myTarget) validated = YES;
  if ([myTarget respondsToSelector:@selector(validateMenuItem)])
  {
    NSMenuItem *myItem = [[NSMenuItem alloc]
        initWithTitle:[self title] action:[self action]
        keyEquivalent:@""];
    validated = [myTarget validateMenuItem:myItem];
    [myItem release];
  }

  if ([self isEnabled] != validated)
  {
    [self setEnabled:validated];
  }
}

@end
```

If there is no valid target, then the button needs to be disabled. So the first thing to do is initialize `validated` to `NO`. The target is determined by using the NSApplication method `-targetForAction:to:from:`. If a target exists, we can tentatively validate the button and set `validated` to `YES`. Next, if the target responds to the menu item validation method `-validateMenuItem:`, we can create a dummy menu item mirroring the button's title and action and then use the `-validateMenuItem:` method to do a final validation. If the final value of `validated` differs from the button's enabled state, then `-setEnabled:` is used to update it.

A simple application to test this class can be created by placing an NSTextView in a window along with three buttons that send `-cut:`, `-copy:`, and `-paste:` to the first responder. Figure 18.3 shows what this looks like.

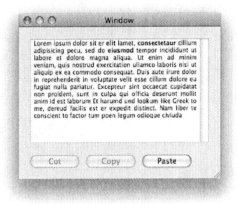

Figure 18.3   `MyValidatingButton` example
interface

Examples in Cocoa

Responder Chains are a central part of Cocoa's design. User input from the keyboard and
mouse is dispatched by the NSApplication object and sent down the relevant Responder
Chain. Keyboard events are passed down the Responder Chain of the key window, while
mouse events can be dispatched to different windows depending on the mouse location
and event type. For example, mouse moved events go to the key window, while mouse
down and mouse scroll events go to the window currently under the mouse pointer.

An extended version of the Responder Chain that includes Responder Chains from
the key and main window and the shared NSApplication and NSDocumentController
instances is used to dispatch action messages sent to a nil target. Menu items are one of
the most common places nil-targeted actions are encountered, considering many menu
commands are intended to operate on whatever view and/or window the user has focused. Any time an action needs to dynamically change its target based on application
context, a nil-targeted action is usually the best solution. Copy and paste, font and color
selection, ruler manipulation, and undo and redo are all examples of actions that are commonly sent down the extended Responder Chain.

Because of the way the Responder Chain is designed, it is possible to easily implement
automatic menu-item validation. The menu item and the targeted object are completely
decoupled because neither is aware of the other until the moment of validation. This
helps to keep validation code both simple and well organized.

Contextual menus also leverage the Responder Chain. If a given view doesn't want to
generate a contextual menu, its superview is given an opportunity to do so. This query can
continue up the Responder Chain. In this way, some views can provide very specific contextual menus while others provide a more general menu. Context help works in exactly
the same way, offering each object in the Responder Chain the opportunity to supply help.

Many of these context-dependent features were not in the original releases Cocoa or its predecessors and were added later. The power and flexibility of the Responder Chain has made it possible to implement these features in an elegant way that usually allows developers to adopt the new features with little, if any, extra work. It is highly likely that future major feature additions to the AppKit will further leverage Responder Chains to present new features that developers can adopt quickly and easily.

Consequences

Cocoa leverages the flexibility of dispatching messages along a chain to automatically provide application features as diverse as keyboard and mouse event dispatch, menu item validation, undo and redo, copy and paste, font selection, contextual menus, and contextual help. Every graphical Cocoa application gets these features and more for free or with very little code thanks to the Responder Chain.

Developers benefit from being able to include all these features in their applications with little to no effort. It is also possible for developers to customize the Responder Chains within their applications and to leverage them to ease the implementation of application-specific, context-dependent behaviors.

19

Associative Storage

Associative Storage is one of the oldest and most used patterns in software development. It organizes data and keys so that data can be quickly and easily accessed using the corresponding keys. Associative Storage promotes flexibility and runtime storage efficiency.

Motivation

Use Associative Storage to accomplish the following:

- Efficiently store arbitrary data associated with objects.
- Promote flexibility by delaying the selection of which data to access until runtime.
- Provide object extensibility per instance instead of per class.
- Work around an Objective-C programming language limitation that prevents addition of instance variables without subclassing.

Solution

The NSDictionary and NSMutableDictionary classes in Cocoa's Foundation framework are the most prominent classes that provide associative storage. An NSDictionary instance maps keys to object values. To retrieve an object value previously stored in a dictionary, use the -objectForKey: method, which returns the object that is associated with a specified key. NSMutableDictionary is a subclass of NSDictionary and provides the -setObject:forKey: method used to create new associations in the dictionary. When keys and values are added and removed from a mutable dictionary, the memory allocated to store objects grows and shrinks automatically. If -setObject:forKey: is called with a key that is already in the dictionary, the object associated with that key is replaced by the new object. Each unique key is stored in each dictionary at most once.

The objects stored in a dictionary are retained when they are added to the collection and released when they are removed. The implications of retaining and releasing objects are described in Chapter 10, "Accessors." The keys that are added to a dictionary are copied, which means that all objects used as keys in a dictionary must conform to the NSCopying formal protocol declared in NSObject.h. In addition to conforming to the NSCopying protocol, objects used as keys in a dictionary must implement the -isEqual: and -hash methods so that any two objects that are considered equal by the -isEqual: method also have the same hash value. The -isEqual: and -hash methods are declared in the NSObject class, which provides basic implementations using the addresses of objects. In other words, two objects are equal if they have the same address, and the -hash value is computed from the address.

Subclasses of NSObject override the inherited implementations of -isEqual: and -hash as needed. For example, instances of the NSString class are compared based on their stored string values rather than merely their addresses, and the value returned from -hash is also computed from the stored strings.

> **Note**
>
> NSDictionary and other Associative Storage features of Cocoa are implemented with hash tables. Hash tables are explained in almost every introductory software data structures text-book. An excellent introduction is available at http://ciips.ee.uwa.edu.au/~morris/Year2/PLDS210/hash_tables.html, and an advanced description is available at http://www.cris.com/~Ttwang/tech/inthash.htm.

Cocoa provides a functional interface for Associative Storage using the NSMapTable data structure and functions that manipulate it. NSMapTable is used in the following example because it provides a little more flexibility than NSDictionary. Dictionaries always copy their keys, but in the following example it is necessary to store keys without copying or retaining them.

Simulating Instance Variables

One limitation of the Category pattern described in Chapter 6, "Category" is that categories can only add methods to a class; instance variables must be declared only in the main class interface. This example shows one way the Associative Storage pattern is used to simulate the addition of an instance variable to Cocoa's NSObject class. The category in this example provides access to a different label for each instance of NSObject or any class that inherits from NSObject. Instances that don't have an assigned label don't consume any extra memory. The following category declares the -mySetLabel: and -myLabel methods:

```
#import <Foundation/Foundation.h>
```

```
@interface NSObject (MYSimulateIVar)
```

```
- (void)setMyLabel:(NSString *)aString;
- (NSString *)myLabel;
```

```
@end
```

Methods like the ones defined in this category are called *accessors*. Accessors are themselves an important pattern described in Chapter 10. The primary purpose of accessors is to funnel all references to each instance variable through a few, usually only two, methods. A nice benefit of using accessors in this example is that even though the labels are not stored as instance variables, programmers using the NSObject class don't need to know that. The accessors shield users of a class from the actual implementation.

```
#import "MYSimulateIvar.h"
```

```
@implementation NSObject (MYSimulateIVar)
```

```
//
static NSMapTable *_MYSimulatedIVarMapTable = NULL;
```

```
+ (NSMapTable *)_mySimulatedIVarMapTable
//
{
  if(NULL == _MYSimulatedIVarMapTable)
  {
    _MYSimulatedIVarMapTable = NSCreateMapTable(
        NSNonRetainedObjectMapKeyCallBacks,
        NSObjectMapValueCallBacks, 16);
  }

  return _MYSimulatedIVarMapTable;
}
```

```
- (void)dealloc
// Possibly risky implementation
{
  NSMapRemove([[self class] _mySimulatedIVarMapTable], self);
  NSDeallocateObject(self);
}
```

```
- (void)setMyLabel:(NSString *)aString
//
{
  NSString       *newLabel = [aString copy];
```

```
  NSMapInsert([[self class] _mySimulatedIVarMapTable], self, newLabel);
  [newLabel release];
}


- (NSString *)myLabel
//
{
  return NSMapGet([[self class] _mySimulatedIVarMapTable], self);
}

@end
```

There are several important elements to the implementation of the MYSimulateIVar category. The +_myRefCountMapTable class method is used to access the NSMapTable data structure that stores labels associated with NSObject instances. The +_myRefCountMapTable method is not declared in the category interface because it is a private implementation detail of the category. The first time +_myRefCountMapTable is called, the data structure is initialized to store nonretained object keys and retained objects as values. It is critical that the keys are not retained because if they are retained it will be impossible to correctly deallocate any instances of NSObject that have associated labels. The table is initialized with sufficient storage for 16 key/value pairs, but that number is arbitrary. The storage for the table automatically increases as keys and values are added. The -dealloc method implemented in the category replaces NSObject's existing implementation. The -dealloc method removes any key/value pair associated with an instance when the instance is deallocated. It is safe to replace NSObject's -dealloc implementation in this case because the replaced version is documented to do nothing except call NSDeallocateObject() as of Mac OS X 10.5. If Apple ever changes the implementation of -dealloc in the NSObject class, the fact that this category bypasses that implementation could have undesirable side effects.

To flesh out support for labels associated with objects, it's necessary to provide encoding and decoding support so that labels are stored along with any other data stored for objects when they are encoded. An example of using existing accessors in the implementation of encoding and decoding methods is provided in Chapter 11, "Archiving and Unarchiving." Support for copying labels when objects are copied should also be supported, and a general technique is described in Chapter 12, "Copying."

Finally, this example is limited to storing labels for objects. A more useful category enables the storage on any amount of data with each object. To enable that, modify the example to store dictionaries of key/value pairs with -mySetUserInfo: and -myUserInfo methods instead of instead of -mySetLabel: and -myLabel methods.

```
 - (void)mySetUserInfo:(NSDictionary *)aDictionary
//
{
  NSDictionary    *newDictionary = [aDictionary copy];
```

```
   NSMapInsert([[self class] _mySimulatedIVarMapTable], self,
       newDictionary);
   [newDictionary release];
}


- (NSDictionary *)myUserInfo
//
{
   return NSMapGet([[self class] _mySimulatedIVarMapTable], self);
}
```

Any number of key/value pairs can be stored in the dictionary associated with each object. To keep the ability to store labels, simply store a label string associated with a key such as @"Label" in each user info dictionary.

Even though Objective-C doesn't support true class variables, this technique can be used to simulate class variables. A generalized implementation of simulated class variables could use nested Associative Storage. The class name can be used as a key to return a dictionary for a particular class. The name of the class variable would then be used as a key to look up the actual value.

Examples in Cocoa

Many Cocoa classes including NSAttributedString, NSFileManager, NSNotification, and NSProcessInfo use the Associative Storage pattern extensively. The pattern can be used to simulate instance variables in your own code. The opposite is possible, too. Cocoa uses the related key value coding system to provide access to instance variables of any object as if the true instance variables were all simulated with Associative Storage. Associative Storage also provides the basis of Cocoa's keyed archiving system described in Chapter 11.

The use of NSDictionary to provide Associative Storage for arbitrary properties of NSNotification and NSFileManager objects has already been mentioned. NSNotification provides the -userInfo method that returns a dictionary containing arbitrary keys and values. NSFileManager's -fileAttributesAtPath:traverseLink: method returns a dictionary that stores the subset of possible file attribute key/value pairs available for a file. Another prominent example is the dictionary of text formatting attributes stored by NSAttributedString instances. Each string can have different attributes, and the set of possible attributes is open-ended. Using a dictionary to store attributes enables the storage of custom application-specific attributes without the need to subclass NSAttributedString. The NSProcessInfo class provides the -environment method that returns a dictionary of environment variable name/value pairs that are defined for a running process. Once again, because the collection of variable names and values is open-ended, using the Associative Storage pattern is the perfect solution.

Reference Counted Memory Management

Cocoa uses the Associative Storage pattern to store the reference count needed to implement reference counted memory management. The following example describes a hypothetical MYRefCounted category of NSObject that stores a reference count for each object using Associative Storage in much the same way it is implemented in Cocoa. The code shows the basic technique and highlights some of the advantages and disadvantages of using Associative Storage:

```
#import <Foundation/Foundation.h>


@interface NSObject (MYRefCounted)

- (int)retainCount;
- (id)retain;
- (void)release;

@end
```

The -retainCount, -retain, and -release methods form the core of Cocoa's reference counted memory management support. Another critical method, -autorelease, and the NSAutoreleasePool class used to support -autorelease are not shown here but are described in Chapter 10.

```
#import "MYRefCounted.h"


@implementation NSObject (MYRefCounted)

//
static NSMapTable *_MYRefCountMapTable = NULL;


+ (NSMapTable *)_myRefCountMapTable
  // Provides access to the table used to store reference counts
{
  if(NULL == _MYRefCountMapTable)
  {
    _MYRefCountMapTable = NSCreateMapTable(
        NSNonRetainedObjectMapKeyCallBacks,
        NSIntMapValueCallBacks, 16);
  }

  return _MYRefCountMapTable;
}
```

```
- (int)retainCount
  // Returns the receiver's current reference count
{
  int              result = 1; // receiver not in table, its count is 1
  void             *tableValue = NSMapGet(
    [[self class] _myRefCountMapTable], self);

  if(NULL != tableValue )
  { // if receiver is in table, its count is the value stored
    result = (int)tableValue;
  }

  return result;
}


- (id)retain
  // Increases the receiver's reference count
{
  // store the increased value in the table
  NSMapInsert([[self class] _myRefCountMapTable], self,
      (void *)([self retainCount] + 1));

  return self;
}


- (void)release
  // Decrease the receiver's reference count and dealloc if it reaches
  // zero
{
  int    currentRetainCount = [self retainCount];

  if(1 == currentRetainCount)
  { // the reference count is about to reach zero so deallocate
    // there is no need to remove receiver from table now because if
    // its reference count is 1, it is not in the table
    [self dealloc];
  }
  else if(2 == currentRetainCount)
  {
    // remove the receiver from the table to indicate that its
    // reference count is 1
    NSMapRemove([[self class] _myRefCountMapTable], self);
```

```
  }
  else
  { store the decreased value in the table
    NSMapInsert([[self class] _myRefCountMapTable], self,
        (void *)(currentRetainCount - 1));
  }
}

@end
```

Objects that are not stored in _MYRefCountMapTable have an implicit reference count of 1. For example, newly allocated objects aren't stored in the table and therefore have a reference count of 1, and no extra storage beyond the storage needed for instance variables is needed. Working on the assumption that at any give time, almost all objects have a reference count of 1, this system makes efficient use of memory.

Each time an object is retained by calling the -retain method, its reference count increases and is stored in the table. Each time an object is released via the -release method, the associated reference count stored in the table is decreased. If the reference count decreases to 1, the association is removed from the table. If the reference count decreases to zero, the object is immediately deallocated.

Key Value Coding

Much of this chapter has focused on simulating additional instance variables with the Associative Storage pattern. Cocoa's Key Value Coding does exactly the opposite. It provides access to an object's instance variables using semantics similar to Associative Storage. Key Value Coding provides access to an object's properties indirectly using string keys rather than through accessor methods or direct instance variable references. Key Value Coding was introduced to simplify the interaction of scripting languages with Cocoa objects, but the technique has value in many contexts. The two principal methods that implement key value coding are -valueForKey and -setValue:forkey:. The -setValue:forKey: method uses the string name specified as a key to identify an accessor method or instance variable name. If a suitable method or variable is identified, its value is set to the value specified. Similarly, the -valueForKey: method returns a value obtained by calling an accessor method or directly accessing the instance variable identified by the key.

Cocoa's existing implementations of -setValue:forKey: and -valueForKey: first try to use an accessor method based on the key name. The set accessor needs to have the form -set<key>: where <key> is the string used as a key. The first letter in the key is made uppercase if it is not already so that Cocoa's method naming convention of capitalizing all but the first word in a method name is preserved. For example, if -setValue:forKey: is called with @"label" as the key, it will try to use an accessor method named -setLabel: to set the value. When getting a value with -valueForKey:, the method tries to use an accessor with the name -<key>. In this case, the first letter of the key is converted to lowercase if necessary so that the method starts with a lowercase letter. For example, calling -valueForKey: with @"label" as the key ends up calling the -label method if it exists.

The key value system is very sophisticated and will fall back to using accessors that start with underscore "_" characters and if all else fails will directly access instance variables with names derived from the strings used as keys. The key value system allows programs to interact with objects as if every object is a dictionary that associates its properties with string keys. Key Value Coding is also described in Chapters 29, "Controllers," and 30, "Code Data Models."

Key Value Coding provides a way for scripting languages to access the values stored in objects at runtime based on the string name of the value. Perhaps more importantly, Key Value Coding is the foundation for Cocoa bindings technology. Key Value Coding applies the Associative Storage pattern to every Cocoa object so that object instance variables or accessors are selected at runtime via string keys.

Consequences

Associative storage is flexible and can be used to implement previously unanticipated features. The uses for a dictionary associated with each NSObject instance are completely open-ended. However, accessing values stored in a dictionary or map table is not as efficient as accessing instance variables directly. An instance variable can typically be accessed from program code with a single machine instruction, but Associative Storage requires multiple method or function calls, calculation of hash values, and indexed memory access into a table. Storing an associated value requires memory for both the key and the value. If every object uses associated storage, the memory required to store all of the keys and values exceeds the memory that would have been required to store the values in instance variables. If the need to store values is rare, using Associative Storage can be a big win. Rather than storing unused instance variables in every instance, memory is only reserved when the values are actually used.

The examples in this chapter use Associative Storage with categories, but the technique is applicable in many circumstances. In fact, the drawbacks of replacing methods like -dealloc with methods in categories are serious. When subclassing is an option, simply adding instance variables in a subclass is probably the best choice. One of the most flexible techniques for using Associative Storage is to provide an NSDictionary object as an instance variable. Cocoa's NSNotification class uses this approach to allow storage of arbitrary data with each instance. The NSFileManager class uses a similar technique to store file system-specific information about files. The flexibility is needed in the case of NSFileManager because each file being managed could be stored in a different file system with different file system-specific attributes. Using a dictionary of attributes enables the storage of pertinent attributes without requiring storage for attributes that don't apply.

Associative Storage is also useful for shortening method names. A complex method that requires many arguments might be better implemented with a single NSDictionary argument instead. If some of the arguments are optional, then there is a temptation to create many convenience methods with shorter names that leave out the optional arguments. By using Associative Storage to pass the arguments, it is possible to avoid a proliferation of methods. Optional keys can simply be omitted when populating the dictionary and the method can supply sensible default values for missing keys. Associative Storage also helps to insulate senders from future changes. If later versions of the method allow for new arguments, there is no need to alter the message. More key/value pairs are simply added to the dictionary. If arguments are removed, any extra keys in the dictionary will be ignored. The downside of this approach is that the sender needs extra code to configure and populate an NSDictionary instance.

20

Invocations

Invocations are a technique for preserving the state of messages, arguments, and return values. Invocations can be used to completely decouple the sender of a message from the receiver. The sender and receiver can be in different processes or separated by time. Invocations are implemented by Cocoa's NSInvocation class and are used in distributed objects, undo and redo support, and scheduled periodic event processing. Invocations can be used in applications to provide a wide range of flexible and dynamic behavior. Invocations are a generalized implementation of the well-known Command pattern described at http://en.wikipedia.org/wiki/Command_pattern.

Motivation

Provide a means of capturing messages so that they can be stored, delayed, rerouted, or treated and manipulated as objects. Allow new messages to be constructed and sent at runtime without requiring a compiler.

Solution

When working with Objective-C, it is important to remember that sending a message to an object is not the same thing as invoking a method. When an object receives a message, usually a method is invoked to handle the message. However, this is not always the case. For example, if an object doesn't implement a particular method, then there is no method that can be invoked, and a runtime exception is raised instead. Because of the flexibility of the Objective-C runtime, it is possible for messages to be delayed, rerouted to other receivers, or even ignored.

It is sometimes useful to think of Objective-C messages as if they were analogous to a real-world message. For example, a secretary might receive messages for a corporate executive. The messages might be handled by the secretary, passed on to the executive as-is, or changed before being passed on. A particularly important message might be copied and sent on to multiple recipients. In Objective-C, all these scenarios are possible.

Chapter 27, "Proxies and Forwarding," demonstrates how many of these situations can be implemented.

At the core of this flexibility is the need to treat a message as if it were an object that can be created and manipulated. The NSInvocation class is designed to represent an Objective-C message. NSInvocation instances encapsulate all the attributes of an Objective-C message. They know the message's receiver, the message name (both the selector and method signature), and all the message's arguments. After invoking an NSInvocation, the message's return value (if there is one) may be retrieved from the NSInvocation.

Method Signatures

One point of confusion for many developers is in how messages are named. Each name has two parts, the selector and the method signature. Both parts are required to properly configure NSInvocation objects. A selector is the message's name without any type information, for example "countOfObjectsOfType:" is a selector. Objective-C also has the data type SEL, which is a unique identifier representing a selector. The Objective-C directive @selector() can be used to obtain a SEL.

Most programmers consider the selector to be the same thing as the message name, and in most cases this is fine. However, selectors do not provide any type information. To build a complete message, the types of each argument and the return value's type need to be known. This type information is known as a *method signature*. The class NSMethodSignature encapsulates this information.

To get an NSMethodSignature instance, typically you would ask an NSObject subclass for the correct signature given a particular selector. This is necessary because the same selector can have a different signature depending on which object is responding. For example, consider two methods with the same selector but different signatures and a message that invokes one of them:

```
- (int)countOfObjectsOfType:(id)objectType; // defined in ClassA
- (NSValue *)countOfObjectsOfType:(int)objectType; // defined in ClassB
value = [myObject countOfObjectsOfType:aType];
```

If the receiver, myObject, is of type id, then this message will create a compiler warning because the compiler won't know for certain which method signature to use when constructing the message. Normally a developer would use static typing on the receiver to tell the compiler what kind of object will receive the message. It is also possible to use a type cast when sending a message. One of these two solutions would be used to eliminate the compiler warning:

```
// if you must use an id type, then use a cast when sending the message
id myObject;
value = [(ClassA *)myObject countOfObjectsOfType:aType];

// otherwise, use static typing instead of a generic id to disambiguate
ClassA *myObject;
value = [myObject countOfObjectsOfType:aType];
```

At runtime, however, the receiver is known, and it is possible to simply ask it for the correct message signature, like this:

```
NSMethodSignature* mySignature = [myObject
    methodSignatureForSelector:@selector(countOfObjectsOfType:)];
```

The designated initializer for `NSInvocation` instances requires a method signature to be provided, so you can't create invocations without first obtaining a method signature. Because the `NSMethodSignature` object also knows the return type to expect, it is additionally needed when retrieving return values from `NSInvocation` instances.

Using `NSInvocation` Objects

To use an `NSInvocation` to send a message, an instance is created and then configured. Once configured, it may be invoked at the appropriate time, causing an Objective-C message to be sent. The return value of the message can then be retrieved from the `NSInvocation` object. `NSInvocation` instances may be invoked multiple times, possibly with changes made to target, arguments, and even message selector between invocations.

To demonstrate how an `NSInvocation` can be created and used, we will create a simple application to perform some basic string manipulations. The user will be able to enter a string, select an operation to be performed, supply the appropriate arguments, and then click a button to send a message that will perform the operation on the string and display the return value. One class, named `InvocationController`, is required. The interface for this class is simple:

```
@interface InvocationController : NSObject
{
  IBOutlet NSTextField    *receiver;
  IBOutlet NSPopUpButton *message;
  IBOutlet NSTextField    *argument1;
  IBOutlet NSTextField    *argument2;
  IBOutlet NSTextField    *result;
}

- (IBAction)inputChanged:(id)sender;
- (IBAction)sendMessage:(id)sender;

@end
```

Figure 20.1 shows the user interface used by this example, including the connections to the controller object.

The pop-up button is configured with an `NSMenuItem` for each operation that will be performed. The title of each item is the selector for the message to be sent. Proper spelling and capitalization is very important. The tag for the menu item is the number of arguments the message requires. For example, the method `-lowercaseString` takes no arguments, so the title is "lowercaseString" and the tag is "0." Figure 20.2 shows all the pop-up button's menu items for this example.

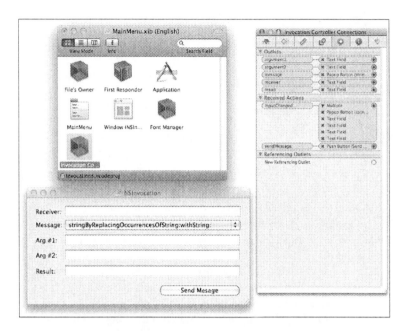

Figure 20.1   `NSInvocation` example interface

Figure 20.2   Menu items found in the pop-up button

The controller's -`inputChanged:` method simply enables or disables the argument text fields based on which menu item has been selected by the user with the pop-up button.

```
- (IBAction)inputChanged:(id)sender
{
  int numberOfArguments = [[message selectedItem] tag];
  [argument1 setEnabled:NO];
```

```
[argument2 setEnabled:NO];
switch (numberOfArguments)
{
  case 2:
    [argument2 setEnabled:YES];
  case 1:
    [argument1 setEnabled:YES];
  case 0:
  default:
    break;
  }
}
```

Now that the interface is in place, it is time for the meat of this example. The
-sendMessage: method of the controller object needs to take the information from the
interface, turn it into an NSInvocation instance, invoke it, and then put the return value
into the interface.

Because the selector is the title of the pop-up button, it is necessary to convert from
an NSString to an Objective-C SEL type. The NSSelectorFromString() function can
convert NSString instances into selectors. Using the receiver and the selector, it is
possible to get the method signature, which can then be used to create an NSInvocation
instance:

```
NSString *receivingString = [receiver stringValue];
NSString *messageString = [message titleOfSelectedItem];
SEL selector = NSSelectorFromString(messageString);
NSMethodSignature *methodSignature = [receivingString
    methodSignatureForSelector:selector];
NSInvocation *invocation = [NSInvocation
    invocationWithMethodSignature:methodSignature];
```

The first step of configuring an invocation is to tell it the message's receiver (or target)
and the selector. The invocation was created with the method signature, so it knows the
type information, but it also needs to know the selector as well:

```
[invocation setTarget:receivingString];  // argument 0 is "self"
[invocation setSelector:selector];        // argument 1 is "_cmd"
```

Every Objective-C method has two hidden arguments. The first and most commonly
used argument is self. The second, containing the selector that invoked the method, is
_cmd. Note that this means it is technically possible to write method implementations
that may be invoked by multiple different selectors. The implementation would use _cmd
to determine which selector was actually used. This works as long as each of the selectors
has the same method signature. This is particularly useful when constructing classes on-
the-fly in a running program, as might be done when bridging between Objective-C and
scripting languages. These hidden arguments are important when building NSInvocation
instances because it is critical that both arguments be supplied. If you forget to use both
-setTarget: and -setSelector:, the invocation will not work.

Returning to the example, the next step is to configure the arguments for the invocation. The -setArgument:atIndex: method of NSInvocation is used for this. The messages being sent can have 0, 1, or 2 arguments, and the tag of the selected pop-up button item tells how many arguments to set up. Because the hidden arguments self and _cmd take up spots 0 and 1 in the argument list, the first argument to the method is actually argument 2. Also when using the -setArgument:atIndex: method, pointers to object pointers must be used instead of just a pointer to the object. Here's the code:

```
int numberOfArguments = [[message selectedItem] tag];
if (numberOfArguments > 0)
{
  NSString *argumentString1 = [argument1 stringValue];
  [invocation setArgument:&argumentString1 atIndex:2];
  if (numberOfArguments > 1)
  {
    NSString *argumentString2 = [argument2 stringValue];
    [invocation setArgument:&argumentString2 atIndex:3];
  }
}
```

Invocation objects by default do not retain their arguments. If the arguments are objects that might be released before the invocation sends its message, then it needs to be sent the -retainArguments message. Given that this example invocation will be used immediately, there is no need to use -retainArguments.

Now that the invocation is created and has all its arguments configured, it can be sent the -invoke message. The return value can then be requested with the -getReturnValue: method, which takes a pointer to void* as its argument. The return value is stored in that pointer, but the method signature must be queried to know how to interpret the data. Here is the code to invoke the message and interpret the return value:

```
[invocation invoke];
void *returnValue = NULL;
[invocation getReturnValue:&returnValue];
const char *returnType = [methodSignature methodReturnType];

if (returnType)
{
  switch (returnType[0])
  {
    case '@':
      [result setObjectValue:(id)returnValue];
      break;
    case 'i':
      [result setIntValue:(int)returnValue];
      break;
    default:
      break;
  }
}
```

The interpretation of return values is based on the Objective-C @encode() directive as described by the documentation for the Objective-C language. Because this is implementation-dependent, it is wise to carefully test any code that uses this information directly, such as this example's switch statement. In this case, because the methods that would be called in the example only return int ("i") or id ("@") types, only two cases are handled. More robust code would attempt to handle all types supported by @encode() or throw exceptions for unsupported types.

Figure 20.3 shows this example program in action. A real program probably wouldn't put method names on a pop-up button directly as is done by this example. Instead, a dictionary or other mechanism might be used to look up method names so that the pop-up button's menu items could have titles that are more user-friendly.

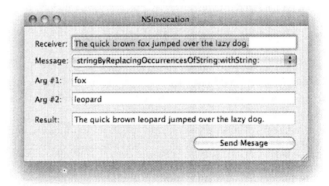

Figure 20.3   The Invocation example while running

Using Timers

For most Cocoa programmers it is rare to actually manipulate NSInvocation objects directly as is done in the previous example. That said, many parts of Cocoa use NSInvocation in their implementation. One example of this is the NSTimer object. A timer takes a target, a message to be sent to that target, and a time interval. Every time the interval elapses, the timer sends the message to the target. This can be used to create uniformly repeating events. The classic example of this would be an animation loop. For example, an animation loop that draws a new frame 24 times per second would use a time interval of 1/24 second (0.0417 seconds). When a timer's time interval has elapsed and it is time to send the message again, the timer is said to "fire," just like a starter fires a gun at the start of a race.

To show an example of how this works, let's create a simple example implementing a stopwatch that counts upward from one number to another number at a user-specified speed. As in the previous example, a controller object is required. The interface for the TimerController class is as follows:

```
@interface TimerController : NSObject
{
  NSTimer               *myTimer;
  IBOutlet NSTextField *startCount;
  IBOutlet NSTextField *endCount;
  IBOutlet NSTextField *interval;
  IBOutlet NSTextField *currentCount;
  IBOutlet NSButton    *startButton;
  IBOutlet NSButton    *continueButton;
  IBOutlet NSButton    *endButton;
  int                   count;
}

- (void)startTimer;
- (void)stopTimer;
- (IBAction)beginTimer:(id)sender;
- (IBAction)continueTimer:(id)sender;
- (IBAction)endTimer:(id)sender;
- (void)count:(id)userInfo;

@end
```

The interface controlled by this object is shown in Figure 20.4.

The controller's implementation does some basic initialization in the -init and -awakeFromNib methods to set up the interface and set the counter to its initial value. The -dealloc method needs to properly shut things down. The Interface Builder actions are simple cover methods that call the -startTimer and -stopTimer methods:

```
- (id)init
{
  if(nil != (self = [super init]))
  {
    count = 0;
  }
  return self;
}

- (void)awakeFromNib
{
  count = [startCount intValue];
  [currentCount setIntValue:count];
  [self stopTimer];
}

- (void)dealloc
```

```
{
  [self stopTimer];
}

- (IBAction)beginTimer:(id)sender
{
  count = [startCount intValue];
  [currentCount setIntValue:count];
  [self startTimer];
}

- (IBAction)continueTimer:(id)sender
{
  if (!myTimer)
  {
    [self startTimer];
  }
}

- (IBAction)endTimer:(id)sender
{
  [self stopTimer];
}
```

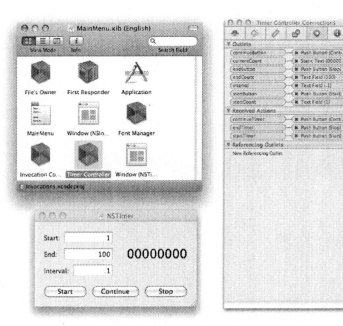

Figure 20.4   The interface for the Timer example

The timer is going to need a message to send to increment the counter. The timer will be configured so that the -count: message will be sent to the controller every time it fires. The -count: method simply increments the count and updates the interface unless the count has reached the last number, in which case it stops the timer. Here is the code to do this:

```
- (void)count:(id)userInfo
{
  if (count >= [endCount intValue])
  {
    [self stopTimer];
  }
  else
  {
    count++;
    [currentCount setIntValue:count];
  }
}
```

Now that the interface is set up and there is a method for the timer to call, it is possible to write start and stop methods.

Because our controller should only have one timer running at a time, it first stops any running timers. Next it creates a new timer and then updates the interface so that only the buttons that make sense to use are enabled. The core of this method is a single message that creates the timer.

Typically, a timer is created and then added to an NSRunLoop, a two-step process. As a shortcut, if you want the timer to be added to the current run loop—which is usually the case—then you create a "scheduled" timer, which is a single step. Here is the code to create and start the timer:

```
- (void)startTimer
{
  if (myTimer)
  {
    [self stopTimer];
  }
  myTimer = [NSTimer scheduledTimerWithTimeInterval:
      [interval doubleValue]
      target:self selector:@selector(count:)
      userInfo:nil repeats:YES];
  [myTimer retain];
  [startButton setEnabled:NO];
  [continueButton setEnabled:NO];
  [endButton setEnabled:YES];
}
```

When setting up the timer, the time interval is specified along with the message to send and whether the timer should repeat. Of course a nonrepeating timer will only fire once, whereas a repeating timer will keep firing until it is stopped.

The message that is sent by the timer must follow a very specific method signature. It returns void and takes a single argument, an object called userInfo. The object itself is arbitrary. When you create the timer, you choose the object that should be sent. It is up to the method the timer invokes to determine what should be done with the userInfo object. Usually it is ignored. Sometimes this object is used to pass data on to the invoked method. If multiple timers invoke the method, then the userInfo object can be used to help identify which timer is doing the invoking. If more than one piece of data needs to be passed, then userInfo can be a dictionary, taking advantage of the Associative Storage pattern discussed in Chapter 19, "Associative Storage."

Although messages are being constructed and sent on-the-fly by the timer, no code involving NSInvocation has to be written. The catch is that only a very specific method signature can be used by the method invoked when the timer fires. If that is unsuitable, it is also possible to create timers that will send any message desired. Instead of specifying a target, selector, and user info object when creating a timer, you can simply pass an NSInvocation object using the +scheduledTimerWithTimeInterval :invocation:repeats: method. While this is more flexible, the downside is that, as seen previously, it can require several lines of extra code to create a suitable NSInvocation instance.

The final method required by the controller object is used to stop the timer. To stop a repeating timer, simply send an -invalidate message. As part of invalidating, it will automatically remove itself from its run loop. Nonrepeating timers automatically remove themselves from their run loop after they fire, so there is no need to invalidate them. The -stopTimer method of the controller simply invalidates the timer and updates the interface:

```
- (void)stopTimer
{
  [myTimer invalidate];
  [myTimer release];
  myTimer = nil;
  [startButton setEnabled:YES];
  if ((count > [startCount intValue]) &&
      (count < [endCount intValue]))
  {
    [continueButton setEnabled:YES];
  }
  else
  {
    [continueButton setEnabled:NO];
```

```
    }
    [endButton setEnabled:NO];
}
```

Delayed Messaging

Sometimes it is useful to delay a message so that it is sent at a later time. Obviously, a nonrepeating NSTimer can be used for this purpose. As a shortcut, Cocoa provides the NSObject methods -performSelector:withObject:afterDelay: and -performSelector:withObject:afterDelay:inModes. The only difference between them is that the first only sends the message when the run loop is in its default mode. In order for the message to be sent in a modal loop or other specific run mode, the latter version needs to be used instead. Both methods create and schedule the appropriate NSTimer instance. Both methods may also be used with any instance of any NSObject subclass to cause a delayed message to be sent.

One interesting use for a delayed message is to use a time interval of zero. In this case, the message will still be delayed, but only until the next pass through the run loop. This can be useful when a message should be sent after the processing of the current event is completed. This "next run loop invocation" is a frequently encountered idiom used by many Cocoa developers.

For example, consider a push button. It is drawn differently, with a "pushed-in" look, when it is clicked. Supposed that the action invoked by clicking the button causes an alert panel to come up. If the normal NSRunAlertPanel() function is called from the code that handles the button push, then the button will remain with the pushed-in look for as long as the alert panel is on the screen. If, instead, a delayed perform with a delay of zero is used, then the button click will finish processing, the button will be drawn to look normal, and only then will the alert panel be placed on the screen.

You can clearly see the difference between these two approaches in Figure 20.5. On the left, NSRunAlertPanel() is run immediately. On the right, a delayed perform is used instead. The code for the two action methods used by the two buttons is very simple:

```
- (IBAction)openAlert:(id)sender
{
  NSRunAlertPanel(@"Alert", @"This is an alert.",
      @"OK", nil, nil);
}


- (IBAction)openDelayedAlert:(id)sender
{
  [self performSelector:@selector(openAlert:)
      withObject:sender afterDelay:0.0];
}
```

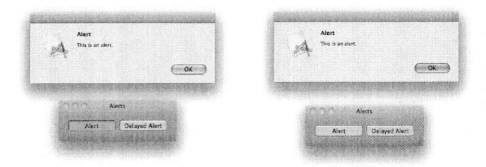

Figure 20.5   Using delayed perform to allow a button to redraw

Examples in Cocoa

Cocoa uses invocations extensively, even though their use is not always immediately obvious. Invocations are used whenever there is a need to manipulate an Objective-C message and make it possible to store, delay, resend, or reroute messages. Invocations are implemented directly with the NSInvocation class.

The NSTimer class uses NSInvocation instances but can create its own invocation objects. This frees most developers from the need to deal with the NSInvocation class directly. NSObject implements -performSelector:... methods that can even eliminate the need to directly manipulate NSTimers instances in some cases. The NSOperation class, new to 10.5, has an NSInvocationOperation subclass that can be used as a generic implementation of operations. The bridges between Objective-C and the Ruby and Python languages also take advantage of invocations internally.

The two most notable uses of invocations in Cocoa are the undo/redo functionality of Cocoa's NSDocument architecture and Distributed Objects. The way these two technologies leverage invocations is important enough that it is discussed in detail in Chapter 27.

Consequences

Invocations package up an Objective-C method so that it can be handled as if it were an object. Using invocations, a developer can create and modify Objective-C messages on-the-fly. Messages can be stored and sent at a later time or repeated periodically. Messages can also be duplicated and can be captured and forwarded to other objects, even objects in other applications, as is described in detail in Chapter 27.

Prototype

A Prototype is an object that is copied to implement application features. In particular, copying an existing object often provides more flexibility than allocating and initializing new instances from scratch. The Prototype pattern avoids the need to hardcode relationships between objects. For example, Cocoa's NSMatrix class displays a grid of objects. As rows and columns are added to a matrix, more objects are created as needed to fill in every grid position. NSMatrix wouldn't be very flexible if it only worked with one kind of object. To provide flexibility, NSMatrix allows you to specify a prototype object that NSMatrix copies as often as necessary to fill in the grid. If you provide a prototype button, you get a grid of buttons. If you provide a prototype text field, you get a grid of text fields.

Motivation

Use prototypes for the following reasons:

- Minimize dependence between objects that create new instances and the types of instances created.
- Allow runtime control of the kind of object created instead of specifying that information at compile time.

Solution

The most essential feature of prototype objects is that they can be copied. Cocoa provides the NSCopying and NSCoding protocols that objects implement to assure interoperability with tools like Interface Builder and classes like NSMatrix.

> Note
>
> The Copying pattern and related NSCopying protocol are detailed in Chapter 12, "Copying." This chapter focuses on the narrow copying requirements of the Prototype pattern.

The NSCopying protocol, documented at /Developer/Documentation/Cocoa/ Reference/Foundation/ObjC_classic/Protocols/NSCopying.html, defines the -copyWithZone: method. Instances of any class that implements -copyWithZone: can be copied. The -copyWithZone: method must return an object with the same state as the object that received the message.

There are two common techniques for implementing -copyWithZone:. The first and most common technique returns a shallow copy. A shallow copy stores exactly the same values as the object being copied. In other words, if the original object stores a pointer to memory, the shallow copy will store another pointer to the same memory. Only the pointer itself is copied; both pointers point to the same thing.

The other technique is a deep copy. A deep copy stores true copies of the values stored in the original. For example, if the original stores a pointer to an object, the deep copy ends up with a pointer to a copy of the object.

The Prototype pattern works best with objects that provide deep copies because the copied objects often need to be truly independent of the original. For example, objects copied from an Interface Builder library need to work long after Interface Builder itself has been quit. However, most Cocoa classes implement the NSCopying protocol to return shallow copies.

It can be tricky to implement deep copies well. The object being copied can send -copy messages to the objects it references via pointers, but if one or more of the referenced objects implements -copyWithZone: to return a shallow copy, the result will be a mix of deep and shallow copies. Such a mix is still not a truly independent copy.

Cocoa's NSCoding protocol and the NSArchiver and NSUnarchiver classes provide a heavy-handed but easy way to create deep copies of arbitrary graphs of interdependent objects. If the object being copied and all of the objects it references conform to the NSCoding protocol, the -copyWithZone: method can be implemented as follows to return a deep copy:

```
- (id)copyWithZone:(NSZone *)aZone
// Return a deep copy of the receiver
{
  id            result;

  // archive self and immedaitly unarchive it to craete a deep
  // copy
  result = [NSKeyedUnarchiver unarchiveObjectWithData:
      [NSKeyedArchiver archivedDataWithRootObject:self]];

  // return a retained object because by convention, the caller
  // is responsible for releasing copied objects
  [result retain];

  return result;
}
```

Interface Builder uses exactly this technique to copy objects from libraries. When an object is dragged and dropped into a `.nib` file under construction, the object is first archived from an existing library instance and then unarchived to create a copy for further editing. When the application under construction is later saved as a `.nib` file, all of the interconnected objects in the application are archived yet again. A `.nib` file is just an archive of objects. When the `.nib` file is loaded into a running application, the objects are unarchived and resume operation right where they left off in Interface Builder.

Chapter 11, "Archiving and Unarchiving," details the Archiving and Unarchiving pattern and explains the `NSKeyedArchiver` and `NSKeyedUnarchiver` classes.

Archiving and then unarchiving is a brute force technique for creating deep copies, and it works well for Interface Builder because the tool is expected to work with almost any object. Interface Builder doesn't know enough about the objects it copies to reliably use any other technique. The `NSMatrix` class only works with `NSCell` subclasses, and `NSCell` implements the `NSCopying` protocol using another technique, the `NSCopyObject()` function.

The `NSCopyObject()` function is documented at /Developer/Documentation/Cocoa/Reference/Foundation/ObjC_classic/Functions/FoundationFunctions.htm. Additional information about copying objects is provided at /Developer/Documentation/Cocoa/TasksAndConcepts/ProgrammingTopics/MemoryMgmt/Concepts/HowToImplCopy.html. `NSCopyObject()` produces a shallow copy of an object by exactly copying the memory that the original occupies. Once the shallow copy is made, `NSCell`'s implementation of `-copyWithZone:` copies various attributes such as the original's stored text or image by sending `-copy` messages to the referenced objects. This mix of deep and shallow copying works for the `NSCell` subclasses provided by Cocoa, but it can be tricky to use with your own subclasses. As long as added attributes in your subclasses are stored as instance variables and the attributes are not pointers, you don't have to write any code to support copying. `NSCell`'s use of `NSCopyObject()` will automatically copy the new attributes along with the inherited ones. However, if you add instance variables that point to other objects or store attributes without using instance variables (See Chapter 10, "Accessors"), you must override `NSCell`'s implementation of `-copyWithZone:`.

> **Note**
>
> The `MYLabelBarCell` class created in Chapter 3, "Two-Stage Creation," works as the Prototype cell for a matrix even without overriding its inherited implementation of `-copyWithZone:` because the only attribute added is a floating point value.

Examples in Cocoa

The objects in Interface Builder's libraries are all Prototypes. When an object is dragged from a library to an application window, the object is copied including its current configuration and state. The set of objects in Interface Builder libraries is open-ended. New libraries can be created at any time. The paradigm of copying objects from libraries into applications enables seamless extension of the Interface Builder tool itself without the need to recompile. As long as library objects can be copied via archiving and unarchiving, Interface Builder will work with them.

Cocoa's NSMatrix class uses a Prototype NSCell instance to define how values are stored and presented. The NSMatrix class implements basic features of spreadsheet or grid style user interfaces. When the matrix needs to add rows or columns, it simply copies the Prototype cell as many times as necessary to fill the new positions. The NSMatrix class has no dependencies on the cells that it uses. Any subclass of NSCell, even subclasses that didn't exist when the matrix was compiled, can be used in a matrix. Furthermore, by configuring the Prototype, it's possible to indirectly specify the initial state of all cells in the matrix; each cell starts with the same state as the copied Prototype.

The Prototype pattern makes NSMatrix an extremely flexible class and greatly expands opportunities for reuse. Figure 3.1 in Chapter 3 shows a matrix filled with instances of the custom MYLabeledBarCell class. The following example shows one way to configure a matrix to copy a Prototype MYLabeledBarCell instance whenever new cells are needed.

Using MYLabeledBarCell Instances as Prototypes

The MYLabeledBarCell class as implemented in Chapter 3 is ready for use with the Prototype pattern. MYLabeledBarCell is a subclass of NSCell, and the NSCell class conforms to the NSCopying protocol. Because NSCell uses the NSCopyObject() function in its own implementation of -copyWithZone:, MYLabeledBarCell's added instance variable, barValue, is automatically copied along with the inherited instance variables from NSCell.

The following code creates a new instance of NSMatrix and a new instance of MYLabeledBarCell that is used as the Prototype cell for the matrix. The matrix is then passed to a scroll view to be used as the scroll view's document view. To test this code, you must create an instance of MYLabeledBarCellTestController in Interface Builder and connect its scrollView outlet to a scroll view.

```
/* MYLabeledBarCellTestController */


#import <Cocoa/Cocoa.h>

@interface MYLabeledBarCellTestController : NSObject
{
  IBOutlet NSScrollView *scrollView;
}

@end


File MYLabeledBarCellTestController.m
#import "MYLabeledBarCellTestController.h"
#import "MYLabeledBarCell.h"
```

```objc
@implementation MYLabeledBarCellTestController
// Just a simple class to test the MYLabeledBarCell class when used in
// a matrix.
// Create an instance of this class in Interface builder.  Connect the
// scrollView outlet to a scroll view.
static const int _MYInitialNumRows = 75;
static const int _MYInitialNumColumns = 5;

- (void)awakeFromNib
// This method is called automatically when an object is unarchived
// from an Interface Builder nib file.
{
    NSMatrix            *newMatrix;
    MYLabeledBarCell    *prototype = [[MYLabeledBarCell alloc]
        initTextCell:@"Prototype...................................."];

    // Set the prototype's value.  All copies will initially have the
    // same value.
    [prototype setBarValue:0.15f];

    // Allocate and initialize a new matrix specifying the prototype to
    // use
    newMatrix = [[NSMatrix alloc] initWithFrame:[scrollView bounds]
        mode:NSRadioModeMatrix prototype:prototype
        numberOfRows:_MYInitialNumRows
        numberOfColumns:_MYInitialNumColumns];

    // The prototype object was allocated in this method so it must be
    // released or autoreleased. The matrix that is using it has already
    // retained it, so it is safe and efficient to just release it now.
    [prototype release];
    prototype = nil;

    // Install the matrix at the document view of the scroll view
    [scrollView setDocumentView:newMatrix];
    // Tell the matrix to resize itself to accommodate all of its cells
    [newMatrix sizeToCells];

    // The matrix was allocated in this method so it must be released or
    // autoreleased. The scroll view has already retained it, so just
    // release it now.
    [newMatrix release];
    newMatrix = nil;
}

@end
```

Using `MYColorLabeledBarCell` Instances as Prototypes

The following `MYColorLabeledBarCell` class is a subclass of `MYLabeledBarCell` that shows how to correctly override -copyWithZone: when object attributes are added in a subclass of `NSCell`. Each `MYColorLabeledBarCell` instance stores a pointer to an `NSColor` instance and uses that color when drawing the bar.

```
#import "MYLabeledBarCell.h"



@interface MYColorLabeledBarCell : MYLabeledBarCell
{
  NSColor         *barColor;       // The color of the bar
}

// Accessors
- (void)setBarColor:(NSColor *)aColor;
- (NSColor *)barColor;

@end

#import "MYColorLabeledBarCell.h"



@implementation MYColorLabeledBarCell

// Overriden Designated Initializer
- (id)initTextCell:(NSString *)aString
{
  self = [super initTextCell:aString];

  if(nil != self)
  {
    [self setBarColor:[NSColor blueColor]];
  }

  return self;
}



- (void)drawBarInRect:(NSRect)aRect
// Draw a bar that fills a portion of aRect specified by barValue
// using the color returned from [self barColor]
{
  aRect.size.width *= barValue;
  [[self barColor] set];
```

```
    NSRectFill(aRect);
}


- (id)copyWithZone:(NSZone *)aZone
{
    id          result = [super copyWithZone:aZone];

    // Ugly hack necessitated by NSCell's use of NSCopyObject()
    // Directly access the copied instance variable and set it to nil
    result->barColor = nil;
    [result setBarColor:[self barColor]];
    return result;
}

// Accessors
- (void)setBarColor:(NSColor *)aColor
{
    [aColor retain];
    [barColor release];
    barColor = aColor;
}


- (NSColor *)barColor
{
    return barColor;
}

@end
```

The key to using an instance of MYColorLabeledBarCell as the prototype cell for a matrix is the implementation of -copyWithZone:. The following lines from that method set the barColor instance variable of the copy to nil before -setBarColor: is called.

```
    // Ugly hack needed because NSCell's uses NSCopyObject()
    // Directly access the copies instance variable and set it to nil
    result->barColor = nil;
```

The copy's barColor variable must be set to nil to avoid a serious memory error. The NSCopyObject() function called by NSCell's implementation of -copyWithZone: copies the pointer stored in the prototype's barColor variable, but the color itself is not retained or copied.

The second line of code in MYColorLabeledBarCell's correctly implemented -setBarColor: method releases the old color pointed to by barColor before assigning the pointer to the new color. If barColor isn't set to nil before calling -setBarColor:, the prototype's color object will be released without any corresponding -retain message having been sent. The extra release has the potential to cause a segmentation fault error. Chapter 10 provides details about the rules for retaining and releasing objects. The necessary implementation of MYColorLabeledBarCell's -copyWithZone: method is a deviation from the otherwise nearly universal rules for Cocoa memory management, and direct access to the copy's instance variable is an unfortunate but necessary violation of good object-oriented programming practices.

In general, the NSCopyObject() function should only be used with classes that do not store pointers. NSCell's use of NSCopyObject() is unfortunate and makes subclassing NSCell to add instance variables that point to objects unnecessarily difficult.

> **Note**
>
> The tricky details of memory management for NSCell copies are avoided by using automatic memory garbage collection introduced with Objective-C 2.0.

Consequences

Copying objects is often as time-consuming as creating new instances with +alloc and -init. This is particularly true when deep copies are used. As an optimization, the NSMatrix class seldom releases copies of its Prototype cell even if the number of cells needed decreases. The extra copies are preserved in case they are ever needed again so that making new copies can be avoided. The drawback to this optimization is that in many cases, memory that could be made available for other uses is consumed storing unneeded copies.

When using the Prototype pattern with your own classes, it's necessary to document the behavior that prototype objects are required to support. For example, the object used as a Prototype cell for an NSMatrix instance must be a subclass of NSCell and correctly implement the NSCopying protocol to produce independent copies. All objects on Interface Builder libraries must conform to the NSCoding protocol.

22

Flyweight

The Flyweight pattern minimizes the amount of memory and/or processor overhead required to use objects. The advantages of object-oriented programming are sometimes outweighed by the overhead of using objects particularly when large numbers of object instances are needed at once. The Flyweight pattern enables instance sharing to reduce the number of instances needed while preserving the advantages of using objects. Classes that implement the Flyweight pattern are called "flyweights."

Motivation

Within Cocoa, flyweights are primarily used for the following three reasons:

- Flyweights encapsulate nonobject data so that the data can be used in contexts where objects are required.
- Flyweights reduce storage requirements when a large number of instances are needed.
- Flyweights act as stand-ins for other objects.

Solution

There are many applications that require large numbers of objects. Consider a spreadsheet that contains 100 rows and 100 columns. If every cell in the spreadsheet is represented by a unique object, 10,000 instances of that object are required. If the spreadsheet has 2,000 rows and 2,000 columns, 4 million instances are required.

The Flyweight pattern is applied to the spreadsheet implementation in several ways. Assuming each spreadsheet cell is represented by an instance of a hypothetical `SpreadsheetCell` class, there are several potential optimizations. First, if many of the cells in the spreadsheet are empty, a single `SpreadsheetCell` instance configured as an empty cell is used to represent all of the empty cells. When the value of an empty cell is set, the shared instance of `SpreadsheetCell` is replaced by a new instance that stores the new value. Second, much of the information stored for each cell is separated out. For example, even with four million cells, perhaps only a dozen different cell formats like line style, font, and color are used. Factor the formatting information out into a hypothetical SpreadsheetCellFormat class. Every SpreadsheetCell instance points to one of the dozen SpreadsheetCellFormat instances instead of storing that information redundantly itself. Third, if there are many cells that store the same value and have the same format, they can all be replaced by a single SpreadsheetCell instance the same way that all empty cells are represented by a single SpreadsheetCell instance.

In the spreadsheet application, the SpreadsheetCell and SpreadsheetCellFormat classes are flyweights. Instances of SpreadsheetCell are shared to reduce the total number of instances needed. The information stored by each SpreadsheetCell instance is minimized by storing some of the information in shared SpreadsheetCellFormat instances.

Examples in Cocoa

Cocoa uses the Flyweight pattern to achieve three goals: to encapsulate nonobject values, to reduce memory usage, and to stand-in for other objects.

Encapsulating Nonobject Values

Cocoa's NSNumber class is a flyweight. Each instance of NSNumber stores a number in one of the C language's numeric data types such as char, short, int, long, float, or double. NSNumber can also store the Objective-C BOOL data type. NSNumber and its superclass, NSValue, provide object wrappers around the nonobject data types for use in situations where Cocoa requires objects. For example, the NSArray class is only able to store objects, so if you need to store float numbers in an NSArray, you use the NSNumber class.

> **Note**
>
> Many object-oriented languages represent everything including numbers as objects. Objective-C is a hybrid of ANSI/ISO standard C and objects. Objective-C provides direct programmatic access to the nonobject types provided by C, and Cocoa provides objects that encapsulate those C data types to enable pure object orientation when you want it. The down-side of the hybrid approach is that you must sometimes convert back and forth between objects and nonobjects. On the up-side, the full computer speed that results from using raw C data types is available when you need it, and it's easy to use existing C libraries with your Objective-C code.

Besides NSValue and NSNumber, other classes like NSDecimalNumber, NSDate, NSCalendarDate, NSString, NSURL, NSFileHandle, NSPipe, and NSAffineTransform all wrap simple nonobject values or data structures. For example, while providing powerful international language support for string processing, NSString effectively wraps ordinary

C arrays of Unicode characters. `NSFileHandle` and `NSPipe` wrap underlying UNIX file descriptor data types. `NSAffineTransform` wraps a 2 x 3 array of C `double` variables used to implement 2D drawing transformations such as rotation.

Reducing Storage Requirements

There may be a lot of `NSNumber` instances in use at any one time in a Cocoa program. Cocoa optimizes storage for `NSNumber` instances by sharing them. Each time you call `[NSNumber numberWithInt:0];`, you are likely to get the same instance returned. Cocoa keeps a cache of recently or frequently used `NSNumber` instances. When you ask for a new `NSNumber` that stores the same value as a cached instance, the cached instance is returned instead of a new instance.

Sharing `NSNumber` instances only works because the `NSNumber` class is immutable. That means that once an instance is created, the value stored by that instance can't be changed. Imagine what would happen if you changed the value stored by a shared `NSNumber` instance. The `NSNumber` instance storing 300 might be shared in many places to store diverse information such as the number of available television stations and a current bank balance. If the value of that shared `NSNumber` instance was changed to 45 when a different cable television provider was selected, somebody might notice the unintended change in the bank balance.

Other Cocoa flyweights like `NSFont` and `NSColor` cache and reuse immutable instances. Each of the standard colors used in Mac OS X interfaces are obtained from the `NSColor` class using methods like `[NSColor redColor];`. Each call to `+redColor` returns the same shared instance of `NSColor`. Similarly, even the most complex text rendering is unlikely to use more than a few different fonts at once. Each time you create an `NSFont` instance with a particular font name and size, that instance is cached. The next time you request an instance of the same font with the same size, the cached instance is returned. The caching of `NSFont` instances provides a significant performance benefit for most applications by reducing the need to read font data from the hard disk.

Cocoa's `NSCell` class is another flyweight. `NSCell` instances are part of the View subsystem when the Model-View-Controller design pattern is used. `NSCell` instances draw user interface components with the assistance of Cocoa's `NSView` class. `NSMatrix` is a kind of `NSView` that's like the hypothetical spreadsheet described in the previous section of this chapter. `NSMatrix` uses flyweight `NSCell` instances to draw each row in each column instead of using more heavyweight subviews. Subviews are explained in Chapter 16, "Hierarchies."

The benefits of using `NSCell` instead of subviews are dramatic. Each `NSCell` instance stores a relatively simple value like a pointer to an `NSString` or a pointer to an `NSImage`. Each `NSCell` instance uses 20 bytes compared to 80 bytes for a basic `NSView` instance. `NSCell` instances draw with very little computational overhead compared with `NSView`. An `NSMatrix` with 2,000 rows and 2,000 columns stores four million instances of `NSCell`, requiring 80MB compared to 320MB of storage required for four million `NSView` instances.

NSMatrix makes minimal use of the Flyweight pattern. It stores cells for every row in every column, but it still benefits. Cocoa's NSTableView class is also superficially similar to a spreadsheet, but NSTableView leverages the Flyweight pattern far beyond NSMatrix. NSTableView stores a single NSCell instance for each column, and the formatting information stored in that cell is applied to every row in the column. As a result, all rows in a single column are formatted the same way. To draw each row in a single column, the NSTableView resets the value stored by the column's NSCell instance to match the row's value, tells the cell to draw at the correct location, and then repeats the process for the next row. An NSTableView with 2,000 rows and 2,000 columns only needs to store 2,000 NSCell instances—one for each column. Reusing the same NSCell instance for every row in a column requires NSCell instances that are mutable; each instance's value can be changed at any time. This is exactly the opposite of the way the immutable NSNumber flyweight is used.

The NSTableView class depends on the Model-View-Controller design pattern in a way that NSMatrix does not. An NSTableView doesn't actually store any of the values it displays. To redraw itself, each NSTableView instance asks another object called its data source to provide the needed values. The data source is typically in the Controller subsystem, and the data provided by the data source is usually stored in the Model subsystem. No matter how many rows or columns the NSTableView instance has, it only asks its data source to provide values for the rows and columns that are visible. Data sources are described in Chapter 15, "Delegates," and Chapter 29, "Controllers," provides more details about the use of the Model-View-Controller pattern with NSTableView.

Standing in for Other Objects

Flyweights often act as temporary placeholders for other more heavyweight objects. For example, displaying text in a user interface can be a complex operation. A single block of text often contains multiple fonts, colors, underlines, alignments, spacing, and such. Editing text in a user interface is even more complex. The attributes of the text may be changed, text may be inserted or deleted causing other text to be repositioned, the current selection and insertion point must be managed, and features like spell checking must be considered. Cocoa provides the NSTextView class to handle text display and input. In reality, NSTextView is just part of a text handling subsystem that includes layout, storage, spell checking and much more implemented by several cooperating classes. As you can imagine, using separate instances of NSTextView and the entire text management subsystem every time a text label is drawn next to a button would be a very heavyweight solution.

Cocoa uses NSCell and its subclasses as flyweight placeholders for the complex text management system. Each Cocoa NSWindow instance provides a single NSTextView instance called the "field editor" for use by cells within the window. NSCell instances share the field editor to draw or edit text. This design works because users only edit one NSCell at a time. When a user starts to edit the text in an NSCell instance, the View hierarchy is temporarily modified so that the cell is replaced by the field editor, which actually handles the editing. When editing completes, the field editor is removed from the

View hierarchy, and the cell is redisplayed. You can read more about the View hierarchy in Chapter 16.

Consequences

Using the Flyweight pattern is always a trade-off between simplicity, storage, and performance. Invariably, using a Flyweight complicates a design. For example, the existence and use of Cocoa's field editor with NSCell instances has consistently generated questions and confusion from programmers learning the frameworks. Even the simplest flyweights like NSNumber increase the complexity of applications slightly compared to straightforward use of built-in C data types as shown in the following two code examples:

```
double        firstFactor = 37.059;
double        secondFactor = -18.112;
double        sum = firstFactor + secondFactor;
```

Versus

```
NSNumber      *firstFactor = [NSNumber numberWithDouble:37.059];
NSNumber      *secondFactor = [NSNumber numberWithDouble:-18.112];
NSNumber      *sum = [NSNumber numberWithDouble:
   [[firstFactor doubleValue] + [secondFactor doubleValue]];
```

Many uses of the Flyweight pattern optimize both storage and performance. Replacing NSView instances with NSCell instances reduces storage and increases drawing performance in almost every case, but not without cost. Cells don't support advanced view features like arbitrary clipping paths, transformed coordinate systems, and Core Animation layers for animation and special effects. Flyweights also have the potential to reduce performance. Allocating and initializing an instance of NSNumber requires hundreds or thousands of times more processing cycles than initializing and storing a built-in C data type. Fortunately, modern processors are fast enough that allocating NSNumber instances seldom reduces application performance perceptibly, and one of the strengths of Objective-C is that you can always fall back to using the built-in types when needed.

Finally, optimization of storage is becoming less and less important as computers get faster and storage becomes cheaper. NSView and NSCell were once used on computers that had 8MB of RAM. Computers with 1GB of RAM are now common and even considered low-end. With 125 times more memory available now than when NSCell was first widely used, many programmers reasonably ask whether the time for using NSCell has passed. Cocoa's NSCollectionView was introduced in Mac OS X 10.5 and displays a collection of NSView instances in a grid much the way NSMatrix displays a grid of NSCells. Because using flyweights increases complexity, avoid creating new flyweight classes in your own applications unless there really is a need to optimize storage or stand-in for heavyweight objects.

23

Decorators

The Decorators pattern adds common reusable capabilities to objects via composition as an alternative to adding capabilities via subclassing. Decorators can be added or configured at runtime in contrast to defining subclasses at compile time. Cocoa's NSScrollView class is a prominent example of the Decorator pattern. Scrolling is a technique that enables users to control which portion of an object is visible when the object is too large to see in its entirety. Rather than reimplement scrolling capability in every object that draws, Cocoa provides scrolling by decorating objects with an NSClipView instance, which in turn is decorated by an NSScrollView instance. The NSClipView hides portions of the view it decorates. The NSScrollView decorates the clip view and provides NSScroller instances as needed. NSScrollView coordinates the clip view and the scrollers to indicate and control the visible portion of object decorated by the clip view. Figure 23.1 illustrates the typical composition of objects used by Cocoa to enable graphical scrolling. The NSScrollView, NSClipView, and NSScroller instances decorate an NSImageView instance by providing a border, clipping, and scrollers that enable user-controlled scrolling.

The Decorator pattern is a special case of the Hierarchies pattern described in Chapter 16, "Hierarchies."

Motivation

Programmers often want to add multiple capabilities to an existing object. If all capabilities are added by subclassing, it doesn't take long before the number of classes needed explodes. Subclassing defines an is-a relationship between the subclass and its base class. For example, a hypothetical RulerText object *is a* Text object with the addition of support for a ruler to indicate dimensions and tab stops. A BorderedRulerText object *is a* RulerText object with the addition of a border. The inheritance hierarchy for the hypothetical BorderedRulerText class is shown in Figure 23.2.

What happens when an application needs a scrolling text object that has a border and a ruler? You end up with a ScrollingBorderedRulerText class. For those occasions when you want scrolling but don't need the border feature, you'll need a ScrollingRulerText class. When no ruler is required, you'll need a

`ScrollingBorderedText` class. The inheritance hierarchy for the combinations of text with and without borders, scrolling support, and rulers shown in Figure 23.3. Some frameworks might attempt to implement a simpler hierarchy using multiple inheritance, but multiple inheritance only changes the inheritance relationships without necessarily reducing the number of classes.

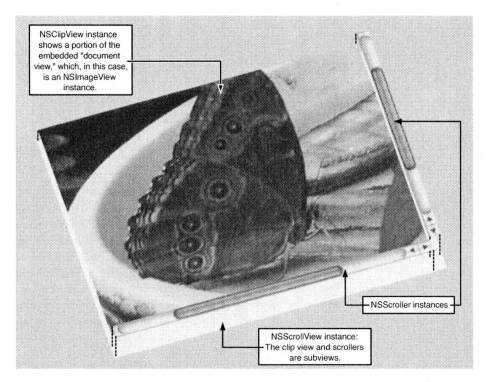

Figure 23.1   The `NSScrollView`, `NSClipView`, and `NSScroller` instances decorate an `NSImageView` instance.

Text ——— RulerText ——— BorderedRulerText

Figure 23.2   The inheritance hierarchy for a hypothetical `BorderedRulerText` class

Use the Decorators design pattern to accomplish the following goals:

- Customize application behavior via composition rather than inheritance.
- Provide runtime flexibility; capabilities can be added and removed dynamically at runtime.

- Add capabilities to individual instances instead of classes.
- Reduce the number of classes needed.

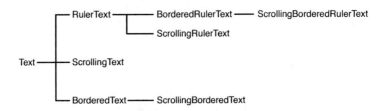

Figure 23.3   An expanded inheritance hierarchy with more combinations and permutations

Solution

In contrast to inheritance, composition defines has–a relationships between objects. The Decorators pattern uses implied has–a relationships. When you say an NSClipView instance decorates its document view, you're really saying that the NSClipView instance *has a* document view. The "document view" might be an NSTextView instance or any other kind of Cocoa view. Each NSScrollView instance decorates an NSClipView instance and therefore *has a* clip view. NSScrollView can be decorated by NSRulerView instances. Figure 23.4 shows the composition of an NSTextView instance decorated by an NSScrollView instance, one NSRulerView instance, and one NSScroller instance.

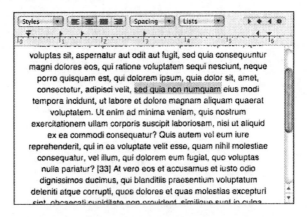

Figure 23.4   The composition of an NSTextView instance with multiple decorators

Composition is typically established and controlled at runtime, so all of the combinations and permutations of document views with and without rulers, scrolling, and other features are available and can even be changed dynamically. If you want, your application can add or remove a ruler at runtime—perhaps based on user selection of a menu item. Adding a ruler to a particular scroll view instance has no effect on other scroll view instances.

NSScrollView provides the -(void)setDocumentView:(NSView *)aView method to programmatically set the embedded clip view's document view. The document view can be any subclass of Cocoa's NSView class, which means you can use your own custom views and any number of subviews. To embed a view or collection of views within a scroll view in Interface Builder, select the views and use Interface Builder's Layout, Embed Objects In, Scroll View menu item.

Examples in Cocoa

Although Cocoa primarily uses the Decorator pattern with objects from the View layer of the Model View Controller architecture, the pattern is by no means limited to that role. Cocoa's NSAttributedString is a Model layer class that decorates ordinary NSString instances with attributes to specify fonts, paragraph styles, tab stop positions, embedded images, or any other user supplied data. The NSAttributedString class provides built-in support for many attributes defined by standards like Rich Text Format (RTF), Hyper-Text Markup Language (HTML), and Microsoft's .doc format. NSAttributedString doesn't modify the decorated string; it just stores additional information along with the string. The approach is similar to the way NSClipView doesn't modify its document view; it just controls which portion of the document view is visible.

The prominent Cocoa classes used as decorators are identified in Table 23.1.

Table 23.1   **Prominent Cocoa Decorator Classes**

Class	Purpose
NSAttributedS tring	Decorates an NSString instance with arbitrary attributes such as font, color, or underline style
NSBox	Decorates an NSView instance with optional borders and a label
NSClipView	Decorates an NSView instance by clipping (hiding) parts of the view
NSRulerView	Decorates an NSView instance by providing configurable rulers that indicate view dimensions, mark positions of interest to a user, and enable users to move positions of interest

Table 23.1 **Prominent Cocoa Decorator Classes**

Class	Purpose
NSScrollView	Decorate an NSClipView by providing optional scrollers that indicate and adjust the visible portion of the view decorated by a clip view
NSSplitView	Decorates NSView instances with a graphical bar that users drag to hide or reveal portions of the decorated views
NSTableHeader View	Decorates an NSTableView instance with optional column labels and provides a way for users to resize and control table columns
NSTabView	Decorates NSViews instances with a border and graphical "tabs" so that users can control which of the decorated views are visible

Accessory Views

Many of Cocoa's standard user interface panels allow you to add your own decorators. For example, the NSSavePanel, NSFontPanel, NSColorPanel, NSAlert, NSRulerView, ABPeoplePickerView, and NSSpellChecker classes all provide a -(void) setAccessoryView: (NSView *) aView method that you use to add any view you want as the "accessory view" displayed on the related panel. The accessory view decorates the panel, and because the accessory view can be any view you provide, you're able to add buttons or any other user interface elements your application needs. The panels automatically resize to make the accessory views fit. Use accessory views to add capabilities to the standard panels without having to subclass the various panel classes. Apple provides an example using accessory views at http://developer.apple.com/documentation/Cocoa/Conceptual/AppFileMgmt/Articles/ManagingAccessoryViews.html.

As of Mac OS X 10.5, Cocoa's NSPrintPanel and NSPageLayout classes provide a new way to manage accessory views, an - (void) addAccessoryController: (NSViewController *) accessoryController method. The new method replaces the deprecated -setAccessoryView: implementations in the print and page layout panels. This change to the class interfaces may indicate the direction that Apple is moving Cocoa. The NSViewController class is part of the Controller subsystem in an MVC application. The change from using accessory views directly to using accessory view controllers encourages consistent use of the MVC pattern and clarifies where you should implement the controller code that mediates between the accessory views and application logic. NSViewController also provides convenient support for bindings, described in Chapter 32, "Bindings and Controllers."

Consequences

Object-oriented inheritance relationships are powerful, but they're also a primary cause of coupling within a design. Inheritance relationships are set statically at compile time and affect all instances of subclasses. Composition using has-a relationships often provides a flexible alternative to subclassing. Extending an object through composition is dynamic at runtime and can be applied per instance. It's possible to add multiple capabilities to the same objects via composition without an explosion in the number of classes needed.

Other frameworks require decorators to have the same interface, for example, public methods, as the object being decorated. That restriction isn't needed when using Cocoa. The dynamism of Objective-C and the Anonymous Object patterns enables you to ask a scroll view for its embedded clip view's document view and dynamically determine the capabilities of the document view. Similarly, the NSRulerView class is able to interoperate with any kind of NSView because NSRulerView will determine which methods are implemented at runtime.

IV

Patterns That Primarily Hide Complexity

One of the goals of object-oriented programming is to hide complexity from programmers. Programmers don't need to know the detailed implementations of every object used. If programmers needed that detailed knowledge, they wouldn't be able to reuse more than a few objects before being overwhelmed by complexity. The same goal applies to patterns involving multiple objects. The patterns in Part IV hide complexity and implementation details so programmers can focus on solving problems.

Chapters in this part of the book include

24

Bundles

A bundle is a collection of executable code and related resources such as images, sounds, strings, and `.nib` files. Ideally, bundles are able to simultaneously store multiple versions of each resource so that you can use one set of executable code with different resource versions based on the language or cultural preferences of the user. The Bundles pattern provides a mechanism for organizing and dynamically loading executable code and resources.

Like most design patterns, the Bundles pattern exists in many object-oriented development environments besides Cocoa. The Java programming language implements the Bundles pattern with JAR (Java ARchive) files that combine compiled Java classes and resources into a single compressed file in the file system. JAR files are easy to copy or download because the complexity of resource file organization is hidden within the JAR file. However, no standards exist for the organization of noncode resources within JAR files, so it's difficult to share JAR files between separately developed applications.

Microsoft's C# programming language and development tools compile resources including sounds, images, and text files into "assemblies" via a program called `resgen.exe`. The assemblies are linked into the executable file for the application or plug-in to create a single file that contains the resources and executable code. However, most developers only include file system paths to resources when compiling assemblies. The paths end up embedded into the application's executable, but the actual resource files exist separately, and users must remember to download or copy the resources along with the application.

Motivation

The Bundles pattern achieves the following goals:

- Keep executable code and related resources together even when there are multiple versions and multiple files involved in the underlying storage.
- Implement a flexible plug-in mechanism that enables dynamic loading of executable code and resources.

Solution

Both the Cocoa frameworks and Apple's nonobject-oriented framework, Carbon, implement the Bundles pattern using file system directories of related files, code, and resources. Such directories are called *bundles* and contain a standard hierarchical organization of files. In Mac OS X, bundles are the preferred way to organize the files that compose applications, frameworks, and plug-ins regardless of the programming language or framework used. Apple defines the Mac OS X bundle directory hierarchy at http://developer.apple.com/documentation/CoreFoundation/Conceptual/CFBundles/Concepts/BundleAnatomy.html. Each bundle must contain an `Info.plist` file that among other things stores a unique bundle identifier string. The `Info.plist` file can be opened in any text editor to obtain information about the bundle without having to actually load the bundle into an application.

Figure 24.1 shows an example of a Cocoa application's bundle as seen in a Finder's browser view. The `Contents` folder contains all the bundle's resources. Within `Contents` is the `Info.plist` file that describes the bundle and folders named `MacOS` and `Resources`. The `MacOS` folder contains the application's executable. The `Resources` folder contains InterfaceBuilder files, graphics, strings, and other resource files needed by the application. Localized versions of resources are placed inside folders whose names end with the `.lproj` extension. All these files are located at very specific places within the bundle. The Apple documentation referenced previously shows diagrams of the expected layout for all the bundle types currently defined by Apple.

Figure 24.1   The layout of a typical application bundle, as might be seen in Finder

Mac OS X's Finder and standard user interface components like the File Open and File Save panels are able to selectively hide the fact that a bundle directory contains many files and instead present the bundle to the user so that it appears to be a single file. Directories that masquerade as single files are called *packages*, and most bundles are also packages. However, users can always choose to see the files within a package via the Show Package Contents item in the context menu that is available when the user right-clicks or control-left-clicks a package in Finder. Users also see the true nature of packages when using the UNIX command line interface.

Mac OS X's use of packages and file system directories to implement bundles has the following advantages:

- Bundle directories contain other directories and ordinary files, which can be viewed with standard file viewers and edited with any application that's appropriate for the resource file type.

- Users can move, copy, or delete bundle directories just like any other directories in the file system.

- Naive users are unlikely to inadvertently modify or delete the individual files within a package because they will most likely never see the individual files.

- The standard bundle hierarchy supports inclusion of multiple language or cultural localizations for resource files and makes it easy to later remove unwanted localized resources to save space.

- Just like bundles contain multiple versions of resources, they can also contain multiple versions of the executable code so that one application bundle works on both PowerPC and Intel-based computers.

- Bundles don't depend on special file system features like resource forks or file system extensions. They can be stored on file servers and nonMac computers running diverse file systems.

It's straightforward to distribute Mac OS X application bundles via CD-ROM; just copy the bundle onto the CD-ROM, and users can copy it from the CD-ROM to their local hard disk. However, enabling users to download bundles over a network sometimes presents some issues. For download, it's desirable to both compress the bundle to reduce download time and avoid any chance of users inadvertently downloading some parts of the bundles and not others. One solution is to create a compressed archive of the bundle using Finder's File, Compress menu or similar tools such as "gzip." A compressed bundle is very similar to a Java JAR file except that the compressed bundle contains the Mac OS X standard directory hierarchy. Another solution is to create a compressed Mac OS X disk image. Disk images are files with the .dmg extension, and when a user double-clicks a .dmg file in Finder, the .dmg file is mounted as a removable disk. The mounted .dmg file looks a lot like a mounted CD-ROM to users, and the user can copy bundles from the mounted .dmg to the local hard disk just like they would copy from a CD-ROM.

You aren't always required to use bundles for your applications. It's possible to make stand-alone Cocoa command line programs with the Foundation Kit framework and produce only a stand-alone executable program with no bundle. However, Cocoa applications that use the Application Kit framework are almost always implemented as bundles, and the Cocoa frameworks are themselves stored in bundles.

When building an application or other bundle, Xcode will automatically put standard resources such as image, sound, .nib, and .strings files where they belong. This is done by the Copy Bundle Resources build phase, as shown in Figure 24.2. If there are other resource files that need to be copied into the bundle, they can be added to this build phase, or a new "Copy Files" build phase can be added to the project.

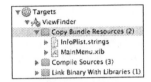

Figure 24.2   The Copy Bundle Resources build phase in XCode

Examples in Cocoa

Cocoa encapsulates bundles with the NSBundle class. Every Application Kit-based application has at least one bundle, the main bundle, which is accessed via the [NSBundle mainBundle] message. Cocoa's NSApplication class automatically loads the Interface Builder .nib file that contains the application's main menu from the main bundle. NSApplication is a Singleton, as explained in Chapter 13, "Singleton," and Interface Builder .nib files are object archives as explained in Chapter 11, "Archiving and Unarchiving."

Use the NSBundle class to dynamically load executable code and resources. The following code fragment obtains the file system path to an image resource called "myImage.tiff" within the main bundle.

```
NSString    *pathToImage = [[NSBundle mainBundle]
    pathForResource:@"myImage" ofType:@"tiff"];
```

Using NSBundle helps you avoid any need to hard code the paths to resources in your applications. If there are many different versions of the resource for different localizations, NSBundle's - (NSString *)pathForResource:(NSString *)name ofType:(NSString *)extension method automatically returns the path to the most appropriate version based on the user's current language and localization preferences. If the resource can't be found, -pathForResource:ofType: returns nil. Note that the extension string you specify to -pathForResource:ofType: should not include the '.' character.

If you need to access a specific version of a resource, NSBundle's - (NSString *)pathForResource:(NSString *)name ofType:(NSString *)extension inDirectory:(NSString *)subpath forLocalization:(NSString *)localizationName method returns the path to the resource version with the specified localization in the specified subdirectory of the bundle. If no such specific version exists, -pathForResource:ofType:inDirectory:forLocalization: returns the path to the closest match if one can be found and nil otherwise.

The NSBundle class is declared in the Foundation framework, but the Application Kit framework extends NSBundle in several ways using categories. The Application Kit adds methods to simplify loading of Interface Builder .nib files, sounds, and images. The most

commonly used methods added by the Application Kit are + (BOOL) loadNibNamed:
(NSString *) aNibName owner: (id) owner, - (NSString *) pathForSoundResource:
(NSString *) name, and - (NSString *) pathForImageResource: (NSString *) name.
You don't need to specify a file extension when you use -pathForSoundResource: and
-pathForImageResource:. Resources can be stored in any supported sound or image file
format, and NSBundle will find the resource and provide the path.

In addition to the main bundle, you can access the bundle that contains the executable
code that defines any class used in your application. The following code fragment returns
the NSBundle instance that encapsulates the Foundation framework's own bundle:

```
// Return the bundle that contains the executable code definition of
// the NSString class
return [NSBundle bundleForClass:[NSString class]];
```

If one of your objects needs to load resources, one approach is to use [NSBundle
bundleForClass:[self class]] within the instance methods that load the resources.
That way, if your class is compiled and linked directly into an application, the bundle returned at runtime will be the application's main bundle. However, if you later decide to
put the class and its associated resources into a framework or plug-in, the bundle returned
at runtime will be the framework or plug-in. Using the +bundleForClass: method
avoids any dependence on the future location of the executable code.

You can obtain an array of all nonframework bundles currently loaded into your application via NSBundle's + (NSArray *) allBundles method. You obtain all of the framework bundles with + (NSArray *) allFrameworks.

Dynamically Loading Executable Code

It's not necessary to explicitly load the code in an application's main bundle or any framework bundles. Those are loaded automatically when the application starts.

You dynamically load other bundles into your application by first creating an
NSBundle instance with NSBundle's + (NSBundle *) bundleWithPath: (NSString
*) fullPath method. The following code fragment loads a bundle named
"myPlugin.bundle" from the application support directory:

```
NSBundle      *bundle = nil;

// Get array of paths to standard application support locations in
// the file system
NSArray       *bundleSearchPaths = NSSearchPathForDirectoriesInDomains(
    NSApplicationSupportDirectory, NSUserDomainMask, YES);

NSString      *currentPath = nil;
NSEnumerator  *pathEnumerator = [bundleSearchPaths objectEnumerator];

// Find the first bundle with the name @"myPlugin.bundle" in
```

```
// bundleSearchPaths
while (nil == bundle &&
   nil != (currentPath = [pathEnumerator nextObject]))
{
  currentPath = [currentPath stringByAppendingPathComponent:
     @"myPlugin.bundle"];

  bundle = [NSBundle bundleWithPath:currentPath];
}

return bundle;  // return the bundle or nil
```

Just creating an NSBundle instance to encapsulate a bundle directory doesn't automatically load the code contained within the bundle. The NSBundle class waits until there is a need to use code within the bundle. One way to force the bundle's executable code to be linked into your application is to call NSBundle's -load method, which returns YES if the load was successful. NSBundle's -principalClass method also forces the linkage of executable code. The -principalClass method returns the class object for the "principal class" within the bundle. The principal class for each bundle can be specified when building the bundle with Xcode or by editing the "Principal class" key of the Info.plist file stored within each bundle. If the principal class is not specified, the -principalClass method returns the first class found within the executable code for the bundle.

The Info.plist file contains key-value pairs that provide information about the bundle. NSBundle's -infoDictionary method returns the keys and values read from the Info.plist file. The following code fragment obtains information about a bundle without actually loading the bundle's executable code into the application:

```
NSBundle       *bundle = [NSBundle bundleWithPath:somePath];

NSDictionary   *infoDictionary = [bundle infoDictionary];
```

Once a bundle's executable code has been loaded, any class defined within the bundle can be accessed using NSBundle's -classNamed: method. For example, the class object for a hypothetical class named MYApplicationPlugin can be loaded by calling [someBundle classNamed:@"MYApplicationPlugin"]. Apple provides an excellent example of a full-featured bundle-based plug-in system at http://developer.apple.com/samplecode/ BundleLoader/index.html.

You can determine whether code had been dynamically loaded from an NSBundle instance via NSBundle's -isLoaded method.

NSBundle provides the -unload method that attempts to unload a bundle's executable code and returns YES if the bundle's code was unloaded. Don't unload executable code that contains Objective-C classes or categories. Apple's documentation states, "It is the responsibility of the caller to ensure that no in-memory objects or data structures refer to the code being unloaded." However, once Objective-C classes and categories have been installed within the Objective-C runtime, it's impractical to find and remove all dependencies on the loaded code. If a class or category is unloaded while other code or the runtime itself still depends on the previously loaded code, your application will most likely crash. Prior to Mac OS X v10.5, the -unload method did nothing and always returned NO.

Consequences

Cocoa's implementation of the Bundles pattern keeps executable code and related resources together and enables you to avoid hard-coded paths to resources within your applications. By using a standard bundle directory hierarchy and providing related development tools like Xcode, Mac OS X simplifies bundle creation. However, use of a directory hierarchy to store resources and code has advantages and disadvantages. One advantage is that users can view each bundle's contents and edit resources with standard applications for each resource type. The corresponding disadvantage is that users can inspect, modify, or delete your applications' resources at any time.

25

Class Clusters

The Class Clusters pattern presents a simple interface to a complex underlying implementation. This pattern is usually used to shield application developers from the details of performance and storage optimizations provided by frameworks. The pattern provides a public class for use in application code, but when applications attempt to allocate instances of the public class, the framework actually provides instances of private subclasses of the public class. Frameworks use information supplied at runtime to select the appropriate private subclass on a case-by-case basis. The Class Clusters pattern is sometimes called the "Abstract Factory" pattern because the public class is abstract. This means instances of the public class itself are never created, and the public class produces instances of other classes.

For example, Cocoa's NSData class is the public interface for a class cluster that exists to efficiently encapsulate arbitrary binary data. The object returned from NSData's `-(id)initWithContentsOfMappedFile:(NSString *)path` method is actually an instance of a hidden NSData subclass. The hidden subclass leverages Mac OS X's virtual memory features to map the data stored in the file into the application's virtual address space. Only a small portion of the binary data stored by the object is present in RAM at any one time. The rest remains on the hard disk. As data is needed, the virtual memory system automatically reads from the file and discards unused data. This approach avoids the need to load unneeded data into RAM or store data that is no longer needed. The data is always recoverable from the source file when needed. In contrast, when NSData's `-(id)initWithBytes:(const void *)bytes length:(NSUInteger)length` method is used, the object returned may contain just the right amount of heap allocated storage for optimum random access performance and memory efficiency.

Your code to access the binary data looks exactly the same regardless of which underlying subclass of NSData actually gets allocated. You usually don't need to know or care how a class cluster is implemented. In the case of NSData, the framework designers make the trade-offs regarding virtual memory versus heap allocation. The trade-off may differ based on the version of Mac OS X or the amount of RAM installed in your system. Your application uses the relatively simple set of methods declared by the NSData class without concern for implementation complexity.

Motivation

The primary motivation for using class clusters in a framework is to shield application programmers from framework implementation complexity. Simple concepts might sometimes require complex implementations for reasons of flexibility or optimization. Class clusters present simple class interfaces that match simple concepts and hide the true complexity. Frameworks hide implementation details and conceal classes as a way to reduce the number of classes that programmers must learn to use the framework.

Class clusters preserve the ability of framework designers to change the underlying implementation of a class cluster without losing compatibility with existing code. Framework designers can add and remove private subclasses without fear of breaking application code.

Solution

Cocoa's implementation of class clusters relies on the Two-Stage Creation pattern introduced in Chapter 3, "Two-Stage Creation." The Two-Stage Creation pattern separates memory allocation from initialization. Creation of a new instance is usually accomplished with code similar to the following examples:

```
// Keep the +alloc and -init messages in the same expression
id          newInstance = [[SomeClass alloc] init];

// Here is a similar example with a more precisely specified type
SomeClass   *anotherNewInstance = [[SomeClass alloc] init];

// This example uses a more complex initializer
NSError     *errorLoadingContents = nil;
NSString    *contentOfFile = [[NSString alloc]
    initWithContentsOfFile:@"/usr/share/dict/words"
    encoding:NSUTF8StringEncoding error:&errorLoadingContents];
```

With Two-Stage Creation, first a pointer to storage for an uninitialized new instance is returned from +alloc. Then the new instance is initialized by some variant of the -(id)init method.

> ## Note
>
> The NSObject's +alloc method calls the "primitive method," +(id)allocWithZone: (NSZone *)aZone. Primitive methods are the small number of methods in each class with which all other methods are implemented. For example, NSCharacterSet adds only one primitive method, -(BOOL)characterIsMember:(unichar)aCharacter, to the methods it inherits from NSObject. All other methods of the NSCharacterSet class are implemented to call -characterIsMember: or an inherited method. Apple documents the convention of primitive methods to make it easier for you to subclass framework classes. Your

subclass can override the primitive methods and be sure that messages that invoke nonprimitive methods will still ultimately invoke your implementations of the primitive methods.

The public interface class in a class cluster overrides +(id)allocWithZone:(NSZone *)aZone with an implementation that doesn't actually allocate any storage. Instead, +allocWithZone: returns a pointer to a shared object that employs the Flyweight pattern explained in Chapter 22, "Flyweight." When any variant of the -init method is later sent to the shared object, the shared object uses the initializer's arguments (if any) to determine which private subclass of the class cluster's public interface class to actually allocate, initialize, and return. The sequence of allocation and initialization with a class cluster is shown in Figure 25.1.

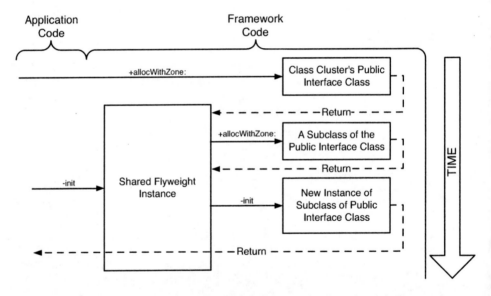

Figure 25.1   The typical sequence of a message sent when creating a new instance via a class cluster

When you use a class cluster, the pointer returned from the initializer method is not the same pointer returned by the preceding +alloc message. For example, NSString is the public interface class of a class cluster. The [NSString alloc] expression returns a pointer to a shared instance of a private class called NSPlaceholderString. The object returned from NSPlaceholderString's - (id)initWithString:(NSString *)string method is an instance of the private NSCFString class. The following small program and the resulting output from Mac OS X 10.5 show each step in the process of allocating and initializing an instance via the NSString class cluster:

```
main()
{
  // First allocate
  NSString     *newInstance = [NSString alloc];
  NSLog(@"After +alloc\npointer value:%p description:%@", newInstance,
      [newInstance description]);

  // Now initialize
  newInstance = [newInstance initWithString:@"silly string"];
  NSLog(@"After -initWithString:\npointer value:%p description:%@",
      newInstance, [newInstance description]);
}
```

```
2009-03-19 19:47:48.321 ClassClusterInstantiation[261:10b] After +alloc
      pointer value:0x103390
      class:NSPlaceholderString
2009-03-19 19:47:48.324 ClassClusterInstantiation[261:10b] After -initWithString:
      pointer value:0x2040
      class:NSCFString
```

Apple encourages application programmers to use a single compound expression to both allocate and initialize new instances as follows: `newInstance = [[NSString alloc] initWithString:@"silly string"];` It is critical to store the value returned from the initializer because, as shown in the preceding example, the returned value may be a different object than the one that received the initializer message. The following code is an error:

```
// First allocate
NSString     *newInstance = [NSString alloc];

// Error: newInstance is initialized but the resulting object is lost
[newInstance initWithString:@"silly string"];
```

> **Note**
>
> Undocumented details like the existence of the `NSPlaceholderString` and `NSCFString` classes are implementation details that may change in between versions of Mac OS X. This chapter introduces `NSPlaceholderString` and `NSCFString` as specific examples of Cocoa's class cluster implementation, but don't rely on `NSPlaceholderString` or `NSCFString` in your own code.

Creating a Class Cluster

Given that class clusters are meant to hide complexity, a complete and usable example of a class cluster is too long and complex to be implemented in one chapter. As a consequence, only skeleton code is presented here.

In the simplest implementation, a class cluster consists of two classes: an abstract superclass and a concrete subclass. To implement a cluster whose abstract class is `MYClassCluster`, define an interface like the following:

```
#import <Cocoa/Cocoa.h>


@interface MYClassCluster : NSObject

// initializers
- (id)initForType:(MYType)type;
- (id)initWithData:(NSData *)data;

// primitive methods here

// derived methods here

@end
```

In the implementation, the initialization methods need to release the allocated instance of the abstract class and then create an instance of the desired concrete subclass that can be returned. The primitive methods are often empty in the abstract class implementation because they are to be implemented by the concrete subclasses. Some developers prefer to have the primitive methods raise exceptions so that if a subclass author forgets to implement one, the omission will be flagged at run time. Finally, any derived methods must be implemented using calls to the primitive methods to do their work. Here is some code showing the initialization methods for a cluster with two concrete subclasses, MYSubclassA and MYSubclassB.

```
#import "MYClassCluster.h"


@implementation MYClassCluster

- (id)initForType:(MYType)type
{
  [self release];
  self = nil;
  if (/* should use MySubclassA */)
  {
    self = [[MYSubclassA alloc] initForType:data];
  }
  else if (/* should use MySubclassB */)
  {
    self = [[MYSubclassB alloc] initForType:data];
  }
  return self;
}


- (id)initWithData:(NSData *)data
{
  [self release];
```

```
  self = nil;
  if (/* should use MySubclassA */)
  {
    self = [[MYSubclassA alloc] initWithData:data];
  }
  else if (/* should use MySubclassB */)
  {
    self = [[MYSubclassB alloc] initWithData:data];
  }
  return self;
}


// primitive methods here — all of them should raise exceptions!

// derived methods here

@end
```

Most class clusters have more than two initialization methods. In many cases, different initializers return different concrete subclasses.

As an optimization, the class cluster implementations in the Cocoa frameworks use an additional intermediate "placeholder" class to avoid allocating and then immediately releasing an instance of the abstract superclass. The placeholder is a cross between a Flyweight and Singleton. There is one instance created for each memory zone in the application, and Associative Storage is used to obtain it. The abstract superclass then overrides +allocWithZone: to return the placeholder for a given zone.

> **Note**
>
> The placeholders should all be created in the application's default zone but have an instance variable that points to the zone they are associated with so that they know from which zone to allocate instances. This way they do not interfere with the destruction of a zone.

The placeholder is required to implement all the initializer methods that are defined by the abstract superclass because all the initialization messages will actually be sent to a placeholder object. The placeholder allocates and initializes an object of the correct concrete subclass and returns it. This moves all the logic for choosing which subclass of the class cluster to use into the placeholder class. The abstract superclass' initialization methods should never be called, so when a placeholder is used they would normally be altered to throw exceptions.

A clever way to throw an exception in an initializer or a primitive method is to send the message [self doesNotRecognizeSelector: _cmd];. This will ensure that the name of the offending method is logged. Alternatively, NSAssert(@"message", NO); can be used to provide a specific message.

For more detailed examples of creating class clusters, including placeholders, see the article at http://www.cocoadev.com/index.pl?ClassClusters.

Examples in Cocoa

The Foundation framework's collection classes like NSString, NSData, NSArray, NSSet, NSDictionary, and their mutable subclasses are the most prominent public interfaces to class clusters. Other Foundation framework class cluster interface classes include NSAttributedString, NSNumber, NSNotification, NSPipe, NSScanner, and NSCharacterSet. As of Mac OS X 10.5, Core Data's NSManagedObject class is the public interface to a class cluster. The existence of class clusters seldom affects application code that merely uses the class clusters, but it can be difficult to correctly subclass the public interfaces to class clusters. NSManagedObject is frequently subclassed in application code, but the other public interfaces to class clusters are seldom subclassed.

Subclassing a Class Cluster's Public Interface Class

To create a new concrete subclass of a class cluster's abstract public interface class, the following rules must be followed:

- The new class must override the superclass' primitive methods.
- The new class must override all the superclass' initializer methods or risk exceptions.
- Every initializer in the new class must call its superclass' designated initializer, which is always either -init or -initWithCoder: for the abstract interface to a class cluster.

Primitive methods provide the core features common to all classes in a class cluster. Apple's class documentation identifies the primitive methods of class clusters. The other methods declared for a class cluster are implemented using the primitive methods. The existence of primitive methods reduces the number of methods that must be overridden in each subclass. Implementing the primitive methods for a class cluster ensures that other inherited methods besides the initializers will continue to operate properly. Implementing the nonprimitive methods is allowed, even though it is not required. This is usually done when a subclass can offer optimizations over the default implementations.

Class clusters require special handling for initializer methods. The public interface classes typically don't implement the declared initializers because instances of the public interface classes are never created. Instead, the placeholder class for each class cluster implements the initializers to allocate, initialize, and return instances of the private classes within the cluster. When you subclass a cluster's public interface class, you must implement all of the declared initializers or risk a runtime exception if one of the unimplemented initializers is ever invoked. In contrast, when you subclass classes that aren't part of a cluster, you aren't required to implement any of the inherited initializers.

In Mac OS X 10.5 and later, there is no practical way to get frameworks to return instances of your custom subclass. For example, if you subclass NSString, you can allocate and initialize instances of your subclass from within your own code. You can even pass instances of your subclass as arguments to framework methods, and everything should work fine. However, there is no way to force the frameworks to return instances of your subclass from framework methods. When you send a messages like NSBundle's - (NSString *)bundlePath or NSString's - (NSString *)stringByAppendingString:(NSString *)aString, the framework will return instances of hidden NSString subclasses instead of instances of your subclass.

> **Note**
>
> Prior to OS X 10.5, you could use NSObject's + (void)poseAsClass:(Class)aClass method to inform the Objective-C runtime that your subclass should be used in any situation where the class cluster's public interface class would otherwise have been used. In that way, you could force the frameworks to return instances of your subclass. The +poseAsClass: method is deprecated in the 32-bit Objective-C runtime for OS X 10.5, and the method is completely missing from the 64-bit Objective-C runtime. Apple has not provided any replacement for +poseAsClass:.

Before creating a subclass of a class cluster's public interface class, consider alternatives. If you need to add methods to a class, the Categories feature of Objective-C might provide the best solution. Categories are explained in Chapter 6, "Category." Even if you need to add instance variables and methods, Chapter 19, "Associative Storage," describes a way of simulating the additional instance variables without subclassing.

As another alternative to subclassing, consider composition or "has-a" relationships. You may be able to accomplish your goals by creating a new class that has an instance of the class cluster's public class and other attributes. For example, do you really need a new NSDictionary subclass, or can your new MYAwsomeDictionary class merely use an instance of NSDictionary to store some of the awesome dictionary's contents? The Decorators pattern in Chapter 23, "Decorators," shows a way to use composition. For example, Cocoa's NSAttributedString class decorates NSString instances with arbitrary attributes such as font, color, or underline style.

If your goal is to keep an instance of a class cluster synchronized with other parts of your application, you may be able to use the Notifications pattern from Chapter 14, "Notifications," or Cocoa Bindings from Chapter 32, "Bindings and Controllers."

The MYShortString Subclass of NSString

Usually when people ask how to subclass a class cluster, the common answer is something like, "Don't do it—it's a waste of time." Often, the work required far exceeds any benefits accrued and other patterns provide alternatives to subclassing. One good reason to subclass a class cluster is to improve performance if profiling shows that a particular cluster causes a bottleneck in your application. But as Cocoa matures, even performance reasons evaporate.

Even after being cautioned, most developers still want to know how to subclass a class cluster even if it's just to satisfy curiosity. Here is an example that demonstrates the process and also shows why you probably don't really want to subclass a class cluster.

Back in the Mac OS X 10.0 days, profiling a particular large Cocoa application revealed that a large percentage of processing time in that application was being spent allocating and deallocating NSString instances. The strings were usually very short, but hundreds of thousands of them were allocated and deallocated every second. The primary requirement of the application was string processing, so a solution to avoid the dynamic allocation of string objects was needed. The MYShortString class presented here and at www.CocoaDesignPatterns.com provided the solution.

MYShortString only handles short strings. Instances of MYShortString are allocated as needed, but they are seldom deallocated. Instead of being deallocated, the MYShortString instances are added to a cache of available instances. When a new MYShortString instance is needed, one of the unused instances in the cache is reused rather than a new one being allocated.

NSString's primitive methods are -(NSUInteger)length and -(unichar)characterAtIndex:(NSUInteger)index. According to the rules for subclassing class clusters, the MYShortString class must implement -length and -characterAtIndex: and any of NSString's initializers that may ever be invoked. The following code declares the class interface for the MYShortString class.

```
#import <Foundation/Foundation.h>


#define _MYMAX_SHORT_STRING_LENGTH (40)

@interface MYShortString : NSString
{
  // storage for the short string
  unichar          _myBuffer[_MYMAX_SHORT_STRING_LENGTH+1];

  // number of unichars not counting null termination
  NSUInteger       _myLength;
}

// Overridden allocator
+ (id)allocWithZone:(NSZone *)aZone;

// Shared resource cleanup
+ (void)cleanup;

// Reuse statistics
+ (NSUInteger)numberOfAvailableInstances;
+ (NSUInteger)totalNumberOfInstances;

// Overridden designated initializer
- (id)init;

// Other initializers
- (id)initWithCharacters:(const unichar *)characters
                  length:(NSUInteger)length;
- (id)initWithUTF8String:(const char *)nullTerminatedCString;
- (id)initWithString:(NSString *)aString;
```

```
- (id)initWithFormat:(NSString *)format, ...;
- (id)initWithFormat:(NSString *)format arguments:(va_list)argList;
- (id)initWithFormat:(NSString *)format locale:(id)locale, ...;
- (id)initWithFormat:(NSString *)format locale:(id)locale
          arguments:(va_list)argList;
- (id)initWithCString:(const char *)bytes length:(NSUInteger)length;
- (id)initWithCString:(const char *)bytes;

// NSCoding
- (void)encodeWithCoder:(NSCoder *)encoder;
- (id)initWithCoder:(NSCoder *)decoder;

// NSCopying
- (id)copyWithZone:(NSZone *)aZone;

// NSMutableCopying
- (id)mutableCopyWithZone:(NSZone *)aZone;

// Overridden NSString primitive methods
- (NSUInteger)length;
- (unichar)characterAtIndex:(NSUInteger)index;

// Overridden NSString performance methods
- (void)getCharacters:(unichar *)buffer;
- (void)getCharacters:(unichar *)buffer range:(NSRange)aRange;

@end
```

The following code fragment shows how `MYShortString` implements `+allocWithZone:` and `-release` to reuse instances:

```
#import "MYShortString.h"


@implementation MYShortString

#define _MYMaxNumberOfCachedInstance (10000)

// Collection of shared instances
static MYShortString
    *_MYShortStringCache[_MYMaxNumberOfCachedInstance];

// Number of instances currently available for reuse
static NSUInteger    _MYAvailableInstances = 0;

// Number of instances currently allocated
static NSUInteger    _MYTotalNumberOfInstances = 0;
```

```
// Used to disable caching during cache cleanup
static BOOL           _MYCacheIsDisabled = NO;


+ (void)cleanup;
// Releases all cached short string instances
{
  _MYCacheIsDisabled = YES; // prevent re-caching when instances
                            // are released

  NSUInteger    i;
  for(i = 0; i < _MYAvailableInstances;  i++)
  {
    [_MYShortStringCache[i] release];
    _MYShortStringCache[i] = nil;
  }
  _MYAvailableInstances = 0;

  _MYCacheIsDisabled = NO;
}


+ (NSUInteger)numberOfAvailableInstances
// Returns number of MYShortString instances available for reuse.
{
  return _MYAvailableInstances;
}


+ (NSUInteger)totalNumberOfInstances
// Returns total number of MYShortString instances currently allocated.
{
  return _MYTotalNumberOfInstances;
}


// Overridden allocator
+ (id)allocWithZone:(NSZone *)aZone
{
  MYShortString        *result = nil;

  if(_MYAvailableInstances > 0 && aZone == NSDefaultMallocZone())
  { // reuse available instance
    _MYAvailableInstances−;
    result = _MYShortStringCache[_MYAvailableInstances];
    _MYShortStringCache[_MYAvailableInstances] = nil;
  }
```

```
  else
  { // create a new instance (Can't use +alloc here without infinite
    // recursion)
    result = NSAllocateObject([self class], 0, aZone);

    _MYTotalNumberOfInstances++;
  }

  return result;
}



- (void)release
// Overloaded to cache unused instances for reuse.
{
  if([self retainCount] == 1 &&
     _MYAvailableInstances < _MYMaxNumberOfCachedInstance &&
     !_MYCacheIsDisabled &&
     [self zone] == NSDefaultMallocZone())
  {
    _MYShortStringCache[_MYAvailableInstances] = self;
    _MYAvailableInstances++;
  }
  else
  {
    [super release];
  }
}

- (void)dealloc
// Clean-up
{
  _MYTotalNumberOfInstances—;

  [super dealloc];
}
```

MYShortString overrides the -release method to store unused instances for later reuse rather than letting them be deallocated. The +allocWithZone: method reuses stored instances rather than creating new ones whenever it can. The number of instances available for reuse is obtained from the + numberOfAvailableInstances method. The total number of instances that have been allocated is returned from the + totalNumberOfInstances method. The +cleanup method is used to release all the instances that are cached.

Note

The approach used to cache MYShortString instances for reuse is incompatible with the automatic memory garbage collection introduced with Objective-C 2.0.

The MYShortString class implements some of NSString's initializers by falling back to the class cluster's implementation. The primary reason to fall back in some cases is that MYShortString can't store strings that are longer than MYMAX_SHORT_STRING_LENGTH (40). If the user of MYShortString tries to store a string that's too long, a suitable NSString instance that can handle the storage is provided. The following code fragment continues the implementation of MYShortString and shows how the initializer methods are implemented:

```objc
// Overridden designated initializer
- (id)init;
{
  if(nil != (self = [super init]))
  {
    _myBuffer[0] = 0;
    _myLength = 0;
  }

  return self;
}


// Other initializers
- (id)initWithCharacters:(const unichar *)characters
    length:(NSUInteger)length;
{
  NSParameterAssert(NULL != characters);

  id      result = nil;

  if(nil != (self = [self init]))
  {
    if(length < _MYMAX_SHORT_STRING_LENGTH)
    {
      memcpy(_myBuffer, characters, (length * sizeof(unichar)));
      _myLength = length;
      _myBuffer[_myLength] = 0;

      result = self;
    }
    else
    {
      [self release];
      self = nil;

      result = [[NSString alloc] initWithCharacters:characters
          length:length];
```

```
    }
  }
  return result;
}


- (id)initWithUTF8String:(const char *)nullTerminatedCString;
{
  NSParameterAssert(NULL != nullTerminatedCString);

  return [self initWithCString:nullTerminatedCString
      encoding:NSUTF8StringEncoding];
}


- (id)initWithString:(NSString *)aString;
{
  id            result = nil;
  const int     length = [aString length];

  if(nil != (self = [self init]))
  {
    result = self;

    if(length < _MYMAX_SHORT_STRING_LENGTH)
    {
      NSRange           copyRange = NSMakeRange(0, length);

      [aString getCharacters:_myBuffer range:copyRange];
      _myBuffer[length] = '\0';
      _myLength = length;
    }
    else
    {
      [self release];
      self = nil;

      result = [[NSString alloc] initWithString:aString];
    }
  }
  return result;
}


- (id)initWithFormat:(NSString *)format, ...;
{
```

```
  NSParameterAssert(nil != format);

  id          result = nil;
  va_list     args;

  va_start(args, format);
  result = [self initWithFormat:format locale:nil arguments:args];
  va_end(args);

  return result;
}

- (id)initWithFormat:(NSString *)format arguments:(va_list)argList;
{
  NSParameterAssert(nil != format);

  return [self initWithFormat:format locale:nil arguments:argList];
}

- (id)initWithFormat:(NSString *)format locale:(id)locale, ...;
{
  NSParameterAssert(nil != format);

  id          result = nil;
  va_list     args;

  va_start(args, locale);
  result = [self initWithFormat:format locale:locale arguments:args];
  va_end(args);

  return result;
}

- (id)initWithFormat:(NSString *)format locale:(id)locale
    arguments:(va_list)argList;
{
  NSParameterAssert(nil != format);

  [self release];
  self = nil;

  return [[NSString alloc] initWithFormat:format
      locale:locale arguments:argList];
}
```

```
- (id)initWithCString:(const char *)bytes length:(NSUInteger)length;
{
  NSParameterAssert(NULL != bytes);

  id       result = nil;

  if(nil != (self = [self init]))
  {
    if(length < _MYMAX_SHORT_STRING_LENGTH)
    {
      int       i;

      for(i = 0; i < length; i++)
      {
        _myBuffer[i] = bytes[i];
      }
      _myLength = length;
      _myBuffer[_myLength] = 0;

      result = self;
    }
    else
    {
      [self release];
      self = nil;

      result = [[NSString alloc] initWithCString:bytes length:length];
    }
  }
  return result;
}


- (id)initWithCString:(const char *)bytes;
{
  NSParameterAssert(NULL != bytes);

  NSUInteger   length = strlen(bytes);

  return [self initWithCString:bytes length:length];
}
```

MYShortString is required to implement NSString's primitive methods: -length and
-characterAtIndex:. The following code fragment shows how:

```
// Overridden NSString primitive methods
- (NSUInteger)length;
```

```
{
  return _myLength;
}


- (unichar)characterAtIndex:(NSUInteger)index;
{
  if(index >= _myLength)
  {
    [NSException raise:NSRangeException format:@""];
  }
  return _myBuffer[index];
}


// Overridden NSString performance methods
- (void)getCharacters:(unichar *)buffer;
{
  NSParameterAssert(NULL != buffer);

  memcpy(buffer, _myBuffer, ((_myLength) * sizeof(unichar)));
}


- (void)getCharacters:(unichar *)buffer range:(NSRange)aRange;
{
  NSParameterAssert(NULL != buffer);

  if((aRange.length + aRange.location) > _myLength ||
      aRange.location < 0)
  {
    [NSException raise:NSRangeException format:@""];
  }
  else
  {
    memcpy(buffer, &_myBuffer[aRange.location],
        (aRange.length * sizeof(unichar)));
  }
}
```

MYShortString isn't required to override the inherited -getCharacters: and
-getCharacters:range: methods shown in the preceding code. The NSString class
includes implementations of -getCharacters: and -getCharacters:range: based on
the primitive methods. However, these two methods are called frequently by other
NSString methods, and, as an optimization, MYShortString's implementation avoids
many unnecessary calls to the primitive methods.

Finally, NSString conforms to the NSCoding, NSCopying, and NSMutableCopying protocols. MYShortString's implementations of the protocol methods follow:

```objc
// NSCoding
- (void)encodeWithCoder:(NSCoder *)encoder;
{
  [encoder encodeValueOfObjCType:@encode(NSUInteger) at:&_myLength];
  [encoder encodeArrayOfObjCType:@encode(unichar)
      count:_myLength at:_myBuffer];
}


- (id)initWithCoder:(NSCoder *)decoder;
{
  self = [self init];
  [decoder decodeValueOfObjCType:@encode(NSUInteger) at:&_myLength];
  [decoder decodeArrayOfObjCType:@encode(unichar)
                          count:_myLength at:_myBuffer];
  return self;
}


// NSCopying
- (id)copyWithZone:(NSZone *)aZone;
{
  id      result = nil;

  if(aZone == [self zone])
  {
    result = [self retain];
  }
  else
  {
    result = [[MYShortString allocWithZone:aZone]
        initWithString:self];
  }
  return result;
}


// NSMutableCopying
- (id)mutableCopyWithZone:(NSZone *)aZone;
{
  return [[NSMutableString allocWithZone:aZone] initWithString:self];
}

@end
```

The MYShortString class can be used directly in application code. Instances are created by calling [MYShortString alloc] and initialized by calling any of the provided initializers. However, Cocoa classes that return strings do not automatically take advantage of the MYShortString class. For example, calling MYShortString's inherited implementation of the +stringByAppendingString: method will return an instance of one of Cocoa's private concrete NSString subclasses rather than an instance of MYShortString.

Lessons from MYShortString

The MYShortString class was originally developed to improve performance by avoiding repeated allocation and deallocation of NSString instances. In the Mac OS X 10.0 days, it accomplished this goal. However, those days are past. The test program at www. CocoaDesignPatterns.com reveals a startling conclusion: The implementation of MYShortString is much slower in practice than the framework-supplied private NSString subclasses. With Mac OS X 10.5, Apple has either optimized allocation and deallocation to the extent that MYShortString is unneeded, or the frameworks already use an optimization approach that is superior to MYShortString.

Avoid creating your own subclasses of class cluster public interface classes. It's difficult to produce a better result than the frameworks already provide. Furthermore, even if your custom subclass surpasses the framework behavior today, the frameworks continue to improve. Using your own subclass could prevent your applications from automatically benefiting from future framework enhancements.

NSManagedObject is a special case that must be subclassed to use Core Data effectively. Chapter 30, "Core Data Models," includes a section about subclassing NSManagedObject to add custom behavior such as extra processing whenever a new instance of your NSManagedObject subclass is inserted into your model.

Consequences

The Class Clusters pattern provides simple programmatic interfaces that solve conceptually simple problems regardless of the underlying complexity of the solution. The pattern minimizes the number of classes that programmers need to learn. However, this pattern complicates the task of creating subclasses.

When debugging Cocoa applications, you may encounter class names that are unfamiliar or undocumented. Such classes are usually undocumented concrete classes within a class cluster. Just remember that all of the classes in a class cluster inherit from the public interface classes, and you can rely on features and semantics of the public interface classes.

The Class Clusters pattern also complicates the implementation of the Archiving and Unarchiving pattern from Chapter 11, "Archiving and Unarchiving." While encoding an object into an archive, it's possible to substitute one object for another. Each private concrete class within a class cluster encodes the name of its public interface class for two reasons: First, the existence of the private subclass is an implementation detail that shouldn't be exposed in the archive and might change in future framework versions, and second, the framework's choice of which concrete private class to use might differ between the computer that encoded the object and the computer that decodes it. For example, two different computers might have different framework versions or different amounts of memory.

26

Façade

The Façade pattern exists to limit the coupling between objects that interact with a complex subsystem and the objects that implement the complex subsystem. The Façade pattern hides complexity. A real-world example of the Façade pattern is the customer interaction when using the phone to order pizza delivery. As a customer, you typically communicate with just the order taker who answered the phone at the pizza parlor, but there may be many people involved in fulfilling your order. Figure 26.1 illustrates the hypothetical relationships between the people, companies, and services that may contribute toward fulfilling your pizza order.

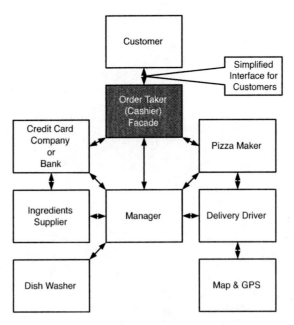

Figure 26.1   Relationships involved in pizza order fulfillment

As a customer, you don't normally need to interact with the entire staff of the pizza parlor. The order taker provides a simplified public face or façade to simplify your interaction. In some unusual circumstances, you might need to communicate directly with the manager, or you might even contest a credit card transaction with the credit card company or bank. In those cases, you might bypass the façade to enable more complicated interactions.

The Façade software design pattern is directly analogous to the pizza parlor example. The pattern is used within Cocoa to simplify your custom code's interaction with complex subsystems like text processing without preventing you from accessing the details when necessary. The philosophy is to keep common interaction simple while making complex interaction possible.

Motivation

Apply the Façade pattern to achieve the following goals:

- Provide a simple interface to a complex subsystem.
- Limit coupling between the objects that use a subsystem and the objects that implement the subsystem.

Use the Façade pattern when sophisticated interaction with a complex subsystem is seldom needed but must be possible.

Solution

Within the pages of a book, it's difficult to show simple sample code for a representative implementation of the Façade design pattern because the pattern exists to hide complexity. A useful example must show all of the complexity that is being hidden to reveal the utility of the pattern. As a compromise to show the concept, the following example leverages the free Google chart generation web service to produce the application shown in Figure 26.2. The code needed to use the web service is just complicated enough to show the benefit of a simple façade.

The `MYDirectoryChartGenerator` class declared in the following code presents a very simple interface. Use the `+sharedGenerator` method to access a shared instance of the `MYDirectoryChartGenerator` class. Once you have the shared instance, use the `- (NSImage *)chartForDirectory:(NSString *)directoryPath` method to obtain the image of a Google-generated chart showing the relative sizes of the files in the specified directory, `directoryPath`.

```
#import <Cocoa/Cocoa.h>


@interface MYDirectoryChartGenerator : NSObject
{
}
```

```
+ (MYDirectoryChartGenerator *)sharedGenerator;

- (NSImage *)chartForDirectory:(NSString *)directoryPath;

@end
```

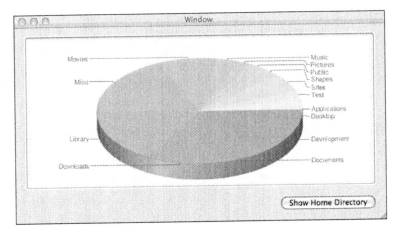

Figure 26.2   An application that displays Google-generated charts

The implementation of `MYDirectoryChartGenerator` contains a couple of helper methods that aren't declared in the class' public interface. The - `(NSString *)delimitedFileNamesForDirectory:(NSString *)directoryPath` method returns a string containing the names of the files in `directoryPath` properly delimited for use by the Google charting web service. The - `(NSString *)delimitedFileSizesForDirectory:(NSString *)directoryPath` similarly returns a delimited string containing the sizes of the file at `directoryPath`. In both cases, the UNIX `popen()` function is used to execute shell commands that supply the necessary file information. The `popen()` function is an example of a nonobject-oriented equivalent of the Façade pattern. The function exposes the complex and sometimes arcane universe of UNIX shell commands to any C program, and yet `popen()` itself could hardly be simpler to use.

```
#import "MYDirectoryChartGenerator.h"


@implementation MYDirectoryChartGenerator

+ (MYDirectoryChartGenerator *)sharedGenerator
{
  static MYDirectoryChartGenerator *sharedInstance = nil;

  if(nil == sharedInstance)
  {
```

```objc
        sharedInstance = [[MYDirectoryChartGenerator alloc] init];
    }
    return sharedInstance;
}


- (NSString *)delimitedFileNamesForDirectory:(NSString *)directoryPath
{
    NSMutableString  *fileNames = [NSMutableString string];
    NSString         *fileNamesCommand = [NSString
        stringWithFormat:@"ls %@\n", directoryPath];
    FILE             *pipe = popen([fileNamesCommand UTF8String], "r");
    int               currentChar;

    while(EOF != (currentChar = fgetc(pipe)))
    {
        [fileNames appendFormat:@"%c", currentChar];
    }
    pclose(pipe);
    pipe = NULL;

    // Add delimiters required by Google's web service
    [fileNames replaceOccurrencesOfString:@"\n" withString:
        @"|" options:NSLiteralSearch range:
        NSMakeRange(0, [fileNames length])];

    // Delete the last delimiter because Google doesn't like it
    [fileNames deleteCharactersInRange:NSMakeRange(
        [fileNames length]-1, 1)];

    return fileNames;
}


- (NSString *)delimitedFileSizesForDirectory:(NSString *)directoryPath
{
    NSMutableString  *fileSizes = [NSMutableString string];
    NSString         *fileSizesCommand = [NSString stringWithFormat:
        @"ls -l %@ | awk '{print $2}'\n", directoryPath];
    FILE             *pipe = popen([fileSizesCommand UTF8String], "r");
    int               currentChar;

    while(EOF != (currentChar = fgetc(pipe)))
    {
        [fileSizes appendFormat:@"%c", currentChar];
    }
```

```
    pclose(pipe);
    pipe = NULL;

    // Add delimiters required by Google's web service
    [fileSizes replaceOccurrencesOfString:@"\n" withString:
        @"," range:NSMakeRange(0, [fileSizes length])];

    // Delete the last delimiter because Google doesn't like it
    [fileSizes deleteCharactersInRange:NSMakeRange(
        [fileSizes length]-1, 1)];

    return fileSizes;
}


- (NSImage *)chartForDirectory:(NSString *)directoryPath
{
    NSString      *names = [self delimitedFileNamesForDirectory:
        directoryPath];
    NSString      *sizes = [self delimitedFileSizesForDirectory:
        directoryPath];
    NSString      *chartServiceURL =
        @"http://chart.apis.google.com/chart?";
    NSString      *chartCommand = [NSString stringWithFormat:
        @       names, sizes];
    NSURL         *url = [NSURL URLWithString:[chartCommand
        stringByAddingPercentEscapesUsingEncoding:NSUTF8StringEncoding]];
    NSImage       *chartImage = [[[NSImage alloc]
        initWithContentsOfURL:url] autorelease];

    return chartImage;
}

@end
```

In this example, available at www.CocoaDesignPatterns.com, the
MYDirectoryChartGenerator hides the details of reading the filenames and file sizes
from a directory and then using the Google web service to generate an image. One
-delimitedFileSizesForDirectory: message hides a page or so of code, but more to
the point, the popen() function and the web service are each in their own way examples
of the philosophy embodied by the Façade pattern. The example in this chapter isn't coupled to the specific implementation of UNIX shell commands or Google's 3D chart
drawing code.

Examples in Cocoa

Cocoa primarily applies the Façade pattern to simplify or reduce the code that must be written to programmatically use sophisticated features in common situations. Façades are also used to decouple the programmatic logic of user interaction from the actual user interface implementations.

The NSTextView and NSImage classes exemplify the Façade pattern's capability to simplify programmatic interfaces. Similarly, Core Data's NSPersistentStoreCoordinator class provides a simple interface that encapsulates potentially complex interactions between multiple data storage types.

The Application Kit's NSColorPanel, NSOpenPanel, NSSavePanel, and NSPrintPanel all isolate your code for the specific user interface representation of the corresponding common panels. For example, it's important for your code to obtain the color selected by a user via the standard Cocoa color panel, but your code shouldn't depend on how the user made the selection. In fact, when future versions of Mac OS X provide new color selection capabilities in the standard panel, your code should continue to work unmodified.

The Text Façade

One of the most compelling implementations of the Façade pattern within Cocoa is the NSTextView class. NSTextView handles all of the details of interactively displaying and editing richly formatted text with multiple fonts, paragraph styles, embedded graphics, multilanguage support, colors, styles, tab stops, and so on. From a programmer's point of view, inserting text for display in a text view is as simple as sending the -insertText: message. The NSTextView that you drag from an Interface Builder library appears to comprise a sophisticated text editor all by itself. In reality, that NSTextView from the Interface Builder library only provides the most common and standard configuration. Most applications only need the standard NSTextView configuration, so the common simple scenario is supported by drag and drop at design time with no new code at all. Figure 26.3 shows a more complete picture of the Cocoa components that interact behind the scenes to implement rich text editing and display.

When you need detailed control over text editing, display, or processing, you are able to customize each and every component of the Cocoa text system. Extremely complex configurations are possible, but true to the goals of the Façade pattern, you seldom if ever need to be concerned about the details.

Cocoa's text subsystem architecture is documented at http://developer.apple.com/documentation/Cocoa/Conceptual/TextArchitecture/Concepts/ArchitectureOverview.html.

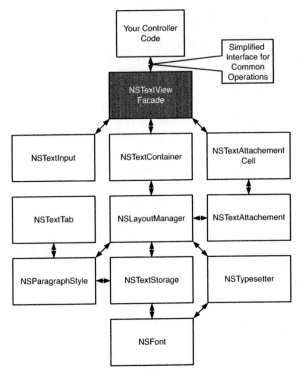

Figure 26.3   Components hidden behind the façade of the NSTextView class

The Image Façade

The NSImage class provides another implementation of the Façade pattern. Most applications that load images can be implemented using the straightforward NSImage methods, + (id)imageNamed:(NSString *)name or -(id)initByReferencingFile: (NSString *)filename. The NSImage class is a façade for a sophisticated and flexible subsystem that supports loading, drawing, and converting a multitude of vector and bitmap image types. When you use NSImage, you don't necessarily need to be aware of the underlying image representation. The image could be Portable Document Format (PDF), Encapsulated PostScript (EPS), Tagged Image File Format (TIFF), Joint Photographic Experts Group (JPEG), Portable Network Graphics (PNG), Graphics Interchange Format (GIF), Device Independent Bitmap (DIB), or a whole host of other formats. The supported formats are listed at http://developer.apple.com/documentation/ Cocoa/Conceptual/CocoaDrawingGuide/Images/chapter_7_3.html.

If all you want to do is load and display the image in your application, you don't need to know or care about the details of the various formats. The NSImage class will communicate with other objects on your behalf and convert between formats as necessary.

`NSImage` will automatically keep track of multiple representations of the same image. For example, `NSImage` might cache a rendered bitmap generated from a vector file format. To draw the best available representation of an image that has already been loaded, use the `- (void)compositeToPoint:(NSPoint)aPoint operation:(NSCompositingOperation)op` method.

If you ever need to create new images from scratch programmatically or use image data with OpenGL or support custom image data formats, you can always access the `NSBitmapImageRep`, `NSCachedImageRep`, `NSCIImageRep`, `NSPDFImageRep`, `NSEPSImageRep`, `NSPICTImageRep`, or `NSCustomImageRep` classes directly. For example, the `NSBitmapImageRep` class provides a method with one of the longest names in Cocoa to enable the maximum degree of programmer control: `- (id)initWithBitmapDataPlanes:(unsigned char **)planes pixelsWide:(NSInteger)width pixelsHigh:(NSInteger)height bitsPerSample:(NSInteger)bps samplesPerPixel:(NSInteger)spp hasAlpha:(BOOL)alpha isPlanar:(BOOL)isPlanar colorSpaceName:(NSString *) colorSpaceName bitmapFormat:(NSBitmapFormat)bitmapFormat bytesPerRow: (NSInteger)rowBytes bitsPerPixel:(NSInteger)pixelBits`. If you need fine control, the options are available, but `NSImage` takes care of the details in the vast majority of cases so that you don't have to be concerned.

More information about image processing in Cocoa is available at http://developer.apple.com/documentation/Cocoa/Conceptual/CocoaDrawingGuide/Images/chapter_7_1.html.

The Persistent Storage Facade

Instances of the `NSPersistentStoreCoordinator` class mediate your application data and the underlying storage representation of the data. `NSPersistentStoreCoordinator` fulfills a role that is conceptually similar to `NSImage`. Just like `NSImage` shields you from the details of specific image file formats, `NSPersistentStoreCoordinator` shields you from the details of multiple persistent data storage formats. Using `NSPersistentStoreCoordinator`, you can load your application data from an XML file and save it to an SQLite database without any effect on the data itself. `NSPersistentStoreCoordinator` handles data storage in ways that make the type of storage unimportant to your code that uses the data.

Additional information about the Core Data architecture is provided at http://developer.apple.com/documentation/Cocoa/Conceptual/CocoaFundamentals/OtherArchitectures/chapter_8_4.html.

User Interaction Façades

Cocoa uses the Façade design pattern to decouple the programmatic logic of user interaction from the actual user interface implementation. For example, Cocoa's `NSColorPanel`

class provides a simple interface for programmers, and yet it supports a wide range of sophisticated color picking user interfaces. The standard color panel supports gray scale, Red
Green Blue (RGB), Cyan Magenta Yellow, blacK (CMYK), and Hue Saturation Bright-
ness (HSB) color formats. There is support for per-user color lists, color wheels, and even
a whimsical "Crayon" interface with named colors, as shown in Figure 26.4.

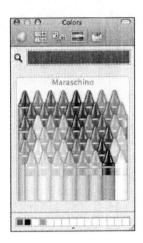

Figure 26.4   The standard Cocoa color panel

Each Cocoa application has a single instance of NSColorPanel that can be obtained
programmatically by sending the [NSColorPanel sharedColorPanel] message. Even
with all of the capability of the color panel, your application code that interacts with the
color panel is usually limited to implementing the - (void)changeColor:(id)sender
action method similar to the following:

```
- (void)changeColor:(id)sender
{
    NSColor *color = [sender color];   // get user chosen color

    // Do something with the color
}
```

Whenever a user picks a color in any of the color panel's modes, the shared
NSColorPanel instance sends the -changeColor: action message using the Target and
Action design pattern described in Chapter 17, "Outlets, Targets, and Actions." The target
of the color panel is usually set to nil, which means that the -changeColor: message is
sent along the Responder Chain to be handled as described in Chapter 18, "Responder
Chain." In most applications, NSColorPanel's - (NSColor *)color method is the only
one you will need to use.

Your code usually has no direct involvement with the multiple picking modes and user interfaces provided by the standard color panel. Even if your application has special needs, you can still control the color panel without direct coupling to the user interface. For example, you can limit the color panel to accept CMYK format colors exclusively without needing to know anything about the look and feel of CMYK color selection. Apple occasionally changes the user interface of standard panels, but application code is seldom broken because the code has no dependence on the specific interface.

Like NSColorPanel, the NSOpenPanel, NSSavePanel, and NSPrintPanel classes similarly isolate application code for the complexities of the corresponding user interfaces.

Consequences

The Façade design pattern hides complexity and reduces code coupling, but the pattern can be misused. When the full complexity of a subsystem is commonly required, a simplified façade adds little value and might actually increase the effort needed to effectively use the subsystem. If the façade interface is too complex or duplicates too many details of the hidden classes, it probably adds no value.

Facade objects are often singletons. For example, Cocoa provides one instance of NSColorPanel per application.

The Class Clusters pattern can sometimes be used as an alternative to Façade. Class clusters also hide implementation complexity for framework users. The Class Cluster's user only sees a relatively simple public interface that hides the fact that multiple specialized subclasses implement the interface on a case-by-case basis.

Proxies and Forwarding

Proxies are objects that stand in for other objects. They are used in any situation where an object is needed but the object is not readily available. For example, when distributed objects are used to provide object-oriented communication between applications, an actual object in one application may be represented as a proxy in another. Messages sent to the proxy are transmitted over the network and received by the actual object. Return values from the actual object are sent back over the network and returned by the proxy.

Forwarding is a feature of the Objective-C runtime that allows an object to capture messages sent to it and then pass these messages on to another object. Proxies use Forwarding in their implementation. Forwarding is more generally applied to implement Cocoa's undo and redo system. The Higher Order Messaging concept explained later in this chapter also uses the Forwarding pattern. Forwarding relies on the Invocation pattern.

Motivation

The Proxy pattern allows messages to be sent to an object that is separated from the message's sender by time or space. Proxies can also control access to or alter the behavior of other objects. Forwarding simplifies the capture of messages as invocations so that they can be resent, delayed, repeated, stored, or altered.

Solution

Forwarding is a feature of the Objective-C language and is built into the runtime's message dispatcher. When a message is sent to an object that doesn't have a corresponding method, the runtime offers the receiving object an opportunity to handle the message before raising an exception.

Implementing Forwarding

NSObject provides Template Methods that you override to tailor message forwarding behavior. See Chapter 4, "Template Method." To forward a message, the runtime first calls the -methodSignatureForSelector: template method to obtain an appropriate method signature to create an NSInvocation instance. Next, the -forwardInvocation: template method is called with a newly created NSInvocation instance as its argument. You must override NSObject's implementation of -forwardInvocation: to provide custom behavior. NSObject's default implementation of -forwardInvocation: sends the -doesNotRecognizeSelector: message to raise an exception. It's not sufficient to override -forwardInvocation:. It is also necessary to override -methodSignatureForSelector: to enable correct forwarding behavior.

For example, suppose the class MYClass wants to forward any message that it doesn't understand to an instance of MYHelperClass. MYClass uses code like the following:

```
- (NSMethodSignature *)methodSignatureForSelector:(SEL)aSelector
{
  if ([myHelperClassInstance respondsToSelector:aSelector])
  {
    return [myHelperClassInstance
        methodSignatureForSelector:aSelector];
  }
  else
  {
    return [super methodSignatureForSelector:aSelector];
  }
}


- (void)forwardInvocation:(NSInvocation *)invocation
{
  SEL aSelector = [invocation selector];
  if ([myHelperClassInstance respondsToSelector:aSelector])
  {
    [invocation invokeWithTarget:myHelperClassInstance];
  }
  else
  {
    [self doesNotRecognizeSelector:aSelector];
  }
}
```

Because a substantial amount of Objective-C code will test to see if an objects responds to a selector before sending a message, it is also a good idea to override the -respondsToSelector: method. In the example of MYClass forwarding messages to MYHelperClass, the code looks like this:

```
- (BOOL)respondsToSelector:(SEL)aSelector
{
  if ([myHelperClassInstance respondsToSelector:aSelector])
  {
    return YES;
  }
  else
  {
    return [super respondsToSelector:aSelector];
  }
}
```

Of course it is possible to customize behavior beyond simple forwarding in a -forwardInvocation: implementation. You can implement -forwardInvocation: to ignore messages. Some forwarding implementations trigger other processing before or after forwarding a message. The NSInvocation instance can be stored or altered, and it can be used to construct a message to be transmitted over the network. Proxy objects are the most common use of forwarding as explained in the next section.

Proxies

A proxy is an object that typically does nothing by itself. It's linked to some other object for which it stands in proxy. Nearly every message sent to a proxy ends up passing through the runtime's forwarding mechanism. For this to happen, the proxy is constrained to implement only a bare minimum of methods. The sequence of messages and return values when passing a message through a proxy is shown in Figure 27.1.

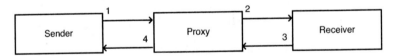

Figure 27.1   A proxy stands between a message sender and receiver.

The NSProxy class is used to implement most proxies. Unlike most Objective-C classes, which inherit from NSObject, the NSProxy class has no superclass. NSProxy implements as few methods as possible, which means that a lot of the NSObject methods that developers take for granted, such as -class, -superclass, and even -init, are not implemented by NSProxy. This helps to ensure that most messages will reach the proxy's -forwardInvocation: implementation.

The following MYJunction class implements a proxy that forwards action messages from a user interface to each object in an array. This overcomes a limitation of the Target/Action design pattern that normally only supports one target. You set the proxy as a target, and the proxy forwards any received action messages on to multiple other objects.

MYJunction requires an NSMutableArray to contain the targets to which it forwards the action messages. The public interface declares two methods, one to add a target and one to obtain a shared instance. This class isn't a strict singleton, so multiple instances are possible. The shared instance is simply provided for convenience when using it in a test application, as will become clear later. Here is the interface declaration:

```
#import <Foundation/Foundation.h>


@interface MYJunction : NSProxy
{
  NSMutableArray *targets;
}


+ (MYJunction *)sharedJunction;
- (void)addTarget:(id)anObject;


@end
```

The implementation of +sharedJunction creates an instance the first time it is called and then returns the same instance thereafter, similar to the code used to create a singleton:

```
+ (MYJunction *)sharedJunction
{
  static MYJunction *sharedJunction = nil;
  if (!sharedJunction)
  {
    sharedJunction = [[MYJunction alloc] init];
  }
  return sharedJunction;
}
```

To manage the targets array, the -init, -dealloc, and -addTarget: methods are required. The -init method creates the targets array while -dealloc disposes of it. The -addTarget: method simply adds a new target to the array.

```
- (id)init
{
  targets = [[NSMutableArray alloc] init];
  return self;
}


- (void)dealloc
{
  [targets release];
  [super dealloc];
}


- (void)addTarget:(id)anObject
{
  [targets addObject:anObject];
}
```

Notice that the -init method does *not* call [super init]. This is because the super-class, NSProxy, doesn't implement an -init method. As an implementation detail, an NSMutableArray was chosen so that the order in which the targets receive messages is determined by the order in which targets are added to the MYJunction instance via -addTarget:. A fully robust implementation should probably ensure that a target is only added to the targets array if it is not already there, unless the ability to have an action message sent to a target twice or more is desired. Using NSMutableSet to store targets guarantees the uniqueness of the targets but doesn't guarantee the order in which messages are forwarded to the targets.

The meat of the proxy implementation lies in the implementation of message for-warding. The following code loops through all the targets, sending the forwarded message to each in turn. Also, if the message sender is one of the targets, then we don't forward the message to that target.

Because this object is primarily interested in forwarding Target/Action messages, it makes some assumptions about the method signature. Remember that every message has two hidden arguments, self and _cmd. Therefore, the first user visible argument is actu-ally the third argument. The following -forwardInvocation: implementation silently ignores messages that don't have a third argument and assumes that the third argument is an object, typically the sender of an action message. For robustness, production code must verify that the third argument is actually an object.

```
- (void)forwardInvocation:(NSInvocation *)anInvocation
{
  if ([[anInvocation methodSignature] numberOfArguments] > 2)
  {
    for (id target in targets)
    {
      id messageSender = nil;
      [anInvocation getArgument:&messageSender atIndex:2];
      if (messageSender != target)
      {
        [anInvocation invokeWithTarget:target];
      }
    }
  }
}
```

This code doesn't check to see if a given target actually responds to the message. A possible improvement is to only send to targets that actually respond to a given message. Another improvement is to keep track of whether or not the message was successfully forwarded to any of the targets and raise an exception if none of them respond.

In order for forwarding to function properly, an implementation of -methodSignatureForSelector: is also required. In this case, another assumption is made. Because only one method signature can be returned, the first target found that can respond to a selector will be used to generate the method signature. If some targets have a different method signature, this implementation may result in run time errors. Again, because the focus is forwarding Target/Action messages, which all have the same signature, this assumption isn't a problem in the example code.

```
- (NSMethodSignature *)methodSignatureForSelector:(SEL)aSelector
{
  for (id target in targets)
  {
    if ([target respondsToSelector:aSelector])
    {
      return [target methodSignatureForSelector:aSelector];
    }
  }
  return nil;
}
```

Finally, implementations of -conformsToProtocol: and -respondsToSelector: are usually needed to ensure the proxy is more generally usable in a wide variety of situations. The following implementation returns YES if any one of the targets returns a YES.

```
- (BOOL)conformsToProtocol:(Protocol *)aProtocol
{
  for (id target in targets)
  {
    if ([target conformsToProtocol:aProtocol])
    {
      return YES;
    }
  }
  return NO;
}


- (BOOL)respondsToSelector:(SEL)aSelector
{
  for (id target in targets)
  {
    if ([target respondsToSelector:aSelector])
    {
      return YES;
    }
  }
  return NO;
}
```

That is all the code that is necessary to make the proxy functional. However, to use it in an actual example application, a little bit more code is necessary. The example application opens four identical windows, each with an NSSlider and NSTextfield. To do this, a window is placed in its own .nib file and the file is loaded four times. All of the sliders and text fields are tied together using a single MYJunction instance so that changing the value of any one of them causes the other seven to update also.

One of the challenges is that our proxy object is a bit confusing to Interface Builder when it comes time to make connections. To work around this, we will use a helper object. The helper object's only function is to make the connections to the MYJunction instance once a .nib file is loaded. The helper needs a single outlet for the object it's managing.

```
@interface MYJunctionHelper : NSObject
{
  IBOutlet id myObject;
}

@end
```

When the helper awakens from a .nib file, it will obtain the shared MYJunction instance and add its object to the target list. Additionally, it will set the junction as the object's target, as follows:

```
#import "MYJunctionHelper.h"
#import "MYJunction.h"


@implementation MYJunctionHelper

- (void)awakeFromNib
{
  MYJunction *junction = [MYJunction sharedJunction];
  [myObject setTarget:junction];
  [junction addTarget:myObject];
}

@end
```

Using this helper object is simple. One helper is instantiated in Interface Builder for every control that sends a message to the junction. Because the window has both a slider and a text field communicating through the junction, two MYJunctionHelper instances are created. Each instance is connected to one of the controls. Finally, each control is connected to the First Responder, and an action message is chosen. For the example application the message -takeDoubleValueFrom: is used. The reason the connection is made to the first responder is so that *any* valid action message known to Interface Builder can be chosen. If it is connected to another object instead, then only action messages implemented by the chosen target are offered as options. Connecting to the first responder actually sets a control's target to nil, but this doesn't matter because the helper object will set the target to be the junction as soon as the interface is loaded into the application.

A final class is used in the example application to open up all four windows when the application finishes launching. The JunctionAppController class is instantiated in the Main.nib file and is a delegate of the NSApplication object. It has an NSMutableArray containing NSWindowControllers for the four windows and implements the method -openAllWindows: to open all the windows at once. The interface is as follows:

```
#import <Cocoa/Cocoa.h>


@interface JunctionAppController : NSObject
{
  NSMutableArray *windowControllers;
}


- (IBAction)openAllWindows:(id)sender;


@end
```

The implementation simply manages the creation of the window controllers and opens all four windows after a brief delay. A delay of zero postpones the -openAllWindows: message until the "next run loop invocation," which means that the windows won't open until after the application's event loop starts running.

```
#import "JunctionAppController.h"


#define NUMBER_OF_WINDOWS 4


@implementation JunctionAppController


- (id)init
{
  if(nil != (self = [super init]))
  {
    windowControllers = [[NSMutableArray alloc] init];
  }
  return self;
}


- (void)dealloc
{
  [windowControllers release];
  [super dealloc];
}
```

```
- (void)awakeFromNib
{
  int i;
  for (i=0; i<NUMBER_OF_WINDOWS; i++)
  {
    NSWindowController *controller = [[NSWindowController alloc]
        initWithWindowNibName:@"JunctionWindow"];
    [windowControllers addObject:controller];
  }
  [self performSelector:@selector(openAllWindows:)
    withObject:self afterDelay:0.0];
}

- (IBAction)openAllWindows:(id)sender
{
  [windowControllers
      makeObjectsPerformSelector:@selector(showWindow:)
      withObject:self];
}

@end
```

This is all the code required to make the example work. When run, the controls will all function together in lock step, as seen in Figure 27.2. This particular example is rather simple. The same effect could have been achieved by using Cocoa bindings technology to bind each control to a single value as explained in Chapter 32, "Bindings and Controllers." Even so, the example shows how to make connections to objects that are in different .nib files and how to send a Target/Action message to more than one object at a time, both of which can be useful in some situations.

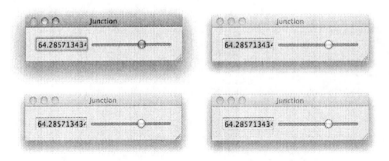

Figure 27.2   MYJunction example interface

There are other ways in which proxies may be used. If an object has expensive initialization, such as fetching data from a database or loading a file off disk, then use a proxy to stand in for the real object until the real object is needed. If the real object is never needed, only the lightweight proxy is ever created. When accesses that require the real object are requested, the proxy initializes the real object and then forwards messages to it.

Proxies are also used as a way to wrap other objects and control or alter access to the objects. Depending on a message's sender, a proxy changes which methods it is willing to forward to the real object. Some messages might be altered before being forwarded, or one message might be substituted for another.

Another way a proxy can be used is to create objects that have new behaviors. For example, a category can add methods to an existing class, but it cannot add instance variables. A proxy can simulate a category with instance variables by defining its own variables and methods and then forwarding everything else to the real object. Furthermore, when a category overrides an object's existing methods, it has no easy way to access the original method, but a proxy can. Proxies are also able to simulate multiple inheritance by forwarding messages to multiple other objects, creating a form of composite object.

Higher Order Messages

In the `MYJunction` example, the application's controller sends a message to the window controller array invoking the `-makeObjectsPerformSelector:withObject:` method. This is a convenient method because it eliminates the need to write loop or iteration code. It has two downsides, however. First, it somewhat obscures the intent of the code by hiding the fact that the *real* message being sent is `-showWindow:`. There's a lot of extra text surrounding the real message. Second, the possible messages that can be sent to every object in the array are limited. A very specific method signature is required. The methods that can be used must all take a single object as an argument. There is no convenient method to send a message that takes, say, four arguments. The following code is much cleaner:

```
// send an arbitrary message to all objects
[[windowControllers makeObjectsPerform] showWindow:self];
```

The key observation here is that what is really wanted is a message that can take another message as its argument. A message that does this is known as a *Higher Order Message* or HOM. The terminology and the basic concept borrow much from the idea of higher order functions in the Lisp programming language.

Until Objective-C supports a language feature called blocks, there is no direct support for methods that take messages or other code as arguments. However, through the use of invocations, forwarding, and proxies, it is possible to capture a message and then use it elsewhere. In the following example, the `-makeObjectsPerform` message returns what is called a *trampoline* object.

A trampoline is a simple proxy object that captures a message and then passes it back to the original object. The trampoline returned by `-makeObjectsPerform` waits until it is asked to forward the `-showWindow:` message. At that time, it calls a private method that takes an `NSInvocation` as an argument. The private method contains the loop that actually sends the message to each object in the array. To see how this is implemented, the previous example is modified to use HOM when opening the windows. The sequence of messages sent when using -makeObjectsPerform in this example is shown in Figure 27.3.

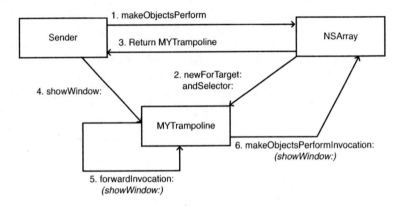

Figure 27.3   Sending a HOM through a trampoline

The first task is to create a class that is used as a trampoline. The trampoline's job is to capture a message as an NSInvocation and then send it to a target object. It should avoid implementing most messages. Therefore, MYTrampoline is a subclass of NSProxy with two instance variables, target and selector. It implements two methods to aid in the creation of trampolines, +newForTarget:andSelector: and -initForTarget:andSelector:.

To allow collections to find method signatures from their contained objects, we add a method named -findMethodSignatureForSelector: to NSObject. The default implementation simply calls -methodSignatureForSelector:, but collection classes can override it to search their collected objects for a signature. The interface file for all this is as follows:

```
#import <Foundation/Foundation.h>


@interface NSObject(MYTrampoline)

- (NSMethodSignature *)findMethodSignatureForSelector:(SEL)aSelector;

@end

@interface MYTrampoline : NSProxy
{
  id  target;
  SEL selector;
```

```
}

+ (id)newForTarget:(id)aTarget andSelector:(SEL)aSelector;
- (id)initForTarget:(id)aTarget andSelector:(SEL)aSelector;

@end
```

The implementation of the trampoline is nearly trivial in comparison to the MYJunction class. The +new... and -init... methods simply set the instance variables to the arguments that are passed in. To forward the invocation, the trampoline sends a message to its target using the preconfigured selector.

```
#import "MYTrampoline.h"


@implementation NSObject(MYTrampoline)

- (NSMethodSignature *)findMethodSignatureForSelector:(SEL)aSelector
{
  return [self methodSignatureForSelector:aSelector];
}

@end


@implementation MYTrampoline

+ (id)newForTarget:(id)aTarget andSelector:(SEL)aSelector
{
  id newTrampoline = [[[self class] alloc]
      initForTarget:aTarget andSelector:aSelector];
  [newTrampoline autorelease];
  return newTrampoline;
}

- (id)initForTarget:(id)aTarget andSelector:(SEL)aSelector
{
  target = aTarget;
  [target retain];
  selector = aSelector;
  return self;
}

- (void)dealloc
{
  [target release];
  [super dealloc];
}
```

```objc
- (NSMethodSignature *)methodSignatureForSelector:(SEL)aSelector
{
  return [target findMethodSignatureForSelector:aSelector];
}

- (void)forwardInvocation:(NSInvocation *)anInvocation
{
  [target performSelector:selector withObject:anInvocation];
}

@end
```

The next step is to implement the actual higher order message using a category on the NSArray class. The category defines two new methods. The first is the HOM -makeObjectsPerform. The second is the method that will be called by the trampoline, -makeObjectsPerformInvocation:. To keep this method semi-private, it is not part of the interface declaration and is only found in the implementation. In this case, the method itself might be more generally useful to other code, so it makes sense to expose it publically.

```objc
#import <Foundation/Foundation.h>

@interface NSArray(HOM)

- (id)makeObjectsPerform;
- (void)makeObjectsPerformInvocation:(NSInvocation *)invocation;

@end
```

The -makeObjectsPerform method, the actual higher order message, only creates and returns a trampoline object. The trampoline calls -makeObjectsPerformInvocation: to loop through all the objects in the array, using the invocation object on each of them.

The implementation must also override the -findMethodSignatureForSelector: method that is used by the trampoline. Because NSArray is a collection object, this method searches all the collected objects for the first object that responds to the selector and then uses it to make a method signature. If no such object is found, then the implementation falls back to trying to get the NSArray object to create a signature.

```objc
#import "NSArray+HOM.h"
#import "MYTrampoline.h"

@implementation NSArray(HOM)

- (NSMethodSignature *)findMethodSignatureForSelector:(SEL)aSelector
{
  for (id object in self)
  {
```

```
   if ([object respondsToSelector:aSelector])
   {
     return [object methodSignatureForSelector:aSelector];
   }
  }
  return [self methodSignatureForSelector:aSelector];
}


- (id)makeObjectsPerform
{
  return [MYTrampoline newForTarget:self
      andSelector:@selector(makeObjectsPerformInvocation:)];
}


- (void)makeObjectsPerformInvocation:(NSInvocation *)invocation
{
  for (id object in self)
  {
    [invocation invokeWithTarget:object];
  }
}
@end
```

With the trampoline object implementation and the HOM category on NSArray completed, the code for -openAllWindows: in the JunctionAppController class is now changed:

```
- (IBAction)openAllWindows:(id)sender
{
  [[windowControllers makeObjectsPerform] showWindow:self];
}
```

In this example, the HOM doesn't have a return value. It is possible to create HOMs that have return values, however. For example, imagine an array populated with person objects. An HOM such as -select might be used to find all the persons matching particular criteria, such as all the person objects that respond YES to the message -livesWithinDistance:ofCity:. In this case, the HOM returns an NSArray containing all the objects that answered YES.

Handling return values properly adds significant complexity to the implementation of trampolines and HOMs. To see examples of how such messages might be implemented, refer to the implementation of HOM found as part of the MPWFoundation framework. It can be downloaded from http://www.metaobject.com/downloads/Objective-C/. This implementation is where HOM was first introduced to the Cocoa developer community.

HOMs do not necessarily have to be covers for looping code, either. Consider the following two messages, one as a normal Cocoa method call and one as a possible HOM:

```
[anObject performSelector:selector(anAction)
    withObject:self afterDelay:1.0];  // old way
[[anObject afterDelay:1.0] anAction:self];  // HOM way
```

HOMs can also be used to simplify common idioms. For example, to send a message to a delegate only if it can respond to the message, an -ifResponds HOM is used. Any time you find yourself writing the same basic code repeatedly, you may have a candidate for HOM.

The Cocoa undo and redo functionality implemented by the NSUndoManager class and its -prepareWithInvocationTarget: method is a form of HOM because it captures the messages required to undo or redo a user action. In this case, the undo manager acts as a trampoline for itself.

Although HOMs aren't common in Cocoa at present, they do offer several advantages. The programmer's intent is made clearer, and less code is required to accomplish the same actions. This leads to fewer errors in code.

Furthermore, because HOMs only accept one message as an argument, using an HOM forces developers to put blocks of code into single methods on the object in question rather than having sequences of messages buried in multiple loops scattered throughout the code base. This reduces coupling and improves the organization of code. In some cases, however, this can lead to an excessive number of extra method implementations. Such a situation signals that either HOM isn't the best solution for the problem or that the design itself is flawed and needs to be refactored.

One negative of HOM is the potential for performance degradation. As implemented here, there is the need to allocate and set up a trampoline and the overhead of capturing a message. For messages that aren't sent very often, this isn't a significant problem. The HOM overhead can be reduced by reusing trampoline objects. Instead of allocating a new trampoline every time one is needed and deallocating after only a single use, keep the old trampoline around after it's done it's job. When a new trampoline is needed, reinitialize the old one and reuse it. By maintaining a pool of trampoline objects, fewer allocations and deallocations are performed. Even without this optimization, however, the advantages to code correctness, readability, and maintainability usually negate any performance concerns about HOM overhead.

When an HOM implies a loop, the HOM overhead is usually not a problem. By pushing the code for loops into the implementation of the HOM, optimizations not normally worth the effort for a typical loop now become worthwhile because the loop is reused many times. The savings that are achieved when the loop is optimized often dwarf the overhead of setting up an HOM. The HOM implementation in MPWFoundation demonstrates several optimizations of this nature.

Examples in Cocoa

Cocoa uses proxies with Distributed Objects (DO). The NSProxy class implements the Proxy pattern. When requesting an object in another process or thread, DO returns an NSProxy instance. Messages sent to the proxy object are captured using Forwarding. DO then transmits the captured messages to the real object, where the message is received. If the return value of a message is another object, then a new proxy may be created automatically and returned to the message sender. If a message uses an object as an argument, a proxy may be automatically created at the receiving end for that argument. It is possible for each of two applications to have proxies that send messages to the other. Sometimes, depending on how a method has been declared, DO may use Archiving to send a copy of an object to the other side of a connection instead of creating a proxy.

The undo and redo features provided by Cocoa use the Forwarding pattern to capture the actions required to undo or redo a user operation. When the -prepareWithInvocationTarget: method is sent to an NSUndoManager instance, the undo manager returns itself, ready to capture the next message sent to itself. The captured message, an NSInvocation, is then added to either the undo or redo stack as appropriate.

Consequences

Forwarding adds tremendous flexibility to Objective-C objects. Messages may be captured and re-sent at a different time, re-sent multiple times, sent to another or multiple other objects, changed or substituted for other messages, conditionally ignored, and so on. Forwarding can also be used to allow an object to take on some or all of the behaviors of a child object.

Forwarding enables the implementation of proxy objects. Proxies represent other objects and stand in for them. This can be used to simplify passing messages between remote objects because the code to send a message is the same no matter whether you are dealing with a proxy or an actual object. Proxies control access to other objects or alter behavior of other objects on an instance-by-instance basis by intercepting messages.

A special kind of proxy, the trampoline, can be used to implement designs where a message wants to use another message as an argument. The undo and redo system in Cocoa is one example of this, but Higher Order Messaging generalizes the concept.

Managers

Managers are classes that manage instances of other classes. Examples of Cocoa manager classes include NSFileManager, NSFontManager, NSInputManager, and NSLayoutManager. Managers simplify the creation and management of reusable resources such as fonts and encapsulate implementation details. For example, the NSFileManager class provides methods for managing files from file systems as diverse as DOS FAT, Apple HFS+, Network File System, UFS, and ISO 9660 without requiring any system-specific code in applications. Some managers also act as controllers within the Model View Controller pattern.

Motivation

Offer a uniform interface for managing the instantiation of and access to a group of related objects. Many managers use and extend the Singleton pattern; they are singletons themselves, and they may ensure that the objects they manage are unique.

Solution

It is common in application design to have a collection of objects that need to be unique but at the same time are not singletons. For example, consider fonts. Because an application may use many different fonts, the object used to encapsulate a font will probably be instantiated multiple times and therefore is not a singleton. At the same time, there is no need for multiple instances all encapsulating the same exact font. It makes sense to control the creation of font instances so that whenever a specific typeface is requested, the same instance is returned.

One approach is to use class methods to ensure that all instances of an object are unique. For example, if an NSImage is obtained using the +imageNamed: class method, the same instance is returned every time a particular name is requested. Associative Storage, Chapter 19, "Associative Storage," is commonly used to keep track of the named instances. One possible implementation for a method like this uses an NSMutableDictionary to track each object as it is created:

```
static NSMutableDictionary *imageTable = nil;

+ (NSImage *)imageNamed:(NSString *)name
{
  NSImage *image;
  if (!imageTable)
  {
    imageTable = [[NSMutableDictionary alloc] init];
  }
  image = [imageTable objectForKey:name];
  if (!image)
  {
    image = /* add code to create new image here */ ;
    [imageTable setObject:image forKey:name];
  }
  return image;
}
```

This approach can be fairly limited, however. Returning to the example of font objects, there are other necessary tasks involving the manipulation of font objects. One such manipulation would be to request the italic version of a font. The font class could be given a method that would look up and return the italic version, but eventually the interface of the font class could become cluttered.

Because the normal and the italic versions of a typeface are actually two different font objects, it makes sense to have a second class involved that can return the desired font object. To get the italic version of a font, the programmer would give this managing class the normal font and request the italic version. In Cocoa, this is exactly how it works. There are the NSFont and NSFontManager classes. The NSFontManager class has several -convertFont... methods that, given an NSFont instance, can be used to obtain different NSFont instances.

The NSFontManager itself is a singleton, and for many manager objects this makes sense. When a class is controlling uniqueness of another class' instances, it needs to be a Singleton to guarantee uniqueness. If there were two manager instances, each would end up maintaining its own set of objects, and duplicates would be possible.

An added advantage of creating a separate class to manage fonts is that the manager class can also act as a controller, handling some applicationwide font related tasks. The NSFontManager class tracks the "current" font so that as text is selected in a Cocoa application, the NSFontPanel can be kept up to date. It also manages the application's Font menu. In effect, the NSFontManager is managing the interaction between NSFont objects and various application objects, hence the name "Manager" for this pattern.

Extending the Singleton Pattern

If we revisit the example given with the Singleton pattern (Chapter 13, "Singleton"), we can extend it into a more general Manager-type class. In the example, an object was created to manage high scores for a game. The assumption was that there would only be one high score table for the game. However, there are many games that have different game settings or gameplay variations. In such cases, it would make sense to have a separate high score table for each game variant. With this in mind, the MYGameHighScoreManager class can be rewritten. Because this manager still needs to be a singleton itself, much of the code presented in Chapter 13 can be retained as-is; most changes will be the addition of new code.

For this example we will assume the creation of a new class, MYHighScoreTable. This new class will contain all the actual high score data. The manager class will manage instances of this new class. In the previous example, the manager has the instance methods -registerScore:playerName: and -scoreEnumerator. Both methods need to be implemented by the new MYHighScoreTable class, but the MYGameHighScoreManager class will also have implementations of them. Part of the manager's job is to know which type of game is being played at the moment and pass score submissions on to the correct table. Assuming that the game has a window for displaying the high scores, MYGameHighScoreManager is responsible for displaying and updating that window. Given all these tasks, we can now create the class interface definition:

```objc
@class MYHighScoreTable;


@interface MYGameHighScoreManager : NSObject
{
  NSString            *currentGameName;
  NSMutableDictionary *highScoreTables;
  IBOutlet NSWindow   *highScoreWindow;
}


@property (readwrite copy) NSString *currentGameName;

+ (MYGameHighScoreManager *)sharedInstance;
+ (BOOL)sharedInstanceExists;
- (MYHighScoreTable *)highScoreTableForGameNamed:(NSString *)gameName;
- (MYHighScoreTable *)highScoreTableForCurrentGame;
- (IBAction)displayHighScoreWindow:(id)sender;
- (void)updateHighScoreWindow;
- (void)registerScore:(NSNumber *)score playerName:(NSString *)name;
- (NSEnumerator *)scoreEnumerator;
@end
```

There are three instance variables. The variable currentGameName tracks which game variant is currently being played or has just been played and will be handled as a property of the class. The dictionary highScoreTables contains all the instances of

MYHighScoreTable that are being managed by the MYGameHighScoreManager. Finally, the outlet highScoreWindow points to the window that is used for displaying high scores. Presumably, this window would be set up in an Interface Builder file. In this example, it will be assumed that the file is called HighScoreWindow.nib. The file would be set up so that an instance of MYGameHighScoreManager is the File's Owner, and a connection would be wired up between the File's Owner and the window. In a real implementation, there might be other outlets in the MYHighScoreTable class to connect to instances of NSTableView or other NSView objects used to display the high scores. For simplicity, those details are omitted here.

Turning to the implementation, all the code to make this class a singleton still applies:

```
static MYGameHighScoreManager *myInstance = nil;

@implementation MYGameHighScoreManager : NSObject


+ (id)hiddenAlloc
{
  return [super alloc];
}

+ (id)alloc
{
  NSLog(@"%@: use +sharedInstance instead of +alloc",
      [[self class] name]);
  return nil;
}

+ (id)new
{
  return [self alloc];
}

+ (id)allocWithZone:(NSZone *)zone
{
  return [self alloc];
}

- (id)copyWithZone:(NSZone *)zone
{
  [self retain];
  return self;
}

- (id)mutableCopyWithZone:(NSZone *)zone
{
```

```
    return [self copyWithZone:zone];
}


+ (MYGameHighScoreManager *)sharedInstance
{
  if (!myInstance)
  {
    NSBundle *mainBundle = [NSBundle mainBundle];
    NSDictionary *info = [mainBundle infoDictionary];
    NSString *className = [info objectForKey:
        @"MYGameHighScoreManagerClass"];
    Class *myClass = NSClassFromString(className);
    if (!myClass)
    {
      myClass = [self class];
    }
    myInstance  = [[myClass hiddenAlloc] init];
  }
  return myInstance;
}


+ (BOOL)sharedInstanceExists
{
  return (nil != myInstance);
}


@end
```

Next, the management of the MYHighScoreTable instances needs to be added to the
class. To do this, an -init method is added to create the dictionary that will contain
all the MYHighScoreTable instances and initialize the other instance variables. An
implementation of the -highScoreTableForGameNamed: method is needed. The
-highScoreTableForGameNamed: method will look and function much like the example
code presented previously for a possible implementation of the -imageNamed: method.

```
- (id)init
{
  if(nil != (self = [super init]))
  {
    highScoreTables = [[NSMutableDictionary alloc] init];
    highScoreWindow = nil;
    currentGameName = @"";
  }
  return self;
}


- (MYHighScoreTable *)highScoreTableForGameNamed:(NSString *)gameName
```

```
{
  MYHighScoreTable *table =
      [highScoreTables objectForKey:gameName];
  if (!table)
  {
    table = [[MYHighScoreTable alloc] initWithName:gameName];
    [highScoreTables setObject:table forKey:gameName];
  }
  return table;
}
```

This code assumes that the MYHighScoreTable class implements an -initWithName: method that will load the high score table's data from disk or network when called. The data for each high score table is also being loaded on demand. Until some application object requests it, the information is not loaded into the application.

Adding Other Manager Features

Next, code is required to handle tracking the current game. Because currentGameName is a property, the @synthesize directive can be used to create set and get instance methods. The -highScoreTableForCurrentGame method is really just for convenience, and the methods -registerScore:playerName: and -scoreEnumerator now forward to the current high score table as shown here:

```
@synthesize currentGameName;

- (MYHighScoreTable *)highScoreTableForCurrentGame
{
  return [self highScoreTableForGameNamed:currentGameName];
}

- (void)registerScore:(NSNumber *)score playerName:(NSString *)name
{
  [[self highScoreTableForCurrentGame] registerScore:score
      playerName:name];
}

- (NSEnumerator *)scoreEnumerator;

{
  [[self highScoreTableForCurrentGame] scoreEnumerator];
}
```

By keeping the methods for registering and enumerating high scores, this new version of the MYGameHighScoreManager class can still function as a drop-in replacement for the previous version and yet have the enhanced ability to manage multiple high score tables.

Now, whenever the player changes the settings of the game or chooses a new game variant, a message should be sent to the `MYGameHighScoreManager` singleton to let it know that a new high score table should be used.

```
// tell the high score system to use a new high score table
[[MYGameHighScoreManager sharedInstance]
    setCurrentGameName:newGameName];
```

Finally, some code is needed to display the high scores window. If the Interface Builder file that contains the window's interface hasn't yet been loaded, then it needs to be loaded first. Then the window itself can be displayed.

```
- (IBAction)displayHighScoreWindow:(id)sender
{
  if (!highScoreWindow)
  { // load the .nib
    [NSBundle loadNibNamed:@"HighScoreWindow" owner:self];
  }
  [self updateHighScoreWindow];
  [highScoreWindow makeKeyAndOrderFront:nil];
}

- (void)updateHighScoreWindow
{
  // code would be placed here as necessary
}
```

The `-updateHighScoreWindow` method's implementation is dependent on the view objects used by the game's high score panel. As such, specific code cannot be shown here. One change that might be necessary, depending on the game's user interface requirements, is to make sure that the `-updateHighScoreWindow` method is called whenever a change is made to the `currentGameName` instance variable. Depending on the needs of other objects in the game, it might also be useful to post a notification when `currentGameName` changes. It may be necessary to write a custom Accessor method instead of using `@synthesize` to add this additional code. For example

```
- (NSString *)setCurrentGameName:(NSString *)newGameName
{
  [currentGameName autorelease];
  currentGameName = newGameName;
  [currentGameName retain];
  [self updateHighScoreWindow];
  [[NSNotificationCenter defaultCenter]
      postNotificationName:@"HighScoreGameNameChanged"
      object:self];
}
```

At this point, the MYGameHighScoreManager class is performing some controller-like functions, but it is also managing instances of MYHighScoreTable. It becomes the central location for the rest of the game's code to use when accessing high scores. Although this example doesn't encapsulate any complex algorithms, some manager classes do. As can be seen, the Manager pattern incorporates elements of the Singleton, Controller, and Façade patterns.

Examples in Cocoa

This pattern is seen most clearly with the NSFontManager class. NSFontManager has two key tasks. The first is to control access to NSFont instances. Additionally, it tracks the current font in use so that it can keep the NSFontPanel and the application's font menu updated appropriately. In this second role, it is acting as part of the application's controller layer.

Another Manager, the NSFileManager class, is used to encapsulate all actions related to the file system. By using this class, an application insulates itself from the details of a specific type of file system. NSFileManager can also return an NSData object containing the contents of a given file. It additionally performs file system operations such as changing file attributes and moving, copying, deleting, and renaming files.

The NSUndoManager class tracks changes made to an application's model and state. As changes are made, it creates objects that record the previous state. The objects can later be used to revert state (undo) or reapply state changes (redo). NSUndoManager decides which state objects to use when an undo or redo request is made and can group multiple state changes together into a single operation. If there are limits set to the undo stack size, then NSUndoManager also controls when its managed objects are released.

In Cocoa not every class whose name ends in "Manager" follows every aspect of this pattern, however. Some of them only encapsulate specific tasks. For example, Core Data has the NSMigrationManager class. It encapsulates the specific task of migrating data from between Core Data persistent stores with different models, but it doesn't manage instances of another class.

Some manager-named classes are merely singletons that encapsulate APIs to applications or features that are provided by Apple as part of Mac OS X. For example, IMAVManager allows applications to provide audio and video to iChat AV. ISyncManager is used to communicate with the iSync engine. The NSAppleEventManager provides an interface to Apple Events within a Cocoa application.

The Cocoa Text system uses two manager classes that encapsulate complex algorithms and behave much like controllers in the MVC pattern. The NSInputManager class works with NSInputServer and NSTextView objects to handle selection and modification of text. The NSLayoutManager class is used to handle layout of text, mediating between NSTextStorage, NSRulerView, and NSTextView objects.

The NSHelpManager class is interesting because it is both a singleton API wrapper and a manager in the sense of this pattern. As an API wrapper, it has methods to open Apple

Help books and search for text in them. But it also associates NSAttributed strings with NSView objects for use in the display of context-sensitive help.

Consequences

The Manager pattern is a hybrid and a generalization of other patterns such as Singleton, Façade, and Controllers. Many managers, such as NSFontManager, NSInputManager, and NSLayoutManager perform controller-like functions within an application. As is the case with NSFontManager and others, some managers are singletons.

Often managers extend the idea of a singleton by controlling access to related instances of another class. For example, NSFontManager is used to obtain NSFont objects. An NSFont is not a singleton because there can be many different NSFont instances. At the same time, however, NSFont instances should be unique. There's no need to have a dozen identical NSFont objects all representing the same typeface. It makes more sense to always use the same instance to represent a specific font. NSFontManager can ensure this is the case by always returning the same NSFont instance whenever a given typeface is requested.

Some managers provide wrappers around APIs. NSFileManager is the preferred means of accessing the file system in Cocoa applications because it decouples a Cocoa application from the file system used by the computer or device running the application.

When encountering a class name ending in "Manager" in Cocoa, one or more of these roles is implied. In custom code, a manager should be used when a class is needed for managing instances of other classes, especially when uniqueness is required.

Controllers

Within the overarching Model View Controller (MVC) design pattern, the Controller subsystem has historically lagged the other subsystems when it comes to object reuse. Controller subsystems are full of "glue" code used to mediate between views and models. In contrast, the Model and View subsystems are replete with standard reuse scenarios. Mature flexible data structures, databases, and algorithms for models were well established decades ago. Standard reusable view objects shipped with the earliest ancestors of Cocoa in 1988 complete with Interface Builder. The Application Kit leverages patterns to almost automate the development of View subsystems. But what about controllers? How are design patterns applied to simplify controllers, promote wide scale controller reuse, and automate controller development? The Controller subsystem in Cocoa has only lately matured and standardized, and the only real explanation for the delay is that it has taken longer to recognize the design patterns that are applicable for controllers.

Consider how controllers differ from views. Conventions and metaphors for user interaction with views are now standard. For example, users understand the concept of the "current selection" within a user interface and that using the "Copy" menu item will copy the current selection and not some other part of the interface. The metaphors and conventions for views had to be established before design patterns like Cocoa's Responder Chain were applied to implement those conventions. Conventions and metaphors for controllers are less clear. Controllers integrate views with models as diverse as games, employee benefits management, weather simulations, and robotic arm manipulation. This chapter explores some common controller tasks and identifies opportunities for reuse in "glue" code. In the process, this chapter exposes the rationale for the various Cocoa `NSController` subclasses and the resulting design patterns.

Motivation

Reduce the need for recurring error prone code when implementing the Controller subsystem of the Model View Controller design pattern. Apply Apple's Interface Builder tool and the Controllers pattern to streamline development of the Controller subsystem for simple applications and substantially reduce the code needed to implement complex applications.

Solution

This section presents the relatively simple MVC MYShapeDraw application example shown in Figure 29.1. The example highlights typical tasks a Controller subsystem needs to perform. Initially, the entire implementation of MYShapeDraw's controller subsystem is in just one class. The example includes the kind of code that has historically been written and rewritten for almost every MVC application. Once the MYShapeDraw application is fully developed, the example's controller is redesigned to make it more general and reusable. By the end of this section, the example's Controller subsystem evolves into a clone of the design used by Cocoa's NSArrayController class. Following the step-by-step reinvention of NSArrayController in this chapter reveals why Cocoa's NSObjectController and its subclasses exist and how they're used in applications.

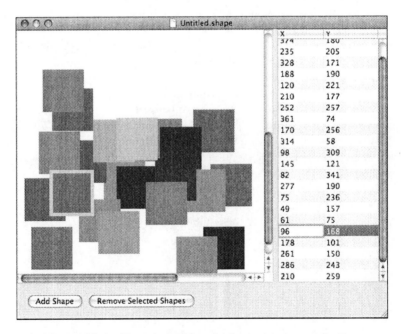

Figure 29.1   The user interface for MYShapeDraw application

The MYShapeDraw example application has the following features/requirements above and beyond the features provided by all Cocoa document-based applications:

- Provide a simple Model subsystem: just an array of shape objects.
- Provide a custom graphical view to display shape objects.
- Provide a way to add shape objects to the model.
- Provide a way to select zero, one, or multiple shape objects.
- Provide a way to reposition selected shape objects in the custom view.
- Provide a way to remove selected shape objects from the model.
- Provide a table view to display information about shape objects.
- When either the model or any of the views change, update the others.

There's a lot of code in this section because controllers can't be analyzed in isolation. It's necessary to develop a minimal model and view just to see how the controller interacts. Some of the code for the Model and View subsystems is omitted from this chapter for the sake of brevity and to keep the focus on the Controller subsystem. All of the code is available at www.CocoaDesignPatterns.com.

MYShapeDraw **Model Subsystem**

The model for this example is just an array of MYShape instances. The MYShape class encapsulates a color and a rectangle that defines the shape's position and size.

> **Note**
>
> The model in this example is deliberately kept simple to preserve the focus on the Controller subsystem. In most applications, properties like rectangles and colors are user interface concerns that don't belong in the Model subsystem. However, in this case, MYShapeDraw is a drawing program. The objects that the user wants to view or edit are shapes. Imagine that the shapes edited by MYShapeDraw actually represent the holes to be cut out of a sheet of metal and the colors represent the color of the wires to be routed through the holes. The model then consists of instructions to be sent to cutting and wire routing machines.

A more full-featured Model subsystem might include subclasses of MYShape to represent circles, text, images, and groups of shapes. However, the following base MYShape class is sufficient for this example:

```
@interface MYShape : NSObject <NSCoding>
{
  NSRect        frame;
  NSColor       *color;
}

@property (readwrite, assign) CGFloat positionX;
@property (readwrite, assign) CGFloat positionY;
```

```
@property (readwrite, copy) NSColor *color;

// Returns the receiver's frame
- (NSRect)frame;

// Moves the receiver's frame by the specified amounts
- (void)moveByDeltaX:(float)deltaX deltaY:(float)deltaY;

// This is a Template Method to customize selection logic.  The default
// implementation returns YES if aPoint is within frame.  Override this
// method to be more selective.  The default implementation can be
// called from overridden versions.
- (BOOL)doesContainPoint:(NSPoint)aPoint;


@end
```

The properties declared for the MYShape class are not identical to the instance variables declared for the class. There's no particular reason for properties and instance variables to coincide, and it's convenient for this example to provide positionX and positionY properties. The Accessor methods (see Chapter 10, "Accessors") for the properties are implemented to calculate values relative to the frame. The implementation of the MYShape class is so simple that it doesn't need to be shown here, but it's available in the example source code.

MYShapeDraw View Subsystem

Based on the requirements for this example, there are at least two different ways to view and interact with the model. A custom NSView subclass is needed to display and select shapes and enable graphical repositioning of selected shapes. An ordinary NSTableView is needed to display information about shapes in a table.

This example doesn't require any code in the View subsystem to use a NSTableView. All of the table configuration is performed in Interface Builder, and the upcoming Controller subsystem provides the data the table needs.

Implementing the custom NSView subclass is almost as straightforward as the model. To start, declare the MYShapeView subclass of NSView as follows:

```
@interface MYShapeView : NSView
{
    IBOutlet id        dataSource;
}

@property (readwrite, assign) id dataSource;  // Don't retain or copy

@end
```

No new methods are needed. The entire functionality of MYShapeView is either inherited from the NSView class, overridden from the NSView class, or provided by the one and only property, dataSource. The dataSource is used to implement the Data Source pattern explained in Chapter 15, "Delegates." MYShapeView instances interrogate their data sources to determine what to draw. The MYShapeView is implemented as follows:

```
@implementation MYShapeView

@synthesize dataSource;


- (void)dealloc
{
  [self setDataSource:nil];
  [super dealloc];
}



// Draw all of the MYShape instances provided by the dataSource
// from back to front
- (void)drawRect:(NSRect)aRect
{
  [[NSColor whiteColor] set];
  NSRectFill(aRect);  // Erase the background

  for(MYShape *currentShape in
      [[self dataSource] shapesInOrderBackToFront])
  {
    [currentShape drawRect:aRect];
  }
}


@end
```

That's pretty much all it takes to draw shapes. MYShapeView overrides NSView's -drawRect: Template Method to get an array of MYShape instances from the dataSource and then send a message to each shape requesting that it draw itself. Template Methods are explained in Chapter 4, "Template Method." An interesting question arises at this point: How do MYShape instances know how to draw themselves in MYShapeView instances? Drawing is clearly part of the View subsystem, but the MYShape class is declared in the Model subsystem. The solution used in this example applies the Category pattern from Chapter 6, "Category," to extend the MYShape class within the View subsystem using the following declaration and implementation:

```
// Declare an informal protocol that MYShape instances must implement
// in order to be displayed in a MYShapeView.
@interface MYShape (MYShapeQuartzDrawing)

// This is a Template Method to customize drawing.  The default
// implementation fills the receiver's frame with the receiver's color.
// Override this method to customize drawing.  The default
```

```
// implementation can be called from overridden versions, but it is
// not necessary to call the default version.
- (void)drawRect:(NSRect)aRect;

@end


@implementation MYShape (MYShapeQuartzDrawing)

// Draw the receiver in the current Quartz graphics context
- (void)drawRect:(NSRect)aRect
{
  if(NSIntersectsRect(aRect, [self frame]))
  {
    [[self color] set];
    NSRectFill([self frame]);
  }
}

@end
```

The MYShapeQuartzDrawing category is implemented right in the same file as the MYShapeView class. Therefore, all of the relevant code for drawing MYShape instances in MYShapeViews is maintained together.

Note

A future MYShapeOpenGLView might draw MYShape instances using Open GL instead of Quartz. The MYShapeOpenGLView class could provide its own category of MYShape to add a `-drawRect:(NSRect)aRect forOpenGLContext:(NSOpenGLContext *)aContext` method. In that way, the Open GL-specific drawing code could be maintained right next to the rest of the MYShapeOpenGLView code.

The MYShapeView class provides basic display of the MYShape instances supplied by a dataSource. The code to support graphical editing features could be added to the MYShapeView class, but sometimes it's handy to have a simple display-only class like MYShapeView. The graphical editing support will be added in a subclass of MYShapeView called MYEditorShapeView later in the example, but for now, MYShapeView provides enough capability to move on to the Controller subsystem.

MYShapeEditor Controller Subsystem

So now that the model and view are established, what does the Controller subsystem need to do? The Controller subsystem needs to initialize the model either from scratch or by loading a previously saved model. The Controller subsystem must set up the view. The Controller subsystem must supply an object that will serve as the table view's data source and an object that will serve as the custom view's data source. The Controller subsystem must enable adding shapes to the model. The Controller subsystem needs to keep track of which shapes are selected and enable removal of selected shapes from the model. Finally, the Controller subsystem must keep the model and all views up to date.

The list of controller tasks fall into two general categories, coordinating tasks and mediating tasks. Coordinating tasks include loading the Model and View subsystems and providing data sources. Mediating tasks control the flow of data between view objects and model objects to minimize coupling between the subsystems, while keeping them synchronized.

Coordinating Controller Tasks

The first step in the implementation of MYShapeEditor's Controller subsystem is to tackle the coordinating tasks. Almost every MVC application must set up a view and initialize a model, and the Cocoa framework provides the NSDocument class for just that purpose. NSDocument declares the -windowNibName Template Method, which allows subclasses to identify an Interface Builder file containing the view objects to be loaded. The -dataOfType:error: and -readFromData:ofType:error: Template Methods support saving and loading model data. There are alternative, more sophisticated ways to use NSDocument, but those three methods are a good fit for this example.

Create a MYShapeEditorDocument subclass of NSDocument, provide a pointer to the array of shapes that will comprise the model, and override the necessary NSDocument methods. The following is just the starting point; it will be fleshed out as the example progresses:

```
@interface MYShapeEditorDocument : NSDocument
{
  NSArray              *shapesInOrderBackToFront; // The model
}

@property (readonly, copy) NSArray *shapesInOrderBackToFront;

@end
```

In the implementation of the MYShapeEditorDocument class, the shapesInOrderBackToFront property is redeclared as readwrite in a class extension also known as an *unnamed category* so that when the property is synthesized, a "set" Accessor method will be generated.

```
@interface MYShapeEditorDocument ()

@property (readwrite, copy) NSArray *shapesInOrderBackToFront;

@end
```

The following implementation of MYShapeEditorDocument takes care of the basic model and view creation:

```
@implementation MYShapeEditorDocument

@synthesize shapesInOrderBackToFront;
```

```
- (NSString *)windowNibName
{ // Identify the nib that contains archived View subsystem objects
  return @"MYShapeEditorDocument";
}


- (NSData *)dataOfType:(NSString *)typeName error:(NSError **)outError
{ // Provide data containing archived model objects for document save
  NSData    *result = [NSKeyedArchiver archivedDataWithRootObject:
      [self shapesInOrderBackToFront]];

  if ((nil == result) && (NULL != outError))
  { // Report failure to archive the model data
    *outError = [NSError errorWithDomain:NSOSStatusErrorDomain
        code:unimpErr userInfo:NULL];
  }

  return result;
}


- (BOOL)readFromData:(NSData *)data ofType:(NSString *)typeName
    error:(NSError **)outError
{ // Unarchive the model objects from the loaded data
  NSArray    *loadedShapes = [NSKeyedUnarchiver
      unarchiveObjectWithData:data];

  if(nil != loadedShapes)
  {
    [self setShapesInOrderBackToFront:loadedShapes];
  }
  else if ( NULL != outError)
  { // Report failure to unarchive the model from provided data
    *outError = [NSError errorWithDomain:NSOSStatusErrorDomain
        code:unimpErr userInfo:NULL];
  }

  return YES;
}

@end
```

The -dataOfType:error: method is called by NSDocument as an intermediate step in
the sequence of operations to save the document to a file. MYShapeEditorDocument
archives the model, an array of shapes, using the Archiving and Unarchiving pattern from

Chapter 11 and then returns the resulting NSData instance to be saved. The
-readFromData:ofType:error: method is called by NSDocument when a previously
saved document is loaded. MYShapeEditorDocument unarchives an array of shapes from
the provided data. The -windowNibName method returns the name of the Interface
Builder .nib file that contains an archive of the objects that compose the View subsystem.
NSDocument unarchives the user interface objects in the named .nib file so they can
be displayed on screen.

That's all it takes to specialize the inherited NSDocument behavior for loading the example's document interface and saving/loading the model. However, it's still necessary to
create an array to store shapes when a new empty document is created. It's also necessary
to clean up memory when documents are deallocated.

NSDocument's -windowControllerDidLoadNib: Template Method is automatically
called after all objects have been unarchived from the document's .nib file but before any
of the objects from the .nib are displayed. If no array of shapes has been created by the
time -windowControllerDidLoadNib: is called, the following implementation of
-windowControllerDidLoadNib: creates an empty array of shapes to use as the model:

```
- (void)windowControllerDidLoadNib:(NSWindowController *)aController
{
  [super windowControllerDidLoadNib:aController];

  if(nil == [self shapesInOrderBackToFront])
  { // Create an empty model if there is no other available
    [self setShapesInOrderBackToFront:[NSArray array]];
  }
}
```

MYShapeEditorDocument's -dealloc method sets the array of shapes to nil thus releasing the model when the document is deallocated.

```
- (void)dealloc
{
  [self setShapesInOrderBackToFront:nil];
  [super dealloc];
}
```

NSDocument is one of the most prominent controller classes in Cocoa. NSDocument
provides lots of features that aren't directly relevant to this example including management of the document window's title, access to undo and redo support, periodic
auto-save operations, printing, and other standard Cocoa features. NSDocument is
straightforward to use, and there are similar document classes in other object-oriented
user interface frameworks. NSDocument encapsulates most of the coordinating controller
features of any multidocument application and leverages Template Methods extensively
to enable customization.

Mediating Controller Tasks (Providing Information to Views)

Cocoa provides several mediating controller classes, and once you understand the roles they can play in your design, they're as easy to reuse as the NSDocument class. However, the reuse opportunities for mediator code aren't always readily apparent. For one thing, every application has a unique model and a different view, so how can the code that glues the different subsystems together be reused in other applications? To answer that question, the example implements specific mediator code to meet the application's requirements and then explores how that code is made reusable.

> Note
>
> The examples in this chapter progressively re-create Cocoa's NSArrayController class. The examples refactor MYShapeEditor's design to reveal why NSArrayController and other Cocoa mediating controllers exist. Follow the sequence of changes to MYShapeEditor to see how reusable mediating controllers work.

To get started and keep the design simple, implement all of the custom mediation code for MYShapeEditor's Controller subsystem right in the MYShapeEditorDocument class. Figure 29.2 illustrates the design.

Each MYShapeEditorDocument instance acts as the data source for an associated custom graphic view and the associated table view. MYEditorShapeView only has one data source method, -shapesInOrderBackToFront, and that's already provided by the @synthesize directive for MYShapeEditorDocument's shapesInOrderBackToFront property. The NSTableView class requires its data source to implement -numberOfRowsInTableView: and -tableView:objectValueForTableColumn:row:, so those methods are added to the implementation of MYShapeEditorDocument as follows:

```
- (int)numberOfRowsInTableView:(NSTableView *)aTableView
{
  return [[self shapesInOrderBackToFront] count];
}
```

```
- (id)tableView:(NSTableView *)aTableView
    objectValueForTableColumn:(NSTableColumn *)aTableColumn
    row:(int)rowIndex
{
  id shape = [[self shapesInOrderBackToFront] objectAtIndex:rowIndex];

  return [shape valueForKey:[aTableColumn identifier]];
}
```

To enable editing in the table view, MYShapeEditorDocument needs to implement the -tableView:setObjectValue:forTableColumn:row: method.

```
- (void)tableView:(NSTableView *)aTableView setObjectValue:(id)anObject
    forTableColumn:(NSTableColumn *)aTableColumn row:(NSInteger)rowIndex
```

```
{
    [self controllerDidBeginEditing];
    id shape = [[self shapesInOrderBackToFront] objectAtIndex:rowIndex];

    [shape setValue:anObject forKey:[aTableColumn identifier]];

    [self controllerDidEndEditing];
}
```

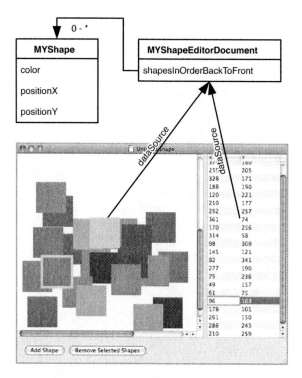

Figure 29.2   The initial design for the MYShapeDraw
application.

The -controllerDidBeginEditing and -controllerDidEndEditing methods
(shown in bold within the implementation of -tableView:setObjectValue:
forTableColumn:row:) are called before and after a shape is modified. Shapes are part of
the model. MYShapeEditorDocument consolidates the code for synchronizing the model,
the table view, and the custom view into just the -controllerDidBeginEditing and
-controllerDidEndEditing methods so that as long as those methods are called before
and after a change to the model, everything is kept updated.

The -controllerDidBeginEditing and -controllerDidEndEditing methods are declared in the following informal protocol, a category of the NSObject base class:

```
@interface NSObject (MYShapeEditorDocumentEditing)


- (void)controllerDidBeginEditing;
- (void)controllerDidEndEditing;


@end
```

The informal protocol means that MYShapeEditorDocumentEditing messages can safely be sent to any object descended from NSObject. Informal protocols are explained in Chapter 6.

MYShapeEditorDocument overrides its inherited -controllerDidEndEditing implementation with the following code:

```
- (void)controllerDidEndEditing
{
  [[self shapeGraphicView] setNeedsDisplay:YES];
  [[self shapeTableView] reloadData];
}
```

MYShapeEditorDocument's -controllerEndEditing method tells shapeGraphicView to redisplay itself at the next opportunity and tells shapeTableView to reload itself from its data source, which indirectly causes shapeTableView to redisplay itself, too. In order for -controllerEndEditing to work, Interface Builder outlets for shapeGraphicView and shapeTableView are needed. Therefore, the MYShapeEditorDocument class interface is updated to the following, and the connections to the outlets are made in Interface Builder to match Figure 29.3.

```
@interface MYShapeEditorDocument : NSDocument
{
  NSArray             *shapesInOrderBackToFront; // The model
  IBOutlet NSView      *shapeGraphicView;
  IBOutlet NSTableView *shapeTableView;
}

@property (readonly, copy) NSArray *shapesInOrderBackToFront;
@property (readwrite, retain) NSView *shapeGraphicView;
@property (readwrite, retain) NSTableView *shapeTableView;


@end
```

Add the corresponding @synthesize directives to the MYShapeEditorDocument implementation:

```
@synthesize shapeGraphicView;
@synthesize shapeTableView;
```

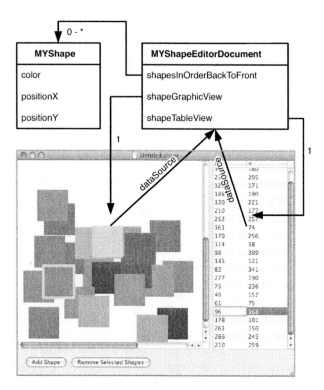

Figure 29.3   MYShapeEditorDocument outlets enable
update of the views.

At this point, the example has produced a bare-bones shape viewer application with
minimal shape editing support provided by the table view. The MYShapeEditor0 folder at
www.CocoaDesignPatterns.com contains an Xcode project with all of the code so far.
Build the project and run the resulting application. Use the application to open the
Sample.shape document provided at the same site. You can double-click the X and Y
coordinates displayed in the table view to reposition the shapes in the custom view.

Mediating Controller Tasks (Selection Management)

The next feature to add to the Controller subsystem is the ability to keep track of the selected shapes in each document. One question to ask is whether keeping track of the
selection is really a controller task at all, or should views perform that function? Storing
selection information in the controller enables designs like the one for MYShapeEditor in
which multiple views present information about the same model, and selection changes
made in one view are reflected in the other views. The Consequences section of this
chapter explains how storing selection information in the controller still makes sense even
when multiple views have independent selections. Add an instance variable to store the

indexes of the selected shapes and selection methods to produce the following
MYShapeEditorDocument interface:

```
@interface MYShapeEditorDocument : NSDocument
{
  NSArray              *shapesInOrderBackToFront;// The model
  IBOutlet NSView      *shapeGraphicView;
  IBOutlet NSTableView *shapeTableView;
  NSIndexSet           *selectionIndexes;        // selection
}

@property (readonly, copy) NSArray *shapesInOrderBackToFront;
@property (readwrite, nonatomic, retain) NSView *shapeGraphicView;
@property (readwrite, nonatomic, retain) NSTableView *shapeTableView;

// Selection Management
- (BOOL)setShapeSelectionIndexes:(NSIndexSet *)indexes;
- (NSIndexSet *)shapeSelectionIndexes;
- (BOOL)addShapeSelectionIndexes:(NSIndexSet *)indexes;
- (BOOL)removeShapeSelectionIndexes:(NSIndexSet *)indexes;
- (NSArray *)selectedShapes;

@end
```

The selectionIndexes variable uses an immutable NSIndexSet to efficiently identify
which shapes are selected. Each MYShape instance in a document can be uniquely identified by the shape's index (position) within the ordered shapesInOrderBackToFront array. If a shape is selected, add the index of the selected shape to selectionIndexes. To
deselect a shape, remove its index from selectionIndexes. To determine whether a
shape is selected, check for the shape's index in selectionIndexes. The selection management methods for the following MYShapeEditorDocument class are implemented as
follows:

```
// Selection Management
- (BOOL)setControllerSelectionIndexes:(NSIndexSet *)indexes
{
  [self controllerDidBeginEditing];
  [indexes retain];
  [selectionIndexes release];
  selectionIndexes = indexes;

  [self controllerDidEndEditing];

  return YES;
}
```

```
- (NSIndexSet *)controllerSelectionIndexes
{
  if(nil == selectionIndexes)
  { // Set initially empty selection
    [self setControllerSelectionIndexes:[NSIndexSet indexSet]];
  }

  return selectionIndexes;
}


- (BOOL)controllerAddSelectionIndexes:(NSIndexSet *)indexes
{
  NSMutableIndexSet  *newIndexSet =
      [[self controllerSelectionIndexes] mutableCopy];

  [newIndexSet addIndexes:indexes];
  [self setControllerSelectionIndexes:newIndexSet];

  return YES;
}


- (BOOL)controllerRemoveSelectionIndexes:(NSIndexSet *)indexes
{
  NSMutableIndexSet  *newIndexSet =
      [[self controllerSelectionIndexes] mutableCopy];

  [newIndexSet removeIndexes:indexes];
  [self setControllerSelectionIndexes:newIndexSet];

  return YES;
}


- (NSArray *)selectedObjects
{
  return [[self shapesInOrderBackToFront] objectsAtIndexes:
      [self controllerSelectionIndexes]];
}
```

All changes to the set of selection indexes are funneled through the
-setShapeSelectionIndexes: method, which calls [self controllerDidBeginEditing]
before updating the selection and [self controllerDidEndEditing] after the update.
As a result, changes to the selection cause refresh of both the custom view and the table
view. A selection change made from one view is automatically reflected in the other.

When the user changes the selection in the table view, NSTableView informs its
delegate and gives the delegate a chance to affect the change via the
-tableView:selectionIndexesForProposedSelection: method. In addition to acting
as the data source for the table view, each MYShapeEditorDocument instance also acts as
the delegate for its table view. The following MYShapeEditorDocument implementation of
-tableView:selectionIndexesForProposedSelection: keeps the controller's selection
up to date.

```
// NSTableView delegate methods
- (NSIndexSet *)tableView:(NSTableView *)tableView
    selectionIndexesForProposedSelection:
    (NSIndexSet *)proposedSelectionIndexes
{
  [self setControllerSelectionIndexes:proposedSelectionIndexes];

  return proposedSelectionIndexes;
}
```

Mediating Controller Tasks (Adding and Removing Model Objects)

Adding new shape instances to the model and later removing selected shapes are best performed by Action methods (see Chapter 17, "Outlets, Targets, and Actions"). Add the following two method declarations to the interface for the MYShapeEditorDocument class:

```
// Actions
- (IBAction)addShape:(id)sender;
- (IBAction)removeSelectedShapes:(id)sender;
```

The Action methods are called by buttons in the View subsystem. Implement the Action methods as follows:

```
- (IBAction)addShape:(id)sender;
{
  [self controllerDidBeginEditing];
  [self setShapesInOrderBackToFront:[shapesInOrderBackToFront
    arrayByAddingObject:[[[MYShape alloc] init] autorelease]]];

  [self controllerDidEndEditing];
}


- (IBAction)removeSelectedShapes:(id)sender;
{
  [self controllerDidBeginEditing];
  NSRange     allShapesRange = NSMakeRange(0,
    [[self shapesInOrderBackToFront] count]);
  NSMutableIndexSet  *indexesToKeep = [NSMutableIndexSet
    indexSetWithIndexesInRange:allShapesRange];
```

```
[indexesToKeep removeIndexes:[self controllerSelectionIndexes]];
[self setShapesInOrderBackToFront:[[self shapesInOrderBackToFront]
    objectsAtIndexes:indexesToKeep]];
[self setControllerSelectionIndexes:[NSIndexSet indexSet]];

[self controllerDidEndEditing];
}
```

The next step is to add graphical selection and editing of shapes to the application.

Extending the `MYShapeDraw` View Subsystem for Editing

Create a subclass of `MYShapeView` called `MYEditorShapeView` with the following declaration:

```
@interface MYEditorShapeView : MYShapeView
{
  NSPoint          dragStartPoint;
}

@end
```

The `dragStartPoint` instance variable is just an implementation detail that supports graphical dragging to reposition shapes with the mouse. The partial implementation of `MYEditorShapeView` that follows is provided to show how the custom view uses its data source to implement selection and editing features, but most of the details aren't important to the Controller subsystem:

```
@implementation MYEditorShapeView

// Overrides the inherited implementation to first draw the shapes and
// then draw any selection indications
- (void)drawRect:(NSRect)aRect
{
  [super drawRect:aRect];

  [NSBezierPath setDefaultLineWidth:MYSelectionIndicatorWidth];
  [[NSColor selectedControlColor] set];

  // Draw selection indication around each selected shape
  for(MYShape *currentShape in [[self dataSource] selectedShapes])
  {
    [NSBezierPath strokeRect:[currentShape frame]];
  }
}

// Select or deselect shapes when the mouse button is pressed.
// Standard management for multiple selection is provided.  A mouse
```

```
// down without modifier key deselects all previously selected shapes
// and selects the shape if any under the mouse.  If the Shift modifier
// is used and there is a shape under the mouse, toggle the selection
// of the shape under the mouse without affecting the selection status
// of other shapes.
- (void)mouseDown:(NSEvent *)anEvent
{
  NSPoint    location = [self convertPoint:[anEvent locationInWindow]
      fromView:nil];

  // Set the drag start location in case the event starts a drag
  // operation
  [self setDragStartPoint:location];

  // ... The rest of the implementation omitted for brevity ...
}


// Drag repositions any selected shapes
- (void)mouseDragged:(NSEvent *)anEvent
{
  [[self dataSource] controllerDidBeginEditing];
  NSPoint     location = [self convertPoint:
      [anEvent locationInWindow] fromView:nil];

  NSPoint     startPoint = [self dragStartPoint];
  float       deltaX = location.x - startPoint.x;
  float       deltaY = location.y - startPoint.y;

  for(MYShape *currentShape in [[self dataSource] selectedShapes])
  {
    [currentShape moveByDeltaX:deltaX deltaY:deltaY];
  }

  [self setDragStartPoint:location];
  [self autoscroll:anEvent];  // scroll to keep shapes in view

  [[self dataSource] controllerDidEndEditing];
}

@end
```

Controllers are responsible for keeping views and models up to date with each other but can't fulfill that role if the model is changed behind the controller's back. Therefore, views must inform the controller about changes made to the model. The two bold lines of code in the implementation of MYEditorShapeView's -mouseDragged: method notify the controller when model objects are modified directly by the view.

You can inspect the full implementation of MYEditorShapeView and the Interface Builder .nib files in the MYShapeEditor1 folder at www.CocoaDesignPatterns.com. Take a little time to explore MYShapeEditor1 application. In spite of the fact that it has taken quite a few pages to describe how it all works, there really isn't very much code. Play with the application.

Redesigning and Generalizing the Solution

MYShapeEditor1 meets all of the example's requirements with straightforward method implementations written from scratch. It might seem like the mediation "glue" code is unique to this example. However, it's pretty common for Model subsystems to store arrays of objects. Certainly, more complex models may use more complex data structures or contain many different arrays of objects, but a class that generalizes the approach used in this example to mediate between any array of arbitrary model objects and multiple views can be reused in a wide variety of applications. So the challenge now is to find and encapsulate the reusable parts of this example to provide that general solution.

Start by creating a new class to implement the general solution and call that class MYMediatingController. Then examine the current implementation of MYShapeEditorDocument and identify features to move to the new class. A general mediating controller must be able to add and remove model objects, so move the -add: and -remove: Action methods to the new class. Selection management is needed in the new class, so move the selectionIndexes instance variable from the MYShapeEditorDocument to the MYMediatingController class. Move all of the selection management methods like - controllerSetSelectionIndexes: and -controllerAddSelectionIndexes: to the new class. Finally, a mediator for an arbitrary array of model objects needs to provide access to that array. Add a method called -arrangedObjects that returns an NSArray pointer. The MYMediatingController declaration should look like the following:

```
@interface MYMediatingController : NSObject
{
  NSIndexSet          *selectionIndexes;        // The selection
}

// arranged content
- (NSArray *)arrangedObjects;

// Actions
- (IBAction)add:(id)sender;
- (IBAction)remove:(id)sender;

// Selection Management
- (BOOL)controllerSetSelectionIndexes:(NSIndexSet *)indexes;
```

```
- (NSIndexSet *)controllerSelectionIndexes;
- (BOOL)controllerAddSelectionIndexes:(NSIndexSet *)indexes;
- (BOOL)controllerRemoveSelectionIndexes:(NSIndexSet *)indexes;
- (NSArray *)selectedObjects;

@end
```

After the redesign, all that's left in the MYShapeEditorDocument interface is the following:

```
@interface MYShapeEditorDocument : NSDocument
{
  NSArray              *shapesInOrderBackToFront; // The model
  IBOutlet NSView      *shapeGraphicView;
  IBOutlet NSTableView *shapeTableView;
}

@property (readonly, copy) NSArray *shapesInOrderBackToFront;
@property (readwrite, retain) NSView *shapeGraphicView;
@property (readwrite, retain) NSTableView *shapeTableView;

@end
```

As the coordinating controller, MYShapeEditorDocument needs a way to configure the mediating controller. Add an outlet called mediatingController to the interface of MYShapeEditorDocument so that document instances can be connected to a mediating controller via Interface Builder. MYShapeEditorDocument also needs a way to be notified when the model is changed via the Controller subsystem, so add a -mediatingControllerDidDetectChange: method to MYShapeEditorDocument. The MYShapeEditorDocument class is now declared as follows:

```
@interface MYShapeEditorDocument : NSDocument
{
  NSArray              *shapesInOrderBackToFront; // The model
  IBOutlet NSView      *shapeGraphicView;
  IBOutlet NSTableView *shapeTableView;
  IBOutlet MYMediatingController *mediatingController;
}

@property (readonly, copy) NSArray *shapesInOrderBackToFront;
@property (readwrite, retain) NSView *shapeGraphicView;
@property (readwrite, retain) NSTableView *shapeTableView;
@property (readwrite, retain) MYMediatingController
    *mediatingController;

- (void)mediatingControllerDidDetectChange:
    (NSNotification *)aNotification;
```

@end

Implement MYShapeEditorDocument's -mediatingControllerDidDetectChange: to synchronize the custom shape view and the table view with the model:

```
- (void)mediatingControllerDidDetectChange:
    (NSNotification *)aNotification;
{
  [[self shapeGraphicView] setNeedsDisplay:YES];
  [[self shapeTableView] reloadData];
  [[self shapeTableView] selectRowIndexes:
      [[self mediatingController] controllerSelectionIndexes]
      byExtendingSelection:NO];
}
```

The MYShapeEditor2 folder at www.CocoaDesignPatterns.com contains an Xcode project with the redesign completed. There is an instance of MYMediatingController in the document .nib, and the dataSource outlets of view objects are connected to the mediating controller. The new design is illustrated in Figure 29.4.

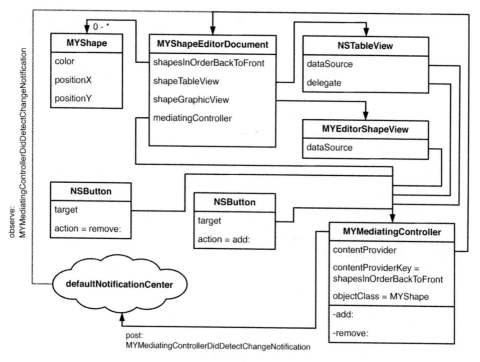

Figure 29.4   The new design of MYShapeEditor

The implementation MYMediatingController shouldn't have any dependencies on other classes in MYShapeEditor, or it won't be reusable in other applications. For example, when MYMediatingController adds new objects to the model, what kind of objects should it add? The class of added objects must be configurable at runtime to keep MYMediatingController general. MYMediatingController also needs a general way to get access to the array of model objects. Add the following instance variable declarations to MYMediatingController:

```
Class          objectClass;        // Class of model objects
IBOutlet id    contentProvider;    // Provider of model array
NSString       *contentProviderKey; // The array property name
```

At runtime, the contentProvider outlet is connected to whatever application-specific object provides the array of model objects. The contentProviderKey variable contains the name of the array property provided by contentProvider. Setting both the provider and the name of the provider's array property at runtime ensures maximum flexibility.

All that remains is to implement the MYMediatingController without any application-specific dependencies. The implementation of selection management and table view delegate methods are the same in MYMediatingController as they were in MYShapeEditorDocument. The rest of the code in MYMediatingController is similar to the code previously implemented in MYShapeEditorDocument, but the new code can be reused in any application. The following implementation of MYMediatingController shows the changes from MYShapeEditorDocument in bold but omits the implementations of methods that are identical in both classes to keep the listing short.

```
@implementation MYMediatingController


@synthesize objectClass;
@synthesize contentProvider;
@synthesize contentProviderKey;

- (void)dealloc
{
  [self controllerSetSelectionIndexes:nil];
  [self setContentProvider:nil];
  [self setContentProviderKey:nil];
  [super dealloc];
}


// arranged content
- (NSArray *)arrangedObjects
{
  return [[self contentProvider] valueForKey:
      [self contentProviderKey]];
}
```

```objc
// Actions
- (IBAction)add:(id)sender;
{
  [self controllerDidBeginEditing];
  NSArray *newContent = [[self arrangedObjects] arrayByAddingObject:
      [[[[self objectClass] alloc] init] autorelease]];

  [[self contentProvider] setValue:newContent forKey:
      [self contentProviderKey]];

  [self controllerDidEndEditing];
}


- (IBAction)remove:(id)sender;
{
  [self controllerDidBeginEditing];
  NSRange    allObjectsRange = NSMakeRange(0,
      [[self arrangedObjects] count]);
  NSMutableIndexSet *indexesToKeep =
      [NSMutableIndexSet indexSetWithIndexesInRange:allObjectsRange];

  [indexesToKeep removeIndexes:[self controllerSelectionIndexes]];
  NSArray *newContent = [[self arrangedObjects]
      objectsAtIndexes:indexesToKeep];

  [[self contentProvider] setValue:newContent forKey:
      [self contentProviderKey]];

  [self controllerSetSelectionIndexes:[NSIndexSet indexSet]];

  [self controllerDidEndEditing];
}


// Editing
- (void)controllerDidEndEditing
{
  [[NSNotificationCenter defaultCenter]
      postNotificationName:MYMediatingControllerContentDidChange
      object:self];
}
```

```
// NSTableView data source methods
- (int)numberOfRowsInTableView:(NSTableView *)aTableView
{
  return [[self arrangedObjects] count];
}


- (id)tableView:(NSTableView *)aTableView
    objectValueForTableColumn:(NSTableColumn *)aTableColumn
    row:(int)rowIndex
{
  id shape = [[self arrangedObjects] objectAtIndex:rowIndex];

  return [shape valueForKey:[aTableColumn identifier]];
}


- (void)tableView:(NSTableView *)aTableView setObjectValue:(id)anObject
    forTableColumn:(NSTableColumn *)aTableColumn row:(NSInteger)rowIndex
{
  [self controllerDidBeginEditing];
  id shape = [[self arrangedObjects] objectAtIndex:rowIndex];

  [shape setValue:anObject forKey:[aTableColumn identifier]];

  [self controllerDidEndEditing];
}

@end
```

Examples in Cocoa

Compare the MYMediatingController class developed in the "Solution" section of
this chapter to Cocoa's NSController and NSArrayController classes documented at
http://developer.apple.com/documentation/Cocoa/Reference/ApplicationKit/Classes/
NSArrayController_Class/Reference/Reference.html. The example in the Solution
section re-invents the NSArrayController class and reveals both why the
NSArrayController class exists and how it can be used in your applications.

NSArrayController mediates between arrays of model objects and your application's
view objects; it also keeps track of selection and provides methods to add and remove
model objects.

NSTreeController is similar to NSArrayController but enables you add, remove, and
manage model objects in a tree data structure. NSTreeController is used with
NSOutlineViews.

NSObjectController mediates between a single model object and your application's view objects. NSObjectController is the superclass of NSArrayController and NSTreeController. NSObjectController provides the concept of a single selected object.

NSUserDefaultsController encapsulates reusable code for mediating between user preferences (the User Defaults system) and your application's views.

Controllers and Bindings

Cocoa's NSArrayController class is more or less a drop-in replacement for the developed MYMediatingController class. However, NSArrayController uses a design that even further reduces the amount of application-specific code needed in MYShapeEditor. As shown in Figure 29.5, MYMediatingController posts a notification that's observed by MYShapeEditorDocument so that MYShapeEditorDocument can keep the views synchronized with the model. Cocoa provides a technology called "bindings" that provides an alternative technique for keeping objects synchronized.

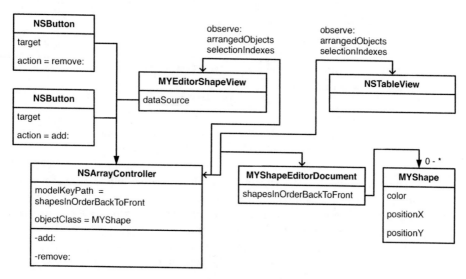

Figure 29.5   MYShapeEditor using NSArrayController

The MYShapeEditor3 folder at www.CocoaDesignPatterns.com implements the MYShapeEditor application with bindings and NSArrayController using the design shown in Figure 29.5. The MYShapeEditorDocument class is simplified in MYShapeEditor3 by removing all of the coordinating code previously used to synchronize views with the model. Bindings configured in Interface Builder replace that functionality.

Bindings are a large enough topic that they deserve their own chapter. Chapter 32, "Bindings and Controllers," describes the Bindings design pattern and its underlying implementation using lower level Cocoa design patterns.

Consequences

Cocoa's NSController subclasses mediate between models and views. The MYShapeEditor example in this chapter identifies some of code that the NSArrayController class replaces in typical applications, but even more controller code can be removed by using Cocoa's NSController subclasses together. Consider the common Master-Detail style of user interface. There is a master list of objects that can be inspected. When one of the objects is selected, details about the selected object are displayed. But what happens when the selected object is complex itself? The details for the selected object might include another list of subobjects used by the selected object. One convenient solution is to chain multiple NSArrayController instances together. The View that displays the selected object's list of subobjects might access the arranged objects of an array controller that that in turn accesses the selected object of another array controller, as shown in Figure 29.6.

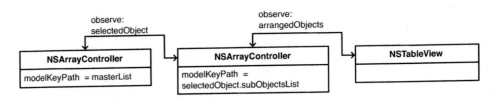

Figure 29.6   Mediating controllers are chained together to control complex relationships.

The pattern of chaining mediating controllers together highlights another reason that it is best to store selection information in the Controller subsystem instead of views. The MYShapeEditor example synchronizes selection between two views, but the example can be modified to enable separate selection in the two views simply by using two separate array controllers that both mediate access to the same array of model objects. The MYShapeEditor4 folder at www.CocoaDesignPatterns.com implements the separate selection design shown in Figure 29.7.

Cocoa's NSController subclasses reduce the amount of code needed to implement Controller subsystems and incorporate a very flexible design. Managing selection information within the Controller subsystem enables controller chaining and even a few other features that haven't been mentioned yet. For example, a button used to remove currently selected objects from the model should probably be disabled if there are no objects selected. NSArrayController already knows about the selection and even provides a canRemove property suitable for "binding" to a button's isEnabled property.

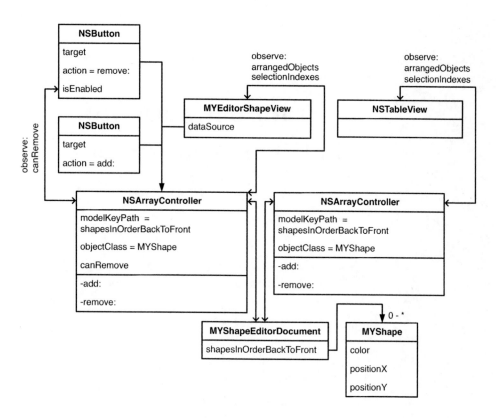

Figure 29.7   Separate NSArrayController instances enable separate selections in the same model.

V

Practical Tools for Pattern Application

This part shows practical applications of the Model View Controller design pattern with examples selected from the Cocoa frameworks.

Chapters in this part of the book include

30

Core Data Models

Core Data is an Apple framework that provides reusable objects to simplify Model sub-system design and development within the overarching Model View Controller pattern. Figure 30.1 shows how Core Data relates to the other prominent Cocoa frameworks.

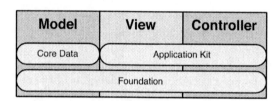

Figure 30.1   Core Data within the Model View
Controller pattern

Apple describes Core Data as "not an entry-level technology," but it's actually not particularly complex. Core Data is considered high level or advanced in part because it uses many lower level design patterns. Some programmers struggle to understand a high level framework like Core Data because the lower level patterns are unfamiliar. Other programmers struggle to understand the lower level patterns because they don't see the utility of the patterns until high-level uses are apparent.

This chapter explains the uses and collaborations between design patterns as they are employed by Core Data. There's no introductory tutorial for using Core Data in this book, but here are some other resources to gently introduce the framework and related tools:

- http://developer.apple.com/documentation/Cocoa/Conceptual/CoreData/ cdProgrammingGuide.html

- http://developer.apple.com/documentation/Cocoa/Conceptual/ NSPersistentDocumentTutorial/00_Introduction/chapter_1_1.html

- http://developer.apple.com/documentation/Cocoa/Conceptual/ CoreDataUtilityTutorial/00_Introduction/chapter_1_1.html

A quick Internet search reveals lots of tutorials available from Apple and third parties, but tutorials generally don't dig into the analysis of how and why a technology works the way it does. Tutorials focus on the basic goal of succinctly explaining how to accomplish tasks. This chapter provides the deeper analysis and explanation.

The Role of the Model Subsystem

Consider the role of the Model subsystem in a Model View Controller application. The model is composed of the objects that provide the unique capabilities and information storage for an application. Models contain the rules for processing application data. Models provide the in-memory representation of application data to be viewed, edited, or processed.

Models are also usually responsible for persistent storage of application data. The model must load or store data in some way. Common forms of persistent storage include files on a disk drive, client-server databases, and more recently, "cloud" computing where data is stored on an anonymous remote server and accessed using Universal Resource Locators (URLs).

Some models need to work with vast amounts of data, and it's not practical to keep all of the data in memory at once. In such cases, models sometimes include search features or filters to limit the amount of data in memory at one time.

Models contain the logic or rules for manipulating data. Some data may be calculated from other data using application-specific algorithms. Data may be constrained to specific types like "dates" or "positive integers." Data values may have defined minimums and maximums. Models provide data validation to ensure that constraints are met.

Models manage relationships between objects. For example, a model that stores information about books and publishers might contain the following rules: "each publisher has a list of zero or more books that have been published," "each book has zero or one identified publisher," and "whenever a book is added to a publisher's list of published books, the book's identified publisher must be set to correspond."

Core Data Terminology

Core Data uses objects to encapsulate data and the operations on the data. However, there isn't necessarily a one-to-one correspondence between the objects in your application and the data that's available. Core Data uses distinct terminology to differentiate between actual application objects and data modeling concepts used to define the available data.

> **Note**
> Core Data is a single-user desktop technology as implemented in Mac OS X 10.5, but it borrows terminology from the world of multiuser client-server database development. Core Data isn't a database, but the use of database terminology strongly suggests a way to map Core Data objects to relational databases. In fact, Core Data is eerily similar to an Apple

technology called Enterprise Objects Framework (EOF) that is used with massive client-server relational databases.

Entity

A Core Data Entity is an abstract description of available data. For example, a drawing program might use Shape entities and Style entities to store information about a drawing. Entities are like classes. They have an inheritance hierarchy. Subentities inherit the characteristics of their superentities just like subclasses inherit superclass characteristics. However, entities aren't necessarily implemented as separate Objective-C classes. By default, Core Data represents all entities at runtime using instances of the NSManagedObject class. You can override the default and use application-specific subclasses of NSManagedObject on a case by case basis.

Attributes

Each Entity defines associated data items called *Attributes*. For example, a Shape entity in a drawing application might have a floating point attribute to specify the shape's line width. Core Data validates attribute values based on constraints you specify. For example, you might constrain a Shape's line width to be greater than or equal to zero. You can also optionally specify an initial default value for each attribute. Some attributes are identified as *transient*, which means they aren't stored along with the other attributes of the entity. Use a transient attribute when the attribute can be calculated on demand from other attributes. For example, a Line entity might have a transient attribute called length that's calculated whenever needed.

Relationships

In addition to attributes, each Core Data entity may have "Relationships" to other entities. For example, each Shape entity might have a relationship to a Style entity that defines the line color and fill color of the shape. Relationships can be made optional or required. Core Data will recognize that an object is invalid if a required relationship has not been assigned. Relationships can be one-to-one or one-to-many. For example, each Shape has exactly one Style, but the same Style entity can be associated with any number of Shape entities. Therefore, the relationship between Style entities and Shape entities is a one-to-many relationship.

Relationships are a two-way street. If each Shape is related to a Style, then each Style must also be related to a Shape. In other words, each relationship has a corresponding reciprocal relationship. Core Data enforces reciprocal relationships. For example, setting the Style of a Shape automatically adds the Shape to the collection of Shapes that use that Style. As a result, you can identify at runtime all the Shapes that have the same Style.

Properties

The term *Properties* describes the collection of attributes and relationships for each Core Data entity. Attributes and relationships are validated differently within Core Data, but they're accessed the same way within your application code. The term Property is used instead of a term like "instance variable" because the underlying storage for properties isn't defined for Core Data entities. Properties may be stored in memory as instance variables or calculated on demand or fetched from persistent storage at the last moment when needed. The term property exists to explicitly inform you that you can't count on any underlying implementation. Figure 30.2 is a partial screen shot of Xcode's data modeling tool showing several entities and their properties. Diagrams produced in Xcode define Core Data models using notation similar to standard Unified Modeling Language (UML) Entity Relationship diagrams.

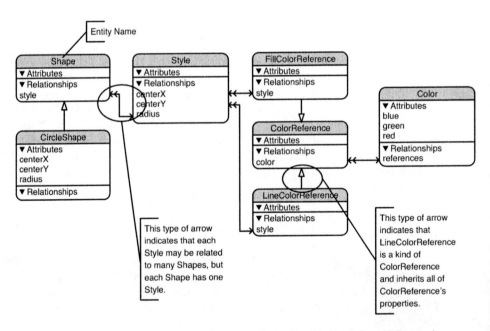

Figure 30.2   Core Data models are usually designed in Xcode's modeling tool.

Collaboration of Patterns Within Core Data

The extremely brief overview of Core Data terminology in this chapter can't prepare you for the actual task of designing a model with entities and properties. There's no substitute for working through some of the Core Data tutorials provided by Apple to get a feeling for how Core Data is used. The remainder of this chapter demystifies the technology by highlighting the practical application of design patterns within Core Data.

Figure 30.3 identifies the most prominent design patterns used in the implementation of Core Data.

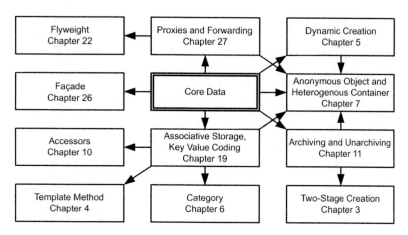

Figure 30.3   Primary Core Data pattern collaborations

NSManagedObject and NSEntityDescription

Instances of Core Data's NSManagedObject class are the objects used at runtime to store the properties defined for the entities in your model. Each NSManagedObject instance references an NSEntityDescription to find out at runtime what properties are available. As a result, each NSManagedObject instance is able to represent any kind of entity described by an NSEntityDescription instance. For example, an NSManagedObject instance might represent a Shape entity described by one NSEntityDescription instance, and another NSManagedObject instance might represent a Style entity described by a different NSEntityDescription instance. However, all NSManagedObject instances that represent Shape entities reference one NSEntityDescription instance that describes the properties of Shape entities. All NSManagedObject instances that represent Style entities reference one NSEntityDescription instance that describes Style entities. Figure 30.4 shows the relationships between three NSManagedObject instances that all represent Shapes and two NSManagedObject instances that represent Style as determined by NSEntityDescription instances.

NSManagedObject uses the Associative Storage pattern described in Chapter 19, "Associative Storage," to decouple access to properties from the underlying storage of properties. For example, when you attempt to access a property of an NSManagedObject instance at runtime, NSManagedObject checks to see whether the property being accessed is one of the properties available for the entity being represented. If the property is available, its value may have to be fetched from persistent storage. Core Data often postpones property fetches until necessary. After all, if certain properties are never accessed, why fetch them into memory at all?

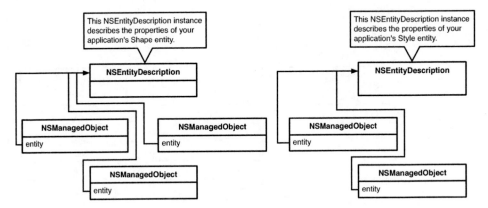

Figure 30.4   Relationships between `NSManagedObject` instances and `NSEntityDescription` instances

`NSManagedObject`'s specific implementation of Associative Storage is provided by Cocoa's Key Value Coding technology.

Another Look at Key Value Coding

Key Value Coding is implemented in Cocoa's Foundation framework as an "informal protocol." An informal protocol is a Category, described in Chapter 6, "Category," that adds methods to the `NSObject` base class so that all objects can be safely assumed to implement the methods. Key Value Coding is described in Chapter 19 and is principally implemented by the `-(id)valueForKey:(NSString *)aKey` and `-(id)setValue:(id)aValue forKey:(NSString *)aKey` methods added to `NSObject`. The default implementation provided by `NSObject` uses the specified string key to lookup an appropriate Accessor method. Accessor methods are explained in Chapter 10, "Accessors." For example, if the specified key is "lineWidth," the default implementation of `-valueForKey:` tries to find a method named "lineWidth" implemented by the receiver of the `valueForKey:` message. If such a method exists, it's called, and its return value is returned by `-valueForKey:`. If no such method exists, `-valueForKey:` looks for other similar methods and as a last resort will directly access any available instance variable named "lineWidth" or "_lineWidth." Finally, if the receiver can't supply a value for the specified key, `-valueForKey:` calls the Key Value Coding method `-valueForUndefinedKey:(NSString *)aKey`, and `NSObject`'s implementation of `-valueForUndefinedKey:` just raises an `NSUndefinedKeyException`.

NSObject's `-setValue:forKey:` method looks for an Accessor method of the form "set<aKey>:" such as `-setLineWidth:`. If necessary, `-setValue:forKey:` will access an appropriate instance variable directly. If there is no Accessor method and no instance variable for the specified key, then `-setValue:forUndefinedKey:` is called, and it raises an `NSUndefinedKeyException`.

> **Note**
>
> `-valueForKey:` and `-setValue:forKey:` make use of the Anonymous Type pattern as described in Chapter 7, "Anonymous Type and Heterogeneous Containers." Anonymous types enable the relatively simple implementation of Key Value Coding, which in turn provides the fundamental mechanism used to implement Core Data. Anonymous types let `NSManagedObject` instances represent any entity regardless of the number or types of attributes and relationships provided by the entity.

The `NSManagedObject` class overrides the `NSObject` implementation of `-valueForKey:` to consult with an `NSEntityDescription` and check whether the requested key corresponds to a property of the entity being represented. If so, `NSManagedObject` does whatever is necessary to obtain the corresponding property's value and return it. Similarly, `NSManagedObject` checks whether properties being set exist within the represented entity.

Accessing Relationships

Entity relationships are accessed via Key Value Coding the same way as attributes. If you access an `NSManagedObject` instance's relationship property, you will get different results depending on the way the relationship is defined by the associated `NSEntityDescription`. If the relationship is a "to-one" relationship, then the accessed value is simply another `NSManagedObject` instance that represents the related entity. If the relationship is "to-many," the accessed property is an instance of `NSSet` that contains a collection of objects corresponding to all of the related entities.

> **Note**
>
> `NSSet` is an unordered Heterogeneous Container described in Chapter 7 and in Apple's documentation at http://developer.apple.com/documentation/Cocoa/Reference/Foundation/Classes/NSSet_Class/Reference/Reference.html.

There are some subtleties to Core Data's implementation of relationships. Consider what happens when an `NSManagedObject` instance has a "to-many" relationship to thousands of other objects. For example, a "Publisher" entity has a "to-many" relationship to thousands of "Book" entities. It's usually not desirable for the Accessor method of a "to-many" relationship to automatically fetch thousands of objects representing all of the related Book entities from persistent storage. As an optimization, the `NSSet` returned from access to a "to-many" relationship usually contains Proxy objects called *faults*. Proxies are described Chapter 27, "Proxies and Forwarding." A proxy is a stand-in for another object, and the proxy only accesses the "real" object as a last resort. That way, if the code that uses a set of proxies only really uses a few objects out of the thousands in the set, only the few proxies ever fetch objects from persistent storage. The proxies themselves implement the Flyweight pattern described in Chapter 22, "Flyweight," and benefit from the memory and performance advantages provided by the Flyweight pattern.

The technique of delaying fetches from persistent storage until necessary is sometimes called faulting in Apple's documentation. Apple describes faulting at http://developer.apple.com/documentation/Cocoa/Conceptual/CoreData/Articles/cdFaultingUniquing.html.

Another key to relationship management is support for inverse relationships. Consider the following rules: "each publisher has a list of zero or more books that have been published," "each book has zero or one identified publisher," and "whenever a book is added to a publisher's list of published books, the book's identified publisher must be set to correspond." Core Data relationships almost always have established inverse relationships. For example, setting the identified publisher for a book automatically adds the book to the identified publisher's list of published books. When you change the identified publisher, Core Data will even take the book out of any other publisher's list of books. Similarly, just adding a book to a publisher's list of books automatically sets the book's identified publisher to match.

Subclassing `NSManagedObject`

When designing a Core Data model, you're able to specify application-specific subclasses of `NSManageObject` to represent each different type of entity if you want. If you specify a particular class for use with a particular entity type, the name of the class is stored in the corresponding `NSEntityDescription` for the entity type. Core Data applies the Dynamic Creation pattern introduced in Chapter 5, "Dynamic Creation," to create instances of the class identified in the `NSEntityDescription`. If you don't specify an `NSManagedObject` subclass for an entity type, Core Data just creates instances of `NSManagedObject` for new entities.

Create subclasses of `NSManagedObject` whenever you want to add application-specific logic to the objects that represent different entity types. For example, you can create a `MYShapeManagedObject` subclass of `NSManagedObject`, specify `MYShapeManagedObject` for use with the `NSEntityDescription` for Shape entities, and implement a `-draw` Template Method (Chapter 4, "Template Method") within `MYShapeManagedObject`. If you have Rectangle and Circle subentities of the Shape entity, you can specify `MYRectangleShapeManagedObject` and `MYCircleShapeManagedObject` subclasses of `MYShapeManagedObject` via the `NSEntityDescription` instances for Rectangle and Circle respectively. Each of your subclasses of `MYShapeManagedObject` can then override the `-draw` method to draw differently.

When you subclass `NSManagedObject` you have the ability to add custom behavior at important moments in the object's lifecycle. For example, to perform extra processing whenever a new instance of your `NSManagedObject` subclass is inserted into your model, override `NSManageObject`'s `-(void)awakeFromInsert` Template Method. The most typical use of `-awakeFromInsert` is to calculate and set default property values at runtime as follows:

```
- (void)awakeFromInsert
{
  [super awakeFromInsert];
  // Set dateInserted property to the current date and time
  [self setValue:[NSDate date] forKey:@"dateInserted"];
}
@end
```

The `-(void)awakeFromFetch` method is called whenever an `NSManagedObject` is fetched from persistent storage. Override `-awakeFromFetch` to establish new transient relationships based on the situation at runtime, but don't modify any pre-existing relation-ships within -awakeFromFetch. Core Data's built-in change validation is disabled while -awakeFromFetch is executing, and as a result, relationships modified within -awakeFromFetch are not being validated, and inverse relationships are not being automatically maintained.

> **Note**
>
> Recall that any time you override a Template Method, you need to know whether you can, should, or must call the inherited superclass implementation. In the cases of -awakeFromInsert and -awakeFromFetch, Apple documents that you must call the inher-ited superclass implementations. Also recall that the key to the Template Method pattern is the "don't call us; we'll call you" philosophy. Don't call -awakeFromInsert and -awakeFromFetch from your own code. The Core Data framework calls those methods at the appropriate times. You override the method implementations to customize Core Data operation at key moments.

Transient relationships and other calculated properties that are established in -awakeFromFetch can be cleaned up in -(void)willTurnIntoFault or -(void)didTurnIntoFault. Core Data calls -willTurnIntoFault when the framework has determined that the object is no longer needed in memory. Implement -willTurnIntoFault to clean up any complex properties such as user preferences or network connections. The -didTurnIntoFault method is called after all of the transient properties known to Core Data have already been cleared out of memory but before the corresponding NSManagedObject instance is actually deallocated or finalized.

Implementing Accessors in NSManagedObject Subclasses

There is usually no need to write custom Accessor methods for properties described by an NSManagedObject's NSManagedObjectDescription. NSManagedObject provides all of the needed logic within its implementations of -valueForKey: and -setValue:forKey:. As of Mac OS X 10.5, Core Data dynamically generates Accessor method implementa-tions at runtime for all entity properties so that the following three lines of code are interchangeable when using Objective-C 2.0:

```
[someObject valueForKey:@"title"];
someObject.title;
[someObject title];
```

Both [someObject valueForKey:@"title"] and someObject.title call [someObject title]. Setting properties also works three ways when using Objective-C 2.0, and the first two ways call the set accessor method:

```
[someObject setValue:@"Cocoa Design Patterns" forKey:@"title"];
someObject.title = @"Cocoa Design Patterns";
[someObject setTitle:@"Cocoa Design Patterns"];
```

As an alternative to runtime-generated accessor methods, you can use the version of Apple's Xcode tool provided with Mac OS X 10.5 to generate source code for correct accessor methods. If you use Xcode to generate code or if for some reason you provide handwritten custom accessor methods in your subclass of NSManagedObject, the compiled accessor methods supersede dynamically generated ones. Custom accessor methods must reimplement all of the logic that NSManagedObject would have dynamically generated. If you don't provide the essential logic, your NSManagedObject subclass will not work correctly with Core Data.

For simple property accessor methods, the essential logic is to call -willAccessValueForKey:, -didAccessValueForKey:, -willChangeValueForKey:, and -didChangeValueForKey: as shown in the following representative example:

```
- (NSString *)title
{
    [self willAccessValueForKey:@"title"];
    NSString *theTitle = [self primitiveTitle];
    [self didAccessValueForKey:@"title"];
    return theTitle;
}


- (void)setTitle:(NSString *)aTitle
{
    [self willChangeValueForKey:@"title"];
    [self setPrimitiveTitle:aTitle];
    [self didChangeValueForKey:@"title"];
}
```

The -willAccessValueForKey:, -didAccessValueForKey:, -willChangeValueForKey:, and -didChangeValueForKey: methods are part of a Cocoa technology called Key Value Observing. They inform NSManagedObject that properties are about to be accessed or have just been accessed. NSManagedObject uses the information to implement automatic undo and redo of changes and lets other interested objects know about accesses too. Key Value Observing is described in Chapter 32, "Bindings and Controllers."

Core Data accessor methods must call "primitive methods" to actually access or modify properties. The primitive methods, -primitiveTitle and -setPrimitiveTitle:, in the preceding example actually fetch properties from persistent storage if necessary. There are more details about Core Data primitive methods at http://developer.apple.com/documentation/Cocoa/Conceptual/CoreData/Articles/cdAccessorMethods.html. In general, throughout Cocoa, the term primitive method is used to describe the small number of methods with which other methods of a class are implemented. In the case of NSManagedObject, Core Data synthesizes/generates primitive accessor methods at runtime by inserting the words "primitive" or "setPrimitive" in the standard accessor method names and capitalizing letters to match Cocoa naming conventions. For example, -title becomes -primitiveTitle, and -setTitle: becomes -setPrimitiveTitle:.

If you need to use attributes of types that Core Data doesn't directly support, you can implement you own "primitive" methods to add support. There are several examples of custom Core Data primitive accessor methods at http://developer.apple.com/documentation/Cocoa/Conceptual/CoreData/Articles/cdZ104NSAttributes.html.

Designing Core Data Models

Apple's Xcode tool includes a graphical Core Data model development capability. The graphical tool is easy to use once you realize that all you are doing is graphically creating and configuring instances of NSEntityDescription. The graphical tool provides a more concise and self-documenting version of the code that you could write if you wanted. You specify the data types and relationships stored in the NSEntityDescriptions that compose your model. When you save your graphical model, the NSEntityDescription instances are archived to files. At runtime, the NSEntityDescription instances are unarchived into your running application. Archiving and Unarchiving are described in Chapter 11, "Archiving and Unarchiving." Just like with Interface Builder, graphical configuration, archiving, and unarchiving avoid the need to write hundreds or thousands of lines of usually repetitive and error-prone code.

Apple provides a tutorial that even includes short videos of the various steps needed to design Core Data models at http://developer.apple.com/cocoa/coredatatutorial/index.html.

All of the NSEntityDescription instances that compose a single model are stored in an instance of Core Data's NSManagedObjectModel class. Each instance of NSManagedObjectModel is a collection of related NSEntityDescription instances. NSManagedObjectModel provides the -(NSArray *)entities method to give you direct access to the entity descriptions if you want them. NSManagedObjectModel loads model descriptions previously saved from within Xcode. It's possible to instantiate NSManagedObjectModel and programmatically add NSEntityDescription instances, but that approach defeats many of the advantages of rapid Core Data application development. Once an NSManagedObjectModel instance is being used to actually access data, the NSManagedObjectModel instance can no longer be changed. Attempts to change an NSManagedObjectModel instance that's in use or any of that NSManagedObjectModel's NSEntityDescription instances generate an exception.

NSManagedObjectContext

An instance of NSManagedObjectContext encapsulates a NSManagedObjectModel and all of the currently existing NSManagedObject instances created from entity descriptions in the NSManagedObjectModel. NSManagedObjectContext is a mediating controller using the pattern explained in Chapter 29, "Controllers." Figure 30.5 illustrates the containment relationship between NSManagedObjectContext, NSManagedObjectModel, NSEntityDescription, and NSManagedObject instances. NSManagedObjectContext keeps the collection of managed objects internally consistent with the context's NSManagedObjectModel.

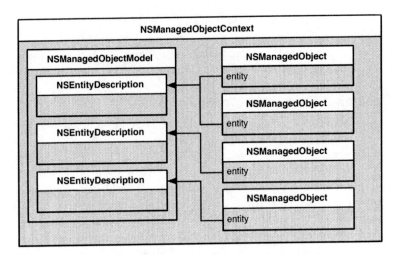

Figure 30.5   Runtime relationships between
NSManagedObjectContext, NSManagedObjectModel,
NSEntityDescription, and NSManagedObject instances

NSManagedObjectContext controls the lifecycle of NSManagedObject instances. It's actually the NSManagedObjectContext that fetches data from persistent storage as needed. NSManagedObjectContext observes changes to managed objects via the NSManagedObject -willChangeValueForKey:, and -didChangeValueForKey: methods described earlier in this chapter. In response to changes, NSManagedObjectContext consults the NSManagedObjectModel to automatically establish, validate, and control reciprocal relationships between objects. NSManagedObjectContext also provides automatic undo and redo.

NSManagedObject isn't very useful outside of an NSManagedObjectContext. Newly created and newly fetched managed objects are therefore always added to an NSManagedObjectContext. Existing managed objects can also be deleted from an NSManagedObjectContext.

NSManagedObjectContext provides one of the keys to the efficiency of Core Data. Changes made within a context only affect the in-memory representation of model data. Changes made in a managed context must be committed to become permanent in the underlying persistent storage.

NSPersistentStoreCoordinator and NSPersistentStore

The last major pieces of the Core Data framework are the NSPersistentStoreCoordinator and NSPersistentStore classes. Core Data supports three basic persistent storage formats: SQLite relational database, binary flat file, and Extensible Markup Language (XML) flat file. NSPersistentStore is an abstract base class that defines methods for reading and writing from the supported persistent file formats. NSPersistentStoreCoordinator is a controller that mediates between your model objects and one or more `NSPersistentStore` instances. `NSPersistentStoreCoordinator` makes it possible to support multiple persistent storage formats simultaneously. For example, you can load your model from an XML file and save it to an SQLite database without any effect on the model itself. `NSPersistentStoreCoordinator` decouples the model from the storage.

`NSPersistentStoreCoordinator` implements the Facade pattern defined in Chapter 26, "Façade." `NSPersistentStoreCoordinator` provides a simple interface that encapsulates potentially complex interactions between multiple storage types and locations. `NSPersistentStoreCoordinator` accesses multiple persistent stores in a way that makes the number and type of stores irrelevant to other parts of your application.

Each `NSManagedObjectContext` needs an `NSPersistentStoreCoordinator` to be able to fetch data or commit changes to data. However, the relationship doesn't need to be one-to-one. You can use a single `NSPersistentStoreCoordinator` with multiple `NSManagedObjectContexts`. For example, your application might provide two views of the same underlying data. One view shows the uncommitted in-memory state of model data as defined by one `NSManagedObjectContext`, while the other view shows the persistent storage state of the same model data as defined by a different `NSManagedObjectContext`. Both managed object contexts fetch data from the same persistent storage, but in-memory changes made in one context have no effect on other context.

Core Data Limitations and Benefits

The most significant limitation of Core Data is that it stores your model data in undocumented formats even when using the XML persistent storage type. Apple presumably keeps the storage formats undocumented to preserve the ability to change formats at some future date. After all, you aren't supposed to need to know details like low-level data format because that's all encapsulated by the reusable framework. However, there may be legitimate reasons why data formats on disk must be fully specified. For example, you may have data retention requirements that mandate the ability to read and process your data via multiple computer systems or decades later when Apple may no longer support Core Data. Core Data is not well-suited when existing data standards or file formats are required. It is not feasible to coerce Core Data to use most standard storage formats.

Another limitation of Core Data is weak support for data translation between model versions. It's generally safe to add entirely new entity descriptions to a pre-existing model. If you only add information, Core Data will likely be able to continue reading data saved with previous model versions. However, if you change your model by modifying existing entity descriptions, you will have to write code to load data stored via the previous model versions into applications that use the new model version. Unfortunately, there is little or no framework support for translating data between model versions.

The most significant benefit of using Core Data is access to the built-in fast, flexible, and efficient data management. Using Core Data has the potential to dramatically reduce the amount of code you write to implement Model subsystems. Core Data also provides straightforward and almost automatic integration with Mac OS X's Spotlight search technology. Finally, Core Data is implemented using modern Cocoa technology like Key Value Coding and Key Value Observing, which support rapid application development.

If you want to rapidly build full-featured Cocoa applications that include complex Model subsystems and support for moderately large amounts of data, Core Data is the right technology. However, you may still need to write code to import and export your data if pre-existing or standard data formats are required—and be very careful when changing your data model to avoid introducing incompatibilities with data stored using prior model versions.

31

Application Kit Views

The Application Kit contains most of the classes that provide user interfaces and graphics for Cocoa applications. This chapter focuses on the key patterns employed the Application Kit. Effective use of the Application Kit often requires the interaction of multiple classes and design patterns. Figure 31.1 shows the relationship of the Application Kit to Cocoa's overarching Model View Controller pattern.

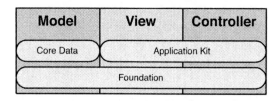

Figure 31.1   The Application Kit within the Model
View Controller pattern

The Application Kit is large and relatively complex, but its organization and use of design patterns keeps it manageable. Within Cocoa, the Application Kit is the oldest subframework. Some of the design patterns described in this book were first recognized by scholars who studied the Application Kit and then later adopted by other frameworks for other platforms. Almost all of the design patterns in this book are used in one way or another by the Application Kit. This chapter briefly explains how the Application Kit uses many of the patterns. An understanding of the interactions between multiple patterns clarifies how the Application Kit works and how patterns are applied in practice.

The Role of the View Subsystem

Within the Model View Controller pattern, the View subsystem presents information and enables user interaction with the information. The View provides the look (appearance) and feel (user interaction) for an application. Cocoa's Application Kit includes default implementations that satisfy almost all standard Mac OS X look and feel expectations including menus, windows, undo and redo, text editing, spell checking, help, standard controls, and more. Frequent developer reuse of default implementations contributes to the Mac's famous consistency and ease of use. Cocoa developers generally have to perform extra work to circumvent the standard look and feel.

Users bring certain expectations when interacting with graphical applications. For example, they understand the concept of a current selection or "focused" user interface component. Menu items affect the current selection. The "focused" user interface component will respond to text typed by the user. Standard Mac OS X's look and feel and user expectations are described in Apple's Human Interface Guidelines (HIG) which are available at http://developer.apple.com/documentation/UserExperience/Conceptual/AppleHIGuidelines/XHIGIntro/chapter_1_1.html. Mac developers need to pay attention to the HIG, but for the most part, HIG-compliance comes "for free" just by using the Application Kit.

Collaboration of Patterns Within Application Kit

Figure 31.2 identifies the key patterns used in the implementation of the Application Kit.

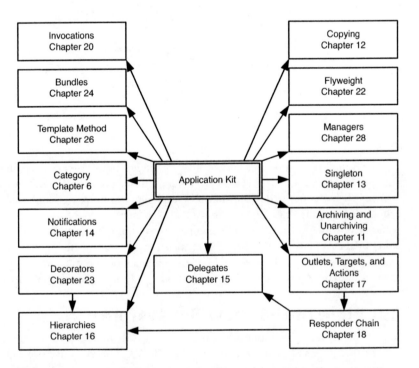

Figure 31.2   Key design patterns used to implement the Application Kit

NSApplication, Events, and the Run Loop

Most graphical user interface toolkits, including the Application Kit, use an event-driven model. That simply means applications react to events that are sent to the application by the operating system. Some events originate from user keyboard or mouse input. Timer events may arrive at periodic intervals. Other input sources like network sockets or inter-thread message queues may produce events.

Cocoa applications receive events from the operating system with the help of the NSApplication and NSRunLoop classes. Every graphical Cocoa application contains one instance of the NSApplication class. NSApplication is a singleton, as described in Chapter 13, "Singleton." The NSApplication instance creates an instance of NSRunLoop to receive events from the operating system. Multithreaded Cocoa application may use up to one NSRunLoop instance per thread.

Run loops monitor input sources that are part of the operating system and block if no input is available. That just means that when there is no input available, the run loop doesn't consume CPU resources. Many other user interface toolkits make the run loop a key focus for developers, but in Cocoa, the run loop plays only a small but crucial role. When input data becomes available, the run loop translates the data into events and sends Objective-C messages to various objects to process the events.

In most cases, Cocoa programmers don't need to access run loops directly because NSApplication takes care of all the details. The Application Kit uses the Hierarchies pattern and the Responder Chain pattern described in Chapters 16, "Hierarchies," and 18, "Responder Chain," respectively. NSApplication uses the hierarchy of objects within your application and the resulting Responder Chain to determine which objects should receive which messages in response to events.

The NSApplication class is seldom subclassed. Instead, the behavior of an application can be modified through the use of an application delegate and notifications. Notification and Delegation are powerful patterns described in Chapters 14, "Notifications," and 15, "Delegates," respectively.

Responders

When keyboard events, mouse events, timer events, or other events are detected by the run loop and the NSApplication instance that manages the run loop, those events are converted into instances of the NSEvent class and dispatched to other objects using Objective-C messages. The use of messaging is an important difference from other user interface toolkits and results in much of the power and flexibility of Cocoa. The Application Kit does not use C-language switch statements or explicit tables of function pointers. The messaging capabilities built into the Objective-C runtime are ideally suited to user interface event dispatching.

Cocoa includes the NSResponder class, which provides basic event handling methods. NSResponder is an abstract class, which means it's not intended for direct use by application programmers. Instead, abstract classes provide functionality that is used by subclasses. Some of the most prominent Cocoa subclasses of NSResponder are NSView, NSWindow, and NSApplication. These subclasses collaborate to manage the flow of events within an application.

The collaboration between the various subclasses of NSResponder within a Cocoa application is so powerful that many applications can be written without any custom event handling code at all. The event processing within the Application Kit framework takes care of almost all events automatically. When application-specific, custom–event handling is needed, one or more of NSResponder's event-processing Template Methods can be overridden in a subclass, as explained in Chapter 4, "Template Method." For example, to perform processing in response to a mouse button-press event, override NSResponder's -(void)mouseDown:(NSEvent *)theEvent template method.

Each of NSResponder's event processing methods accepts a single argument, which is an instance of the NSEvent class. Within the event processing methods, the NSEvent instance can be interrogated to obtain more information about the event such as the location of the mouse or which modifier keys were pressed. The NSEvent class documentation describes the information obtainable. The NSResponder class documentation identifies the event processing methods that you may want to override in subclasses.

The NSEvent passed to each event-processing method is only valid until the next event. NSEvent is implemented using the Flyweight pattern from Chapter 22, "Flyweight." The Cocoa frameworks sometimes reuse existing NSEvent instances. To preserve the information in an NSEvent instance, copy it or store the information in a separate data structure. Simply storing and retaining a pointer to the Application Kit provided NSEvent instance for later use is not sufficient. NSEvent conforms to the NSCopying protocol and can be copied using the approach described in Chapter 12, "Copying."

The Responder Chain

Each instance of the NSResponder class stores a pointer to another instance of NSResponder called the *next responder*. NSResponder provides Accessor methods for setting and getting the next responder. Responders are chained together from next responder to next responder and collectively form a data structure called the Responder Chain. If an instance of NSResponder doesn't process a message that it receives, the message can be passed on to the next responder. The message travels along the chain until the message is either processed or there is no next responder. Details about the Responder Chain are presented in Chapter 18.

The Responder Chain plays a crucial role in applications that use the Application Kit. Many powerful features such as automatic menu validation, context-sensitive menus, text entry, and automatic spell checking depend on the Responder Chain. The Responder Chain also provides opportunities for programmers to insert context-sensitive custom logic and event handling into applications.

Whichever object gets the first chance to respond to an event message is called the *first responder*. The first responder is the first link in the Responder Chain. Interface Builder provides an icon that represents the first responder so that you can make graphical connections and specify application messages that should be sent via the Responder Chain.

One of the keys to using this is understanding which responder will be the first responder in different circumstances.

The Responder Chain and the first responder are managed by three NSResponder subclasses: NSApplication, NSWindow, and NSView. An instance of the NSApplication class receives events from the operating system. The events are either sent on to a window represented by an NSWindow instance or consumed by the application object itself. Every window in an application stores a pointer to the window's first responder. The first responder for a window can change based on user actions or program code. The initial first responder in each window can be set in Interface Builder or through an NSWindow instance method.

Sometimes the first responder for a window is the window itself. When a window receives an event from the application object, the event is either forwarded to a responder within the window or consumed by the window. The responders within a window are typically instances of NSView subclasses.

The first responder to receive an event message depends on the application object, the window that is most appropriate for the event, and a responder (view) within the window. Chapter 18 details the event message processing sequence within windows and between windows. In some cases, the delegates of each window in the Responder Chain are automatically included in the Responder Chain. Similarly, the NSApplication object's delegate is sometimes automatically part of the Responder Chain.

NSWindow **Overview**

The NSWindow class is a subclass of NSResponder and extends the capabilities of responders to provide an area of the display for drawing. In Cocoa applications, every window onscreen is an instance of the NSWindow class or one of its subclasses such as NSPanel. A window is needed to display graphical output from an application. Windows have a position and size on screen. Following Mac OS X's standard Quartz graphics conventions, each window's position is defined by the screen coordinates of the window's lower-left corner. The window's size is the width and height of the window in screen coordinates.

Windows are composed of three major parts: an optional title bar, optional resize control, and the content view. The title bar and resize control are standard Decorators as described in Chapter 23, "Decorators." The title bar optionally contains a title and controls to minimize, fit content, or close the window. NSWindow instances automatically manage these controls in accordance with Apple's HIG. The resize control is also managed by the window itself. The content view is the portion of a window that contains your application's unique interface and is controlled by your application's code.

Each window takes advantage of the NSApplication singleton's connection to the operating system to draw onscreen. The pixels drawn by a window are stored in memory that can be shared by the operating system and the window. Because the operating system has direct access to the pixel memory, the operating system can move and uncover windows without intervention by the application that owns the window. For example, a window can be dragged while the application that owns it is busy performing other computations. The shared memory is also used by the operating system to implement transparency effects, shadows, and other Quartz graphics features.

The NSApplication class manages all the windows in an application. In addition to a list of all the application's windows, NSApplication keeps track of which window, if any, is the *key* window and which is the *main* window. The key window and the main window are the windows in which the user is currently working. The key window receives keyboard events. The main window is the window that is affected by actions in the key window. The key window and the main window are usually the same, but in some cases they might be different.

The key window and main window have darker gray title bars with deeper shadows, and all other windows have light gray title bars with smaller shadows. The key window is the only window to which keyboard events are sent. Windows become the key window and main window automatically as the result of the user actions. If the main window and key window are different, the main window becomes key if the current key window is closed or minimized. In most cases, the user can make a window become the key window by clicking the mouse within the window.

Application developers can prevent a window from becoming the key window by subclassing NSWindow and overriding NSWindow's - (BOOL) canBecomeKeyWindow method to always return NO. However, NSWindow is seldom subclassed for this purpose because the NSPanel class already provides the desired behavior when configured as a "utility" window in Interface Builder. A window can also be made the key or main window by calling NSWindow's - (void) makeKeyWindow or - (void) makeMainWindow methods, respectively. The - (void) makeKeyAndOrderFront: (id) sender method is available to make a window the front-most or top-most window and also the key window in one operation.

Windows in the Responder Chain

NSWindow is a subclass of NSResponder and can be part of a Responder Chain. The role that a window plays in the Responder Chain depends on the state of the application that owns the window. Windows are also integral to event distribution. Most events received by the application are sent on to a window. NSApplication selects the window to receive an event based on the type of the event.

Mouse events inside a window but outside the window's content view are handled automatically by the window. No programmer intervention is required to resize windows or manage the controls in the window's title bar. The NSWindow class handles all those details automatically and sends notifications and/or delegate messages to let other application objects intervene by constraining the window's size or saving the contents of the window before the window closes.

Mouse-down and mouse-move events are sent from the application object to the top-most window under the mouse pointer. The NSWindow class then distributes received mouse events to a responder within the window or consumes the events itself. Mouse-up and mouse-drag events are always sent to the object that received the corresponding mouse-down event even if the mouse has been moved outside the window. Keyboard events are always sent to the first responder in the key window.

NSView **Overview**

The NSView class extends the event-handling capabilities of NSResponder to add drawing and printing capabilities. NSView is an abstract class meaning that instances of NSView are seldom used directly. Instead, many subclasses of NSView exist to implement particular combinations of event handling and drawing behavior. Almost everything drawn in a Cocoa application is drawn by a subclass of NSView. For example, buttons, text fields, sliders, and even the backgrounds of windows are directly or indirectly subclasses of NSView. The most prominent subclasses of NSView include NSControl, NSTextView, NSTabView, NSSplitView, NSScrollView, and NSBox.

The NSView class cannot draw without the help of a graphics context, and that context is usually provided by a window. When a view is drawn, it writes the data for pixel colors into memory. A window's context provides the memory that stores the pixel data. NSWindow and NSView cooperate to implement user interfaces. Every NSWindow instance has at least one associated NSView instance, the content view. The content view is used to draw the content of the window.

View Hierarchy

NSView instances exist in a tree data structure also known as a hierarchy. A view can contain any number of subviews. NSView instances are normally added to a window by making each view a subview of the window's content view. Each view has a reference to the view that contains it. The containing view is called the superview. Complex user interfaces are composed of many views arranged in a hierarchy of superviews and subviews.

Subviews are always drawn after their superview, resulting in subviews always appearing on top of their superview graphically. Views graphically clip their subviews so that no part of a subview can be drawn outside its superview. The order in which views with the same superview are drawn was not defined in Mac OS X prior to version 10.5. So-called sibling views should not be overlapped in early versions of Mac OS X because undefined drawing order might produce incorrect display.

Each view can have its own coordinate system. By default, a window's content view has its origin in the lower-left corner and has a width and height equal to the width and height of the window's content area in pixels. The positive-X axis is to the right, and the positive-Y axis is up. Views store two rectangles to define both the area of the view in its superview's coordinate system and the area of the view in its own coordinate system. The area of a view in its superview coordinate system is called its *frame*. The same area stored in the view's coordinate system is called the *bounds*. The view's frame, its bounds, and a transformation matrix define the coordinate system used by a view. The coordinate systems used by views are described in detail at http://developer.apple.com/documentation/Cocoa/Conceptual/CocoaViewsGuide/Coordinates/chapter_3_3.html.

Note

Apple's Core Animation framework provides a "Layer-Tree" hierarchy that is very similar to the view hierarchy. The Layer-Tree is described at http://developer.apple.com/documentation/Cocoa/Conceptual/CoreAnimation_guide/Articles/LayerTreeHierarchy.html. Core Animation is a framework for developing Open GL-based high performance 2D graphical animations and special effects. The Layer-Tree reuses many of the patterns applied within the Application Kit and achieves many of the same goals. Complex animation "layers" are composed of multiple simpler layers. Each layer defines its own graphical coordinate system relative to its parent layer. And layers can be used as decorators that are added, removed, and rearranged dynamically at run time.

Because `NSView` is a subclass of `NSResponder`, `NSView` instances participate in the Responder Chain. Most responders in an application are actually subclasses of `NSView`. The next responder of a view is usually the view's superview. Arbitrary responders can be added to the Responder Chain by calling `NSResponder`'s `- (void) setNextResponder:(NSResponder *)theResponder` method, and that technique can be used to insert responders in the Responder Chain between a view and its superview. If an event-processing message is sent to a view that doesn't handle the message, the message is sent to the view's next responder, and its next, and so on until the window's content view, the ultimate superview of all views in a window, receives the message.

The first view to receive an event-processing message depends on the type of the event. The first mouse-down event within a window that is not the key window is usually consumed by the window itself to make the window into the key window and bring it to the front. This behavior can be modified in several ways. For example, a subclass of `NSView` can override the `- (BOOL) acceptsFirstMouse:(NSEvent *)theEvent` method to return YES based on the mouse event. Returning YES means that the view is able to use the first mouse click in an inactive window.

`NSWindow` sends mouse-down and mouse-move event messages to the top-most view under the mouse. Subviews are drawn after their superview. The top-most view under the mouse is therefore usually the most deeply nested view under the mouse. Mouse-move events occur frequently and are seldom used. `NSWindow` does not send mouse move event messages to views by default. If a subclass of `NSView` needs to receive mouse-move events, it must tell `NSWindow` to send them. `NSWindow`'s `- (void) setAcceptsMouseMovedEvents:(BOOL) acceptMouseMovedEvents` method is used to tell the window to send mouse-move event messages to views. Mouse-drag and mouse-up event messages are sent to the view that received the corresponding mouse-down event. Keyboard event messages are sent to the first responder within the window. The `NSView` class implements the `- (BOOL) acceptsFirstResponder` method to always return NO. As a result, most views never become the first responder within a window.

Subclasses of `NSView` that implement text processing such as `NSTextView` override the `- acceptsFirstResponder` template method to return YES. If a view accepts becoming the first responder, the first mouse-down event within the view automatically makes that view the first responder unless the current first responder refuses to resign its status. The rules for changing the first responder are explained in http://developer.apple.com/documentation/ Cocoa/Conceptual/EventOverview/EventHandlingBasics/chapter_4_6.html.

Targets and Actions

Some of the most powerful features of the Application Kit are provided by the Target and Action pattern described in Chapter 17, "Outlets, Targets, and Actions." Objective-C messages that have one object argument are called *actions*. The one argument is usually the sender of the action message. A *target* is an object that can receive action messages. Targets and actions are defined programmatically or in Interface Builder. The Target and Action pattern is a key mechanism with which user interface elements respond to user actions. The Target and Action pattern is implemented with four parts, the NSApplication class, the Responder Chain, the NSControl class, and the NSActionCell class. NSApplication and the Responder Chain have already been introduced in this chapter. NSControl is a subclass of NSView that adds support for the Target and Action pattern. NSActionCell is a subclass of the NSCell Flyweight and adds support for the Target and Action pattern. Almost all user interface elements such as menu items, buttons, and text fields are implemented as subclasses of either NSControl or NSActionCell. For example, buttons in a user interface are represented by instances of the NSButton class, which is a subclass of NSControl, which in turn is a subclass of NSView.

When a user presses a button, the button sends its action message to its target object. Because both the target and action are variables, button instances can be very flexibly configured. For example, a button can be configured to send the - (void) selectAll: (id) sender action message to a target object that displays editable text. Another button might be configured to send the - (void) deleteSelectedText: (id) sender action message to the same text object target.

One of the strengths of the Target and Action pattern is that actions are sent as Objective-C messages using the standard Objective-C messaging system. Other user interface toolkits use integer event IDs along with large switch statements or tables of function pointers. Some other toolkits use specialized "command" classes that must be subclassed for each different command and receiver combination. The Objective-C runtime eliminates the need for extra code and tables. Even more importantly, the Target and Action pattern used by the Application Kit takes advantage of the Responder Chain to enable a tremendous amount of flexibility.

When a user interacts with a user interface element that is derived from the NSControl class or the NSActionCell class, the user interface element asks the shared NSApplication object to send an action to a target by calling NSApplication's - (BOOL) sendAction: (SEL) anAction to: (id) aTarget from: (id) sender method. When an action is sent using -sendAction:to:from:, the to: argument is the target of the action, and the from: argument is the object that is sending the action. The -sendAction:to:from: method sends the action message to the target, passing the sender as the argument. The target of an action message can use the sender argument to obtain additional information. For example, when the user moves a slider, the slider sends an action message to its target with the slider itself as the argument. The receiver of the action message can ask the sender for more information such as the current value of the slider.

The role of the shared `NSApplication` object in the target-action implementation is important. If the target of a user interface element is specified, the shared application object just sends the action message to the target directly. However, if no target is specified (the `to:` argument is nil), `-sendAction:to:from:` uses the Responder Chain to select the object that receives the action message. Setting the target of a user interface element to `nil` makes the target context-sensitive.

If the `to:` argument to `-sendAction:to:from:` is nil, `NSApplication` searches the Responder Chain for an object that can respond to the action message. The search begins with the first responder in the key window. If the first responder can't respond to the action message, the next responder is checked and so on until the key window itself is reached. After the key window gets a chance, the key window's delegate is checked. If the key window's delegate can't respond to the action message, and the main window is different from the key window, the first responder in the main window is checked. The search for an object that responds to the action continues up the main window's Responder Chain to the main window itself and then the main window's delegate. If no target has been found, the application object is tried. Finally, if the application object can't respond to the action, the application object's delegate is given a chance.

> **Note**
> When the target of a user interface element is set to the First Responder in Interface Builder, the target is actually set to `nil` so that the expanded Responder Chain is used to select the target at runtime.

The Responder Chain enables flexible, dynamic message processing that is context-sensitive in conjunction with the Target and Action pattern. For example, the target of a `-(void)copy:(id)sender` action sent from a menu item depends on the current first responder. If the first responder in the key window is an editable text object with selected text, pressing the Copy menu item places the selected text on the application's pasteboard. If the first responder has selected graphics, the graphics are placed on the pasteboard. The result of pressing the Copy menu item depends on the user's current selection identified by the first responder.

> **Note**
> When Cocoa's document architecture including the `NSDocument` class is used, the `NSDocument` instance and the document's delegate are automatically added to the Responder Chain for action messages.

Archived Objects and Nibs

Chapter 11, "Archiving and Unarchiving," explains the Archiving and Unarchiving pattern. Most Application Kit objects can be archived and unarchived. Archiving and unarchiving are frequently used to implement copy-and paste-operations, drag-and-drop operations, and distributed object messaging. When interconnected objects are encoded as data into a block of memory or a file, the data is called an archive. User interface elements and their interconnections can be stored in just such an archive.

The objects stored in an archive are conceptually freeze-dried. Each freeze-dried object was running in memory at one time but is now in cold storage. It can be unarchived and revived so that it begins running right where it left off at the time it was frozen. In fact, when a user interface is designed in Interface Builder, the file that is saved is an archive of freeze-dried objects. Interface Builder names files that contain such archives with the extension `.nib`. Nib originally stood for NeXT Interface Builder, but the term has become generic and now just refers to an archive of user interface objects. When an application loads a `.nib` file, the objects are unarchived to the same state they where in when archived.

Most object-oriented environments include a visual tool for laying out user interfaces. Such tools usually generate code and resources that must be edited and compiled. Cocoa's Interface Builder generates freeze-dried objects instead of code. This is an important distinction. Generating code is a static approach, whereas the freeze-dried objects present a dynamic solution. The static approach mimics the dynamic solution but lacks much of its underlying power. Freeze dried objects retain all their interconnections including delegates, targets, actions, superviews, current displayed values, and so on. It's possible to create nontrivial applications entirely with Interface Builder and run them in Interface Builder's Test Interface mode without ever compiling.

Interface Builder could have been called Object Connector because in addition to positioning and sizing graphical objects, Interface Builder enables the interconnection of objects. Interface Builder is not limited to editing the objects that Apple provides with Cocoa. Any object can be instantiated and have outlets and actions that are set within Interface Builder. Interface Builder plug-ins can be created to enable more complex editing and configuration as well.

It's possible to write Cocoa applications without using Interface Builder or any `.nib` files, but loading `.nib` files is so convenient and powerful that almost every application uses them. Unless the programmer intervenes, Cocoa applications automatically load a main `.nib` file when launched. The main `.nib` file contains the objects that define the application's menu bar. The name of the main `.nib` file is usually `MainMenu.nib`, but the name can be changed in Xcode.

The File's Owner

When you need direct communication between objects unarchived from a `.nib` file and objects outside the `.nib`, the `.nib` file's owner enables that communication. The file's owner represents an object that is outside of the `.nib` file. Connections to the outlets and actions of the file's owner can be set in Interface Builder, but the actual object that is used as the file's owner is not specified until the `.nib` is loaded.

In many cases, direct connections between objects can be avoided by using notifications and the Responder Chain. For example, an object decoded from a `.nib` can register to receive notifications from within its `-(void)awakeFromNib` implementation. Objects can also send notifications to anonymous receivers or to the current first responder. Objects within a .nib can use the singleton NSApplication instance via the NSApp global variable or calling [NSApplication sharedApplication].

The objects in a .nib file are usually unarchived into an application by calling the + (BOOL) loadNibNamed: (NSString *) aNibName owner: (id) owner method of the NSBundle class. The NSBundle class is explained in the context of the Bundles pattern in Chapter 24, "Bundles."

The +loadNibNamed:owner: method is actually declared in a category that is part of the Application Kit. The Category pattern is discussed in Chapter 6, "Category." Because the +loadNibNamed:owner: method is added by the Application Kit, .nib files cannot be unarchived by programs that do not link to the Application Kit even if the .nib file being loaded doesn't contain any objects that depend on the Application Kit.

The owner argument to +loadNibNamed:owner: is the object that is used as the file's owner for the .nib. Any connections made to the file's owner within the .nib are made to the owner specified when the .nib is loaded. Connections that cannot be made because of inconsistencies between the owner used when the .nib is loaded and the outlets and actions specified for the file's owner when the .nib was created are discarded. The -awakeFromNib method is also sent to the file's owner specified with -loadNibNamed: owner:. The file's owner is not technically part of the .nib, but a .nib's owner can implement -awakeFromNib to perform any logic needed after a .nib has been loaded. If several .nibs are loaded using the same owner, that owner's -awakeFromNib method is called multiple times.

The application's main .nib is loaded automatically by the NSApplication object when the application is launched. The NSApplication object itself is the file's owner of the main .nib.

NSWindowController Overview

The NSWindowController class is often used as the file's owner when loading a .nib containing the definition of a window. The NSWindowController class can be used to customize a window's title, preserve the window's position and size in the user's defaults database, cascade windows onscreen, and manage the window's memory when the window is closed. NSWindowController isn't used in every Application Kit-based application, but it's available for use when appropriate and can eliminate lines of code that would otherwise be repeated in many applications. NSWindowController can be used to manage windows that are created programmatically and windows loaded from .nibs. The NSWindowController class can be used along with Cocoa's document architecture classes to implement flexible multidocument support in applications as detailed at http://developer.apple.com/documentation/Cocoa/Conceptual/Documents/Documents.html. Cocoa also provides the NSViewController class, which manages views. Like NSWindowController, NSViewController can be used with views that are programmatically created or loaded from .nibs.

Undo and Redo

The Application Kit includes a powerful and flexible system to implement undo and redo operations by taking advantage of the **Invocations** pattern (Chapter 20, "Invocations") to record the messages sent to objects and play them back later. Many Application Kit classes including text views already implement undo and redo.

The built-in undo and redo capability is provided by the NSUndoManager class. NSUndoManager is actually part of the Foundation framework because nongraphical applications might include undoable operations. NSUndoManager uses instances of the NSInvocation class to store Objective-C messages and their arguments.

By default, all the messages that are stored in an undo manager within one iteration of the run loop are grouped into a single undoable operation. This is a sensible policy because all the messages that result from a single user action should be undoable by a single user action. Redo is automatically supported whenever an operation is undone. Just as messages for undo are recorded when an operation is originally performed, undoing the operation records messages that enable redo. Redo is essentially implemented as undoing undo.

Cocoa's undo and redo design are explained in more detail at http://developer.apple.com/documentation/Cocoa/Conceptual/UndoArchitecture/UndoArchitecture.html.

Managers

The NSUndoManager class is a perfect example of the Managers pattern. Objects that are managers control the lifetime and accessibility of other objects. The NSUndoManager creates NSInvocation instances, stores them, invokes them as necessary, and destroys them when they are no longer needed. When you implement undo and redo for your own classes, you don't need to worry about managing NSInvocation instances yourself because NSUndoManager takes care of the details.

The Application Kit provides several other managers to handle the details of common View layer features. The NSFontManager class is a singleton that juggles all of the NSFont instances your application may be using. As a behind the scenes optimization, NSFontManager caches font information and makes sure that your application only has one instance of NSFont to describe each font face and size that's in use. NSFontManager also provides interaction with the standard Cocoa Font panel. NSHelpManager is a singleton that handles the details of interoperation with Mac OS X's standard online help system. The NSInputManager class hides the details of interacting with the many different text input techniques and language/cultural localizations supported by Mac OS X. NSInputManager hides the details so well that very few Cocoa applications ever use the class directly. NSLayoutManager converts Unicode characters into the graphical "glyphs" that represent the characters on screen. Management of glyphs is one of the trickiest parts of providing rich text display with support for many languages. It's common for a single character to be represented by multiple glyphs, and sometimes multiple characters are condensed into a single glyph. The rules for mapping characters to glyphs and the sheer number of glyphs needed make `NSLayoutManager` one of the workhorse Application Kit classes.

Application Kit Limitations and Benefits

The Application Kit contains standard implementations of almost all the View layer features that are common to standard Mac OS X desktop graphical applications. The patterns employed by the Application Kit provide ample hooks and reuse opportunities to let you extend standard features and provide application-specific features. With the exception of a few classes like `NSView` that are intended to be subclassed, most applications create very few subclasses of Application Kit classes. Remember that subclassing is one of the tightest forms of software coupling, and coupling is the enemy of flexible reuse. The multitude of patterns in the Application Kit all exist in part to decouple objects, and the scarcity of Application Kit subclasses in your applications demonstrates a level of success.

You should use the Application Kit when you want to create full-featured applications that conform to Apple's HIG for Mac OS X. It makes sense to use portions of the Application Kit such as the `NSApplication`, `NSRunLoop`, and custom `NSView` subclasses even for full-screen games that draw everything with Open GL and/or Core Animation. However, the Application Kit is not well-suited to implementing complex user interfaces that differ substantially from Apple's HIG. The Application Kit doesn't exactly enforce the standard look and feel, but implementing alternate user interfaces with the Application Kit requires tremendous subtlety and sophistication. The design of the Application Kit makes it easy to produce standard applications and difficult to deviate from standards.

32

Bindings and Controllers

Chapter 29, "Controllers," describes the roles of Coordinating Controllers and Mediating Controllers within Model View Controller design pattern that permeates Cocoa. Coordinating Controllers initialize, load, and save the Model and View subsystems. Mediating Controllers manage the flow of data between view objects and model objects to minimize coupling between the subsystems. Cocoa supplies the NSApplication, NSDocumentController, NSDocument, NSWindowController, and NSViewController classes among others to provide reusable implementations of most common coordinating tasks. Cocoa also includes NSObjectController, NSArrayController, NSTreeController, and NSUserDefaultsController, which provide reusable implementations of some common mediating tasks.

Cocoa's reusable Controller subsystem classes go a long way toward simplifying the design and development of traditional "glue" code needed to meld a model and a view into a cohesive application. The MYShapeDraw example in Chapter 29 shows how patterns like Outlets, Targets and Actions, Notifications, and Data Sources are used in combination with the Controllers pattern to implement full-featured Controller subsystems. However, starting with Mac OS X version 10.3, Cocoa Bindings technology has enabled a higher level of abstraction for Mediating Controllers. Bindings further reduce the amount of code needed to implement Controller subsystems and can be configured in Interface Builder to nearly eliminate code for mediating tasks.

Role of Bindings and Controllers

Bindings and Controllers work side-by-side with other patterns like Targets and Actions, Data Sources, and Notifications. You can use Bindings to reduce the amount of mediating "glue" code in your applications, but as always, there is a trade-off. Look at each application design situation on a case-by-case basis to decide which approach makes the most sense. This chapter provides the information you'll need to evaluate whether to use Bindings and Controllers or other patterns or some mixture.

Bindings keep model objects and view objects synchronized so that changes in one subsystem are automatically reflected in the other. Like almost all Cocoa technology, bindings are implemented to reduce or eliminate coupling between objects. Bindings are based on the string names of object properties as opposed to compiled addresses or offsets, and bindings are configurable at design time and runtime.

NSController classes are valuable components of any Cocoa application that uses the Model View Controller pattern, whether bindings are used. In contrast, bindings should only be used in combination with controller objects like NSObjectController and NSArrayController. Whenever two objects are bound, at least one of them should be a controller. Controllers can be bound to each other. View objects can be bound to a controller. Model objects can be bound to a controller. Avoid binding View subsystem objects directly to Model subsystem objects. Don't bind view objects together or model objects together.

> **Note**
>
> There is nothing in the bindings technology that prevents direct binding from View subsystem objects to Model subsystem objects or binding View objects to other view objects or binding model objects together. However, direct bindings without the intervention of a controller are an anti-pattern as explained in "The Importance of Using Controllers with Bindings" section of this chapter.

The simplest example of binding within a Model View Controller application is shown in Figure 32.1, which depicts a text field with has its own floatValue property bound to the floatValue property of whatever object is selected by an instance of NSObjectController. Chapter 29 explains the concept of selection within controllers. The NSObjectController's content outlet is set to an instance of MYModel, which provides a floatValue property. The content of an NSObjectController instance is just one object unlike an NSArrayController which uses an array of objects as its content. The selection provided by an NSObjectController is always the content object.

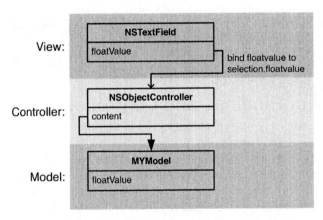

Figure 32.1   Binding within a Model View
Controller application

The binding shown in Figure 32.1 keeps the `floatValue` of the text field synchronized with the `floatValue` of the MYModel instance. If the value in the text field is changed by the user, the change is reflected in the bound MYModel instance. Just as importantly, if the value in the bound MYModel instance is changed, the bound text field is automatically updated.

A slightly more complex binding is shown in Figure 32.2. Both a text field and a slider are bound to the `floatValue` property of a MYModel instance. If the user moves the slider, the `floatValue` of the MYModel instance is updated, which in turn causes the text field to be updated. If the user enters a value in the text field, the `floatValue` of the MYModel instance is updated, which in turn causes the slider to be updated. If the `floatValue` of the MYModel instance is changed programmatically through an appropriate Accessor method, both the slider and the text field are automatically updated to display the new value.

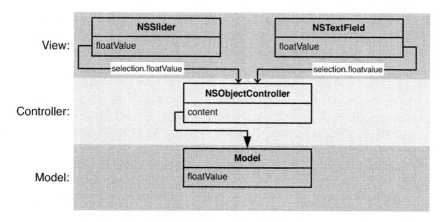

Figure 32.2   More binding within a Model View Controller application

Bindings are used in much more elaborate ways than shown in Figure 32.1 and Figure 32.2. The value of bindings is magnified when you have more complex models and more complex views. Core Data models, complex views, and the NSController classes integrate well with bindings and provide opportunities to almost eliminate traditional controller glue code. Nevertheless, the bindings technology is not dependent on Core Data or complex views, and all of the Cocoa technologies can be used without bindings.

Bindings Avoid Coupling

Bindings are defined by string keys that identify the objects and properties to bind. Key Value Coding (described in Chapter 19, "Associative Storage") provides the underlying mechanism used to obtain the runtime values of properties from associated keys. The use of string keys avoids any need for the objects that are bound together to know anything about each other. Any two properties of any two objects can be bound together, and as long as properties corresponding to the string keys can be found at runtime, the binding will function. String keys minimize coupling between bound objects and allow dynamic changes at runtime. For example, if you bind a text field's value to a property of an array controller's selection, the text field will be automatically updated any time the selection changes or the value of the selected object's bound property changes. In other words, the text field isn't bound to any specific object. It's bound to whatever object is selected by the controller at any particular moment.

> **Note**
>
> Many bindings provide optional placeholder values. For example, when an object's property is bound to the selection of an array controller, it's possible to specify a placeholder value to use when there is no selection and another placeholder to use when there is multiple selection.

String keys provide even more flexibility by supporting key paths. A key path is a series of `'.'` separated keys that specify a sequence of properties to access. For example, if each employee object has a name property and a department property, and each department object has a manager who is also an employee, you could bind the value of a text field to the "`selection.department.manager.name`" key path of an array controller. At runtime, the text field's value is then synchronized to the name of the manager of the department of the selected employee. The selection is an employee object. The binding asks for the selected employee's "department" property. It then asks for the department's "manager" property. It then asks for the manager's "name" property.

It's also possible to use operators, which provide synthetic properties. For example, if each department has an array property called "employees," you can create a binding to "`selection.department.employees.@count`". The `@count` operator returns the number of objects in the array obtained from the employees property of the department property of the selected employee. A description of the operators supported for use with Cocoa collection classes is available at http://developer.apple.com/documentation/Cocoa/Conceptual/KeyValueCoding/Concepts/ArrayOperators.html.

The Importance of Using Controllers with Bindings

Chapter 1, "Model View Controller," made the case that application data shouldn't be stored in the user interface. Instead, the Model View Controller design pattern partitions the application and stores application in a Model that's independent of any View. If you bind the properties of two View objects directly together, you are most likely diluting the benefits of Model View Controller design pattern. In the worst case, you're right back to storing crucial application data in the user interface. Therefore, it's best to bind View objects to other objects outside the View layer.

But why not bind View objects directly to Model objects? One reason is that Cocoa's `NSController` subclasses all implement the `NSEditorRegistration` informal protocol. Informal protocols are explained in Chapter 6, "Category." The `NSEditorRegistration` protocol provides methods for view objects to inform a controller when editing is underway.

It's important for controllers to have that information so that partial edits can be validated and changes can be saved without requiring the user to explicitly commit every edit that's started. NSControllers keep track of which view objects have unfinished edits and can force the view objects to request completion of each edit or discard the intermediate values. For example, if a user is typing in a text field and then closes the window containing the text field, the relevant NSControllers update the Model with the contents of the text field. The Model update causes the document to be marked as needing to be saved and then you are offered a chance to save changes before the window closes. If you don't include a controller in each binding between a View object and a Model object, then you must replace the NSEditorRegistration protocol functionality, and Model objects are a poor place to implement requests for completion of edits taking place in the View. Therefore, you need a controller to mediate between the View and the Model.

> **Note**
>
> Chapter 29 contains an example class similar to NSArrayController to show how and why reusable controller objects work. The example includes a MYShapeEditorDocumentEditing informal protocol similar to NSEditorRegistration and shows how the protocol enables coordination of changes between Model View Controller subsystems.

Another reason to include controllers in your bindings is that NSControllers keep track of the current selection and sometimes provide placeholder values for bound properties. Being able to bind to the current selection as opposed to a specific object makes bindings very flexible.

Finally, spaghetti bindings are as much of a problem as spaghetti code and lead to similar maintenance hassles. The discipline of including NSControllers in every binding clarifies the relationships between objects and serves as visual documentation for bindings. If you inspect a controller object in Interface Builder, there is a visible list of all bindings that involve that controller object, as shown in Figure 32.3. It's straightforward to inspect the controller objects whenever you open an unfamiliar .nib file. If bindings exist between other objects, the only way you can find them is by inspecting each end every object in the .nib. Religiously including controllers in bindings is a wise design guideline and serves the same purpose as coding standards: it reduces the number of places programmers need to look to understand the system.

Collaboration of Patterns Within Bindings and Controllers

Once the behavior of binding has been explained, programmers commonly want to know how bindings work. Although bindings are an advanced topic, there's really no magic. Interface Builder sends -(void)bind:(NSString *)binding toObject: (id)observableController withKeyPath:(NSString *)keyPath options: (NSDictionary *)options messages when it establishes bindings, and you can send the same messages to establish bindings programmatically.

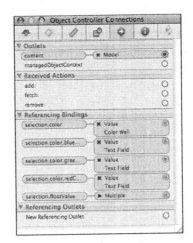

Figure 32.3   Inspecting bindings with
Interface Builder

Key Value Coding and Key Value Observing technologies underlie bindings. Key Value Coding is briefly described in Chapter 19 and again in Chapter 30, "Core Data Models." It is a variation of the Associative Storage pattern, which lets you access the properties of objects as if every object were a simple dictionary of key/value pairs. See Apple's conceptual documentation for Key Value Coding at http://developer.apple.com/documentation/ Cocoa/Conceptual/KeyValueCoding/KeyValueCoding.html. Key Value Observing is a variation of the Notification pattern from Chapter 14, "Notifications." Key Value Observing monitors the values of object properties on behalf of other objects that are interested observers. The underlying implementation of Key Value Observing is somewhat different from the Notification pattern, but in essence, Key Value Observing serves the same function: Register to receive messages when something of interest happens. Apple's conceptual documentation for Key Value Observing is at http://developer.apple.com/documentation/ Cocoa/Conceptual/KeyValueObserving/KeyValueObserving.html.

Key Value Observing is implemented by the NSKeyValueObserving informal protocol, which adds methods to NSObject from which almost all Cocoa objects inherit. Hidden deep behind the scenes, Cocoa maintains a collection of some kind that lists all of the objects that currently observe other objects' properties. Apple is deliberately vague about the specific implementation of that collection because it wants to preserve the flexibility to change the implementation in the future. You add an object to the list of objects that observe a property by calling NSKeyValueObserving's -addObserver:forKeyPath: options:context: method. To remove an observer from the list, use NSKeyValueObserving's -removeObserver:forKeyPath:.

What Happens in `-bind:toObject:withKeyPath:options:`?

Sending the `-bind:toObject:withKeyPath:options:` message to an object creates a bi-directional set of Key Value Observing associations. Somewhere inside Apple's `-(void)bind:(NSString *)binding toObject:(id)observableController withKeyPath:(NSString *)keyPath options:(NSDictionary *)options` implementation, the following code or something similar is executed:

```
[self addObserver:observableController forKeyPath:binding
    options:(NSKeyValueObservingOptionNew|NSKeyValueObservingOptionOld)
    context:nil];

[observableController addObserver:self forKeyPath:keyPath
    options:(NSKeyValueObservingOptionNew|NSKeyValueObservingOptionOld)
    context:nil];
```

There isn't much more involved with the establishment of bindings. Apple documents the available options at http://developer.apple.com/documentation/Cocoa/Reference/ApplicationKit/Protocols/NSKeyValueBindingCreation_Protocol/Reference/Reference.html. If a key path has multiple '.' separated properties, `-bind:toObject:withKeyPath:options:` adds observers for all of the individual properties in the path as needed. You can get information about existing bindings via the `-(NSDictionary *)infoForBinding:(NSString *)binding` method. Sending the `-(void)unbind:(NSString *)binding` message results in corresponding calls to NSKeyValueObserving's `-(void)removeObserver:(NSObject *)anObserver forKeyPath:(NSString *)keyPath` method.

Given that bindings are a relatively thin veneer on Key Value Observing, the magic of bindings resides within Key Value Observing.

How Does Key Value Observing Detect Changes to Observed Properties so That Observing Objects Can Be Notified?

The answer is that changes to observed properties need to be bracketed by calls to `-(void)willChangeValueForKey:(NSString *)key` and `-(void)didChangeValueForKey:(NSString *)key`. If you write your own code to programmatically modify the values of observed properties, you may need to explicitly call `-willChangeValueForKey:` and `-didChangeValueForKey:` like the following method that sets the "counter" property without calling an appropriate Accessor method:

```
- (void)incrementCounterByInt:(int)anIncrement {
    [self willChangeValueForKey:@"counter"];
    counter = counter + anIncrement;
    [self didChangeValueForKey:@"counter"];
}
```

Inside NSObject's default implementation of the NSKeyValueObserving informal protocol, `-willChangeValueForKey:` and `-didChangeValueForKey:` are implemented to send messages to registered observers before and after the property value changes.

It's not necessary to explicitly call -willChangeValueForKey: and -didChangeValueForKey: within correctly named Accessor methods. When you use Objective-C 2.0's @synthesize directive to generate Accessor method implementations, the details are handled for you. Even if you hand-write Accessor methods, Cocoa provides automatic support for Key Value Observing through a little bit of Objective-C runtime manipulation briefly described at http://developer.apple.com/documentation/Cocoa/Conceptual/KeyValueObserving/Concepts/KVOImplementation.html. At runtime, Cocoa is able to replace your implementation of each Accessor method with a version that first calls -willChangeValueForKey:, then calls your implementation, and finally calls -didChangeValueForKey:.

When Key Value Coding's -(void)setValue:(id)value forKey:(NSString *)key or -(void)setValue:(id)value forKeyPath:(NSString *)keyPath methods are used to modify an observed property, the appropriate Accessor methods (if any) are called, and the Accessor methods take care of calling -willChangeValueForKey: and -didChangeValueForKey:. If there aren't any available Accessor methods, -setValue:forKey: and -setValue:forKeyPath: call -willChangeValueForKey: and -didChangeValueForKey: directly. In summary, you only need to explicitly call -willChangeValueForKey: and -didChangeValueForKey: if you change the value of an observed property without using Key Value Coding and without using an appropriately named Accessor method.

> **Note**
>
> As recommended in Chapter 10, "Accessors," if you consistently use Accessor methods to access or mutate properties, you will save yourself a lot of work. In addition to the memory management advantages of using accessors, you'll also avoid the need to ever explicitly call -willChangeValueForKey: and -didChangeValueForKey:.

What Message Is Sent to Notify Registered Observers When an Observed Property's Value Is Changed?

By default, the -didChangeValueForKey: method sends the -(void)observeValueForKeyPath:(NSString *)keyPath ofObject:(id)object change:(NSDictionary *)change context:(void *)context message to all registered observers after an observed property changes value. You can configure the -willChangeValueForKey: method to send notification before each change if you specify the NSKeyValueObservingOptionPrior option in the options: argument used to register an observer. The options: argument also governs whether the change notification includes only the previous value, only the new value, or both the old and new values.

Most Cocoa View subsystem classes already implement -observeValueForKeyPath:ofObject:change:context:. You need to implement that method in your custom View objects if you want them to work correctly with bindings. You may also need to implement -observeValueForKeyPath:ofObject:change:context: in model objects if you want to perform special logic whenever observed properties change. Unfortunately, implementing -observeValueForKeyPath:ofObject:change:context: is one of the least elegant aspects of using Cocoa.

Note

You are able to specify an Objective-C selector that identifies the message you want to receive when you use Cocoa's NSNotificationCenter. Selectors are explained in Chapter 9, "Perform Selector and Delayed Perform," and NSNotificationCenter is explained
in Chapter 14. In contrast Key Value Observing always notifies observers via the
-observeValueForKeyPath:ofObject:change:context: method.

You almost invariably have to implement -observeValueForKeyPath:
ofObject:change:context: by using string comparisons to determine what logic to
invoke based on which key path changed. The following code is a trivial example implementation of -observeValueForKeyPath:ofObject:change:context::

```
- (void)observeValueForKeyPath:(NSString *)keyPath
    ofObject:(id)object change:(NSDictionary *)change
    context:(void *)context
{
    if ([keyPath isEqualToString:@"floatValue"]) {
        NSNumber    *newValue = [change
            objectForKey:NSKeyValueChangeNewKey];
        if(0.0 > [newValue floatValue]) {
            // Perform special logic for negative values here
        }
        [self setNeedsDisplay:YES];
    }

    // be sure to call the super implementation
    [super observeValueForKeyPath:keyPath
        ofObject:object change:change
        context:context];
}
```

The need to perform explicit string comparisons like [keyPath isEqualToString:
@"floatValue"] in -observeValueForKeyPath:ofObject:change:context: is inele-
gant. It's easy to imagine an implementation of -observeValueForKeyPath:
ofObject:change:context: that has to perform hundreds of string comparisons after
every observed property change to control application logic. Objective-C selectors and
the Perform Selector pattern from Chapter 9 exist to make string comparisons in branch
logic unnecessary. It's unfortunate that Apple didn't take advantage of the pre-existing
patterns like NSNotification and the use of selectors when implementing Key Value
Observing.

Note

The Associative Storage pattern is a prominent building block of Key Value Coding,
Key Value Observing, and Bindings. Dictionaries containing key/value pairs specify the
options to binding methods. A dictionary provides information about changes in

-observeValueForKeyPath:ofObject:change:context:. And Key Value Coding is itself a variation of the Associative Storage pattern.

One way to make -observeValueForKeyPath:ofObject:change:context: a little
bit more elegant is to use key path strings as notification names as follows:

```
- (void)observeValueForKeyPath:(NSString *)keyPath
    ofObject:(id)object change:(NSDictionary *)changeDictionary
    context:(void *)context
{
    // copy the change dictionary and add the context to it
    NSMutableDictionary *infoDictionary = [NSMutableDictionary
        dictionaryWithDictionary:changeDictionary];
    [infoDictionary setObject:context forKey:@"MYBindingContext"];

    // post a notification to interested observers using the key path as
    // the notification name
    [[NSNotificationCenter defaultCenter] postNotificationName:keyPath
        object:object userInfo:infoDictionary];

    // be sure to call the super implementation
    [super observeValueForKeyPath:keyPath
        ofObject:object change:change
        context:context];
}
```

If you use the approach of converting Key Value Observation notifications into
NSNotifications, you can have any number of observers that each register a different selector for the same key path. Unfortunately, the NSNotification approach has problems
of its own. Using key path strings as notification names is not ideal because key paths are
specified in Interface Builder and must be duplicated exactly in your code that registers
for notifications. A simple change in Interface Builder could necessitate changes to notification code in multiple disparate places within your application. The compiler can't detect errors in the key path strings, so you must test at runtime to detect key path errors.
Nevertheless, NSNotificationCenter provides at least one way to circumvent the use of
explicit string comparisons in your own code.

Bindings and Controllers Limitations and Benefits

A common criticism of bindings is that there is too much magic happening that the programmer can't see. This chapter dispels some of the magic. Bindings are hard to document
because they typically aren't visible in code. The same criticism can be made for Targets,
Actions, and Outlets that are configured in Interface Builder. However, due in part to the
flexibility and potential complexity of bindings, the need to document bindings is even
greater than the need to document Targets, Actions, and Outlets.

The use of string keys avoids coupling between objects. Any two properties of any two objects can bind together as long as properties corresponding to the string keys can be found at runtime. Of course, the corresponding down side is that the compiler can't determine correctness of bindings. You have to wait until runtime to test bindings.

Bindings interoperate with features like Value Transformers that aren't covered in this chapter (see http://developer.apple.com/documentation/Cocoa/Conceptual/ ValueTransformers/Concepts/TransformersAvail.html). Bindings have the potential to replace code that would otherwise need to be written. Chapter 29 culminated with an example use of Bindings. That example highlights the code that's replaced when bindings are used.

Resources

This appendix contains a list of resources Mac developers should find handy. Here, you'll find our favorite books, and yes, even links to some of Apple's documentation that we feel is a must-read for newcomers to Mac development.

Apple Documentation

While Apple's Technical Publications (TechPubs) group spits out over 10,000 pages of documentation on everything ranging from Mac and iPhone development to managing OS X Server, here are the docs we think every Mac developer should take a peek at:

Apple Human Interface Guidelines (better known as "The HIG") *http://developer.apple.com/documentation/UserExperience/Conceptual/AppleHIGuidelines/OSXHIGuidelines.pdf*

Application Kit Framework Reference *http://developer.apple.com/documentation/Cocoa/Reference/ApplicationKit/ObjC_classic/AppKitObjC.pdf*

Cocoa Fundamentals Guide *http://developer.apple.com/documentation/Cocoa/Conceptual/CocoaFundamentals/CocoaFundamentals.pdf*

Core Data Programming Guide *http://developer.apple.com/documentation/Cocoa/Conceptual/CoreData/CoreData.pdf*

Foundation Framework Reference *http://developer.apple.com/documentation/Cocoa/Reference/Foundation/ObjC_classic/FoundationObjC.pdf*

Garbage Collection Programming Guide *http://developer.apple.com/documentation/Cocoa/Conceptual/GarbageCollection/GarbageCollection.pdf*

Interface Builder User Guide *http://developer.apple.com/documentation/DeveloperTools/Conceptual/IB_UserGuide/IB_UserGuide.pdf*

Key-Value Coding Programming Guide *http://developer.apple.com/documentation/Cocoa/Conceptual/KeyValueCoding/KeyValueCoding.pdf*

Object-Oriented Programming with Objective-C *http://developer.apple.com/documentation/Cocoa/Conceptual/OOP_ObjC/OOP_ObjC.pdf*

The Objective-C 2.0 Programming Lanuguage *http://developer.apple.com/documentation/Cocoa/Conceptual/ObjectiveC/ObjC.pdf*

Reference Library *http://developer.apple.com/referencelibrary/*

Xcode Overview *http://developer.apple.com/documentation/DeveloperTools/Conceptual/Xcode_Overview/Contents/Resources/en.lproj/Xcode_Overview.pdf*

Xcode Project Management Guide *http://developer.apple.com/documentation/DeveloperTools/Conceptual/XcodeProjectManagement/Xcode_Project_Management.pdf*

Xcode Workspace Guide *http://developer.apple.com/documentation/DeveloperTools/Conceptual/XcodeWorkspace/Xcode_Workspace.pdf*

Books

The following books are recommended reading both for Mac development and for learning more about design patterns:

The C Programming Language, Second Edition, by Brian W. Kernighan, Dennis M. Ritchie (ISBN: 978-0-131-10362-7).

Cocoa Programming for Mac OS X, Third Edition, by Aaron Hillegass (ISBN: 978-0-321-50361-9).

Design Patterns: Elements of Reusable Object-Oriented Software, by Erich Gamma, Richard Helm, Ralph Johnson, John M.Vlissides (ISBN: 978-0-201-63361-0).

Head First Design Patterns, by Elisabeth Freeman, Eric Freeman, Bert Bates, Kathy Sierra (ISBN: 978-0-596-00712-6).

The iPhone Developer's Cookbook, by Erica Sadun (ISBN: 978-0-321-55545-8).

OpenGL ES 2.0 Programming Guide, by Aaftab Munshi, Dan Ginsburg, Dave Shreiner (ISBN: 978-0-321-50279-7).

OpenGL Programming on Mac OS X, by Robert P. Kuehne, J. D. Sullivan (ISBN: 978-0-321-35652-9).

Programming in Objective-C 2.0, Second Edition, by Stephen G. Kochan (ISBN: 978-0-321-56615-7).

Xcode 3 Unleashed, by Fritz Anderson (ISBN: 978-0-321-55263-1).

Mailing Lists

The following mailing lists and groups provide a great wealth of information for Mac developers of all skills:

Apple's cocoa-dev mailing list—*http://lists.apple.com/mailman/listinfo/cocoa-dev*

Apple's objc-language mailing list—*http://lists.apple.com/mailman/listinfo/objc-language*

Apple's xcode-users mailing list—*http://lists.apple.com/mailman/listinfo/xcode-users*

OmniGroup's MacOSX-dev list—*http://www.omnigroup.com/mailman/listinfo/macosx-dev*

Uli Kusterer's Mac-GUI-Dev mailing list—*http://tech.groups.yahoo.com/group/mac-gui-dev/*

User Groups

CocoaHeads user groups can be found in most major cities in the U.S. and also in nearly 30 cities around the world. Whether you are looking for help or wanting to present some code you're working on, there's most likely a CocoaHeads near you— *http://www.cocoaheads.org.*

Online Groups

iPhone Application Developers (Google Groups) *http://groups.google.com/group/iphoneappdev*

In addition to CocoaHeads, many Mac user and developer groups can be found in the online groups from Google and Yahoo!. Just go to the group pages listed here and search for groups on Cocoa, iPhone, and/or Mac development—*http://groups.google.com* and *http://groups.yahoo.com.*

Conferences/Training

Apple's Worldwide Developer's Conference (WWDC). Moscone West, San Francisco, California (typically held the second week of June). *http://developer.apple.com/wwdc*

Big Nerd Ranch. Run by Aaron Hillegass, former NeXT and Apple employee and best-selling author of *Cocoa Programming for Mac OS X*. Based in Atlanta, Georgia, the Big Nerd Ranch offers training for Cocoa and iPhone developers of all levels. *http://www.bignerdranch.com*

C4. Organized by Jonathan "Wolf" Rentzsch, typically held in Chicago, Illinois, in August or September. Check the website for updates. *http://rentzsch.com/c4*

NSConference. Organized by Steve "Scotty" Scott and Tim Isted in Hatfield, UK. The first conference was held April *2009*. At the time of this printing, the conference organizers are planning to hold NSConference in the future and possibly in more locations, so check the web site. *http://www.nsconference.com*

A

N

O

FREE Online Edition

Your purchase of **Cocoa Design Patterns** includes access to a free online edition for 45 days through the Safari Books Online subscription service. Nearly every Addison-Wesley Professional book is available online through Safari Books Online, along with more than 5,000 other technical books and videos from publishers such as Cisco Press, Exam Cram, IBM Press, O'Reilly, Prentice Hall, Que, and Sams.

SAFARI BOOKS ONLINE allows you to search for a specific answer, cut and paste code, download chapters, and stay current with emerging technologies.

Activate your FREE Online Edition at
www.informit.com/safarifree

> **STEP 1:** Enter the coupon code: XEJIZAA.

> **STEP 2:** New Safari users, complete the brief registration form.
> Safari subscribers, just log in.

If you have difficulty registering on Safari or accessing the online edition, please e-mail customer-service@safaribooksonline.com

Praise for *Cocoa Design Patterns*

Cocoa
Design Patterns

"This long-needed book is a great resource for Cocoa newcomers and veterans who want to get the *why* behind the *what*. The list of patterns gives historical perspective and answers many developer questions and the last three chapters—covering Core Data, AppKit, and Bindings—are a must-read; they reveal insights that might otherwise require hours of discussion with Apple engineers or access to source code."

—*Tim Burks*, Software Developer and Creator of the Nu Programming Language,
www.programming.nu

"This book is a comprehensive and authoritative treatment of design patterns and their practical applications in Cocoa projects. I recommend this book to anyone who wants to advance from intermediate to expert proficiency as a Macintosh developer."

—*John C. Randolph*, Vice President Engineering, Stealth Imaging, Inc.

"*Cocoa Design Patterns* is a fantastic book that will show you the ins and outs of software design patterns, how Cocoa makes use of them, and how to apply them to your own applications for better, more robust, and more maintainable software."

—*August Trometer*, Owner of FoggyNoggin Software

"*Cocoa Design Patterns* is superb! It is highly readable, thoroughly enjoyable, and filled to the brim with wisdom that will make you a more efficient and effective programmer. The authors utilize a consistent and self-contained approach to each chapter, making it easy to return to use as a reference. However, the material is so interesting and vital to Cocoa programmers that you'll want to read it from cover to cover."

—*David Mandell*, Independent Developer

"Erik and Donald's book really helped me out with the conceptual side of programming. It caused me to realize where I was going wrong in my code and helped me sort out my design issues."

—*Eoin Houlihan*

"This book is recommended for any programmer interested in a deeper understanding of Cocoa. Reading it might have helped me become a better software engineer in any object-oriented language. I'll keep it handy as a constant reference and look forward to reading it again more carefully."

—*Daryl Spitzer*